𝕿𝖍𝖊 𝕮𝖆𝖓𝖙𝖊𝖗𝖇𝖚𝖗𝖞 𝖆𝖓𝖉 𝖄𝖔𝖗𝖐 𝕾𝖔𝖈𝖎𝖊𝖙𝖞

GENERAL EDITOR: A. K. McHARDY

M.A., D.Phil.

ISSN 0262-995X

PROVINCE OF CANTERBURY

CANTERBURY AND YORK SOCIETY VOL. LXXVIII

The Register of

John Morton

ARCHBISHOP OF CANTERBURY

1486–1500

VOLUME II

EDITED BY

CHRISTOPHER HARPER-BILL

ST MARY'S COLLEGE,
STRAWBERRY HILL

The Canterbury and York Society

The Boydell Press

1991

First published 1991

A Canterbury and York Society publication
published by The Boydell Press
an imprint of Boydell & Brewer Ltd
PO Box 9, Woodbridge, Suffolk IP12 3DF, UK
and of Boydell & Brewer Inc.
PO Box 41026, Rochester, NY 14604, USA

ISBN 0 907239 47 1

British Library Cataloguing-in-Publication Data
The register of John Morton, Archbishop of Canterbury,
1486–1500: Vol. II. – (Canterbury and York Society)
    I. Harper-Bill, Christopher   II. Series
    282.09
    ISBN 0-907239-47-1

Library of Congress Cataloging-in-Publication Data
(Revised for vol. 2)
Catholic Church. Province of Canterbury (England). Archbishop (1486–1500 :
    Morton)
    The register of John Morton, Archbishop of Canterbury, 1486–1500.
    (Canterbury and York Society, ISSN 0262-995X ; vol. 75   )
    Contains entries relating to the diocese of Canterbury and the province in
general.
    Vol. 2 has imprint: [Leeds?] : Canterbury and York Society ; Woodbridge,
Suffolk, UK ; Rochester, NY, USA : Boydell Press.
    Includes bibliographical references and indexes.
    1. Catholic Church. Diocese of Canterbury—History—Sources. 2. Canterbury
Region (England)—Church history—Sources. I. Morton, John, 1420?–1500. II.
Harper-Bill, Christopher. III. Canterbury and York Society. IV. Title. V. Series:
Canterbury and York Society (Series) ; v. 75, etc.
BX5013.C3A5 vol. 75, etc.   283',41 s   89-135147
[BX1495.C35]   [282'.4223]
ISBN 0-907239-47-1 (hardback : v. 2 ; acid-free paper)

Details of previous volumes available from Boydell & Brewer Ltd

The paper used in this publication meets the minimum requirements
of American National Standard for Information Sciences —
Permanence of Paper for Printed Library Materials, ANSI Z39.48-1984

Printed in Great Britain by
St Edmundsbury Press Ltd, Bury St Edmunds, Suffolk

CONTENTS

FOR THE VINCENTIAN FATHERS OF
THE CONGREGATION OF THE MISSION AT
STRAWBERRY HILL

ACKNOWLEDGEMENTS

The main obligations which have been incurred in the preparation of this edition are detailed in the introduction to the first volume. All of these are now acknowledged again, with renewed thanks. In addition, I wish to express my gratitude to the Revd Professor G. Dunstan, Peter Heath and Dr Robert Swanson for help on various points, and to Professor Brian Kemp for much assistance with the proofs.

The dedication of this volume is an expression of a long-standing debt of which I become increasingly conscious as the years pass. It is the Vincentian community at Strawberry Hill which, against all the odds in this present age, makes the college a place in which both scholarship and conviviality still prevail. I could not be more grateful for the privilege of working alongside the priests of the Congregation of the Mission.

ABBREVIATIONS

To the list of abbreviations listed on pp. xxiv–xxv of volume i of this edition, add the following.

English and Welsh Counties

Ang.	Anglesey
Flints.	Flintshire
Glam.	Glamorgan
I.o.W.	Isle of Wight
Mon.	Monmouthshire
Nb.	Northumberland
Nt.	Nottinghamshire
Pem.	Pembrokeshire

Other abbreviations

chw.	churchwarden
cur.	curate
inh.	inhabitant
ord.	ordinand
par. chap.	parochial chaplain
pn.	parishioner
prop.	proprietor
stip.	stipendiary

INTRODUCTION

Among the most important rights of the archbishop of Canterbury within his province was the administration of vacant sees. Upon the death or translation of a diocesan, custody of the temporalities passed to the crown, spiritual jurisdiction and revenues to the metropolitan. This metropolitical right was not standard practice on the continent and had not gone uncontested in England. In the thirteenth and fourteenth centuries five chapters had succeeded in reducing, to a varying degree, the archbishop's freedom of action during vacancies.[1] Although by the fifteenth century the situation had stabilised, there is still evidence during the archiepiscopate of John Morton of resistance to the rights claimed by the church of Canterbury. The monks of Winchester bitterly contested at the court of Rome the archbishop's attempt during the vacancy of 1492–93 to take the revenues of parish churches appropriated to the episcopal *mensa*;[2] in 1496 the dean and chapter of Lichfield protested their immunity from episcopal visitation, which was considered to extend to the archbishop's *sede vacante* jurisdiction (395), and in 1492 the levying of procurations was resisted by St Nectan's abbey at Hartland and by Launceston priory during the visitation of Exeter diocese (285–6).

Morton's register is remarkable for the proportion of its folios which are filled by *sede vacante* material. The records are far from complete. In a period when vacancies were multiplied by frequent translations orchestrated by the king, thirteen have left no trace in the register. Yet for those dioceses where the Official's *sede vacante* register was bound up at Lambeth there is a wealth of detail, especially on the financial administration of the vacant sees.[3]

The archbishop's determination to exercise the closest control over his province is revealed by the situation in dioceses where *sede vacante* administration was regulated by ancient composition. At London in 1489 Morton

---

[1] For discussion of *sede vacante* rights and administration, see I. J. Churchill, *Canterbury Administration* (1933) i, 161–240. The compositions reached between Archbishop Boniface and the chapters of Lincoln, London, Salisbury and Worcester, and between Archbishop Meopham and the monks of Norwich, are printed ibid. ii, 41–68.

[2] *Reg. Morton* i, nos 221–266; cf. C. Harper-Bill, 'Archbishop John Morton and the Province of Canterbury', *Journal of Ecclesiastical History* xxix (1978), 15–17.

[3] Financial accounts must always have been produced by Officials *sede vacante*, but before Morton's archiepiscopate they were rarely bound up in the Lambeth registers; but see Reg. Courtenay, fo. 173, for an account from St Asaph in 1389–90. In Morton's and Warham's registers it is standard for accounts to be included. For recent work on the neglected topic of spiritual income, see R. N. Swanson, 'Episcopal Income from Spiritualities in the Diocese of Exeter in the Early Sixteenth Century', *Journal of Ecclesiastical History* xxxix (1988), 520–30, and 'Episcopal Income from Spiritualities in Later Medieval England: the Evidence for the Diocese of Coventry and Lichfield', *Midlands History* xiv (1989), 1–20, both of which notice the material in this register.

chose from the nominees of the chapter Mr Richard Lichfield, and in 1496 Mr Thomas Jane.[4] Both men were well-known to the archbishop and had served as his commissaries on various occasions. At Lincoln in 1495, after discussion with his councillors concerning the validity of the Boniface composition, he chose from the chapter's nominees Mr John Walles, but insisted that because of the size of the diocese he should associate with him four commissaries – two of these were the archbishop's own clerks (135). At Worcester in 1498 the prior, who by the terms of the Boniface composition automatically served as Official, issued a commission, irrevocable during the vacancy, delegating all his powers to the archbishop's clerk, Mr Roger Church, who was appointed by Morton as Official of the consistory court (452–7). At Salisbury in 1499 Mr Lawrence Cokkys, canon-residentiary nominated by the chapter and chosen by the archbishop, similarly delegated his functions to Mr Church (511, 558). At Norwich the Meopham composition stipulated that the archbishop should freely appoint the Official but should be obliged to accept the nominee of the prior and convent as visitor of the diocese. In 1499, however, the visitor, a monk of the cathedral priory, delegated his functions to two secular clerks, one of whom, again Roger Church, was the archbishop's Official *sede vacante*.[5] In effect, therefore, the compositions for which the chapters had fought so hard were rendered innocuous to the archbishop, and administration of all vacant sees was during Morton's time conducted by men well-known to and trusted by him.

It was normal practice to conduct a visitation of a vacant see, and this compensated for the fact that Morton never, apparently, undertook a metropolitical visitation of his province. Unfortunately for the historian, the *comperta et detecta* of the visitation, and the subsequent injunctions and sentences, were ephemeral matter, especially when the visitation was not that of the diocesan bishop, for the archbishop's commissaries would in all probability never return. This material was, therefore, seldom bound up in the register. The chance survival of the visitation returns for the archdeaconries of Suffolk and Sudbury in 1499 reveals how serious is this loss.[6] Although no programme of questions has survived for these visitations, it is possible to reconstruct the pattern of interrogation from the answers of the clergy and the *inquisitores* or jurors (senior representatives of the parish, normally including the churchwardens) who were cited to appear before the visitor. The mandate directed to the archdeacon or his Official ordered him to instruct all clergy within his jurisdiction to produce their letters of ordination and, in the case of incumbents, of institution. Religious houses to which parish churches were appropriated were to produce authorisation for each such appropriation, and chantry chaplains should have available the foundation deeds and statutes of their chantries.[7] He was also to cite all incumbents to

[4] *Reg. Morton* i, nos 33–4; PRO, Significations of Excommunication, C85/23/42.

[5] *Reg. Morton* iii (forthcoming), nos 253–7.

[6] Ibid. nos 293–798; see also C. Harper-Bill, 'A Late Medieval Visitation: the Diocese of Norwich in 1499', *Proceedings of the Suffolk Institute of Archaeology and History* xxxiv pt i (1977), 35–47.

[7] The amount of work involved for the scribe is revealed by the large corpus of papal, archiepiscopal and royal grants and confirmations relating to the appropriation of

appear, and non-residents, or their proctors, were to produce dispensations or licences. In the course of the visitation the archbishop's commissary endeavoured to discover if any incumbent was absent from his cure without a papal dispensation or a licence from his diocesan, whether the clergy, both beneficed and unbeneficed, were sufficiently well-trained to serve a cure of souls and to administer the sacraments, and whether there was any suspicion of clerical concubinage or immorality. This information was extracted both by examination of the clergy and by questions put to the parishioners. The visitor was also concerned with the physical state of the church and attempted to discover if the rector was maintaining the manse and chancel and the congregation the nave, if the churchyard was properly fenced so as to exclude stray animals, and if the books, ornaments and vestments were in reasonable condition. More important still, he needed to ensure that the church and cemetery had not been polluted, so as to require reconciliation. He asked the incumbent or his representative whether the parishioners were prompt in the payment of tithe and their other dues, and the curate was required to denounce any who were notorious for their failure to attend church or for their irreverent behaviour within it, for heretical or superstitious beliefs, for malicious behaviour towards their neighbours, or for perjury in any form. He sought out any wills which had not been proved by the lawful ecclesiastical authority because the executors were attempting to misappropriate the goods of the deceased. Finally, the visitor required information about any notorious sexual offences in the parish, ranging from prostitution to illicit relations before marriage. The detailed moral code incorporated in the canon law of the Church combined with the perennial inclination to titillating gossip within a closed community to render this last category by far the most productive of accusations.

To understandable suspicions that these *sede vacante* visitations were not very thorough, because the commissaries were burdened by a great volume of work which had to be accomplished in a short time, the *comperta et detecta* of 1499 from Norwich diocese, to be published in volume III of this edition, provide a salutary corrective. They suggest that, although such a voluminous record has not survived elsewhere, the visitors were extremely diligent in their inquisition into parochial life. The necessary speed of operations may, however, be illustrated in the itinerary of Mr Robert Sherborne in the archdeaconry of Exeter in June 1492. On 1 June he visited the cathedral church, where he examined the eight resident canons and thirty-two other clergy. On 2 June he visited the deanery of Christianity, which contained eighteen churches. On the following Monday, 4 June, he visited the priory of St Nicholas, and the next day both St John's, Exeter, and Polsloe priory. On Wednesday eighty-nine jurors were summoned from the deaneries of Kenn and Dunsford, in which thirty-four churches were served by forty-nine clergy. On Thursday he visited the deanery of Aylesbeare in the college of St Mary Ottery, and next day he examined the clergy of the collegiate church before moving on Friday night to Honiton, where on Saturday he examined the clergy and parishioners

parish churches and the foundation of chantries transcribed by the registrar during Archbishop Warham's visitation of the diocese of Canterbury in 1511 (Reg. Warham, fos 90–158). It is rare for such documentation to be preserved in a register.

of the twenty-seven churches of the deaneries of Honiton and Dunkeswell. On Saturday evening he returned to Exeter and did not recommence the visitation until 14 June, when in three days he examined the clergy and parishioners of two deaneries and the nuns of Canonsleigh (265–81).

In the archdeaconry of Lincoln in 1495, Mr Ralph Haines visited seventeen deaneries between 27 February and 14 April and in only one, Holland, did he spend more than one day in examination (138). Easily the best example of the energy expended in visitation is, however, provided by Mr Roger Church, In Bath and Wells diocese in 1495 he visited eleven religious houses between 30 January and 27 February, and also perambulated the deaneries (341–56). The following year in Coventry and Lichfield diocese between 8 March and 23 June he visited twenty-seven religious houses and the five archdeaconries (369–409). Before the end of the year he was in Rochester, where November was occupied in the visitation of the single archdeaconry and five religious houses, including the cathedral priory (441–8). In the diocese of Worcester in 1498, between 26 October and 22 December he visited eighteen deaneries and fifteen monasteries; between 26 October and 27 November alone he examined a theoretical total of 343 clergy from 175 churches (458–88). In the diocese of Norwich in 1499 he personally visited twenty-one religious houses between 14 March and 12 June, and between 15 April and 27 July he held court sessions for the probate of wills and the hearing of cases arising from the visitation of the archdeaconries of Norfolk and Norwich at twenty-nine spearate locations apart from Norwich itself.[8] In autumn 1499 he was delegated to conduct a visitation of the diocese of Salisbury (558).

Little documentary evidence has survived from this tremendous activity. The Norwich material, which is quite exceptional, will receive separate treatment, but for other dioceses information concerning the condition of the parishes is extremely meagre. The lists of parochial clergy from the archdeaconry of Exeter and from nine deaneries of the diocese of Worcester, copied into the register from the returns of the rural deans, have some value as an illustration of the staffing of parish churches and the proportions of graduates to be found among incumbents and the unbeneficed, but they lack the colour of full visitation returns (267–75, 478–88); the information therefrom is summarised below in table 2. From the diocese of Worcester the only positive information concerning the visitor's enquiries that can be gleaned is that he found one churchyard with broken fencing, two incontinent chaplains and two cases of lay immorality (485–7).

Rather more informative are some of the accounts of the visitation of religious houses and collegiate churches. For many of these, in the dioceses of Bath and Wells (347–8), Coventry and Lichfield (374–403), Rochester (442–7) and the archdeaconry of Surrey (83–4), the information to be derived from the register is merely prosopographical, yet even this is not without value, providing evidence of levels of recruitment to the religious life in the generation before the initial impact of Lutheranism. On the evidence of numbers alone, the larger communities appear still to have been healthy and viable institutions. For Exeter diocese (276–96) and the archdeaconry of Winchester (127–34) many of the *comperta et detecta* are extant, while for Repton

8 *Reg. Morton* iii (forthcoming), nos 258–92, 198–252.

priory in 1496 there are injunctions (380). Much interesting detail is provided by these documents, but they do not supply any evidence which should modify judgements based on the more extensive material for Coventry and Lichfield, Lincoln and Norwich dioceses which is already in print.[9] The general picture to be drawn from Archbishop Morton's *sede vacante* visitations of religious houses is one of generally conscientious observance of Rule and statutes, punctuated by occasional minor scandals and more frequent back-biting, and rendered more difficult in smaller communities by economic difficulties leading to indebtedness. The perennial problem was nicely encapsulated in the testimony of one monk of Winchester cathedral priory: at every visitation there was much talk of reform, which in some matters was effective for a while, but the long-term results were negligible (127). The conscientious attempts of the archbishop and his officials to effect reform by whatever means were appropriate may, however, be summarised by two contrasting documents: the appointment in 1493 of a financial coadjutor to the aged prior of Reigate (92) and the draconian measures threatened in 1495 against an allegedly incompetent and malicious prior of St Frideswide's (263). It must never be forgotten, moreover, that the positive and beneficial elements of later medieval monasticism, both spiritual and social, find no reflection in records such as are here printed.

The primary purpose of the visitation was, of course, to examine the state of the church in the vacant diocese, but there can be little doubt that the inevitability of *sede vacante* visitation was due in part to the consequent right to levy procurations from religious houses and rural deaneries. This accounts, too, for the determination of the archbishop's commissaries to conduct visitations in the winter months, which the diocesan and his officials normally regarded as a close season.[10] If the visitation was not accomplished immediately, a new bishop might be provided before the spring and the procurations lost for many years, until the next vacancy. The total procurations collected during the ten vacancies which are recorded in Morton's register was £996 5s 11d from parish churches and £413 6s 8d from religious houses. Many vacancies were not recorded, and the sum total of procurations certainly represented a considerable addition to archiepiscopal revenue. Such *sede vacante* visitations were, moreover, much more profitable than a metropolitical visitation of the province, for which the archbishop was forbidden by a decree of Pope Innocent IV to take procurations from parish churches, which for the ordinary provided the greater part of such revenue.[11]

[9] P. Heath, ed., *Bishop Geoffrey Blythe's Visitations*, c. *1515–1525*, Staffordshire Record Society 4th series, vii (1973); A. Hamilton Thompson, ed., *Visitations of the Diocese of Lincoln, 1517–31*, Lincoln Record Society xxxiii, xxxv, xxxvii (1940–47); A. Jessopp, ed., *Visitations of the Diocese of Norwich, 1492–1532*, Camden Society, 3rd series, xliii (1888).
[10] Winter visitations are recorded at Winchester in 1492, Bath and Wells in 1495, Rochester in 1496 and Worcester in 1498. At Lincoln in 1495 and Coventry and Lichfield in 1496 visitation began in the late months of winter.
[11] Potthast, *Regesta Pontificum Romanorum* ii, 1206; cf. Churchill, *Canterbury Administration* i, 290 n. 4. This bull was in 1492 transcribed at the end of Bishop Courtenay's Winchester register, fo. 43v, following an institution dated 12 Sept. 1492. It is possible that the archbishop was intending to make a metropolitical visitation, but far more

The method of calculating procurations is obscure and deserves further study. It varied considerably from diocese to diocese. In Ely and Norwich dioceses 3d in the pound was levied according to the valuation of each parish church in the *Taxatio* of 1291.[12] In the diocese of Chichester the same system was adopted, but the rate was 4d in the pound.[13] In the dioceses of Bath and Wells, Coventry and Lichfield, Lincoln and Worcester and in the archdeaconry of Winchester each rural deanery was assessed at five marks, with isolated exceptions for very small deaneries (40, 76, 98, 228, 230, 232, 238, 244, 247, 251, 359, 429, 503-4). In the archdeaconry of Surrey, however, assessment was by individual churches and there is no discernible relationship to the taxable valuation (106); in the deanery of Southwark, for example, all churches, from St Mary Magdalen valued at £4 to Lambeth valued at £30, and in the deanery of Ewell all churches from Esher valued at £8 to Kingston valued at £80, paid the same 7s 7½d. In Rochester procurations were listed by deanery, but there was no standard sum (449), while in the diocese of Exeter they were assessed on individual churches, were extremely variable and bore no relationship to the *Taxatio* (332-6). These varying methods of calculation were obviously based on local custom, but it is perhaps surprising that the rate of procurations finds no mention in the synodal statutes of the thirteenth century.

The archbishop during vacancies received all other spiritual revenues due to the diocesan *sede plena*. As the accompanying table I shows, the most profitable dues apart from procurations were the receipts from the episcopal *mensae* (the collection of which in the diocese of Winchester was the cause of prolonged litigation with the prior and convent), the accumulated pensions which had over the centuries been stipulated by successive diocesan bishops when they had authorised the appropriation of parish churches to religious houses, the payments or *praestationes* payable in certain dioceses to the bishop by the archdeacons, and the probate fees normally taken by the bishop. In addition, in the diocese of Norwich, according to a unique custom, a considerable sum accrued from the first fruits of the benefices of newly-instituted incumbents.[14] These revenues were supplemented by synodals, financial penalties imposed by judicial sentence, institution fees and the standard charges imposed for the granting of licences, letters dimissory and other concessions. In some cases the Official *sede vacante* was responsible for the probate of wills pertaining to the prerogative of the church of Canterbury (105b, 324-31, 338, 438) but this revenue did not, of course, accrue as a result of the vacancy.

The various accounts reveal a fairly standard pattern of fees. Half-a-mark was charged for institution,[15] and also for an inquisition into the right of

likely, in view of the subsequent litigation, that there was some convenient confusion at Winchester between the right of the archbishop as metropolitan and as ordinary *sede vacante*.

[12] *Reg. Morton* iii (forthcoming), nos 188-91; Canterbury, Dean and Chapter Library, Reg. R, fo. 49ff.

[13] *Reg. Chichele* iv, 147-8.

[14] *Reg. Morton* iii (forthcoming), no. 196; cf. P. Heath, *English Parish Clergy on the Eve of the Reformation* (1969), 43.

[15] The only exception in the register is no. 104, an institution to the church of Chale, I.o.W.

patronage, when this was necessary (360). Confirmation of the election of a religious superior was more expensive, ranging from £5 to £10 (363, 432). Letters dimissory cost the applicant 3s 4d (220), and the clerk who wished to undergo purgation to clear his name had to part with 6s 8d for the issuing of the commission (225). The reconciliation of a church or cemetery polluted *effusione sanguinis seu seminis*, for which the services of a suffragan bishop was necessary, cost five marks (362). The register also lists a large number of probate fees; for a small proportion of these, forty spread over three dioceses, all under the administration of Mr Church, the total of the inventory of the goods of the deceased is given (254, 438).[16] In a period for which relatively few inventories are extant, these figures are valuable as an indication of the extent to which the archbishop's officials observed the scale of fees set down by Lyndwood earlier in the century.[17] For twenty-six of these wills the fees charged were within Lyndwood's scale, and for two below it; but in twelve cases the fees were higher than that norm, in seven of them very much in excess of the scale. The variation in the fees suggests that charges were levied according to the amount of work involved in probate.

Two of the registers provide some slight indication of the expenses involved in visitation, which is valuable since such references are rare. In the diocese of Exeter in 1492 Mr Sherborne incurred expenses of £13 19s 4d on his visitation, while a further £7 19s 6d was paid out to the thirty-one rural deans, who presumably acted as apparitors (338). In Bath and Wells diocese in 1495 Mr Church's expenses in visitation were £12, while £2 6s 8d was paid to preachers (365). When set against receipts for procurations these figures emphasise the profitability of *sede vacante* visitation.

A large number of documents and references in the accounts illustrate the various tasks assigned to an Official or keeper of the spiritualities. In short, he was responsible for the exercise, as the archbishop's delegate, of all the jurisdictional functions of the ordinary, but since he was not a bishop, the sacramental offices of the diocesan had to be performed by a suffragan, who was normally resident within the diocese. Such would be required to conduct ordinations, to reconcile churches and to confer the veil of chastity upon a pious widow (21). A particularly good example of the vital function of the suffragan bishop is provided by Thomas Cornish, warden of the collegiate church of Ottery St Mary and bishop of Tenos *in partibus infidelium*. He conducted ordinations during the vacancies of the sees of Bath and Wells in 1491-92 and 1495 and of Exeter in 1492 (53, 65, 75, 323, 357). During the first vacancy at Bath and Wells, a large number of candidates from Exeter diocese presented themselves, because their bishop, Richard Fox, was constantly engaged in governmental business as Keeper of the Privy Seal. There were also candidates from Llandaff and Salisbury dioceses. It appears

[16] *Reg. Morton* iii (forthcoming), no. 195.
[17] W. Lyndwood, *Provinciale seu Constitutiones Angliae* (Oxford 1679), 181; cf. M. Bowker, 'Some Archdeacons' Court Books and the Commons' Supplication against the Ordinaries', in *The Study of Medieval Records*, ed. D. A. Bullough and R. L. Storey (Oxford 1971), 296-302.

that Cornish was exercising the sacramental functions of a bishop for the whole of south-west England.

The Official himself was responsible for the collection of revenue due to the archbishop and for the appointment of collectors of any taxation which might be voted by Convocation to the king (60, 67). It was his obligation to root out heresy in the diocese (57, 550-1) and to claim convicted clerks from the secular justices and where appropriate offer them compurgation (56, 225, 552-7). Often the Official *sede vacante* was himself commissioned to preside, alone or with another, in the consistory court (81, 368). He might issue exemplifications of documents emanating from other authorities, notably in this register of an earlier decision in the diocesan consistory in an interesting matrimonial cause (30) and of three dispensations granted by the papal penitentiary (35-7). He instituted to benefices and if necessary organised inquisitions into the rightful possession of the advowson (71-2, 360). He examined and confirmed the election of religious superiors, unless that prerogative was specifically reserved to the archbishop himself (19, 262). He presided over synods of the diocesan clergy, and issued licences for non-residence, marriage other than in a parish church (224) and study away from their cure by beneficed clergy (20, 31). He granted probate of all testaments which normally fell under the bishop's jurisdiction, and sometimes also was entrusted with the local exercise of the authority of the prerogative court of Canterbury (105B; 324-31, a group of transcripts of wills; 338, 438).

All these routine tasks were accomplished in addition to the considerable burden of visitation, and the prevailing impression left by the *sede vacante* registers is one of sustained and conscientious activity. As with the archbishop himself in his wider policies for his province, the maximisation of revenue and the implementation of reform were not necessarily incompatible. Experience as an Official *sede vacante* provided a splendid training for episcopal responsibilities, and that eminently successful bishop of Chichester, Robert Sherborne, acquired under Morton valuable experience in that role. Yet there were other qualifications more obviously essential for a late medieval bishop, and Roger Church, who appears from the register to have been the most overworked of the archbishop's officials, was never to attain the dignity of prelacy.[18]

[18] For further discussion of the careers of those engaged in *sede vacante* administration, see C. Harper-Bill, 'The *Familia*, Administrators and Patronage of Archbishop John Morton', *Journal of Religious History* x (1979), 236-52.

TABLE 1: ARCHIEPISCOPAL REVENUES FROM VACANT SEES, 1490-99[1]

	COVENTRY & LICHFIELD 30 Sept. 1490– Dec. 1491[2]	BATH & WELLS May 1491– 8 Feb. 1492	EXETER 8 May 1492– 1 Mar. 1493	WINCHESTER 22 Sept. 1492– Easter 1493	BATH & WELLS Christmas 1494– Christmas 1495
PROCURATIONS OF PARISH CHURCHES	76 13 4	39 6 8	147 14 2	70 9 6	40 0 ●
PROCURATIONS OF RELIGIOUS HOUSES	16 0 0	26 13 4	2 6 8	48 13 4	33 6 ●
PENSIONS FROM APPROPRIATED CHURCHES	26 16 8		2 0 0	1 3 4	13 ●
PENSIONS FROM ARCHDEACONS				33 6 8	
PROBATE FEES	6 5 1		28 5 2	7 0 8	13 10 1●
BENEFICES APPROPRIATED TO EPISCOPAL MENSAE	30 0 0			62 10 0	
VACANCIES OF CHURCHES & INSTITUTION FEES	3 6		9 13 4	16 8	13 13 ●
FIRST FRUITS OF BENEFICES					
REVENUES FROM LICENCES, CORRECTIONS ETC				10 4	10 0 ●
SYNODALS	24 5 4				
TOTAL	£180 3 11*	£ 66 0 0	£189 19 4	£224 10 6*	£110 4 ●

[1] No attempt has been made to correct minor arithmetical mistakes of the scribes.
[2] This vacancy lasted until February 1493, but the accounts cover only the first year.

LINCOLN	COVENTRY & LICHFIELD	ROCHESTER	WORCESTER	NORWICH
30 Dec. 1494– 6 Nov. 1496	29 Feb.– 8 Oct. 1496	4 Nov. 1496– 21 May 1497	25 Aug.– 24 Dec. 1498	15 Feb. 1499– 20 July 1499
257 6 8	90 0 0	28 8 3	92 3 4	182 0 11
178 6 8	40 13 4	12 6 8	44 6 8	
120 10 8	26 14 8	16 15 4	24 1 0	53 5 6
216 6 8				
67 12 11	13 13 10		3 16 8	52 15 4
76 13 4	34 14 0		57 1 8	
30 0 3	12 3 4[3]	1 0 0	5 0 0	12 13 4
				254 19 5
20 0 10				
	23 10 0		6 9 10	29 12 3
£966 9 2	£241 9 2	£ 58 10 3	£232 19 2	£585 6 10

[3] This is a composite figure for various revenues, including institutions, collected by the archdeacon of Chester and paid to the Official.

* Accounts incomplete in Register.

TABLE 2: THE SECULAR CLERGY OF WORCESTER AND EXETER DIOCESES

The information which can be derived from these visitation returns is extremely disappointing compared with that for the diocese of Norwich, but it is possible to draw some conclusions with relation to the secular clergy.

Archdeaconry of Exeter, 1492

Deanery	No. of churches[1]	Appropriated[2]		Beneficed (G)[3]		Unbeneficed (G)[3]	
Exeter	20	3	(1)	17	(4)	17	
Kenn	18	3	(3)	18	(2)	10	
Dunsford	16	5	(5)	16	(4)	5	
Aylesbeare	20	10	(8)	17	(2)	14	
Honiton	17	4	(4)	15	(1)	6	
Dunkeswell	10	6	(4)	8	(1)	5	(1)
Plymtree	15	4	(4)	15	(6)	15	(1)
Tiverton	16	5	(4)	16	(6)	18	(1)
Cadbury	16	4	(4)	15	(5)	8	
	148	44	(37)	137	(31)	98	(3)

[1] Total churches, includes chapels.
[2] Figure in brackets – vicarages.
[3] Figure in brackets – number of graduates.

Diocese of Worcester, 1498

Deanery	No. of churches	Appropriated		Beneficed (G)		Unbeneficed (G)	
Powick	22	6	(5)	19	(5)	12	
Gloucester	32	13	(11)	18	(6)	35	
Dursley	22	6	(5)	19	(8)	22	(1)
Bristol	26	11	(9)	24	(15)	59	(3)
Hawkesbury & Bitton	28	8	(8)	26	(10)	19	(1)
Stonehouse	27	7	(6)	24	(13)	23	
Cirencester	22	7	(5)	17	(2)	18	(2)
Fairford	11	8	(8)	15	(6)	6	
Stowe	28	11	(8)	24	(7)	13	
	218	77	(65)	187	(72)	207	(7)

Percentage of Graduate Clergy

	Beneficed	Unbeneficed
Canterbury[1]	34%	–
Exeter	22.5%	3%
Norwich[2]	27%	4.5%
Worcester	38%	3%

[1] Calculated from *Reg. Morton* i, *passim*.
[2] Calculated from *Reg. Morton* iii (forthcoming), *passim*.

VACANCY OF THE SEE OF COVENTRY AND LICHFIELD, 1490–1491

[fo. 55] VACANCY OF THE EPISCOPAL SEE OF COVENTRY AND LICHFIELD THROUGH THE DEATH OF THE LORD JOHN HALSE OF GOOD MEMORY, LATELY BISHOP OF THE CATHEDRAL CHURCHES OF COVENTRY AND LICHFIELD, WHICH VACANCY BEGAN ON THE MORROW OF MICHAELMAS 1490 A.D., AND IN THE FIFTH YEAR FROM THE TRANSLATION OF THE VERY REVEREND FATHER IN GOD AND LORD JOHN, BY GOD'S GRACE ARCHBISHOP OF CANTERBURY, PRIMATE OF ALL ENGLAND AND LEGATE OF THE APOSTOLIC SEE.

> *Note*: William Smith was granted custody of the temporalities by the king on 30 Mar. 1491 (*CPR 1485–94*, p. 335). The delay in provision provoked Henry VII to write in strong terms to the pope in Dec. 1491 (*CSP Venetian*, i, no. 614). Smith was eventually provided to the see on 1 Oct. 1492.

1.　　　　Commission, with powers of canonical coercion, to Mr William Wareham, D.C.L., Mr John Thowre, D.C.L., Mr Henry Edyall, archd. of Rochester, Mr Robert Shyrborne, M.A., and Mr John Sharp, Decr. B., as vicars-general and guardians of the spirituality of the see of Coventry and Lichfield in the vacancy following the d. of bp. John Halse, with the following powers:

(i) to enquire or cause enquiry to be made into vacancies of benefices and to admit, institute and issue mandates for induction to all benefices where institution normally pertains to the bp.

(ii) to sequestrate or cause to be sequestrated the fruits of ecclesiastical benefices and other goods of any persons in the cities and dioc. where law or custom decrees that they should be so sequestrated, and to retain custody of such goods.

(iii) to receive oaths of canonical obedience from any subjects within the cities and dioc. who *sede plena* should render such oaths to the bp.

(iv) to visit the cath. chs. of Coventry and Lichfield and all monasteries, abbeys, priories and other pious places, both religious houses and hospitals, and the clergy and people of the cities and dioc.

(v) to enquire in person or by deputy into the excesses, faults, sins and crimes of any persons which may have been or may be committed during the vacancy of the see, cognizance and punishment of which pertains to the diocesan by law or custom, and to correct and canonically to punish the same.

(vi) to examine, approve and finally expedite exchanges of ecclesiastical benefices in the dioc. during the vacancy.

(vii) to inhibit under threat of ecclesiastical censure any action by deans, chapters, convs., archds., rural deans and others exercising jurisdiction which may be prejudicial to the abp.'s visitation of the cities and dioc.

(viii) to register and grant probate of testaments of any persons dying in the cities and dioc. where registration and probate pertain *sede plena* to the bp. or to deans, chapters, convs., archds., rural deans or others; to commit

1

administration of the goods of such deceased and of any others who may die intestate to the executors nominated in the testaments or to other persons to whom, in accordance with law, administration may be committed and who seem suitable, to receive the accounts of executors or administrators and finally to acquit them.

(ix) to suspend in the name of the abp. the jurisdiction of any inferior authority in the cities and dioc. for the duration of the visitation, and if necessary to restrain such inferiors.

(x) to request, receive and retain custody, whenever there is need, of clerks indicted or accused before secular justices or judges in cases of blood or felony, according to the liberty hitherto granted to such clerks or to the clerical order.

(xi) to remove from benefices, offices or ecclesiastical administration those who according to law should be so removed.

(xii) to punish those illicitly farming or receiving at farm ecclesiastical benefices.

(xiii) to issue letters dimissory and letters of recommendation and to grant commission and licence to any catholic bp. who has received the blessing of the apostolic see for the exercise of his office for ordination to minor and holy orders, at the normal times, of regular and secular clerks in the cities and dioc., and to examine such ordinands or cause them to be examined, as pertains to the diocesan *sede plena*.

(xiv) to enquire or cause enquiry to be made concerning the appropriation of any ecclesiastical benefices, portions or pensions in the cities and dioc. by any person, monastery or other place, and to certify the abp. of the names of the benefice and the appropriator, of accusations lodged in this matter and of the reasons for the appropriation.

(xv) to compel rs. and vs. of parish chs. in the cities and dioc., by any ecclesiastical censures, to reside in person.

(xvi) to exercise, maintain and defend, in the name of the abp. and of his ch., all spiritual and ecclesiastical jurisdiction which pertains to the diocesan *sede plena* and to the abp. *sede vacante*.

(xvii) to seek and receive all spiritual and ecclesiastical revenues which pertain to the abp. and his ch. by reason of the vacancy of the see, to issue letters of acquittance for such receipts, to revoke and reform by any legitimate means usurpations and attempts against these revenues, to proceed against usurpers, attempters of usurpation and transgressors and canonically to punish and coerce rebels by ecclesiastical censure.

(xviii) to do all other things necessary or expedient for the above.

Lambeth [undated]

2.   [fo. 55v] Inst.[1] of Nicholas Benteley, pr., to vic. of Shirley (*Shyrley*), Db., vac. by res. of John Moore. P. abbot and conv. of Darley (*Derleigh*). I. archd. of Derby. Assignment for the term of his natural life of an annual pension of 4 marks from the fruits of the vic. to John Moore, payable in equal instalments at the feasts of the Invention of the Holy Cross [3 May] and All Saints [1 Nov.], to the fulfilment of which payment Nicholas Benteley swore upon the Holy Gospels. Lichfield, 10 Nov. 1490.

[1] This inst. was performed by Mr Shirborne and Mr Sharp. Subsequent insts. to no. 18 are noted as performed by the keepers of the spiritualities.

3.	[fo. 56] Inst of Mr Thomas Harrys, Decr. B., to ch. of Stoke-upon-Tern (*Stoke super Tyrne*), Sa., vac. by d. of William Bodon. P. Thomas marquis of Dorset, lord Ferrers, Groby and Astley. I. archd. [of Shrewsbury]. Coventry, 16 Nov. 1490.

4.	Inst. of James Saperton, pr., to ch. of Cubley, Db., vac. by d. of Thomas Broune. P. Sir Nicholas Mountgomery, kt. I. archd. [of Derby]. Lichfield, 22 Nov. 1490.

5.	Inst. of Richard Ardern, chap., to ch. of Northenden (*Northerdene*), Chs., vac. by d. of James Hall. P. Henry Trafford, esq., on this occasion by virtue of the concession of the advowson by the abbot and conv. of St Werburgh, Chester. I. archd. [of Chester]. Lichfield, 3 Dec. 1490.

6.	Inst. of Thurstan Sayer, pr., to vic. of Sedgley (*Seghley*), St., vac. by d. of Richard Sharp. P. Cornelius Wyott of the parish of Sutton Coldfield, Wa., Godfrey Sayer of Adbaston, St., and Roger Sayer of Dudley (*Dudeley*), Wo., on this occasion by virtue of the concession of the advowson by the prior and conv. of St James, Dudley. I. archd. [of Stafford]. Lichfield, 10 Dec. 1490.

7.	Inst. of John Hoo, chap., to perpetual chantry of B.V.M. in ch. of Quatt, Sa., recently founded by Thomas Crowther, once rector, vac. by res. of Thomas Heth. P. Thomas Whiche of Quatt and Hugh and Humphrey Rolowe of Bridgnorth (*Brignorth*), Sa. I. archd. [of Stafford]. Lichfield, 12 Nov. 1490.

8.	[fo. 56v] Inst. of Thomas Swynerton, chap., to vic. of Drayton in Hayles, Sa., vac. by d. of Thomas Condon. P. prior and conv. of Sheen, Sy., O. Carth. I. archd. [of Shrewsbury]. Lichfield, 12 Nov. 1490.

9.	Inst. of Thomas Palmer, pr., in the person of his proctor Robert Woode, to ch. of Berrington (*Beryngton*), Sa., vac. by res. of William Lutte. P. abbot and conv. of St Peter, Shrewsbury. I. archd. of Shrewsbury. An oath was taken by Palmer to render certain pensions or portions to the abbot and conv. of Shrewsbury and to others to whom they were due, and most especially to render an annual pension of 6 marks to William Lutt for the duration of his life, so as to provide for his essential food and clothing, the first payment to be made within a month of the feast of the Annunciation of the B.V.M. [25 Mar.] 1491. The guardians of the spiritualities enjoined him and his successors in this benefice to render the said pension, on pain of excommunication and sequestation of the fruits of the benefice. Repton, 6 Dec. 1490.

10.	Inst. of John Morgan, pr., to vic. of Lilleshall (*Lillyshyll*), Sa., vac. by res. of Thomas Taylor. P. abbot and conv. of Lilleshall. I. archd. [of Shrewsbury]. Lichfield, 14 Jan. 1491.

11.	Inst. by the abp. of Mr Henry Borste, S.T.B., to prebend in the coll.

ch. of Gnosall (*Gnowsale*), St., lately held by Mr Christopher Urswyke and vac. by his res. P. the king.[1] I. Thomas Hande and Thomas Huntbache, curates of the coll. ch. Knole, 11 Jan. 1491.

[1] Pres.: *CPR 1485–94*, p. 338, dated 7 Jan. 1491.

12.   Inst. of Edmund Poole, subdeacon, to perpetual chantry of SS Nicholas and Catherine at Crich (*Criche*), Db., vac. by d. of William Woodruffe. P. Ralph Pole, esq. I. archd. [of Derby]. Lichfield, 8 Mar. 1491.

13.   [fo. 57] Inst. of Mr Robert Legge, Decr. B., in the person of his proctor *dominus* Richard Walton, to ch. of Weddington (*Weddyngton*), Wa., vac. by res. of the same Richard Walton. P. Thomas marquis of Dorset, lord Ferrers, Groby and Astley. I. archd. [of Coventry]. Lichfield, 8 Mar. 1491.

14.   Inst. of John Lacy, chap., to perpetual chaplaincy of the hospital of St Thomas the Martyr, Birmingham (*Brymyngham*), Wa., vac. by d. of Thomas Smalwode. P. Thomas Brymyngham, esq. I. archd. [of Coventry]. Lichfield, 28 Mar. 1491.

15.   Inst. of Thomas Power, chap., to ch. of Normanton, Db., vac. by d. of Richard Bolyngton. P. Sir Ralph Langford, kt. I. archd. [of Derby]. Lichfield, 30 Mar. 1491.

16.   Inst. of Henry Archer, chap., as perpetual v. of prebendal stall of Milverton in coll. ch. of Astley (*Asteley*), Wa., vac. by res. of Thomas Waren. P. Mr John Waren, prebendary of Milverton. I. John Sadeler, chap. Coventry, 11 Apr. 1491.

17.   Inst. of Thomas Bolston, chap., to ch. of Egginton (*Eginton*), Db., vac. by d. of Mr Ralph Forth. P. Ralph Pole, esq., of Radbourne (*Rodborne*), Db., and Thomas Babington, esq. I. archd. of Derby. Lichfield, 16 Apr. 1491.

18.   Inst. of Roger Arnold, pr., to vic. of St Mary, Derby, vac. by d. of John Lenton. P. abbot and conv. of Darley (*Derley*). I. archd. of Derby. Lichfield, 6 June 1491.

19.   [fo. 57v] In the chapter house of the nunnery of St Mary, Chester, O.S.B., in the presence of Mr Christopher Talbott, archd. of Chester, Mr Thomas Twemloo, his Official, Mr Henry Reynford, Decr. B., Mr John Goodefelawe, Decr. D., and of many others, Mr Robert Shyrborne, one of the vicars-general of the dioc. appointed by the abp., confirmed the election as prioress of Margery Pasmeche, nun of the same conv. After she had taken an oath of canonical obedience, the archd. of Chester was ordered to induct or install her. Chester, 1 Mar. 1491.

20.   Licence granted by the vicars-general to Mr Henry Reynforde, r. of Holy Trinity, Chester (*Cestr'*), to study for three years in an English university

in the faculty of arts, theology or laws, and to receive the fruits of his benefice for his maintenance during his study, provided that he should appoint a suitable deputy to discharge the obligations of the benefice to the ordinary and that the cure should be properly served. Lichfield, 21 Apr. 1491.

21.   Commission to Robert bp. of Achonry (*Achaden*)[1] to administer the oath of perpetual chastity to Cecily, widow of Sir Thomas Gerard, kt., late of the parish of Winwick (*Wynwyk*), La., and to invest her with the veil, ring and mantle which customarily signify this state. Lichfield, 22 May 1491.

[1] Robert Wellys, O.F.M. bp. of Achonry, provided on 14 July 1473, never obtained possession of his see. He carried out the majority of ordinations in the dioc. of Coventry and Lichfield from 23 Dec. 1475 to 18 Sept. 1490 (Lichfield Joint Record Office, B/A/1/12, fos 210r–291r *passim*).

22.   Commission by the abp. to Mr Thomas Reynold, canon residentiary in the cath. ch. of Coventry and Lichfield [*sic*] as vicar-general and guardian of the spiritualities of the dioc. of Coventry and Lichfield, with authority to receive all spiritual revenues pertaining to the ch. of Canterbury by virtue of the vacancy, to issue letters of acquittance, to account to the abp. for these revenues and to conduct all other business which pertains to the office of vicar-general. Lambeth, 1 May 1491.

23.   [fo. 58] Inst.[1] of Mr Christopher Norres, pr., in the person of his proctor Robert Colett, chap., to ch. of Aldford (*Aldeforde*), Chs., vac. by d. of Mr Robert Oldom. P. Richard Norres, esq., on this occasion by virtue of the concession of the advowson by John Stanley, esq. I. archd. of Chester. Lichfield, 20 June 1491.

[1] Henceforth all institutions are noted as performed by the keeper of the spiritualities.

24.   Inst. of Christopher Ermethstede, pr., to vic. of Elmton (*Helmetone*), Db., vac. by d. of Thomas Derby. P. prior and conv. of Thurgarton, York dioc. I. archd. of Derby. Lichfield, 1 July 1491.

25.   Inst. of William Walkedene, pr., to vic. of Mayfield (*Mafeld*), St., vac. by res. of Robert Hawkesby. P. prior and conv. of Tutbury. I. archd. [of Stafford]. Assignment of an annual pension of 5 marks payable by Walkedene and his successors in the vic. to Hawkesby for the duration of his natural life, payable in equal instalments at Christmas, the Annunciation of the B.V.M. [25 Mar.], the Nativity of St John the Baptist [24 June] and Michaelmas [29 Sept.]. Lichfield, 13 July 1491.

26.   [fo. 58v] Inst. of Mr Edward Hasley to prebend of Cotton (*Coton*) in coll. ch. of Tamworth (*Tameworth*), St., vac. by d. of Mr Richard Balder. P. the king. I. archd. of Stafford. Lichfield, 9 Aug. 1491.

27.   Inst. of Henry Sydecoke to vic. of Abbots Bromley (*Bromley Abbatis*), St., vac. by res. of Thomas Power. P. abbot and conv. of Burton on Trent. I. archd. [of Stafford]. Lichfield, 20 Aug. 1491.

28.   Inst. of Roger Salter, B.A., in the person of his proctor Mr Robert Sandsone, notary public, to wardenship of coll. ch. of SS Mary and Nicholas, Newport, Sa., vac. by res. of Richard Porter. P. abbot and conv. of SS Peter and Paul, Shrewsbury (*Salop'*). I. archd. [of Shrewsbury]. Lichfield, 20 Aug. 1491.

29.   Recitation of dispensation granted to Roger Salter, B.A., by Adrian Castellesi, protonotary of the apostolic see and papal collector in England, that he may be ordained pr. and hold any ecclesiastical benefice with cure of souls, although he is only 23 years old, issued by virtue of the faculty granted by the pope to Castellesi thus to dispense persons over 22 years of age,[1] and dated at his residence at St Paul's, London, 13 Aug. 1491. Lichfield, 20 Aug. 1491.

        [1] *CPL*, xiv, 54.

30.   [fo. 59] Exemplification issued by authority of Mr Thomas Reynold, J.U.B., vicar-general of the abp. presiding in the consistory court of Lichfield, in the presence of Mr Thomas Colt, notary public and his scribe, John Deyne, chap., John Kyrke and John Gays, and at the request of Mr Robert Prat, proctor of Sir William Troutbeke, kt., of the sentence of annulment of marriage promulgated by Mr Richard Salter, Decr. D., Official of the consistory court of Lichfield:

Letters testimonial of Mr Salter, official of the consistory court *sede vacante* by authority of the abp., rehearsing his verdict in a matrimonial cause between Joan Troutbeke *alias* Butler of the parish of Winwick (*Wynwyke*), La., petitioner, and Sir William Troutbeke of the parish of Bromborough (*Bromebrogh*), Chs., respondent, brought first before Mr Humphrey Hawardyn, D.C.L., Official of the consistory court, and subsequently before Mr Salter. The tenor of the *libellus* produced on behalf of Joan is recited:

She asserts that although she, Joan, and William contracted marriage, or rather a parody of marriage, and obtained its solemnisation, or rather its profanation, by the church, and had lived together for some considerable length of time as man and wife, or rather as adulterers, the marriage and its solemnisation are not in accordance with law, since Joan and William are related in the third and fourth degrees of consanguinity and no dispensation has been obtained; all this is public knowledge. Therefore she requests that the pretended marriage should be annulled, that they should be separated and divorced one from the other, and that perpetual silence should be imposed upon William in this matter by definitive sentence of the judge. She begs that no allegation on the part of William be allowed to interfere with her intention in this matter.

Having taken the advice of men learned in the law, the Official invalidated the pretended marriage and divorced Joan and William one from another, and ordered a public instrument to be drawn up by Mr Thomas Colt, notary public. Sentence was promulgated in the cath. ch. of Lichfield on 30 July 1491 in the presence of Mr Thomas Reynold, J.U.B., canon residentiary of Lichfield and vicar-general of the abp., Mr Richard Shirborne, archd. of Shrewsbury and canon residentiary of Lichfield, and Mr Robert Sampson, notary public.

Notarial exemplification of the foregoing by Thomas Colt, clerk of

Coventry and Lichfield dioc., and notary public by apostolic authority. Lichfield, 12 Aug. 1491.

31.　　[fo. 60] Licence granted by Mr Thomas Reynold to Roger Salter, B.A., warden of coll. ch. of SS Mary and Nicholas, Newport, Sa., according to the terms of the constitution *Cum ex eo*,[1] to study for seven years at Oxford, Cambridge or any other university and to receive the fruits of his benefice as if he were residing in person provided that he shall be ordained subdeacon within a year of institution to the wardenship, that the church shall be adequately served, a proctor shall be appointed to discharge his obligations to the bp. and the chancel and other buildings shall be maintained in good repair. Lichfield, 17 Sept. 1491.

　　[1] c. 34 VI i 6.

32.　　Inst. of James Williamson, chap., to perpetual chantry of William de Allesley in ch. of Holy Trinity, Coventry, vac. by res. of Mr Richard Leylond, S.T.P. P. prior of cath. priory of B.V.M., Coventry. I. archd. of Coventry. Lichfield, 16 Oct. 1491.

33.　　Inst. of Richard West, chap., to perpetual chantry of Sir Thomas Ardyngton, kt., and Jocosa his wife in the parish ch. of Aston near Birmingham (*Assyngton*), Wa., vac. by d. of William Horne. P. Gilbert abbot of Leicester, Lincoln dioc. I. archd of Coventry. Lichfield, 15 Dec. 1491.

34.　　Inst. of John Fox, chap., to perpetual chantry of B.V.M. in ch. of Crich (*Cruche*), Db., vac. by d. of Thomas Cowper. P. Ralph Pole. I. archd. [of Derby]. Lichfield, 22 Dec. 1491.

35.　　Exemplification issued by authority of Mr Thomas Reynold of a notification addressed to the bp. of Coventry and Lichfield of a dispensation granted by Julian, cardinal bp. of Ostia (*Ostien'*), and papal penitentiary, to John Asshehurst and Margaret Longtre, of Coventry and Lichfield dioc., for the celebration of marriage between them despite their relationship in the fourth and fourth degrees of consanguinity, dated at Rome on 4 Dec. 1490 and bearing the seal of the penitentiary. Lichfield, 31 Aug. 1491.

36.　　Exemplification issued by authority of Mr Thomas Reynold of a dispensation granted by Julian, cardinal bp. of Ostia (*Ostien'*) and papal penitentiary, to Hugh Shirbourne and Anne Talbot of Coventry and Lichfield dioc., who had obtained a dispensation from the apostolic see for their marriage despite their relationship in the fourth degree of consanguinity. They feared, however, that this dispensation was invalid because one of them was descended in the third and the other in the fourth degree from a common ancestor, and they had not mentioned in their petition that one of them stood at only three removes from the common ancestor. The papal penitentiary, recalling that Pope Clement VI had validated dispensations in similar cases where it had been omitted to mention that one of the parties stood at three removes from a common ancestor,[1] by apostolic authority declares the dispensation to be valid. Sealed with the penitentiary's seal and dated at Rome, 5 Nov. 1490.

7

Wherefore Mr Reynold, by the authority of this letter, after due inquisition that they wished to marry and that Anne had not been seized from another man, authorised them to contract marriage and declared that their children should be legitimate, declaring that according to the decision of Pope Clement VI the dispensation should be valid as if mention had been made of the third degree. Lichfield, 31 Aug. 1491.

[1] *Acta Clementis Papae VI, 1342–52*, ed. A.L.Tautu (Rome, 1960), no. 325, 31 Aug. 1349, *Cum vos ad partes Armeniae*.

37.   Exemplification issued by authority of Mr Thomas Reynold of a dispensation granted by Julian, cardinal bp. of Ostia and papal penitentiary, to James Lawe, scholar of Coventry and Lichfield dioc., that he may be ordained pr. and hold a benefice, notwithstanding his illegitimacy, in that he is the son of a pr., providing that he is not an imitator of his father's incontinence but is of good life and conversation and sufficiently learned, and that when he obtains a benefice he shall be ordained and shall reside in person. Sealed with the penitentiary's seal and dated at Rome, 27 May 1491.

The dispensation was confirmed by Mr Reynold after due enquiry had been made into his morals and learning. Lichfield, 23 Sept. 1491.

[fo. 61] ACCOUNTS OF RECEIPTS DURING THE VACANCY OF THE SEE OF COVENTRY AND LICHFIELD, 1490–1491.

38.   RECEIPTS FOR PETER'S PENCE AND SYNODALS.

Note: there is a gap of three inches, and the account begins with receipts for Peter's Pence from the prebends of the cath. ch. of Lichfield within the archdeaconry of Stafford, wrongly described as in the archdeaconry of Derby; cf. *Valor Ecclesiasticus*, iii, 149, 134, 115, 102, and below, no. 430b.

a. From prebends of Colwich (*Colwyche*), 10s; Longdon, 5s; Baswich (*Berkeswyche*), 8s; Eccleshall, 20s; Brewood (*Brewode*), 8s.   Total: 51s.

b. Peter's Pence from archdeaconry of Coventry:
Dys. of Coventry (*Coven'*), 46s 8d; Marton (*Merton*), 40s; Stoneleigh (*Stonley*), 46s 8d; Arden (*Ardena*), 60s.   Total: £9 13s 4d.

c. Peter's Pence from the archdeaconry of Derby:
Dys. of Derby (*Derb'*), 48s 8d; Ashbourne (*Ayssheborne*), 26s 8d; High Peak (*Alto Pecco*), 26s 8d; Scarsdale (*Scarvesdale*), £4 6s 8d; Castellar (*Castillar'*), 26s 8d; Repton (*Repyngdon*), 22s. 8d.   Total: £11 18s.

d. Synodals[1] from archdeaconry of Coventry at Michaelmas and Easter:
Dys. of Coventry, 16s; Marton, 32s; Stoneleigh, 26s 8d; Arden, 40s.
Total: £5 14s 8d.

[1] MS: Denarii sancti Petri, but cf. no. 38b above.

e. Synodals from archdeaconry of Derby at Easter:
Dys. of Derby, £3 2s; Ashbourne (*Assheborne*) and High Peak, 42s 8d; Scarsdale, £3 2s; Castellar and Repton, 56s 8d.   Total: £11 3s 4d.

8

f. Peter's Pence from archdeaconry of Shrewsbury at Michaelmas:
Dys. of Shrewsbury (*Salop'*), £4; Newport (*Novi Burgi*), 40s.   Total: £6.

g. Synodals from archdeaconry of Shrewsbury at Michaelmas and Easter:
Dys. of Shrewsbury, 40s; Newport, 26s 8d.   Total: £3 6s 8d.

h. [fo. 61v] Peter's Pence from archdeaconry of Stafford at Michaelmas:
Dys. of Lapley and Trysull (*Trysill*), 42s; Alton (*Alneton*) and Leek (*Leke*), 32s;
Stafford and Newcastle-under-Lyme (*Novo Castro*), 50s; Tamworth (*Tomworth*)
and Tutbury, 28s.   Total: £7 12.

j. Synodals from archdeaconry of Stafford at Michaelmas and Easter:
Dys. of Lapley and Trysull, 26s 8d; Alton and Leek, 20s; Stafford and
Newcastle-under-Lyme, 26s 8d; Tamworth and Tutbury, 17s 4d.
                                                    Total: £4 10s 8d.

39.   PENSIONS DUE FROM CHURCHES.

a. Archdeaconry of Coventry:
Dean and chapter of Astley (*Asteley*) for ch. of Hillmorton (*Hulmerton*), Wa.,
13s 4d; abbot of Lavendon (*Lavenden*) for ch. of Shotteswell (*Shotwell*), Wa.,
3s 4d; prior of Maxstoke for chs. of Bishop's Itchington (*Ichynton*), Maxstoke,
Shustoke, Wa., 20s; prior of Clattercote (*Chaltercote*) for ch. of Ratley (*Roteley*),
Wa., 6s 8d; master of St Lawrence Poultney (*Pulteney*) [for ch. of Napton,
Wa.],[1] 3s 4d; prioress of Markyate (*Markeyate*) for ch. of Kingsbury
(*Kynnesbury*), Wa., 6s 8d; prior of St Anne's, Coventry (*iuxta Coven'*), for ch. of
Wolverton (*Wolverheton*), Wa., 13s 4d; warden of Warwick (*Warr'*) coll. for ch.
of Wolfhampcote (*Wolfamcote*), Wa., 13s 4d; abbot of Merevale (*Meryvall*) for
ch. of Mancetter (*Mancestr'*), Wa., 13s 4d; abbot of Sulby for ch. of
Wappenbury (*Wapynbury*), Wa., 6s 8d.   [Total: £5]

    [1] cf. no. 434a below.

b. Archdeaconry of Derby:
Master of Newark coll., Leicester (*Leicestr'*), for ch. of Duffield, Db., 40s;
abbot of Dale for ch. of Ilkeston (*Ilveston*), Db., 6s 8d; res. of Darley (*Derley*) for
ch. of Darley, Db., 6s 8d; prior of Tutbury for ch. of West Broughton
(*Broughton*), Db., 13s 4d; abbot of Beauchief (*Beauclyffe*) for ch. of Dronfield,
Db., 13s 4d; [prior of Mount Grace][1] for ch. of Beighton (*Boughton*), Db.,
3s 4d; [r. of Eckington][2] for ch. of Eckington (*Ekyngton*), Db., 13s 4d; abbot of
Dale for ch. of Heanor (*Henore*), Db., 6s 8d.   [Total: £5 5s 4d]

    [1] cf. no. 435c below.   [2] cf. no. 434c below.

c. Archdeaconry of Shrewsbury:
Abbot of Haughmond for chs. of Hanmer (*Hannemere*), Stanton (*Staundon*) and
Ryton (*Ruyton*), Sa., 36s 8d; master of Battlefield (*Batilfeld*) coll. for ch. of
Idsall (*Edyshale*), Sa., 13s 4d; master of Tong (*Tonge*) coll. for ch. of Lapley,
St., 4s; abbot of St Peter's, Shrewsbury, for ch. of Great Ness (*Ness Strange*),
Sa., 13s 4d.   [Total: £3 7s 4d]

d. [fo. 62] Archdeaconry of Stafford:
Abbot of Bordesley for ch. of Kinver (*Kynsare*), St., 6s 8d; dean of Windsor
(*Wyndesoure*) for ch. of Uttoxeter (*Otoxhatre*), St., 10s; prior of Stone for ch. of

Madely (*Maddeley*), St., 13s 4d; prior of St Thomas by Stafford (*iuxta Staff'*) for chs. of Bushbury (*Buysshebury*), Weston-upon-Trent (*Weston*) and Baswich (*Barkeswyche*), St., 44s; abbot of Hulton for chs. of Audley and Biddulph (*Bedulffe*), St., 33s 4d; abbot of Burton for ch. of Austrey (*Aldestre*), Wa., 20s.

[Total: £6 7s 4d]

e. Archdeaconry of Chester:
Master of Manchester (*Mancestr'*) coll., La., 40s; master of Bunbury coll. for ch. of Bunbury, Chs., 10s; prior of Penwortham (*Pentwurtham*) for ch. of Leyland (*Leylonde*), La., 40s; warden of coll. of Stoke in Wirral (*Wirall*) for pension from same ch., 6s 8d; dean of St John's, Chester (*Cestrie*), for ch. of Plemonstall (*Plegmonestowe*), Chs., 13s 4d; v. of Croston (*Crostone*) for ch. of Croston, La., 6s 8d; warden of King's College, Cambridge, for ch. of Prescot (*Prescerte*), La., 13s 4d; prior of Arbury (*Erderbury*) for ch. of Leigh, Chs., 6s 8d.

[Total: £6 16s 8d]

40.   PROCURATIONS DUE TO THE ABP. BY VIRTUE OF HIS VISITATION.

a. Archdeaconry of Coventry:
Cath. ch. of Coventry (*Coventren'*), £6 13s 4d; coll. ch. of Astley (*Asteley*), 20s; dys. of Coventry, £3 6s 8d; Marton, 46s 8d; Stoneleigh, 46s 8d; Arden, 46s 8d.   Total: £21.

b. Archdeaconry of Derby:
Dys. of Derby (*Derbei*), Ashbourne, High Peak, Scarsdale, Castellar, Repton, 66s 8d each.   Total: £20.

c. Archdeaconry of Shrewsbury:
Dy of Shrewsbury, 66s 8d; dy. of Newport, 66s 8d; ch. of St Chad (*sancti Cedde*), Shrewsbury, 26s 8d.   Total: £8.

d. Archdeaconry of Stafford:
Priory of Sandwell (*Sandewall*), 20s; coll. ch. of Tamworth (*Tomworth*), 66s 8d; coll. ch. of Gnosall (*Gnowsale*), 26s 8d; dys. of Lapley, Alton and Leek, Stafford and Newcastle, Tamworth and Tutbury, 66s 8d each. Total: £19.[1]

> [1]*Marginal note in later hand*: Deducting procurations of monasteries and coll. chs., there remains £13 6s 8d.

e. Archdeaconry of Chester:
Proprietors of chs. with cure in the archdeaconry, 66s 8d; dys. of Wirral (*Wyrall*), Frodsham (*Fordesham*), Middlewich (*Medii Wici*), Macclesfield (*Macfild*), Nantwich (*Wico Malbano*), Malpas, 66s 8d each; coll. ch. of St John, Chester, 26s 8d.   Total: £24 13s 4d.

41.   RECEIPTS FOR VACANCY OF A CHURCH:
From Richard Phelip, v. of Etwall (*Etvall*), Db., for vacancy of a mediety of the ch. of Eckington (*Ekyngton*), Db., from feast of Eleven Thousand Virgins[1] to 18 Apr. 1491.   Total: 3s 6d.

> [1] 22 Aug. or 21 Oct. (*Handbook of Dates*, p. 62).

42.   RECEIPTS FROM CHS. APPROPRIATED TO EPISCOPAL MENSA:
For revenues of parish ch. of Wybunbury, Chs., £20; of parish ch. of Denford, Np., £10.   Total: £30.

43.   [fo. 62v] RECEIPTS FROM PROBATE OF TESTAMENTS:
For probate of John Curson, 10s; Henry Laycrofte, 40s; Henry Glover, 20d; Robert Bidworth, 20d; Hugh Laurence, 20s; Henry Tomkynson, 2s 8d; William Bate of Cheddleton (*Chedelston*), St., 6s 8d; Nicholas Sondell of Leek (*Leke*), St., 8d; Christopher Halkewurth of Osmaston, Db., 3s 4d; Roger Byrley of Leek (*Leeke*), St., 8d; Hugh Alleyn, 6s 8d; John Cholmeley of Wirral (*Wyrall*), Chs., 5s; John Colton, 5s; John Goodeale of Rowton (*Reuton*), St., 12d; William Eyton of Stafford, 8d; Thomas Tirlaund of Stafford, 8d; Roger Woode of Shropshire (*in comitatu Salop'*), 12d; Joan Wiston, widow of Coventry, 10s; John Bolton of Newcastle-under-Lyme (*Novo Castro*), St., 11d; Richard Heth of Leek, St., 6s; John,[1] bp. of Coventry and Lichfield, £20; Thomas Oteley, £15.   [Total: £41 5s 1d]

    [1] MS. Richard.

        [Total receipts listed from vacancy of the see: £253 8s 3d.]

VACANCY OF THE SEE OF BATH AND WELLS, 1491–1492

[fo. 63] REGISTER OF THE VENERABLE MASTERS JOHN GUNTHORP, DEAN OF THE CATHEDRAL CHURCH OF WELLS, ROBERT SHERBORNE, THOMAS HARRYS AND WILLIAM BOKETT, OFFICIALS OR GUARDIANS OF THE SPIRITUALITIES OF THE CITY (*sic*) AND DIOCESE OF BATH AND WELLS IN THE VACANCY OF THE SEE THROUGH THE DEATH OF ROBERT OF GOOD MEMORY, LAST BISHOP OF THOSE CATHEDRAL CHURCHES, SPECIALLY AND LEGITIMATELY DEPUTED TO ACT JOINTLY AND SEVERALLY BY THE MOST REVEREND FATHER IN CHRIST AND LORD JOHN, BY GOD'S GRACE ARCHBISHOP OF CANTERBURY, PRIMATE OF ALL ENGLAND AND LEGATE OF THE APOSTOLIC SEE.

> *Note*: the see became vacant by the death of Robert Stillington on 15 May 1491 and was filled by the translation of Richard Fox on 8 Feb. 1492. All institutions below were conducted by Mr Thomas Harrys, unless otherwise stated. All places are in Somerset unless otherwise stated.

44.   Commission with powers of canonical coercion from the abp. to Mr John Gunthorp, dean of Wells, Mr Robert Shyrborne, M.A., treasurer of Hereford, Mr Thomas Harrys and Mr William Bokett, as vicars-general and guardians of the spiritualities of the dioc. of Bath and Wells in the vacancy following the death of bp. Robert Stillington, with the powers specified in no. 1, with the omission of clause xi.

     [fo. 64 wanting]

45.   [fo. 65] Inst. of Alan Glasion, pr., to ch. of Stoke Pero, vac. by res. of Mr Edmund Walshe. P. Robert Forster, esq. I. archd. of Taunton. Wells, 20 July 1491.

46.   Letters dimissory for ordination to minor and holy orders granted to John Aisshe of Taunton. Wells, 27 July 1491.

47.   Inst. of Thomas Cutboll, pr., to vic. of the prebendal ch. of Ashill (*Aisshehull*), vac. by res. of Thomas Marys. P. John Waynsford, subdean of Wells and prebendary of Ashill. I. dean of Wells. Wells, 29 July 1491.

48.   Inst. of Walter Redyng, pr., to ch. of Pyle (*Pulle*), vac. by d. of Richard Beram. P. John Bourchier, lord Fitzwarren. I. archd. of Wells. Wells, 1 Aug. 1491.

49.   [fo. 65v] Inst. by Mr Shirborne of Stephen Pomeroy, pr., in the person of his proctor John Hilton, literate, to perpetual chantry in the ch. of Nettlecombe (*Netlecombe*), vac. by res. of Thomas Cawlecott. P. John Trevilian, esq., senior. I. archd. of Taunton. Wells, 9 Aug. 1491.

50.   Inst. of David Howell, pr., to vic. of prebendal ch. of Bathwick, vac.

by res. of Thomas Ryall. P. Mr Thomas Smith, M.A., prebendary of Bathwick in the conventual ch. of the nuns of Wherwell, Winchester dioc. I. archd. of Bath. Wells, 11 Aug. 1491.

51.   Inst. of Thomas Lewes, pr., to ch. of Christon (*Criston*), vac. by res. of John Algar. P. Isabelle lady Newton, widow. I. archd. of Wells. Wells, 13 Aug. 1491.

52.   Inst. of John Thomlyns, pr., to vic. of Kilmersdon (*Kymnerdon*), vac. by res. of John Shoper. P. Br John Eglesfeld, preceptor of Beverley and deputy of the prior of the hospital of St John of Jerusalem in England. I. archd. of Wells. Wells, 30 Aug. 1491.

53.   [fo. 66] Ordinations celebrated in the conventual ch. of the hospital of St John the Baptist, Wells, on the abp's authority, by Thomas bp. of Tenos (*Tinen'*) on 24 Sept. 1491.

a. *Accolites*

John Chapman, Thomas Wyther, John Anell, Walter Hoore, John Tyly, William Philips.
William Birport of Salisbury dioc., by l.d.
Stephen Rounell, John Arvener, David Thomas, Walter Smyth, William Rewes, all of Exeter dioc., by l.d.

b. *Subdeacons*

Henry Colmer, m. of Glastonbury.
William Cory and Thomas Bristowe, ms. of Athelney.
Thomas Burnell, m. of Buckland (*Bucland*), Exeter dioc.
John Howell, can. regular of St Augustine's, Bristol (*Bristoll'*).
John Gaskyn, O.P. of Bristol.
John Neele, vic. choral of Wells cath., to t. of his stall.
John Mecy and Richard Bryan, to t. of Montacute (*Montis Acute*) priory.
William Keepe, to t. of Bermondsey (*Barmundesey*) abbey, Winchester dioc.
Thomas Trowbridge, B.A., to t. of Taunton priory.
John Hayes, to t. of Cerne (*Serne*) abbey, Salisbury dioc.
Walter Hoore, to t. of Cleeve (*Cliva*) abbey.
Simon Roche, to t. of Montacute priory.
Richard Hervy, to t. of Worspring (*Worspryng*) priory.
David Haywode, to t. of hospital of St John the Baptist, Bath.

c. [fo. 66v]

Nicholas Mownt, to t. of Taunton priory.
Thomas Juker, to t. of priory of Burtle in Sprawlesmede.
Nicholas Benett of Salisbury dioc., by l.d., to t. of Cerne (*Serne*) abbey.
John Lovebond, to t. of Stavordale (*Staverdale*) priory.
John Rise, to t. of hospital of St John the Baptist, Wells.[1]
John Danyell, to t. of hospital of St John the Baptist, Bridgewater (*Briggewater*).[2]
John Gale, to t. of Taunton priory.

Thomas Asshe, to t. of Muchelney (*Mochelney*) abbey.

Reginald Peers of Exeter dioc., by l.d., to t. of Plympton priory.

Thomas Jurden of Exeter dioc., by l.d., to t. of Bodmin (*Bodminie*) priory.

Br Malinus de Flandria, O.E.S.A. of Bristol.

[1,2] noted by pointing hand in margin.

d. *Priests*

John Brent, m. of Glastonbury (*Glaston'*).

John Alford, Richard Bowge, John Clipwell, cans. regular of Bruton (*Brewton*).

John Bonwey, can. regular of Worspring (*Worspryng*).

John Peers, can. of St Augustine's, Bristol.

John Geryng of Exeter dioc., by l.d., to t. of Totnes (*Totnesse*) priory.

John Shepard of Exeter dioc., by l.d., to t. of hospital of St John the Baptist, Wells (*Wellen'*).

Robert Paynter of Exeter dioc., by l.d., to t. of Launceston priory.

John Lewes, to t. of Milton (*Myddleton*) abbey, Salisbury dioc.

Benedict Yong of Exeter dioc., by l.d., to t. of Bodmin (*Bodminie*) priory.

William Smyth and William Tayllor of Exeter dioc., by l.d., to t. of Buckfast (*Bucfast*) abbey.

John Michell of Exeter dioc., by l.d., to t. of Osney abbey, Lincoln dioc.

Richard Malpas of Lincoln dioc., by l.d., to t. of hospital of St John the Baptist, Wells.[1]

Hugh Croke of Llandaff dioc., by l.d., to t. of Margam (*Morgan*) abbey.

Nicholas Wiliam of Exeter dioc., by l.d., to t. of Launceston priory.

John Hugh and Henry Freman of Exeter dioc., by l.d., to t. of Newenham (*Newham*) abbey.

Robert Flede, to t. of Taunton priory.

John Middelham, to t. of St Nicholas's priory, Exeter.

Richard Martyn, to t. of Newenham abbey, Exeter dioc.

William Deere of Llandaff dioc., by l.d., to t. of Margam (*Morgan*) abbey.

Richard Davy of Exeter dioc., by l.d., to t. of Launceston priory.

John Feyrehere, to t. of Muchelney (*Mochelney*) abbey.

Thomas Godolgham of Exeter dioc., by l.d., to t. of Glasney college, Penryn.

William Glase of Llandaff dioc., by l.d., to t. of Neth (*Neth*) abbey.

[1] noted by pointing hand in margin.

54.   [fo. 67] Letters dimissory granted to Edmund Scyb of Porlock (*Porlok*), clerk of Bath and Wells dioc. 26 Sept. 1491.

55.   [fo. 67v] Inst. of John Shoppare, pr., to ch. of Hinton Blewett (*Henton Blewett*), vac by res. of John Thomlyns. P. John Seward, esq. I. archd. of Bath. Wells, 28 Sept. 1491.

56.   Mandate directed to the rural dean of Bridgewater (*Briggewater*), the curate of Stogursey (*Stokecursy*) and John Bartholomew, literate of Wells and sub-apparitor-general of the dioc., to cite objectors to the compurgation of John Lemyng, chap., lately of Stogursey (*Stokcursy*) who, as he himself alleges, was indicted before the king's justices on the charge that on Wednesday 10

December 1488 he broke into the house of Robert Peers in *Wyke* in the parish of Stogursey and feloniously took and carried away fifteen pounds of gold and silver, twelve silver spoons worth 40s and two silver mazers worth £3 of the goods and chattels of the said Robert Peers, and on account of this was imprisoned by the lay power until at last he was delivered by the king's justices to be judged in the ecclesiastical court by Robert bp. of Bath and Wells, according to canon law, as he is a literate clerk. He desires to purge himself of this infamy and to declare his innocence, and has implored the vicar-general to allow him purgation. The mandatories are ordered to cite peremptorily all those claiming an interest in this matter who wish to oppose his purgation, making proclamation in the market-place of Wells on Saturday next and in the parish ch. of Stogursey on the next Sunday or convenient festival. Objectors are to appear before Mr Harrys or another guardian of the spiritualities on Monday 17 Oct. in the chapel of St Mary by the cath. cloister to advance reasonable cause for their objection. The mandatories are to certify the action taken by them. Wells, 7 Oct. 1491.

57. [fo. 68] *Abjuration of heretical pravity made by John Dawnsy of Rode.*
In the name of God Amen. Before yow Masters John Gunthorp dean and Thomas Harrys thresurer of the cathedrall chirch of Wellys, officials or kepers of the spiritualite of the bisshopryke of Bath and Wellys, the seys of the chirches of Bath and Wellys aforesaide nowe being voyde, by the most reverend fadre in God John, by the grace of God archebisshopp of Caunterbury, primat of all Englond and of the sede apostolike legate specially ordeyned and deputed, I John Dawnsy, layman and carpenter of the town and parissh of Roode in the diocese of Bath and Wellys aforesaide and jurisdictioun of the saide mooste reverend fadre and yours as his officers, in this parte detected and denunced to you officialles or kepers beforenamed gretely suspect of heresie, errours and other articles evyll sownyng, beyng in dome and jugement before yow, understanding, knowing and wele perceyving that before this ower I the said John Dawnsy have openly holde, tought, declared, preched, affermyd and expressed diverse articles and oppynyons right erroneous and again the feyth of all Holy Chirche and contrary to the determinacioun of the same, and especiall evyll sownyng to the erys of well disposed Cristenn men:
Firste, that for all the prestis whisteryng, that God was not at the awter when the preste speketh softli in his memento.
Also, that it nedeth not a childe to be cristened that is bigotten betwene a Christen mann and a Cristen woman.
Also, that it nede not to be confessed of preste, but that one mann may be confessed of another.
Also, that it nede not a man to make any obesaunce to any crosse but as to a mann spredyng his armys, for that is the crosse that God made.
Also, that a synfull man may never be dampned thorough his synfull luvyng, for then Criste must nedis dampne his owne flessch and blode that He toke of the Virgin Mary.
Wherefor I John Dawnsy before yow, Masters John Gunthorp and Thomas Harrys officialles and kepers abovenamyd, truly and faithfully enformed, knowlege and knowe wele that the articles above reherced be erroneus and

again the trewbileve faith and determynacioun of Holy Chirche and right evyll sownyng to the erys of well disposed Cristen peple. Willing with a puer harte and fre will to forsake the said errours, heresies and erroneous oppinions beyng again the trew faith and determynacioun of Holy Chirche and to turne to the unite and determynacioun of the said Holy Chirch, and to byleeve frohensforthward after the teching of all Holy Chirch and determynacioun therof. Furthermore the said errours, errourous oppinions and evyll sowning articles as is abovesaide, and all other maner errours, heresies, articles, oppinions and doctrine that is again the trewe feyth and determynacioun of all Holy Chirche I forsake, renunce and abiure, and I swere upon this booke that after this hower I shall never openly nor prively holde, declare ne teche heresie n'other errours ne no maner doctrine again the faith and determynacioun of Holy Chirche, ne I shall resceyve, favor nor counsaill, ne defend, socour nor supporte by myself or any other maner person, prively nor openly, them that holdeth, techeth or maynteyneth any suche maner of fals doctrine nor felishippe with them wittyngly nor comfort them nor resceyve them into my howse nor geve them mete ne drynke, clothe nor money ne noon otherwise socour them. Furthermore I swere if that I may knowe any persons, menn or women, suspect of errours and heresies, or fautors, councellors, confortors, defendors, receptors or that make any privatt conventicles contrary to the comyn doctrine of Holy Chirche, I shall denounce them to the saide moost reverend Fadre or to hys officers or to their ordinaries as sone as I goodly may. So helpe me God and the Holy Dome. And my wittenes and recorde hereof I subscribe me + .

58.   [fo. 68] Inst. of William Rogers, clerk, in the person of his proctor John Rogers, literate, to ch. of Dunkerton, vac. by d. of Richard Cooper. P. Walter Enderby, esq. I. archd. of Wells. Wells, 5 Nov. 1491.

59.   Inst. of William Brigeman, pr., to perpetual chantry at the altar of St Martin in the cath. ch. of Wells, founded for the souls of Ralph of Shrewsbury, sometime bp. of Bath and Wells, John de Somerton, sometime abbot of Muchelney, their successors, kin, benefactors and all the faithful departed, vac. by d. of Roger Janys. P. abbot and conv. of Muchelney. I. dean of Wells, or in his absence the subdean or president of the chapter. Wells, 9 Dec. 1491.

60.   Mandate addressed by Mr Thomas Harrys to the prior and conv. of Montacute (*Montis Acute*), O.Cist. [*sic*].[1] Recitation of royal writ, dated at Westminster, 4 Dec. 1491, directed to guardian of the spiritualities of Bath and Wells dioc., ordering the appointment of collectors of the first moiety of the subsidy granted to the king by the Convocation of Canterbury which sat from 21 June to 8 Nov. 1491. The names of the collectors are to be returned to the Treasurer and Barons of the Exchequer by 21 Jan. 1492. Terms and exemptions are as for the second moiety of the subsidy.[2] Mr Harrys, by the authority of this writ, appoints the prior and conv. of Montacute as collectors of the tenth payable at the feast of the Purifiction [2 Feb.], which is to be collected from assessed benefices and those not assessed but customarily paying a tenth, according to the attached schedule listing their true annual

value. The following are to be exempt: the poor nuns of Cannington (*Canyngton*) and Barrow Gurney (*Barogh*), the poor religious of the priories of Worspring (*Worspryng*) and Barlinch (*Berlynch*), and the prebend of Whitchurch, because of their poverty and the ruinous state of their buildings, together with other benefices in the dioc. assessed in the attached schedule but because of their poverty exempt on this occasion according to the terms of the grant made by Convocation. Wells, 24 Jan. 1492.

[1] Montacute was a Cluniac house which became denizen in 1407.
[2] *CFR 1485–1509*, no. 433.

61.　　[fo. 70v] Inst. of Richard Hawky, pr., in the person of his proctor Mr Robert Tydworth, Decr. B., to perpetual chantry in ch. of Combe Florey (*Combflory*), vac. by res. of Richard Hampstede. P. on this occasion Robert Stowell, esq., John Moore and John Carnok, clerk, I. archd. of Taunton. Wells, 29 Jan. 1492.

62.　　Mandate addressed by Mr Thomas Harrys to Mr John Dyer, J.U.B., Official of the archd. of Wells, to collect in the archdeaconry, either in person or by his commissaries, the charitable subsidy[1] granted to the abp. of Canterbury in the last Convocation held from 21 June to 8 Nov. 1491, which is due on 1 March 1492 and is to be collected and paid to the abp. by 1 Apr. The mandate rehearses that of the bp. of London, dated at Fulham, 22 Dec. 1491, which in turn rehearses the mandate of the abp. to the bp. of London, dated at Lambeth, 9 Dec. 1491, ordering him to communicate to the bps. of the province and the Officials *sede vacante* of the diocs. of Coventry and Lichfield and Bath and Wells instructions for the collection of the subsidy. Details as for the charitable subsidies of 1487 and 1489,[2] with the following additional exemptions:
Richard Hall, chap., scribe of the acts of the present Convocation.
All those otherwise liable to the payment of the charitable subsidy who are burdened with payment of a benevolence to the king before 1 April. Wells, 18 Feb. 1492.

[1] F. R H. Du Boulay, 'Charitable subsidies granted to the Archbishop of Canterbury, 1300–1489', *Bulletin of the Institute of Historical Research* xxiii (1950), 147–64. The grant of 1491 is not there discussed.
[2] *Reg. Morton* i, nos. 95, 124.

63.　　[fo. 72] Inst. of Richard Forster, pr., in the person of his proctor John Standewyke, clerk and notary public, to ch. of St Lawrence, Rode (*Roode*), vac. by res. of John Waty. P. Sir John Trefry, kt. I. archd. of Wells. Wells, 11 Mar. 1492.

64.　　Inst. of Eugenius Dale, pr., to vic. of Hinton Monachorum (*Henton Monachorum*). P. Mr Thomas Overay, precentor of Wells cath. I. archd. of Wells. Wells, 17 Mar. 1492.

65.　　Ordinations celebrated in the conventual ch. of the hospital of St John the Baptist, Wells, on the abp.'s authority, by Thomas bp. of Tenos (*Tinen'*) on 18 Mar. 1492.

a. *Accolites*

Robert Penney, John Asshe, John Wylmott, Thomas Legatt, Humphrey Dyker, William Nasshyng.

Henry Bray, John Dokett, John Perkyn, Thomas Harry, Michael Richard, John Varyatt, William Penrose, all of Exeter dioc., by l.d.

Thomas Apwiliam, William Wylett, Thomas Gylyngham, all of Llandaff dioc., by l.d.

b. [fo. 72v] *Subdeacons*

John Whytyng, m. of Glastonbury (*Glaston'*).

Robert Pavy, John Cowper, ms. of Bath (*Bathon'*).

Br Robert Cooke, can. regular of Worspring (*Worspryng*).

John Michelson, m. of Witham (*Wytham*).

John Broughyng, v. choral of Wells cath., to t. of his stall.

William Albone, r. of Chelworth, to t. of his benefice.

John Blakdon, B.A., to t. of Stavordale (*Staverdale*) priory.

John Hunt, to t. of Muchelney (*Mochelney*) abbey.

John Treworga of Exeter dioc., by l.d., to t. of Tywardreath (*Tywardreth*) priory.

Henry Bonour, to t. of Newenham (*Newham*) abbey, Exeter dioc.

John Wey, to t. of Montacute (*Montis Acute*) priory.

William Brightwin of Llandaff dioc., by l.d., to t. of Llantarnam (*Lanternam*) priory.

William Benett of Exeter dioc., by l.d., to t. of Plympton priory.

Alexander Vernay, to t. of hospital of St John the Baptist, Bridgewater (*Briggewater*).[1]

John Tregonwell of Exeter dioc., by l.d., to t. of Bodmin (*Bodmine*) priory.

David ap Philip ap Thomas of Llandaff dioc., by l.d., to t. of Llantarnam abbey.

John Wade of Exeter dioc., by l.d., to t. of Launceston priory.

John Wynne of St Asaph dioc., by l.d., to t. of Tavistock (*Tavistok*) abbey, Exeter dioc.

William Roger, r. of Dunkerton, to t. of his benefice.

John Collys, to t. of Bruton (*Brewton*) priory.

Henry Josepp of Exeter dioc., by l.d., to t. of Glasney coll.

Hugh Preest, to t. of Muchelney (*Mochelney*) abbey.

John Durban of Llandaff dioc., by l.d., to t. of Llantarnam abbey.

Richard Grobham, to t. of hospital of St John the Baptist, Wells.[2]

Robert Mylward of London dioc., by l.d., to t. of Newenham abbey, Exeter dioc.

John Chapman, to t. of Worspring priory.

John Deere, to t. of Taunton priory.

John Pawle of Exeter dioc., by l.d., to t. of Tywardreath (*Tywardreeth*) priory.

Mr Laurence Dottson, M. A., of Exeter dioc., by l.d., to t. of Launceston priory.

[1,2] noted by pointing hand in margin.

c. [fo. 73] *Deacons*

Henry Colmer [as no. 53b].
Thomas Bristowe, William Cory [as no. 53b].
John Jurden, to t. of Dunkeswell abbey, Exeter dioc.
Richard Skebiria of Exeter dioc., by l.d., to t. of Bodmin (*Bodminie*) priory.
John Thomas of St Davids dioc., by l.d., to t. of St Dogmell's (*Sancti Dogmaelis*) abbey.
William Thomas of Exeter dioc., by l.d., to t. of Bodmin priory.
William Barry, to t. of Muchelney abbey.
Robert Oune of Exeter dioc., by l.d., to t. of Dunkeswell abbey.
Eugenius Dale of Norwich dioc., by l.d., to t. of hospital of St John the Baptist, Wells.[1]
David Haywode, to t. of Kington St Michael (*Kington*) priory, Salisbury dioc. [cf. no. 53b].
John Chymowe of Exeter dioc., by l.d., to t. of Plympton priory.
William Kepe [as no. 53b].
William Harrys, to t. of Cleeve (*Cliva*) abbey.
John Gaale, to t. of Taunton priory [cf. no. 53c].

[1] noted by pointing hand in margin.

d. *Priests*

Henry Pynne, m. of Glastonbury.
John Worcetur, John Compton, ms. of Bath.
John Peynter, m. of Cleeve (*Cliva*).
John Neele [as no. 53b].
Richard Bryan [as no. 53b].
John Rodde of Exeter dioc., by l.d., to t. of Launceston priory.
John Hayes [as no. 53b].
Thomas Trowbridge [as no. 53b].
John Mey [as Mecy, no. 53b]; Simon Roche [as no. 53b].
Thomas Asshe [as no. 53c].
John Stratton of Salisbury dioc., by l.d., to t. of Mottisfont (*Mottesfont*) priory, Winchester dioc.
Walter Hoore [as no. 53b].
Reginald Peers [as no. 53c].
Br Robert Bradcomb of the house of friars at Plymouth.

66.   [fo. 73v] Mandate directed to the prior and conv. of Taunton, O.S.A., to collect in the dioc. the second tenth granted by Convocation and payable to the Exchequer by the feast of St George [23 April]. Wells, 22 Mar. 1492.

67.   [fo. 74] Certificate of Mr Thomas Harrys to the Treasurer and Barons of the Exchequer, acknowledging receipt of the royal writ for the collection of a second tenth, dated at Westminster, 24 Feb. 1492,[1] notifying the appointment of the prior and conv. of Taunton as collectors in the dioc. and listing exemptions from payment: the priories of Cannington (*Canyngton*), Barrow Gurney (*Barowe*) and Worspring (*Worspryng*) and the hospital of St John the Baptist, Bridgewater (*Briggewater*), because of their poverty, and the

19

prebend of Whitchurch (*Whitchurche*) in the cath. ch. of Wells because of the ruin of the buildings attached to that prebend, and other benefices taxed in the attached schedule which because of their poverty are exempt on this occasion according to the terms of the concession. Wells, 24 March 1492.

¹ *CFR 1485–1509*, no. 433.

68.   Letters dimissory for ordination to minor, major and holy orders granted to William Nasshyng of Bishop's Lydeard (*Lydyard Episcopi*). 2 Apr. 1492.

69.   Letters dimissory for ordination to major and holy orders granted to William Roger, subdeacon, r. of Dunkerton. 3 Apr. 1492.

70.   Letters dimissory for ordination to major and holy orders granted to Alexander Vernay, subdeacon of Bridgewater (*Brigewater*). 4 Apr. 1492.

71.   Mandate addressed by Mr Thomas Harrys to Mr Robert Pemberton, Decr. B., and Mr Walter Morys, J.U.B., jointly or severally to enquire into the advowson of the free chapel of Claverham (*Clareham*). John Asshefeld, esq., and William Woode, *generosus*, have recently presented John Wode, pr., to the free chapel of Claverham (*Clareham alias Claversham*) in the parish of Yatton, vac. by the d. of Mr William Choke, last master or warden, and have claimed that the presentation pertains to them on this occasion. So that he may deal justly with those presenting and presented, Mr Harrys wishes to ascertain details of the right of patronage and the nature of the vacancy, and therefore commissions the recipients of this mandate, after they have summoned those who according to law should be summoned, to enquire diligently into these matters; they are to examine under oath at least six rectors or vicars and six other trustworthy men likely to have knowledge of these matters and to ascertain the true patron or patrons, who presented the last master, to whom right of presentation pertains on this occasion, by what title and for what reason, from when the chapel had been vacant, and all other matters which according to custom are to be determined. They are to take with them a notary public with no prior interest in this matter and to do all else necessary or expedient, exercising powers of canonical coercion, and they are to certify Mr Harrys or another guardian of the spiritualities as soon as possible by letters close. Wells, 10 Mar. 1492.

72.   [fo. 74v] Certificate of the above mandate by Mr Pemberton and Mr Morys. On 5 Apr. they held an inquisition in the parish ch. of Backwell (*Bacwell*) in the dy. of Redcliffe (*Radclyff*), in which dy. the free chapel of Clàverham is situated. There appeared before them Thomas Morys, r. of Wraxall (*Wroxdale*), John Squyer, r. of Clapton in Gordano (*Clopton*), William Corbett, r. of Backwell, Matthew Hardyng, r. of Chelvey, William Kyngman, r. of Brockley (*Brockeley*), John Turner, r. of Weston in Gordano (*Weston*), Robert Keyton, v. of Clevedon (*Clyvedon*), John Hurlysfrensche, v. of Tickenham (*Tykenham*), and Richard Thurbarn and John Passy of Yatton, Robert Feylond, Thomas Vowles and John Pasty of Backwell, John Wheler of Nailsea (*Naylesey*) and William Harrys of Chelvey, neighbours who might be expected to have knowledge of such matters. They stated on oath that the

chapel was vac. by the d. of Mr William Chok, last master or warden, that John Charles and Matilda his wife had last presented Mr Chok to the chapel and that John Rodenay, esq., was the true patron on this occasion, or that it was his turn on this occasion. They stated also that John Asshefeld, esq., and William Wode, *generosus*, were now presenting to the chapel John Wode, pr., by right and title of the advowson granted to them by John Rodenay, esq., as appeared more fully in the charter of advowson sealed with his armorial seal, and by virtue thereof they were the true patrons. The report of this inquisition was sealed pendant with the seals of the dean of Redcliffe and of those by whom the inquisition was taken. Proceedings were conducted in the presence of Mr John Standerwike, notary public. Backwell, 5 Apr. 1492.

73.   [fo. 75] Inst. of John Woode, pr., to the free chapel of Claverham, vac. by d. of Mr William Chok. P. John Asshefeld, esq., and William Wode, *generosus*, by virtue of the grant of the advowson on this occasion by John Rodenay, esq. I. Mr Walter Morys, v. of the prebendal ch. of Yatton, and Mr Robert Pemberton, Decr. B. Wells, 6 Apr. 1492.

74.   Grant by John Rodenay, esq., lord of Backwell (*Bacwell*), of the first and next advowson, presentation, donation or nomination to a rectory, vicarage, chantry, free chapel or any other ecclesiastical benefice in the county of Somerset in his gift to John Asshefeld, esq., and William Wood, so that when any such benefice shall fall vacant, they or one of them shall present a suitable person to the diocesan, or if it is a benefice of such a nature they shall grant it to a suitable clerk, as fully and freely as he himself might had he not made this grant, and so that after this next presentation free disposal shall revert to him and his heirs and the present writing shall be void. Sealed at his manor of Rodney Stoke (*Stoke Rodenay*), 24 Mar. 1491.

75.   [fo. 75v] Ordinations celebrated in the conventual ch. of the hospital of St John the Baptist, Wells, on the abp.'s authority, by Thomas bp. of Tenos (*Tinen'*) on 21 Apr. 1492.

a. *Accolites*

John Pewe, Hugh Gwynne

b. *Subdeacons*

Richard Wynterbourne, Nicholas Wedmore, ms. of Glastonbury.
Robert Farthyng of Exeter dioc., by l.d., to t. of St German's priory.
Thomas Harry [as no. 65a], to t. of Bodmin priory.
Henry Durgin of Exeter dioc., by l.d., to t. of Plympton priory.
John Gowle of Salisbury dioc., by l.d., to t. of Abbotsbury abbey.
Thomas Belly of Exeter dioc., by l.d., to t. of Plympton priory.
Nicholas Say, to t. of hospital of St John, Bath.

c. *Deacons*

John Broughing [as no. 65b].
Hugh Dowles, v. choral of Wells cath., to t. of his stall.
William Albone [as no. 65b].
Humphrey Dyker, to t. of hospital of St John, Bath.[1]

Thomas Legatt, John Wylmott, to t. of Montacute priory.

John Varyatt [as no. 65a], to t. of Bodmin priory.

John Fynde of London dioc., by l.d., to t. of Bindon abbey, Salisbury dioc.

John Deer, to t. of Worspring priory [cf. no. 65b].

John Wey [as no. 65b].

William Nasshing, to t. of Dunkeswell abbey, Exeter dioc.

John West of Exeter dioc., by l.d., to t. of St Nicholas's priory, Exeter.

John Collys [as no. 65b].

Richard Wythypoll, fellow of New College, Oxford, to t. of the college.

John Myghelson [cf. Michelson, no. 65b].

William Penrose, William Drewe, both of Exeter dioc., by l.d., to t. of Hartland abbey.

Richard Grobham,[2] John Chapman [as no. 65b].

John Dyere, B. A., fellow of New College, Oxford, to t. of the college.

        [1, 2,] noted by pointing hand in margin.

d. [fo. 76] *Priests*

Mr Laurence Dotson [as no. 65b].

Robert Bayly, v. choral of Wells cath., to t. of his stall.

John Tregonwell, John Tregarwa [as no. 65b].

John Powle [as Pawle, no. 65b].

John Gybbys of Exeter dioc., by l.d., to t. of Cornworthy priory.

William Rogers [as Roger, no. 65b].

William Kepe [as no. 53b].

Geoffrey ap Ienkyn of St Davids dioc., by l.d., to t. of Neath abbey, Llandaff dioc.

Richard Milward [as Robert Mylward, no. 65b].

John Huntt [as Hunt, no. 65b].

David Haywode [as Haywode, no. 65c].

John Blacdon [as Blakdon, no. 65b].

John Wade, Alexander Vernay[1] [as no. 65b].

John Ryse [as Rise, no. 53c].

        [1] noted by pointing hand in margin.

76.   [fo. 76v] Procurations due to the abp, from the dioc. of Bath and Wells *sede vacante*.

a. Religious houses:

From the prior of Bath (*Bathon'*), abbot of Keynsham (*Keynesham*), prior of Bruton, abbot of Athelney, abbot of Muchelney (*Mochelney*), prior of Taunton, prior of Barlinch (*Barlinche*), and abbot of Glastonbury (*Glaston'*), 66s 8d each.
                                    Total: £26 13s 4d.

b. Deaneries:

From the deans of Stalls (*Stallis*), Redcliffe (*Ratclyff*), Axebridge (*Axebrige*), Frome, Ilchester (*Yelve*), Crewkerne (*Crokherne*), Taunton, Bridgewater (*Briggewater*), Cary and Marston (*Merston*), 66s 8d each; from the dean of Pawlett, 53s 4d.   Total: £39 6s 8d.

        [fo. 77 is blank.]

VACANCY OF THE SEE OF WINCHESTER, 1492–1493

[fo. 78] ACTS AND PROCEEDINGS CONDUCTED IN THE VISITATION OF THE
CITY AND DIOCESE OF WINCHESTER DURING THE VACANCY OF THE SEE DUE
TO THE DEATH OF PETER COURTENAY OF REVEREND MEMORY, LATE BISHOP
OF THE CATHEDRAL CHURCH OF WINCHESTER, BY THE AUTHORITY OF THE
VERY REVEREND FATHER IN CHRIST AND LORD JOHN, BY GOD'S GRACE
ARCHBISHOP OF CANTERBURY, PRIMATE OF ALL ENGLAND AND LEGATE OF
THE APOSTOLIC SEE, IN THE YEAR 1492 A.D. AND THE SIXTH YEAR OF THE
TRANSLATION OF THAT VERY REVEREND FATHER.

> [*Note*: the see became vacant by the death of Peter Courtenay on 22 Sep.
> 1492 and was filled by the provision of John Langton on 13 Mar. 1493.]

77.   Commission with powers of canonical coercion to Mr Robert
Shyrborne, treasurer of the cath. ch. of Hereford, and Mr Michael Cleve,
Decr. D., as vicars-general and guardians of the spiritualities of the see of
Winchester in the vacancy following the death of bp. Peter, with the powers
specified in no. 1. Lambeth, 20 Oct. 1492.

78.   [fo. 78v] Mandate directed by the abp. to Thomas Somer, apparitor-
general in the province of Canterbury, and Luke Frankyssh, apparitor in the
city and dioc. of London. It is common knowledge and has come to the abp.'s
attention that in the borough of Southwark (*Southwerk*), Sy., in Winchester
dioc., which *sede vacante* is under archiepiscopal jurisdiction, gross sins are
daily committed by clergy and people; brothels exist openly and in these
prostitution, fornication, adultery, debauchery, incest and other manifest sins
are each day damnably and impiously committed, so that clergy and people
greatly require the exercise of visitation. The apparitors are therefore to cite
the prior and conv. of St Mary Overy (*Overey*), O.S.A., the master and
brethren of the hospital of St Thomas the Martyr, the rs. or appropriators, or
their deputies, of the chs. of St Olave, St Mary Magdalene Bermondsey (*iuxta
monasterium sancti Salvatoris*), St Mary Magdalene Southwark, St Margaret and
St George, and all other chaps., both cantarists and stipendiaries, celebrating
in these chs., together with four of the more worthy and honourable
parishioners of each ch., to appear before the abp. or his commissaries in the
conv. ch. of St Mary Overy at 9 a.m. on Thursday next, and they are to
certify the abp. of the execution of this mandate, attaching a schedule
containing the names of those summoned. Lambeth, 23 Oct. 1492.

79.   [fo. 79] Certificate by Thomas Somer, literate, of the receipt of the
foregoing mandate, with attached schedule of those cited.

Priory of St Mary Overy:
John Reculver, prior; William Kempe, John Hale, John Whyte, Walter
Carre, Richard Holand, John Elyngton, Richard Heyward, John Robson,
prs.; Richard London, Thomas Archer, William Goodewyn, Thomas

Ewstase, Hamilectus Agoldicar, John Wilcokkes, John Corcar, professed cans.

Hospital of St Thomas the Martyr:
John Burneham, master; William Beele, lately master; Richard Richardson, Gerard Peerson, William Kelde, John Wakelyn.

Parish of St Olave:
Mr Richard Gryme, r.; Mr Robert Saluse, par. chap.; Mr John Surdyvale, William Chambyr, William Grenehyll, Paschal [blank], John Forlere, stips.; David Chapman, John Hyll, chws.; Thomas Hoore, Gerard Skynner, pns.

Parish of St Margaret:
Prior and conv. of St Mary Overy, prop.; William Philipp, cur.; William Bremond, John Damsell, Thomas Sylson, chaps.; William Hunt, John Driffeld, chws.; William Purscote, Thomas Kebbys, pns.

Parish of St Mary Magdalene, Southwark:
Prior and conv. of St Mary Overy, prop.; John Whyte, par. chap.; William Braunche, John Mayne, chws.; Peter Lawnson, Thomas Moton, pns.

Parish of St Mary Magdalene, Bermondsey:
Robert Ward, r.; Hugh Newton, stip.; Thomas Cooke *alias* Bayly, James Dukke, chws.; Thomas Johnson, John Sandon, pns.

Parish of St George:
Mr Peter [blank], r.; John Drayton, par. chap.; Robert Reed, stip.; Robert Sparow, Thomas Godfrey, Richard Knyght, Richard Goodeman, chws.; William Steler, Gerard Harryson, pns.

[Undated.]

80.   [fo. 79v] Commission with powers of canonical coercion to Mr Ralph Hannyes, clerk, to visit the religious houses and parish chs. of the archdeaconry of Surrey, with power to enquire into and to punish crimes and excesses, to inhibit any action prejudicial to the visitation, to register and grant probate of testaments and to examine the accounts of executors, to suspend any inferior jurisdiction, to receive procurations and other revenues due to the abp., to receive oaths of canonical obedience and to enquire into appropriations. Visitation of the religious houses of Chertsey (*Chersey*) and Merton is reserved to the abp. in person. Lambeth, 27 Oct. 1492.

81.   [fo. 80] Commission with powers of canonical coercion to Mr Michael Cleve, Decr. D., to proceed in all ecclesiastical causes and business, *ex officio*, promoted or at the instance of parties, in the consistory court of Winchester during the vacancy of the see, to terminate such cases and to do all else that pertains to the office of Official-Principal of the consistory court. Lambeth, 28 Oct. 1492.

82.   [fo. 80v] The abp. conducted his visitation in the priory of St Mary Overy after a sermon had been preached in the vernacular by Mr John

24

Camberton, S.T.P., on the text *Ve civitati sanguinum*[1] and the certificate [no. 79] had been exhibited. Southwark, 24 Oct. 1492.

    [1] Ezekial 24, 6.

83.   Citation of the prior and conv. of Merton, O.S.A., to submit to visitation on 16 Nov. Lambeth, 28 Oct.[1] 1492.
Certificate of the prior dated 15 Nov., with a schedule of those cited:
John [Gisbourne], prior; William Sandwiche, subprior; William Ball, John Byrde, Robert Doo, John Moore, John Richemond, John Berde, William London, Godfrey Westmestre, Robert Stone, Thomas Bell, William Iche, John Salter, William Salyng, Andrew Panell, William Russell, John Mershall, William Daurford, Clement Saunderson, John Laberone, James Newlond, Arnold Byrchester, Br Robert Sturgeon, Br Walter Burton.

    [1] MS: 28 Nov.

84.   [fo. 81] Citation of the abbot and conv. of Chertsey (*Chertesey*), O.S.B., to submit to visitation on 14 Nov. Lambeth, 28 Oct. 1492.
Citation received 8 Nov. Certificate of the abbot dated 8 Nov., with a schedule of those cited:
Thomas Pygott, abbot; Robert Render, prior; John Blunt, John Parker, John Kuc, John Bury, Thomas Marshall, William London, Richard Dolphynby, Simon Wallyngton, John Peerson, Henry Brydok, Thomas Sloon.

85.   Commission with powers of canonical coercion to Mr Thomas Cooke, D.C.L., the abp.'s chancellor and special commissary in this matter, to visit the religious houses of Chertsey and Merton and to correct and punish any crimes and excesses which he may discover, as the abp. is occupied by pressing business which will prevent his visitation in person. Lambeth, 12 Nov. 1492.

86.   [fo. 81v] Mr Thomas Cooke, D.C.L., the abp.'s chancellor and auditor of causes, sitting judicially in the chapter house of Merton priory, accepted the foresaid commission, which was read publicly by William Potkyn, notary public. The prior presented his certificate, swore canonical obedience to the abp., exhibited evidence of his own title and the constitution of his house, and in other matters did what is customary. All cans. of the priory appeared in person and likewise swore canonical obedience. Mr Cooke then visited the priory in head and members and thus fulfilled the terms of the commission. Merton, 16 Nov. 1492.

87.   Mr Cooke in like manner visited the abbot and conv. of Chertsey. Chertsey, 14 Nov. 1492.

88.   Res. by Mr William Eliott, in the person of his proctor, Martin Ferrers, *generosus*, into the hands of the abp. as his ordinary during the vacancy of the see of Winchester, of the mastership of God's House and St Nicholas's hospital, Portsmouth (*Portesmouth*), Ha. Notarial exemplification by Mr John Barett of these proceedings conducted in an upper chamber of the residence of Mr Ralph Hethecote in the manor of Thomas bp. of Salisbury in Fleet Street

(*Fletestrete*), in the presence of Mr Ralph Hethecote, clerk of Salisbury dioc., and Thomas Bak, literate of Winchester dioc. London, 9 Feb. 1493.

89.   [fo. 82] Pres. to the abp. by Thomas bp. of Salisbury, postulated to the see of Winchester, by virtue of the royal grant of the temp. of that see,[1] of Mr John Ryse, abp.'s clerk, to mastership of God's House, Portsmouth, with his consent to the provision from the fruits of the benefice of an annual pension to be paid to Mr William Eliott for his better sustenance. 9 Feb. 1493.

> [1] *CPR 1485–94*, p. 412.

90.   Inst. by the abp. of Mr John Ryse to mastership of God's House, Portsmouth, after he had taken an oath to pay to Mr Eliott the pension that should be ordained. Lambeth, 11 Feb. 1493.

91.   [fo. 82v] Ordination by the abp., with the consent of the bp.-postulate of Winchester and of Mr John Ryse, of an annual pension to be paid from the revenues of God's House, Portsmouth, to Mr William Eliott for the duration of his life. He is to receive £20 *per annum* in four equal instalments at Easter, the Nativity of St John the Baptist [24 June], Michaelmas [29 Sept.] and Christmas, to be delivered to him or his proctor in the cath. ch. of Exeter; the first payment is to be made next Easter. Mr Ryse has sworn to observe this ordinance, and as long as Mr Eliott shall live each of his successors as master shall at his inst. take a similar oath before the abp., his successor or the bp. of Winchester, special mention of this oath being made in the letters of inst., and if this is not done the inst. shall be null and void. Before his induction each master shall renounce all privileges and liberties, civil or ecclesiastical, which might stand against payment of the pension and shall also renounce any future appeal against such payment. If Mr Ryse or any of his successors neglect this ordinance or hold it in contempt, and more specifically if any instalment is not paid within forty days of the specified date, the fruits of the house shall be sequestrated by the bp. of Winchester or his Official until full payment is made to Mr Eliott, together with any expenses which he may have incurred because of default of payment, and no man may by any authority gainsay this sequestration, so long as provision is made from the fruits of the house for divine service and the ordinary and extraordinary obligations of the house are in the meantime discharged. Lambeth, 15 Feb. 1493.

92.   [fo. 83v] Commission to Mr Ralph Hainyes, can. of Reigate (*Reygate*), O.S.A., to manage the financial affairs of that house, owing to the decrepitude of the prior. Lambeth, 26 Feb. 1493.[1]

> [1] Duplicate of vol. i, no. 83.

93.   [fo. 84] Inst. by Mr Sherborne of Mr Ralph Hethercote, Decr. B., to canonry in the cath. ch. of Salisbury and prebend of Hurstbourne (*Husborne*), Ha. P. Thomas bp. of Salisbury, by virtue of the vacancy of the see of Winchester.[1] Lambeth, 5 Feb. 1493.

> [1] For collation of the prebend of Hurstbourne and Burbage by the bp. to
> Hethecote, dated 30 Dec. 1492, see *Reg. Langton*, no. 373; custody of temp. of
> the see of Winchester was not granted to Langton until 12 Jan. 1493. (*CPR*

1485–94, p. 412); for an exchange of prebends between Hethecote and Mr Adrian de Bardys on 17 Apr. 1493, see *Reg. Langton*, nos 402–3.

94.   Inst. by the abp. of Mr Adrian de Bardys, clerk, to ch. of Sherborne St John (*Shirborne*), Ha., vac. by res. of Mr Ralph Hethecote.[1] P. Thomas Kyngeston, esq. I. archd. of Winchester. Knole, 20 Apr. 1493.

> [1] On 17 Apr. 1493 the ch. of Wroughton, Wlt., was collated to Hethecote, following the res. of de Bardys (*Reg. Langton*, no. 400).

95.   Inst. by the abp. of Mr Richard Wall, M.A., to vic. of Farnham, Sy., vac by d. of Mr Robert Huberd. P. Mr Oliver Dynham, archd. of Surrey. I. archd. of Surrey. Lambeth, 20 Nov. 1492.

96.   Inst. by the abp. of Robert Horneby, chap., to vic. of St Lawrence, Morden, Sy., vac. by d. of Robert Wyrkysworth. P. abbot and conv. of Westminster. I. archd. of Surrey. Lambeth, 16 Jan. 1493.

97.   [fo. 84v] Inst. by Mr Michael Cleve of Mr John Cowley, clerk, to vic. of Crondall (*Crondale*), Ha., vac. by d. of John Smalwoode. P. Mr Robert Shirborne, treasurer of Hereford, master of hospital of St Cross near Winchester and r. of Crondall. Lambeth, 5 Mar. 1493.

RECEIPTS BY AND DUES TO ROBERT SHIRBOURN DURING THE VACANCY OF THE SEE OF WINCHESTER, WHICH BEGAN ON 22 SEPTEMBER 8 HENRY VII AND LASTED UNTIL EASTER OF THE SAME REGNAL YEAR.

98.   PROCURATIONS.

a. Religious houses:
St Swithun's Winchester, Hyde (*Hyda*), St Mary's Winchester, Romsey (*Rumsey*), Wherwell (*Wharwell*), St Denys, Breamore (*Brymore*), Mottisfont (*Mottisfontt*), Southwick (*Suthwyke*), Christchurch Twynham, 66s 8d each.
                                                          Total: £33 6s 8d.

b. Dys. in archdeaconry of Winchester:
Andover (*Andevere*), Basingstoke (*Basyngstoke*), Droxford (*Drokenesford*), Fordingbridge (*Fourde*), Winchester (*Winton'*), Southampton, Sombourne (*Sombourn*), Alresford (*Alresfourde*), Isle of Wight (*Insula Vecta*), 66s 8d each.
                                                          Total: £33 6s 8d.

c. [fo. 85] [Churches in Hampshire exempt from archidiaconal jurisdiction.] Winnall (*Wynhale*), 3s 4d; Twyford (*Twyfourde*), 7s 5½d; Compton (*Cumpton*), 6s 8d; Chilcomb (*Chilcumbe*), Morestead (*Morestede*), St Faith [Winchester], 3s 4d each; Bishop Stoke (*Stoke Episcopi*), 6s 8d; Hursley (*Hurseley*), South Stoneham (*Stoneham Episcopi*), Chilbolton, Houghton, Wonston, Overton, 7s 5½d each; North Waltham, Hannington (*Hannyngton*), Baughurst (*Baghurste*), 6s 8d each; Upham, 7s.   Total: 105s 10½d.

99.   APPROPRIATIONS OF CHURCHES IN ARCHDEACONRY OF WIN-
CHESTER.
From ch. of Newchurch (*Nyghchurch in Insula Vecta*), I.o.W., 13s 4d; ch. of
Arreton, I.o.W., 10s.   Total: 23s 4d.

100.   CHURCHES APPROPRIATED TO BISHOPRIC OF WINCHESTER.
From ch. of Hambledon (*Hamyldon*), £24; ch. of East Meon (*East Mean*), £38
10s.   Total: £62 10s.

101.   PENSIONS DUE NEXT EASTER.
For archdeaconry of Winchester, £20; for archdeaconry of Surrey, £13 6s 8d.
                                                         Total: £33 6s 8d.

102.   RECEIPTS FOR CITATIONS.
For certain citations at Romsey, Southampton, Winchester, Basingstoke
(*Basyngstoke*) and elsewhere in archdeaconry of Winchester. Total: 10s 4d.

103.   LETTERS OF ADMINISTRATION IN ARCHDEACONRY OF WIN-
CHESTER.
Letters for Robert Knyght, 2s; for sealing same, 2s.   Total: 4s.

104.   RECEIPTS FOR INSTITUTIONS.
Inst. of Richard Slater, v. of Romsey (*Rumsey*), 6s 8d; inst. to ch. of Chale,
I.o.W., 10s.   Total: 16s 8d.

105.   [fo. 85v] RECEIPTS FOR PROBATE OF TESTAMENTS.

a. In archdeaconry of Winchester, by virtue of vacancy of the see:
For probate of John Clouth of Southampton (*Suth'*), 3s; Nicholas Massymere
of Southampton (*Suthampt'*), 2s 8d; Thomas Trussel of Southampton, 20d;
Robert Fourde of Romsey, 2s 8d; Peter Pecok of the New Forest (*nove foreste*),
3s; William Cosshe of Portsmouth (*Portysmewe*), 23d; John Harryes of
Allington (*Ellyngton*), 24d; Richard Hyde of Allington, 4s 2d; John Wodecock
of Wherwell (*Wharwell*), 6s 8d; Richard Boston of Mottisfont (*Motisfont*),
3s 10d; William Hanyngton of Winchester, 13s 6d; Robert Jay of Houghton,
11s 4d; John Warner and Joan his wife of Nether Wallop (*Netherwallopp*),
26s 8d; William Skynner of Winchester, 4s 4d; Richard Radon of Winchester,
20d; John Cristemas of Winchester, 7s 11d; William Batell of Winchester,
16s 8d; Robert Chesthull of Godshill (*Goddeshull*), I.o.W., 13s 4d; Elizabeth
Smyth of Godshill, 20d; John Hamond of Winchester, 7s 10d.
                                                         Total: £6 16s 8d.

b. Receipts for probate [of testaments pertaining to the prerogative
jurisdiction of Canterbury]:
For probate of John Maners of Warwick, 14s; Thomas Banastre of Idsworth
(*Iddeswourthe*), Ha., 8s; Bartholomew Underwoode of Salisbury (*Sar'*), Wlt.,
20s; John Brokes, 14s 4d; bp. Peter Courtenay, £13 6s 8d; Thomas Dalamere,
13s 4d.   Total: £16 16s 4d.

106.　[fo. 86] PROCURATIONS DUE TO THE ARCHBISHOP IN THE ARCH-DEACONRY OF SURREY RECEIVED BY MR SHIRBORN FROM 22 SEPTEMBER 1492 TO EASTER 1493.

a. Dy. of Southwark (*Southwerk*):
Wandsworth (*Wannysforth*), Battersea (*Batersey*), Clapham (*Clompham*), Streatham (*Streteham*), Camberwell (*Camerwell*), Lambeth (*Lamehith*), St George Southwark (*Suthwerke*), St Margaret Southwark, St Mary Magdalene Bermondsey, St Olave Southwark, Rotherhithe (*Redreth*), 7s 7½d each.
Total: [£4 3s 10½d].

b. Dy. of Ewell:
Ewell, Kingston (*Kingeston*), Esher (*Esshere*), Long Ditton (*Longdytton*), 7s 7½d each; Ashstead (*Asshetede*), 6s 8d; Cobham (*Coveham*), Leatherhead (*Lederede*), Mickleham (*Mykylham*), Epsom (*Ebbisham*), Cuddington (*Codyngton*), Morden (*Mordon*), Carshalton (*Crashalton*), Beddington (*Bedyngton*), Mitcham (*Mycheham*), 7s 7½d; Merton, 7s 6d; Stoke d'Abernon (*Stoke Daberun*), 6s 8d; Malden (*Maldon*), 4s; Sutton, 6s 8d; Reigate, Betchworth (*Blecgeworth*), 7s 7½d; Buckland (*Bocland*), Walton-on-the-Hill (*Walton*), 6s 8d; Lingfield (*Lyngefelde*), 7s 7½d; Godstone (*Wolkestede*), 6s 8d; Blechingley (*Blechingleigh*), Nutfield (*Nuttefelde*), 7s 7½d; Gatton, 6s 8d; Chipstead (*Chipstede*), Coulsdon (*Cullusdon*), 7s 7½d; Woodmansterne (*Wodmershom*), 6s 8d; Banstead (*Banstede*), 7s 7½d; Crowhurst, Tandridge (*Tanrigge*), Oxted (*Ockstede*), 6s 8d; Horley, 5s 6½d; Caterham (*Chaterham*), Chaldon (*Chalfendon*), Warlingham (*Warlyngham*), 7s 7½d; Titsey (*Tichesey*), 6s 8d; Farley (*Farleigh*), 3s; Sanderstead (*Sounderstede*), 7s 7½d.　Total: [£14 9s 8½d].

c. [fo. 86v] Dy. of Guildford (*Gildeforde*):
Holy Trinity Guildford, St Mary Guildford (*Guldeforde*), 5s; St Nicholas Guildford, 7s 7½d; Stoke-next-Guildford, 5s; West Clandon (*Clandon Regis*), West Horsley (*Westehorsely*), 7s 7½d; Merrow (*Merewe*), East Clandon (*Clandon Abbatis*), 5s; Great Bookham (*Bocam*), Fetcham (*Feccham*), Dorking (*Dorkyng*), 7s 7½d; Abinger (*Abyngworth*), 6s 8d; Ockley, Ewhurst (*Iwerst*), 7s 7½d; Cranleigh (*Cranley*), 7s 6d; Chiddingfold (*Chidingfeld*), 6s 8d; Witley, Wilton (*Wolton*), Shere (*Shire*), 7s 7½d; Albury (*Aldbury*), 6s 8d; Shalford (*Chalford*), 7s 7½d; Hambledon (*Hamolden*), 3s; Godalming (*Godalmyn*), 7s 7½d; Compton, Puttenham (*Puttynham*), 6s 8d; Ash (*Asshe*), Woking (*Wockyng*), Send (*Sende*), Wonersh (*Wogners*), Leigh (*Ligh*), 7s 7½d; Newdigate (*Nudegate*), 6s 8d; Peper Harow (*Pepurharow*), 3s; Effingham, 7s 6d; Worplesdon (*Warphisdon*), Chertsey, Chobham (*Chabham*), Egham (*Egam*), 7s 7½d; Windlesham (*Windesleham*), 3s; Walton-on-Thames (*Walton*), 6s 8d.
Total: [£13 3s 5d].

d. Religious houses:
Tandridge (*Tanrigge*), Reigate (*Reygate*), Newark (*Newerke*), 20s; St Mary Overy (*Overey*), 100s; hospital of St Thomas the Martyr, Southwark (*Suthwerke*), 40s; Chertsey (*Chertesey*), 66s 8d; Merton, 40s.
Total Procurations in archdeaconry of Surrey: £47 17s 5d.[1]

　　[1] *Added in later hand*: Total procurations excluding those of religious houses: £32 10s 7d.

107. [fo. 87v] Inst. by Mr Shirborne of Richard Walkfelde, chap., to ch. of All Saints, Winchester, vac. by res. of John Dodson, and in the abp.'s collation by virtue of vacancy of see. I. Matthew Delamer, clerk. 17 Oct. 1492.

108. Inst. by Mr Shirborne of Thomas Moren, chap., to vic. of East Wellow (*Welow*), Ha., vac. by d. of Thomas Martyn, chap. P. abbot and conv. of Netley. I. archd. of Winchester. 18 Oct. 1492.

109. Inst. by Mr Shirborne of William Goodyer to vic. of Ashley (*Asheley*), Ha., vac. by res. of Richard Wroxton, chap. P. prior and conv. of Mottisfont. I. archd. of Winchester. 1492.

110. Inst. by Mr Shirborne of Richard Sklater, chap., to vic. of Romsey, Ha., vac. by d. of Edmund Colman, clerk. P. abbess and conv. of Romsey. I. archd. of Winchester. 3 Jan. 1493.

111. Inst. by Mr Shirborne of John Malton, Premonstratensian can. of Titchfield (*Tychefeld*), legitimately dispensed, to ch. of Chale (*Shale*), I.o.W., vac. by res. of William Jenyvere, chap. P. Thomas Langford, esq. I. archd. of Winchester. Lambeth, 7 Jan. 1493.

112. [fo. 88] Inst. by Mr Michael Cleve of Mr Robert Shirborne to mastership of the hospital of St Cross, Winchester, vac. by surrender of Mr John Lychefeld, D.C.L. P. the king, by virtue of vacancy of the see.[1] I. Richard Waren, chap. Winchester cath., 19 Dec. 1492.

   [1] For pres., see *CPR 1485–94*, p. 411.

113. Inst. by Mr Shirborne of Mr Michael Cleve, Decr. D., to prebend and prebendal ch. of Holy Trinity, Wherwell, vac. by surrender of Mr William Smyth. P. abbess Juliana Overey and conv. of Wherwell. I. archd. of Winchester. 22 Jan. 1493.

114. Inst. by Mr Shirborne of [*blank*] Syll, chap., to vic. of St Swithun's, Combe, Ha., vac. by d. of William Fillerey. P. dean and chapter of free chapel of St George in Windsor castle. I. archd. of Winchester. Lambeth, 18 Jan. 1493.

115. Inst. by Mr Cleve of Richard Iremonger to ch. of Linkenholt (*Lynkynholt*), Ha., vac. by res. of Mr David Knollys, Decr. B. P. abbot and conv. of St Peter's, Gloucester. I. archd. of Surrey [*sic*]. 30 Jan. 1493.

116. Inst. of Gervase Ketyll, chap., to ch. of St Lawrence, Wathe (*Southwath*), I.o.W., vac. by d. of Mr John Hayfeld. P. John Cottysmore, esq. I. archd. of Winchester. 5 Feb. 1493.

117. [fo. 88v] Inst. by Mr Cleve of John Grenewoode, chap., to vic of Shipton Bellinger (*Shipton*), Ha., vac. by d. of William Medcalfe. P. prior and

conv. of Guildford New Place (*novo loco iuxta Gilford*). I. archd. of Winchester. 25 Feb. 1493.

118.   Inst. by Mr Shirborne of Robert Wolfe, chap., to ch. of Chilbolton, Ha., vac. by d. of Mr Richard Docheson. P. Thomas bp. of Salisbury, postulate of Winchester, by virtue of the grant to him by the king of temp. of the see. I. Mr William Stephins, chap. of same ch. 23 Mar. 1493.

119.   Inst. by Mr Shirborne of John Bacon, chap., to ch. of Swarraton (*Swarveton*), Ha., vac. by d. of br. William Corner, chap. P. John Kendall, prior of the Hospital of St John in England. I. archd. of Winchester. 29 Mar. 1493.

120.   Inst. by Mr Shirborne of Mr John Nicholl, clerk, to ch. of St Thomas the Martyr, Winchester, vac. by d. of last incumbent, and in the abp.'s collation by virtue of vacancy of the see. I. Mr John Wyott. 23 Mar. 1493.

121.   Inst. of Mr Adrian de Bardys, clerk, to prebend of Hurstbourne Priors (*Husborne Prioris*), Ha., vac. by res. of [*blank*] Cokkys.[1] P. Thomas bp. of Salisbury. I. cur. of same prebendal ch. 25 Apr. 1493.

> [1] Over erasure; *recte* Ralph Hethecote; cf. no. 93 above and *Fasti 1300–1541, Salisbury*, p. 64. For collation by Thomas bp. of Salisbury, see *Reg. Langton* no. 403.

122.   Inst. by Mr Shirborne of William Cutston, chap., to vic. of [*blank*], vac. by res. of Mr James Whitstonys. P. prior and conv. of Southwick. I. archd. of Winchester. [No date].

123.   [fo. 89] Inst. by Mr Shirborne of John Pope, chap., to vic. of Sopley (*Sopeley*), Ha., vac. by res. of John Ray. P. William Ryngeborne, esq. At the urgent petition of John Ray, Mr Shirborne decreed that for the duration of his life the ch. should be charged with an annual pension of ten marks, payable in two equal instalments, the first being due next Christmas, and he issued letters of attestation dated 4 July [*sic*]. 4 June 1493.

124.   Letters of attestation by the abp. that on 22 [*sic*] Dec. 1492[1] Mr Michael Cleve, Decr. D., instituted Mr Robert Shirborne, clerk, treasurer of the cath. ch. of Hereford, to the mastership of the hospital of St Cross, Winchester, vac. by res. of Mr John Lychefeld, D.C.L., to which he had been presented by the king, the rightful patron by virtue of the vacancy of the see. Lambeth, 6 Feb. 1493.

> [1] Cf. no. 112 above.

125.   Inst. by Mr Shirborne of Robert Horneby, chap., to vic. of St Lawrence, Morden, Sy., vac. by d. of Robert Wyrkysworth, pr. P. abbot and conv. of Westminster. I. archd. of Winchester [*sic*].[1] 20 Jan. 1493.

> [1] Cf. no. 96 above.

126.   Inst. by Mr Shirborne of William Leghmore, chap., to ch. of Lasham (*Lasseham*), Ha., vac. by d. of William Blakborne, chap. P. Sir Reginald Bray, kt. I. archd. of Winchester. 18 June 1493.

[fo. 89v] VISITATION CONDUCTED BY MR ROBERT SHIRBORNE, VICAR-GENERAL, GUARDIAN OF THE SPIRITUALITY AND COMMISSARY OF THE ARCHBISHOP IN THE DIOCESE OF WINCHESTER *SEDE VACANTE*, WHICH BEGAN ON 29 OCTOBER 1492.

127.   Visitation of the cath. priory of St Swithun, Winchester, on 29 Oct. 1492. The commissary proceeded to the chapter house, where a collation and his commission were read. The certificate of his citation was presented, with a schedule containing the names of the brethren cited, in order of their profession, and the commissary ordered them to be summoned by name and proceeded to make enquiry into the matters customary in such an inquisition. The prior was summoned first, and the commissary put to him many articles concerning the constitution of the house and matters requiring reform, and he and his brethren replied in the following form:

The prior made no deposition, but stated that all things in the house were laudably observed.

William Silkstede, subprior, deposed that although food was provided in the customary quantity, the quality was very poor, especially that of the mutton and beef.

John Wode deposed that as far as he knew all was managed well in the monastery.

John Floure agreed with the subprior in his deposition.

Thomas Gardyner agreed, and also deposed that there was no inventory of the possessions of the ch., and that through negligence a very valuable ring had been lost; he asked that a search should be made for it and that greater security should be maintained in the future. By similar negligence the foot of the cross of the reliquary which was the gift of the late bp. William had also been lost. The prior, against laudable custom, kept in his own hands the offices of almoner, third prior and *anniversarius*. There should be 46 monks, and there were now only 30.

John Chechestre agreed about the quality of the food. He also deposed that the treasurer did not keep an account in the customary manner and that there was no inventory of the ornaments and jewels of the ch. He also stated that at every inquisition there was much talk of reforming many things and there was some correction or reformation for a time, but it was not maintained.

John Dorsett agreed that the quality of the food was not good, but neither was the quantity sufficient. The humanity which once used to be shown to the brethren in the augmentation of their diet had now fallen into oblivion. No inventory had been made of the goods of the ch., and many depositions were made at inquisitions but no correction was made, as John Chechestre had deposed.

John Pury complained of bad provisioning and that the food was badly prepared and served by the servants. He also deposed that one pound of wax had been withdrawn from certain of the officials, together with many other of the things which used by long-established custom to be provided for them.

John Lawnson deposed that the dormitory was neither extensive, clean, quiet nor in good repair, and the stalls in the cloister were badly exposed to the weather. A certain Philip the treasurer had given £10 to the conv. so that meals might be improved, but to what use this money was put was not known. Due provision was not made for the sick lying in the infirmary, and the ornaments on the altar in Wykeham's chapel were of very poor quality and were broken. He asked that the books in the library might be seen, for free access was not given to them. The foot of a cross had been removed and the man who took it had paid the prior 10 marks for it, for which the prior had not rendered account to the conv., but had retained the money himself. A ring of great value had been lost or alienated by the prior's negligence, to the grave prejudice of the monastery.

John Fetipase, the treasurer, deposed that no inventory of the goods of the ch. had been made by the sacrist.

John Marlborowe deposed that no better provision was made for the sick than for others, notwithstanding the allowance made for them. There was no inventory of the goods of the ch., nor was account rendered by the officials.

Richard Anceline, the sacrist, complained of the food, as above.

Philip Yonge complained that the various offices were not divided among the monks, and that the seats in the refectory were not suitably arranged or repaired. He asked that two offices should not be held by the same man, because this was contrary to their Rule [religionem].

Richard Lacy deposed that no inventory had been made, and petitioned that one monk should be sent to a house of studies, and that due pronouncement should be made against delinquents according to the Rule.

Richard Arundell complained of the poor food.

John Stoughton, John Gympany, John Woodeson and Richard Manhode made no deposition.

Walter Hill deposed that some persons had been introduced by his fellow-monks, and their introduction had resulted in the diminution of the accustomed alms.

John Beste deposed that the vessels for wine and water for the altars were not properly covered and that neither the linen cloths nor the ornaments on the altars were clean.

Thomas Knyght agreed with him, and also deposed that the sacrist did not pay the brethren the customary payment due to them for celebration of the second mass. He also asked that the prior should treat the monks honourably, and that they should maintain decency in their speech.

John Westbury deposed that the proper hours at which the bells should be rung for matins and the other hours were not kept, and that the food was not properly prepared by the servants in the kitchen.

Peter Marlowe deposed that the prior used many dishonourable words to the monks and the conv., and that inadequate provision was made for the sick by the infirmarer.

Arnold Gilbard, Robert Bury and John Mean made no deposition.

128.   [fo. 90] Visitation of the abbey of St Mary, Winchester [no date].
Joan Ligh, abbess, made no deposition.

Catherine Dyngley asked that the nuns's quarters should be repaired at the charge of the house.

Margaret Exestre, subprioress, made the same request.

Anne Seint John, sacrist, made the same request. She also said that the king and the abp. of Canterbury might nominate one sister of the house.

Agnes Tisted also asked for repairs, as above.

Anne Tailard also asked for repairs, as above.

Christina Whytington made no deposition.

Margaret Bawdewyn asked for the reapir of the pavement in the dormitory and the place where their clothes and linen were washed.

Agnes Trussell, Margery Fawkentre and Agnes Awstell made no deposition.

Anastasia Holand deposed that the prioress did not use honourable words to the sisters.

Alice Tisted complained that the curate of the parish ch. of St Roaldus had struck her in the presence of Agnes Tisted, Margaret Somerfounde and *dominus* William Thornton. She also asked for repairs with the others.

Elia Pitt and Agnes Procher made no deposition.

129.   Visitation of Hyde (*Hyda*) abbey, 3 Nov. 1492.

Richard Hall, abbot, deposed that the prior was very remiss in his office and was too free in granting licence to the brethren to go beyond the bounds of the monastery.

Walter Enfourde, prior, deposed that Thomas Barkeley was an apostate, and had been for two years. There were of old 29 brethren in the house, but now the number had decreased to [*blank*]. Each year there should be an account presented to the prior and two of the brethren, with publication of the same when it had been agreed, but this account had neither been seen by him nor published. The chs. of Pewsey (*Peuesey*), Wlt., and Chisledon (*Shisilton*), Wlt., were appropriated to the monastery for certain purposes, but their original appropriation was not maintained, for it had been declared to what uses the revenues should be put when the appropriation was obtained by abbot Strowde, and by his constitution, which had long been observed, it had been ordained that 14 boys should stay in the conv. and should each morning sing mass in the chapel of the B.V.M. and should afterwards attend grammar school, but this provision had fallen into disuse. The advowsons of the chs. of Pewsey and St Lawrence, Ha., had been conceded to Dr Glyn and Dr Lichefeld. There remained in the hands of the abbot £10 for the construction of a new library, which was not yet begun, and it was not known where the money was. The sacrist should make an inventory of the goods and ornaments of the ch.

Thomas Miller and Thomas Stokes agreed with the prior's deposition.

John Hide asked that some of the monks might be admitted to knowledge of the house's revenues, for none of the brethren knew their true value. The office of vintner had fallen into abeyance; on other points he agreed with the prior.

John Moreston deposed that the sick were not properly cared for by the infirmarer in the infirmary. The abbot had begun to build a parlour, which in all probability would take a long time to complete.

William Hendrede agreed with Moreston's deposition.

Richard Rumsey deposed that the food for the monks was not properly provided, nor were essential repairs to the ch. effected.

John Laveyndre asked that the accustomed offices should be divided among the monks.

William Salisbury asked that the prior should have and maintain his house in the customary manner.

William Sheltenham, Thomas Glowcestre, Roger Wherwell and William Chesilden made no deposition.

John Forest asked that better provision should be made for the sick than was now the case, for in the past there used to be an allocation made by the abbot of 1½d, and a similar sum by the infirmarer, and even then the diet of those lying in the infirmary was not good.

130.   [fo. 90v] Visitation of Romsey (*Rumsey*) abbey [no date].

Elizabeth Broke, abbess, stated that she owed to Terbocke a great sum, that is £80, as appeared in a schedule produced by her. She requested that no nun should keep her own house or domicile, or should receive any man or woman without licence from the abbess. She also deposed that nuns were suspected of going into town by the church door. She requested that they should not frequent taverns and other suspect places and that they should not go outside the monastery without her licence. She requested that an injunction be made that she should not pay a corrody of 50s or more, because there appeared to be no reason why it should be paid.

Isabelle Morgan, prioress, deposed that the nuns frequented taverns and continually went into town without licence. She stated that the nuns, impelled by fear, had consented to the sealing of an instrument, and that for three years the said Terbock had held, in part-payment of a debt which the abbess admitted that she owed him, a manor valued at £40. She deposed that the abbess favoured Terbock too much. She prayed that the intention of the founder might be observed in the celebration of masses, since the number of priests was now diminished, first as regards the infirmary, and secondly the chapel of St Nicholas. She requested that an account should be rendered for the sale of woods or groves. She stated that nothing should be sealed with the common seal unless it were done with the advice of some prudent man associated with the house. She requested that an injunction be issued to the abbess and sisters that they choose no man as auditor without consulting the abp. of Canterbury. She deposed that the abbess, as far as it lay with her, had granted a prebend to *dominus* Adrian.[1] She requested that those men who were familiars of Terbock should be driven from the house, especially one called Write. She deposed concerning a cross and many other things given to Terbock by the abbess. She requested that the account rolls might be seen for those years during which Terbock was steward.

Anabel Dunsley deposed with the prioress, and requested that John Write be forbidden continual access to the abbess, because it was said that from her he begged money for Terbock. She deposed that the abbess sealed certain indentures with her private seal.

Cecily Snede deposed that she had not consented to the sealing of the writing in favour of Terbock, and that all the perversion and ill-repute of the house was caused by him.

Joan Skilling deposed with the prioress. She prayed that the conventual beer might be improved. She also deposed concerning two mills valued at 10 marks, which had been withdrawn by the abbess for two years, whereas the profits should be rendered to the sisters.

Joan Paten deposed that she had told the abbess that she did not wish to be involved in the writing delivered to Terbock concerning the office of receiver. She requested that the beer might be improved, and complained of repairs left unattended in the monastery. She also requested that the nuns should observe divine office, especially those who were in the house of the abbess; she also stated that they did not serve in the refectory on the days when they were bound so to do. She requested that a nun who had been brought in should be restored to the place of her profession. She deposed that they had no priest in the infirmary, and also that the abbess had said that when the inquisition was finished she would do as she had done before. She said that all things such as jewels belonging to the place were alienated and pledged to *dominus* Dynham[2] and Mr Borton and some, such as silver dishes and many other silver vessels, to others. She requested that words should be had with *dominus* Ralph French (*Gallicus*), because he did not celebrate in his parish ch., and she said that she had no suitable confessor. She deposed that the doors were not closed at the tenth hour, and also that none of the sins committed by the nuns had been punished for seven years. She requested that nobody should go out of the choir without licence, and stated that people stood chattering in the middle of the choir.

Thomasina Assheley said that she had spoken against the sealing, and in other matters she agreed with Joan Paten.

Edith Howell deposed that due reverence was not shown to the officials, nor was divine service observed. In other things she agreed with Joan Paten. She also stated that she did not consent to the sealing in word or spririt.

Anne Rowse deposed that she had never consented to the sealing of Terbock's office. The prioress did not observe divine office or the canonical hours by day or by night, and the abbess did nothing towards the observance of religion. There was no correction of delinquents.

Joyce Rowse agreed with Joan Paten. She deposed that Terbock had a house belonging to the monastery which was not repaired, and indeed was almost in ruins.

Joan Sutton agreed with Joan Paten in all things.

Ellen Tawke deposed that *dominus* John Dameram had given 20 marks for the repair of the chapel of St Mary, and it was thought that this money had been squandered by the abbess. In other things she agreed with Joan Paten.

Christina Moore deposed that religion was not maintained. In other things she agreed with Joan Paten. She deposed that they used to be in the dormitory at the eighth hour, but that now they had no fixed hour.

Mary Tisted agreed with Joan Paten.

Margaret Strowde deposed as her sisters.

Agnes Haynowe stated that the lamps were not maintained, by the fault or negligence of the sextoness. She also deposed that money was lost which the abbess should share in common but was accustomed rather to consume in drink. In other things she agreed with Joan Paten.

Agnes Skilling deposed with Joan Paten.

Agnes Hervy agreed with the other sisters. She complained of the beer and asked that entry should not be allowed in future to the chapel of St Mary, so as to avoid further danger and evil. She deposed that Howell fed his horses in the ploughed fields and meadows of the monastery. She prayed that the doors of the house be closed day and night, unless urgent necessity should dictate otherwise. She prayed that in entering and leaving the choir they should go modestly and without noise.

Emma Conney had only been in the place for half a year.

Alice Widenstall agreed with Joan Paten. She deposed that the abbess kept three nuns in her own house, and also that one sick nun was not cared for as was fitting.

Elizabeth Rowthale agreed with Joan Paten.

> [1] Probably Adrian de Bardis, clerk to the papal collector, who was extensively beneficed in this region; see nos 93–4, 121 above.
>
> [2] Mr Oliver Dinham, prebendary of St Lawrence Major in Romsey abbey (*BRUO*, p. 618).

131.　[fo. 91v] Visitation of Southwick (*Sothewicke*) priory, 7 Sept. 1492.
Philip Stanbroke, prior, deposed that all the cans. were religious men of good morals and disposition. He also deposed that two tenements in the town of Southwick belonging to his house were [*blank*] by the last strong wind.

John Lawder, John Wolman, William Pile, Thomas Atle, Thomas Skete, William Whight, John Burges, Robert Cole and Walter Chapman made no deposition.

132.　Visitation of the priory of St Denys near Southampton (*sancti Dionisii iuxta Southampton*).
John Foster, John Somersett and Nicholas Dunche made no deposition.

William Thurley asked that they might have a secular or lay servant to ring at the canonical hours.

George Blake and Thomas Wardell asked that the food and drink might be improved.

133.　Visitation of Christchurch, Twynham (*Twyniham*), 12 Nov. 1492.
John Draper, prior, made no deposition.

John Gawge, subprior, made no deposition.

Thomas Selby deposed that the conventual beer was very weak.

John Warner, Richard Skogin, Nicholas Britte, Thomas Colgile, Walter Lagge, Thomas Wymborn, William Eyre, John Eyre, John Gravy, John Quatpry, John Baker, Thomas Greteham, William Bever, William Eleot, William Welles and Robert Salisbury made no deposition.

134.　[fo. 92] Visitation of Breamore (*Brymora*) priory, 13 Nov. 1492.[1]
John Harpy, prior, deposed that there were various pensions or annuities to the value of £12 17s 8d *per annum* conceded by his predecessor, which were a burden to the conv.

William Fromond, William Bodenham and William Fromond [*sic*, repeated] agreed with the prior.

Richard Grey deposed that a certain Richard Cliffe, layman, fed his dogs and horse at the conv.'s expense.

Denis Coventre agreed with this and also deposed that a certain John Dibbe, servant of the prior . . . [ends thus].

[1] MS: 1494.

[fos 92 and 93 blank.]

Note: the see became vacant on the d. of bp. John Russell on 30 Dec. 1494. William Smith, bp. of Coventry and Lichfield, was translated to Lincoln on 6 Nov. 1495.

135.　　[fo. 94] The cath. ch. of St Mary, Lincoln, being vac. by the d. of bp. John Russell, who died at his manor of Nettleham (*Nettilham*) near Lincoln on 30 Jan. 1495 [*sic*],[1] and whose body was honourably buried beneath the cath., the dean and chapter, according to the composition made between their predecessors and abp. Boniface,[2] sent letters to the abp. nominating Henry Apjohn, precentor, and John Walles and Thomas Hille, residentiary cans., humbly praying that the abp. would choose one of them as his Official in the dioc. and keeper of the spirituality for the duration of the vacancy. These letters were presented with due reverence by Mr Apjohn and Mr Walles to the abp., who received and inspected them and deliberated for a day. He and his counsellors discussed with the cans. the force and validity of the composition, and finding that it had been applied by his predecessors in the ch. of Canterbury and wishing to preserve inviolate the rights of the chs. of Canterbury and Lincoln and of the dean and chapter, and to bestow upon the said dean and chapter the greatest favour because of his love for God and the Immaculate Virgin Mary, the patron of the ch. of Lincoln in which he himself in times gone by had held ecclesiastical benefices, he appointed Mr John Walles his Official and keeper of the spirituality, and issued to him letters of commission under his great seal. Mr Walles took an oath to exercise faithfully the office committed to him and to account fully to the abp. for all revenues due to him during the vacancy. The abp. repeatedly urged him and obliged him before God to exercise the office in the dioc. of Lincoln, which he believed to be very extensive, both personally and through the agency of other suitable men whom he should depute, and to proceed diligently in all things to the glory and honour of Almighty God and His exalted mother Mary, to the furtherance of the salvation of souls and in accordance with the abp.'s conscience and his own. Having given these instructions, the abp. dismissed Mr Walles with his blessing.

[1] Cf. *Handbook of British Chronology*, 3rd ed., 256.
[2] Churchill, ii, 42–47.

136.　　[fo. 94v] In the chapel of St Catherine the Virgin in Lincoln cath. the letters of commission were exhibited on the abp.'s behalf before Mr Walles as he sat judicially. He accepted them with due reverence, ordered them to be read publicly and accepted execution of the commission. He announced the extent of his jurisdiction and at the abp.'s command appointed Mr William Miller, clerk and notary public, as his registrar and scribe of the acts. Mr Walles declared that he would visit the religious houses and the clergy and people of the dioc. at suitable and convenient times, and as he kept major residence in the cath. because he was a can. residentiary, and because of the wide extent of the dioc. and the large number of persons within the spiritual jurisdiction, by the express command of the abp. he appointed Mr Edward Shuldham, D.C.L., Mr John Veysye, D.C.L., Mr Roger Churche, Decr. D., and Mr Ralph Hanneys, Decr. B., jointly and singly as his commissaries to visit the clergy and people of the dioc. and to exercise other jurisdictional functions, as fully stated in the letters of commission under the Official's seal. Lincoln, 27 Jan. 1495.

137. Commission, with power of canonical coercion, to Mr John Walles as Official in the city and dioc. of Lincoln to exercise episcopal jurisdiction during the vacancy of the see according to the terms of the composition and in accordance with the oath which he had taken. Reservation to the abp. of collation of benefices *pleno iure sive iure devoluto*. Lambeth, 13 Jan. 1495.

138. [fo. 95] Citation directed by Mr Walles to the archd. of Lincoln or his Official for the visitation of the archdeaconry on the dates specified below. All incumbents, other chaps. and four or six parishioners, according to the extent of each parish, are to be cited to appear. Any action prejudicial to the visitation is hereby inhibited. Lincoln, 20 Jan. 1495.
The dy of Yarborough (*Jordeburgh*) is to be visited in the ch. of Keelby (*Keleby*) on Friday 27 Feb.; dy. of Grimsby (*Grymesby*) in ch. of St James, Grimsby, on Saturday 28 Feb.; dy of Wraggoe (*Wraghou*) in ch. of Wragby on Thursday 5 Mar., dy. of Loutheske and Ludborough (*Louthburgh*) in ch. of Louth on Tuesday 10 Mar.; dy. of Horncastle (*Horncastre*), Hill (*Hille*) and Gartree (*Gartre*) in ch. of Horncastle on Tuesday 17 Mar.; dy. of Candleshoe (*Candeleshou*) in ch. of Partney (*Partenay*) on Wednesday 18 Mar.; dy. of Calcewaith (*Calcewath*) in ch. of Alford on Thursday 19 Mar.; dy. of Bolingbroke in ch. of Bolingbroke on Monday 23 Mar.; north part of Holland (*Holand*) at Boston on Tuesday 24 Mar.; south part of Holland at ch. of Spalding (Spaldyng) on Thursday 26 Mar.; dy. of Ness (*Nesse*) and Stamford (*Staunford*) at Stamford on Wednesday 1 Apr.; dy. of Aveland (*Avelond*) in ch. of Bourne (*Burne*) on Friday 3 Apr.; dy. of Beltisloe (*Beltislawe*) in ch. of Bitchfield (*Bilchefeld*) on Saturday 4 April; dy. of Lafford in ch. of Sleaford (*Sleford*) on Tuesday 7 Apr.; dy. of Grantham (*Graham*) in ch. of Grantham on Wednesday 8 Apr.; dy of Lovedon (*Loveden'*) in ch. of Ancaster (*Ancastr'*) on Thursday 9 Apr.; dy. of Longoboby (*Langhouboby*) and Graffoe (*Grafhou*) in ch. of Navenby on Friday 10 Apr.; dy. of Walshcroft (*Walescrofte*) in ch. of East Rasen (*Estrasen*) on Tuesday 14 Apr.
On 27 Feb. in the parish ch. of Keelby, before Mr Ralph Hanneys, Decr. B., commissary of the official, sitting judicially for the visitation of the dy. of Yarborough, *dominus* [*blank*], perpetual v. of Thornton, appeared on behalf of Mr Henry Apjohn, Official of the archd. of Lincoln, and presented letters of certification sealed with the Official's seal and dated at Lincoln, 22 Feb. 1495.

139. [fo. 96] Similar citation and inhibition directed to the archd. of Stow or his Official. Lincoln, 20 Jan. 1495.
The dy. of Lawres (*Laures*) is to be visited in the ch. of Torksey (*Torkeseye*) on Tuesday 17 Feb.; dy. of Coringham (*Coryngham*) in ch. of Gainsborough (*Gaynesburgh*) on Wednesday 18 Feb.; dy. of Manlake (*Manlak*) in ch. of Messingham on Friday 20 Feb.; dy. of Aslacoe (*Aslakhou*) in chapel of Spital-in-the-Street (*Spitel of the Strete*) on Monday 13 Apr.

On 17 Feb. in the parish ch. of Torksey, before Mr Hanneys, letters of certification dated 12 Feb. were returned by Mr Richard Stokes, Official of the archd. of Stow.

140.   [fo. 96v] Similar citation and inhibition directed to the archd. of Northampton or his Official and to the dean of Peterborough (*Burgo*), for visitation of the dy. of Peterborough on Tuesday 31 Mar. Lincoln, 25 Feb. 1495.
On 31 Mar. in the parish ch. of Peterborough, before Mr Hanneys, letters of certification dated 12 Mar. were returned by the dean.

141.   [fo. 97] Similar citation and inhibition directed to the archd. of Leicester or his Official. Lincoln, 1 Mar. 1495.
The dy. of Framland is to be visited in the ch. of Melton Mowbray (*Melton Moubray*) on 25 Apr.; dy. of Akeley (*Akle*) in ch. of Loughborough (*Louthburgh*) on 26 Apr.; dy. of Sparkenhoe (*Sperkenhou*) in ch. of Bosworth (*Boseworth*) on 30 Apr.; dy. of Leicester (*Leicestr'*) in ch. of St Martin, Leicester, on 2 May; dy. of Goscote in ch. of Belgrave on 4 May; dy. of Guthlaxton (*Gudlaxton*) in ch. of Lutterworth on 5 May; dy. of Gartree (*Gartre*) in chapel of Market Harborough (*Harborowe*) on 6 May.
On 25 Apr. in the ch. of Melton Mowbray, before Mr Hanneys, letters of certification dated 20 Apr. were returned by Mr John Shorman, Official of the archd.

142.   [fo. 97v] Citation of the abbot of St Mary de Pratis, Leicester, O.S.A., to submit to visitation on 12 Feb. Lincoln, 14 Jan. 1495.
On 20 Jan. 1495 at Lincoln similar citations were despatched to other superiors: to prior of Torksey (*Torkeseya*), O.S.A., for visitation on Tuesday 17 Feb.; prior of Elsham (*Ellesham*), O.S.A., for 23 Feb.; abbot of Thornton, O.S.A., for Wednesday 25 Feb.; prioress of Nun Cotham (*Nuncoton*), O. Cist., for Thursday 26 Feb.; abbot of Grimsby *alias* Wellow, O.S.A., for Saturday 28 Feb.; abbot of Bardney (*Bardenay*), O.S.B., for Friday 6 Mar.; prioress of Stixwould (*Stikeswolde*), O. Cist., for 9 Mar.; prioress of Legbourne (*Legborn*), O. Cist., for 12 Mar.; prioress of Greenfield (*Grenefeld*), O. Cist., for 20 Mar.; warden of coll. ch. of Tattershall (*Tateshall*) for 23 Mar.; prior of Spalding, O.S.B., for 26 Mar.; abbot of Croyland, O.S.B., for [*blank*].

[Fos 98v–101v are blank.]

INSTITUTIONS EXPEDITED BY MR JOHN WALLES
    Note: mandates for induction were directed to the appropriate archd. or his Official, unless otherwise stated.

[fo. 102] ARCHDEACONRY OF LINCOLN

143.   Inst. of Robert Everyngham, pr., in the person of his proctor Thurstan Smyth, literate, to vic. of Killingholme (*Kelingholme*), vac. by res. of

Thomas Robynson. P. abbot and conv. of Newsham *alias* Newhouse. Lincoln, 26 Jan. 1495.

144.   Inst. of William Oldham, pr., to ch. of Silk Willoughby (*Northwillugby* alias *Silkwillughby*), vac. by res. of Augustine, bp. of Lydda (*Liden'*). P. John Stanlowe, esq. Lincoln, 30 Jan. 1495.

145.   Inst. of Thomas Rowse, pr., to perpetual chantry founded in honour of B.V.M. in parish ch. of Welton le Marsh (*Welton*), vac. by res. of John Beverley. P. Thomas Rigge of Welton. Lincoln, 2 Mar. 1495.

146.   Inst. of Ralph Bollis, acolyte, to ch. of Old Somerby (*Somerbye*), vac. by d. of Richard Owre. P. John Colvylle, *generosus*. Lincoln, 2 Mar. 1495.

147.   Inst. of William Grave, pr., to ch. of Ulceby [near Alford] with ch. of Fordington (*Forthington*) united and annexed to the same, vac. by res. of Br William Halton. P. abbot and conv. of Croyland. Lincoln, 1 Apr. 1495.

148.   Inst. of Richard Hogeson, pr., to vic. of Saleby, vac. by d. of Thomas Walton. P. prior and conv. of Sixhills. Lincoln, 7 Apr. 1495.

149.   Inst. of Robert Bothe, pr., to vic. of Ulceby [near Barton on Humber], vac. by d. of Robert Hygdon. P. abbot and conv. of Thornton. Lincoln, 21 Apr. 1495.

150.   Inst. of Mr Peter le Pennok. D.C.L., in the person of his proctor Mr Simon Stalworth, subdean of cath., to prebend of North Kelsey in cath. ch. of Lincoln, vac. by res. of Mr Christopher Urswyk. P. the king.[1] I. dean and chapter of Lincoln. Lincoln, 2 May 1495.

        [1] *CPR 1494–1509*, p. 14.

151.   [fo. 102v] Inst. of John Taylour, pr., to ch. of Bag-Enderby (*Bagendirby*), vac. by res. of John Inglyssh. P. George Gednay of Bag-Enderby. Lincoln, 27 May 1495.

152.   Inst. of Mr Thomas Madiow, pr., to ch. of St Peter, Conisholme (*Conyngesholm*), vac. by res. of John Hardyng. P. John viscount Welles. Lincoln, 3 June 1495.

153.   Inst. of John Hardyng, pr., to ch. of St Michael Major, Stamford (*Staumforth*), vac. by res. of Mr Thomas Madiow. P. abbot and conv. of Croyland. Lincoln, 3 June 1495.[1]

        [1] *Note*: nos 152 and 153 constitute an exchange.

154.   Inst. of Richard Lucas, pr., in the person of his proctor Mr Richard Lucas, notary public, to ch. of Silk Willoughby, vac. by res. of William Oldeham. P. John Stanlowe, esq., and Margaret his wife. Lincoln, 25 June 1495.

155.   Inst. of Thomas Dey, pr., to ch. of Greatford (*Gretford*), vac. by d. of Mr Nicholas Major. P. abbess and conv. of St Mary, Winchester. Lincoln, 18 July 1495.

156.   Inst. of Thomas Forestar, pr., to ch. of St Michael Major, Stamford, vac. by res. of John Hardyng. P. abbot and conv. of Croyland. Croyland, 20 July 1495.

157.   Inst. of Mr Richard Norton, pr., in the person of his proctor Gregory Karre, literate, to ch. of Islip (*Islyppe*), Ox., vac. by res. of Mr Simon Stalworth. P. abbot and conv. of Westminster. Boston, 24 July 1495.

158.   Inst. of William Westwode, pr., to vic. of Fotherby (*Foterby*), vac. by d. of John Carlell. P. prior and conv. of North Ormsby (*Nunormesby*). Louth, 29 July 1495.

159.   Inst. of George Paythnoll, pr., to vic. of Calceby, vac. by res. of Simon Barow. P. prior and conv. of Kyme. Lincoln, 7 Aug. 1495.

160.   [fo. 103] Inst. of Richard Elande, can. of Haverholme, to vic. of Anwick (*Anwyk*), vac. by d. of Thomas Mayne. P. prior and conv. of Haverholme. Lincoln, 11 Aug. 1495.

161.   Inst. of Mr Robert Odelby, pr., to ch. of Toft (*Tofte*), vac. by d. of Mr Nicholas Major. P. abbot and conv. of Croyland. Lincoln, 14 Aug. 1495.

162.   Inst. of William Mareshall, pr., to perpetual chantry of St Nicholas in ch. of Heckington,[1] vac. by res. of John Lowden. P. Sir Marmaduke Constable, kt. Lincoln, 18 Aug. 1495.

> [1] MS: *Helyngton* and *Hollington*, but cf. no. 219a.

163. Inst. of John Gryndell, pr., to ch. of Braceborough (*Brasborogh*), vac. by d. of Mr Nicholas Maior. P. master and brethren of Burton Lazars. Lincoln, 12 Sept. 1495.

164.   Inst. of Richard Whiteby, can. of Bullington (*Bollyngton*), to vic. of West Torrington, vac. by res. of William Pownswet. P. prior and conv. of Bullington. Lincoln, 15 Sept. 1495.

165.   Inst. of Richard Norwich, pr., in the person of his proctor John Cook, literate, to moiety of the ch. of Sedgebroke (*Segbroke*), vac. by res. of Alexander Deynys. P. prior and conv. of Eye, Norwich dioc. Lincoln, 23 Sept. 1495.

166.   Inst. of William Perkyn, pr., to vic of Ashby, vac. by deprivation of Robert Leydes.[1] P. prior of the Hospital of St John of Jerusalem in England. Lincoln, 25 Sept. 1495.

> [1] Cf. no. 219a.

167.   Inst. of Robert Kocke, pr., to ch. of Kirkby St Denis, vac. by res. of Henry Sleford. P. John Stanlowe, esq., and Margaret his wife. Lincoln, 7 Oct. 1495.

168.   Inst. of William Dortour, pr., to ch. of All Saints, Wainfleet (*Wayneflete*), vac. by d. of Mr William Hode. P. Geoffrey Symeon, chancellor of the cath. ch., and John Cutler, clerk. Lincoln, 28 Oct. 1495.

169.   [fo. 103v] Inst. of Thomas Chymylby, pr., in the person of his proctor Alexander Knolles, literate, to ch. of Tetford, vac. by d. of Thomas Wodthorp. P. Richard Chymylby, esq. Lincoln, 15 Dec. 1495.

170.   Inst. of Mr Humphrey Fitzwilliam, M.A., to ch. of Ingoldmells (*Ingolmellis*), vac. by d. of Mr John Bell. P. Agnes Skypwith, widow of Sir William Skypwith, kt. Lincoln, 20 Dec. 1495.

171.   Inst. of John Belenden, can., in the person of his proctor Mr Robert West, to vic. of All saints, Sixhills (*Syxhill*), vac. by d. of William Okes. P. prior and conv. of Sixhills. Lincoln, 1 Jan. 1496.

172.   Inst of Ralph Pole, pr., to ch. of Careby (*Coreby*),[1] vac. by d. of William Warde. P. Henry Grymsby, esq., and Elizabeth Pole, widow of Ralph Pole, esq. Lincoln, 19 Jan. 1496.

>   [1] Cf. no. 223a below, and A. H. Thompson, *Associated Archaeological Societies Reports* xl (1930–1), 36.

173.   Inst. of Robert Thomeson, pr., to vic. of Edlington, vac. by d. of Robert Thorp. P. abbot and conv. of Bardney. Lincoln, 26 Jan. 1496.

174.   Inst. of Robert Hemslay, pr., in the person of his proctor William Sixhill, literate, to vic. of Burgh Marsh (*Burgh*), vac. by d. of William Bonde. P. prior and conv. of Bullington. Lincoln, 1 Feb. 1496.

175.   Inst. of John Wryght, pr., in the person of his proctor Thomas Candeler, to ch. of Fleet, vac. by d. of William Westlonde. P. prior and conv. of Castle Acre. Lincoln, 5 Feb. 1496.

ARCHDEACONRY OF STOW, Li.

176.   [fo. 104] Inst. of Edward Colinson, can. of Welbeck, to vic. of Coates by Stow (*Coytes*), vac. by d. of John Hirst. P. abbot and conv. of Welbeck. Lincoln, 13 Mar. 1495.

177.   Inst. of William Lincoln, pr., to perpetual chantry of St Mary and St Catherine in the parish of Epworth, vac. by res. of John Mawe. P. Elizabeth duchess of Norfolk. Lincoln, 2 June 1495.

178.   Inst. of Thomas Wamyslay, pr., to third part of the perpetual chantry in the north part of parish ch. of Gainsborough (*Gaynesburgh*), vac. by d. of John Whyte. P. Sir Thomas Cornewaile, kt. Lincoln, 4 Sept. 1495.

179.   Inst. of William Tupholme, pr., to ch. of Waddingham St Mary (*Staynton Wadyngham*), vac. by d. of Richard Heilde. P. Sir Guy Fairfax, kt., William Rowkeshawe, clerk, and William Rilston, esq. Lincoln, 15 Dec. 1495.

ARCHDEACONRY OF NORTHAMPTON

180.   [fo. 104v] Inst. of Thomas Williamson, pr., to ch. of Glendon, vac. by d. of Richard Stafford. P. prior of the Hospital of St John of Jerusalem in England. Lincoln, 3 Mar. 1495.

181.   Inst. of Thomas Cotys, pr., in the person of his proctor Mr William Miller, notary public, to ch. of St Peter, Rushton, vac. by res. of William Poole. P. John Cresham, esq. Lincoln, 17 Mar. 1495.

182.   Inst. of Alexander Deyns, pr., to ch. of Cottesbrook (*Cottisbroke*), vac. by d. of John Medycok. P. John Markham, esq. Lincoln, 14 Apr. 1495.

183.   Inst. of John Palady, pr., to vic. of Harrowden (*Haroden*), vac. by res. of Thomas Style. P. abbot and conv. of St Mary, Sulby. Lincoln, 3 June 1495.

184.   Inst. of Henry Wollaston, pr., to vic. of Desborough (*Desburgh*), vac. by d. of Laurence Kynge. P. prior and conv. of St John the Baptist, Rothwell. Lincoln, 12 Aug. 1495.

185.   Inst. of William Hasulwode, pr., in the person of his proctor Mr Richard Grene, notary public, to vic. of Little Houghton [near Northampton], vac. by d. of John Gough. P. prior and conv. of St Andrew's Northampton. London, 12 Oct. 1495.

186.   Inst. of Richard Nycholl, pr., to ch. of Holcot, vac. by res. of William Lilly. P. prior of the Hospital of St John of Jerusalem in England. London, 13 Nov. 1495.

187.   Inst. of Mr Henry Horneby, pr., to ch. of Thrapston, vac. by d. of Mr John Mesaunt. P. abbot and conv. of Bourne. London, 20 Nov. 1495.

188.   Inst. of Robert Wyham, pr., to vic. of Helpringham, Li., vac. by res. of the same Robert Wyham [*sic*]. P. abbot and conv. of Bourne. I. archd. of Northampton [*sic, recte* of Stow]. London, 10 Nov. 1495.

ARCHDEACONRY OF LEICESTER

189.   [fo. 105] Inst. of John Milner, pr., to vic. of Hose (*Howes*), vac. by d. of Thomas Kirkman. P. Richard Mariot and Thomas Milner. Lincoln, 22 Mar. 1495.

190.   Inst. of Mr John Davy, Decr. B., to ch. of Kimcote (*Kylmyncote*), vac. by res. of John Ranowdon. P. the lady Joan Talbot, widow. Lincoln, 17 June 1495.

191.   Inst. of Mr Edward Shuldam, D.C.L., in the person of his proctor Thomas Parys, literate, to fifth prebend in coll. ch. of Newark, Leicester, vac. by res. of Thomas Rydley. P. the king. I. dean and chapter of Newark. Lincoln, 4 July 1495.

192.   Inst. of Thomas Barford, pr., to ch. of Ashby Parva, vac. by res. of Mr Thomas Dalby. P. prior of the Hospital of St John of Jerusalem in England. Lincoln, 15 Jan. 1496.

193.   Inst. of John Hamond, pr., to ch. of Withcote (*Withcok*), vac. by res. of William Sotherey. P. William Smith, *generosus*. Lincoln, 22 Jan. 1496.

194.   Inst. of Richard Claybroke, clerk, to ch. of Frowlesworth (*Frollew-orth*), vac. by d. of Robert Claybroke. P. Robert Walsall, *generosus*. 28 Jan. 1496.

ARCHDEACONRY OF OXFORD

195.   [fo. 105v] Inst. of Robert Occulshawe, pr., to ch. of Holton (*Halton*), vac. by res. of John Coldale. P. Joan Fowler, widow. Lincoln, 19 Mar. 1495.

196.   Inst. of George Harryson, pr., to ch. of Tusmore (*Turvesmer'*), vac. by d. of John Cottismore. P. Thomas Langston, esq. Lincoln, 1 Apr. 1495.

197.   Inst. of David Biford, pr., to ch. of Wilcote (*Wibilcote*), vac. by d. of Robert Coly. P. Jasper, duke of Bedford and earl of Pembroke. Lincoln, 14 May 1495.

198.   Inst. of Mr Simon Stalworth, can. of Lincoln, in the person of his proctor John Robynson, literate, to ch. of Algarkirk (*Algerkirke*), Li., vac. by res. of Mr Richard Norton. P. Thomas Grey, marquis of Dorset, lord Ferrers, Astley and Groby of Harrington and Bonville. Boston, 24 July 1495.

199.   Inst. of William Walweyn, pr., in the person of his proctor John Morwyn, literate, to vic. of Charlbury (*Chorlebury*), vac. by res. of John Slatter *alias* Wynyngton. P. John Holford. Lincoln, 12 Oct. 1495.

ARCHDEACONRY OF HUNTINGDON

200.   [fo. 106] Inst. of John Porter, pr., to vic. of King's Langley (*Langley Regis*), Hrt., vac. by d. of Richard Wylly. P. prioress and conv. of Dartford (*Derteford*), Lincoln, 6 Mar. 1495.

201. Inst. of William Kynnardesley, pr., in the person of his proctor Thomas Paryse, literate, to ch. of Knebworth, Hrt., vac. by d. of Thomas Jordan. P. Anne Burgchyer, widow of Sir Thomas Bourgchier, kt. Lincoln, 22 Mar. 1495.

202.   Inst. of Walter Prior, pr., to ch. of All Saints, Huntingdon (*Huntyngdon*), vac. by d. of Mr John Elys. P. abbot and conv. of Thorney. Lincoln, 15 Apr. 1495.

203.   Inst. of James Carwardyn, pr., in the person of his proctor Walter ap Morgan, literate, to ch. of Ayot St Lawrence (*Eyate sancti Laurencii*), Hrt., vac. by res. of William Kynnardesley. P. Sir Richard de Labere, kt., Thomas Cornewayle, esq., and Edward Haugner, esq. 6 June 1495.

204.   Inst. of Mr Thomas Hutton, Decr. D., pr., to ch. of Warboys (*Wardeboys*), Hu., vac. by d. of Mr Richard Burton. P. abbot and conv. of Ramsey. Lincoln, 29 Aug. 1495.

205.   Inst. of John Hunte, pr., in the person of his proctor Mr William Miller, clerk and notary public, to vic. of Tilsworth (*Tillysworth*), Bd., vac. by res. of Robert Clerk. P. prioress and conv. of St Giles in the Wood (*Sancti Egidii in Bosco*), Flamstead. Lincoln, 12 Sept. 1495.

206.   Inst. of Mr Thomas Heide, S.T.B., in the person of his proctor Mr Oliver Stalys, clerk and notary public, to ch. of St Mary, Orton Waterville (*Chercoverton*), Hu., vac. by d. of Mr William Rawson. P. warden and fellows of Pembroke College, Cambridge. Lincoln, 20 Sept. 1495.

207.   Inst. of Richard Warde, pr., to ch. of Folksworth (*Folkysworth*), Hu., vac. by res. of Thomas Cartwryght. P. abbot and conv. of Croyland. Lincoln, 6 Oct. 1495.

208.   [fo. 106v] Inst. of Thomas Cade, pr., to ch. of Buckworth (*Bukworth*), Hu., vac. by d. of Mr Thomas Stokke. P. Edward, earl of Wiltshire. London, 28 Oct. 1495.

209.   Inst. of Mr William Thornburgh, D.C.L., in the person of his proctor Mr William Pykerell, clerk and notary public, to ch. of St Faith, Kelshall (*Kelsall*), Hrt., vac. by res. of Mr Geoffrey Scrope. P. bp. of Ely. London, 28 Oct. 1495.

210.   Inst. of Mr Matthew Knyveton, M.A., to vic. of Ashwell (*Asshewell*), Hrt., vac. by res. of Mr Robert Middleton. P. abbot and conv. of Westminster. London, 14 Nov. 1495.

211.   Inst. of Thomas Hobbys, M.A., to ch. of Wood Walton (*Walton*), Hu., vac. by d. of Mr Richard Burton. P. abbot and conv. of Ramsey. London, 26 Nov. 1495.

212.   Inst. of Richard Oliver, pr., to vic. of St Mary, St Neots (*sancti Neoti*), Hu., vac. by d. of Richard Wolley. P. Robert Arnold. Lincoln, 15 Jan. 1496.

ARCHDEACONRY OF BEDFORD

213.   Inst. of John Lewes, pr., to ch. of Potsgrove (*Pottesgrave*), vac. by d. of last incumbent. P. abbot and conv. of St Albans. Lincoln, 2 July 1495.

214.   [fo. 107] Inst. of Robert Lefe, pr., to ch. of Isenhampstead Chenies (*Isnamstede*), vac. by d. of Richard Newland. P. David Philippe, esq., and Anne his wife, lords of Isenhampstead Chenies, and John Couper, *generosus*, and Roger Flecher. Lincoln, 13 Mar. 1495.

215. Inst. of Robert Talys, M.A., in the person of his proctor John Presgrave, literate, to ch. of Alwalton, Hu., vac. by d. of Mr John Ely. P. abbot and conv. of Peterborough. Lincoln, 9 Dec. 1495.

[Fos 107v–109v are blank.]

[fo. 110] ACCOUNT RENDERED BY MR JOHN WALLES, OFFICIAL *SEDE VACANTE*, FOR EPISCOPAL REVENUES IN THE ARCHDEACONRIES OF LINCOLN, STOW AND LEICESTER DUE TO THE ARCHBISHOP AND THE CHURCH OF CANTERBURY BY VIRTUE OF THE VACANCY OF THE SEE, FROM 12 JANUARY TO 1 NOVEMBER 1495.

216.   PENSIONS IN THE ARCHDEACONRIES OF LINCOLN AND STOW, Li.

a. At feast of the Purification of B.V.M. [2 Feb.]:
from ch. of Legbourne (*Legburn*), 3s 4d

b. At feast of the Annunciation of B.V.M. [25 Mar.]:
from ch. of Leake (*Leeke*), 20s

c. At Easter:
from chs. of Ailby (*Aylesby*), 6s 8d; Theddlethorp All Saints (*Thedilthorp*), 20s; Frodingham (*Frothingham*), 20s; Northorpe (*Northorp*), 6s 8d; Wrawby (*Wrauby*), 5s; Wootton (*Wotton*), 20s; Theddlethorp St Helen (*Thebilthorp*), 3s 4d; Fulstow (*Fulstowe*), 20s; Harpswell (*Harpeswell*), 5s; Grayingham (*Geryngham*), 6s 8d; Ulceby (*Ulseby*), 2s; Wainfleet St Mary (*Wayneflete Marie*), 10s; Heckington (*Hekyngton*) and Hale, 66s 8d; Swaton, 60s; Quadring (*Quadryng*), 13s 4d; Boston (*Bostone*), 26s 8d.   Total: £14 12s

d. At the Nativity of St John the Baptist [24 June]:
from chs. of Ewerby (*Iwardby*), 6s 8d; Frampton, 13s 4d; Spalding (*Spaldyng*), 3s 4d; Spridlington (*Sprydlyngton*), 3s 4d.   Total: 26s 8d

e. At Michaelmas [29 Sept.]:
from chs. of Helpringham, 20s; Coleby (*Colby*), 10s; Syston (*Siston*), 6s 8d; Harnston (*Harneston*), Mere and Hackthorn (*Hakthorn*), 16s 8d; Irby in the Marsh (*Irby*), 2s; Leake (*Leeke*), 20s; Heckington and Hale, 66s 8d; Great Stretton (*Magna Stretton*), with vic. of Stainton Burneth (*Steynton Burneth*) and mediety of Rasen Tupholme, 40s; Wainfleet (*Wayneflete*), 10s; Woodhall (*Woodehyll*), 3s; Horncastle (*Hornecastre*), 13s 4d; Theddlethorp All Saints, 20s; Frodingham, 20s; Stickford (*Stikford*), 3s 4d; Spilsby (*Spillisby*), 26s 8d; Great Carlton (*Carleton Magna*), 6s 8d; Fulstow (*Fullestowe*), 20s; Alvingham (*Allvyngham*) and Garthorpe (*Garnthorpe*), 6s 8d; Clee, 6s 8d; Keelby (*Keleby*), 10s; Brocklesby (*Brokelesby*), 3s 4d; Wrawby, 5s; Scawby (*Scalby*), 40s; Owston

(*Ouston*), 50s; Boston, 26s 8d; Northorpe, 6s 8d; Torksey St Peter (*Torkesey*), 3s 4d; Quadring, 13s 4d; Cadney, 2s; Hogsthorpe (*Hoggesthorp*), 20s.
Total: £25 0s 8d

TOTAL PENSIONS IN ARCHDEACONRIES OF LINCOLN AND STOW:
£42 2s 8d

217.   PENSIONS IN THE ARCHDEACONRY OF LEICESTER, Lei.

a. At feast of the Annunciation of B.V.M. [25 Mar.]:
from chs. of Higham on the Hill (*Higham*), Irchester (*Irchestre*) and Rand (*Randes*), 50s; Arnesby (*Ernesby*), 13s 4d; Dishley (*Dyxley*), 3s. Total: 66s 8d

b. At Easter:
from chs. of Buckminster (*Bukmynster*) and Twyford, 20s; Ragdale (*Rakedale*), 6s 8d; Little Dalby (*Dalby Parva*), 10s; Castle Donington (*Casteldonyngton*), 30s.
Total: 66s 8d

c. [fo. 110v] At the Nativity of St John the Baptist [24 June]:
from chs. of Higham on the Hill, Irchester and Rand, 50s; King's Norton (*Norton*) and vic. of Owston (*Oselweston*), 22s; Shackerstone (*Shakerston*), 13s 4d; priory of Ulverscroft (*Ulvescrofte*) and Charley, 6s 8d. Total: £4 12s

d. At Michaelmas [29 Sept.]:
from chs. of Thingden, 40s; Twyford (*Twiford*), 10s; Ragdale, 6s 8d; Cransley (*Cranesley*), 13s 4d; Hungerton and Humberstone (*Humbreston*), 40s; Castle Donington, 30s; Sileby, 3s 4d; Market Overton (*Overton*), 20s; Loddington (*Lodyngton*), 2s; hospital of St John, Leicester, 10s; Wistow (*Wistowe*), 6s 8d.
Total: £9 2s

TOTAL PENSIONS IN ARCHDEACONRY OF LEICESTER: £20 7s

TOTAL OF ALL PENSIONS IN ARCHDEACONRIES OF LINCOLN, STOW AND LEICESTER: £62 9s 8d

218.   PAYMENTS FROM ARCHDEACONS OF LINCOLN, STOW AND LEICESTER

a. At Easter:
Lincoln, £22; Stow, 70s; Leicester, £14 13s 4d.   Total: £40 3s 4d

b. At Michaelmas:
Lincoln, £22; Stow, 70s; Leicester, £14 13 4d.   Total: £40 3s 4d

TOTAL PAYMENTS FROM ARCHDEACONS: £80 6s 8d

219.   RECEIPTS FOR INSTITUTIONS   [standard fee: 6s 8d]

a. Archdeaconry of Lincoln, Li.:
Vic. of Killingholme (*Kelyngholme*), 26 Jan., by res.; vic. of Saleby, 7 Apr., by d.; Silk Willoughby (*Silk Willuby*), 30 Jan., by res.; Somerby (*Somerby*), 2 Mar., by d.; chantry at Welton, 2 Mar., by res.; Ulceby, 1 Apr., by res.; vic. of Ulceby, 21 Apr., by d.; prebend of North Kelsey, 3 May, by res.;

Bagenderby, 27 May, by res.; Conisholme (*Conyngisholme*), ch. of St Peter, 3 June, by res.; Stamford, ch. of St Michael, 24 June, by res.; Silk Willoughby (*Silkwillughby*), 24 June, by res.; Greatford, 18 July, by res.; Stamford (*Stamfordie*), ch. of St Michael, 20 July, by res.; Algarkirk (*Algarkyrke*), 24 July, by res.; vic. of Fotherby (*Foterby*), 29 July, by res.; vic. of Calceby, 7 Aug., by res.; vic. of Anwick (*Anwik*), 11 Aug., by d.; Toft (*Tofte*), 14 Aug., by d.; chantry at Heckington (*Hekyngton*), 17 Aug., by res.; Braceborough (*Brasbourgh*), 11 Sept., by d.; vic. of West Torrington (*Westrington*), 15 Sept., by res.; moiety of Sedgebroke (*Segbroke*), 23 Sept., by res.; Ashby (*Asseby*), 25 Sept., by res. [cf. no. 166 above]; Kirkby St Denis (*Kyrrkeby Dionisii*), 6 Oct., by res. Total: £8 6s 8d

b. [fo. 111] Archdeaconry of Stow, Li.:
Vic. of Coates by Stow (*Coots*), 13 Mar., by d.; chantry at Epworth, 2 June, by res.; third part of chantry in north part of ch. of Gainsborough, 4 Sept., by d. Total: £1

c. Archdeaconry of Leicester, Lei.
Vic. of Hose (*Howse*), 3 Mar., by d.; Kimcote (*Kilmerdcote*), 16 June, by res.; fifth prebend of Leicester, 4 July, by res.; prior of cell of Breedon, 17 Oct., by d. Total: 26s 8d

d. Archdeaconry of Northampton, Np.:
Glendon, 3 Mar., by d.; Rushton (*Russhton*), 17 Mar., by res.; Cottesbrook (*Cottysbroke*), 14 Apr., by d.; vic. of Harrowden (*Harouden*), 3 June, by res.; vic. of Desborough (*Desburgh*), 12 Aug., by d. Total: 33s 4d
In addition, vic. of Little Houghton (*Houghton Parva*), 21 Oct., by d. Total: 40s

e. Archdeaconry of Bedford, Bd.:
Potsgrove (*Pottesgrave*), 3 July, by d.; vic. of Tilsworth (*Tylesworth*), 12 Sept., by res. Total: 13s 4d

f. Archdeaconry of Buckingham, Bu.:
Isenhampstead Chenies (*Isenhamstede*), 13 Mar., by d., 6s 8d

g. Archdeaconry of Oxford, Ox.:
Holton (*Halton*), 19 Mar., by res.; Tusmore (*Turvesmore*), 1 Apr., by d.; Wilcote (*Wyvelcote*), 13 Mar, by d.; Islip (*Islepe*), 24 July, by res.; vic. of Charlbury (*Chorlebury*), 12 Oct., by res. Total: 33s 4d

h. Archdeaconry of Huntingdon:
Vic. of King's Langley (*Langley*), Hrt., 6 Mar., by d.; Knebworth, Hrt., 22 Mar., by d.; Ayot St Lawrence, Hrt., 6 June, by res.; Huntingdon, ch. of All Saints, 15 Apr., by res.; Warboys (*Wardeboys*), Hu., 29 Aug., by d.; Orton Waterville (*Cheryovorton*), Hu., 20 Sept., by d.; Folksworth (*Folkesworth*), Hu., 6 Oct., by res. Total: 46s 8d

TOTAL RECEIPTS FOR INSTITUTIONS: £17 13s 4d

220. [fo. 111v] RECEIPTS FOR LETTERS DIMISSORY
Thomas Hill, Thomas Draper, Mr Thomas Wigtofte, Thomas Carter, William Pynder, Robert Barker, 3s 4d each. Total: 20s

221.   RECEIPTS FROM ALMS COLLECTORS
For hospital of St Anthony, in archdeaconry of Lincoln, 6s 8d; for hospital of
St Thomas the Martyr in Rome (*in urbe*), in archdeaconry of Leicester, 3s 4d.
Total: 10s

222.   RECEIPTS FOR TESTAMENTS PROVED BEFORE MR WALLYS AND FOR
MORTUARIES

a. Archdeaconry of Lincoln:
Probate of r. of Somerby [near Brigg], 13s 4d; price of one cow for his
mortuary, 6s 8d; probate of Robert Reed of Alford, 6s 8d; Alexander Brigge,
5s; Robert Higden, v. of Ulceby, 66s 8d; price of one portas for his mortuary,
20s; probate of Alexander Gymmyll, 40s; William Pynder, 10s; Richard
Butler, 20d; Richard Grantham, 20d; John Newland, 10s; Agnes Raye,
3s 4d; Henry Chapleyn, 12d; William Herberd, 6s; Emma Oxton, 3s;
William Grene, 3s 4d; price of one robe for mortuary of r. of Greatford,
13s 4d; probate of Richard Gilbert, 33s 4d; John Nicholl, 6s 8d; Thomas
Alanson, 3s 4d; Robert Deth, 13s 8d; Robert Waltham, 6s 8d; John Pethell,
3s 4d; John Jakson, 2s; Henry Jakson, 9s; John Houson, 5s; John Wright,
3s 4d; Margaret Jaybard, widow, 16s 8d; Henry Marable, 16s 8d; John
White, 16d; Thomas Howton, 5s; John Goneld, 13s 4d; Robert Cokke, 4s;
Richard Cousyn, 2s; Joan Grantham, widow, 3s; John Halefax, 2s; Nicholas
Hall, 4s; price of one portas for mortuary of v. of Anwick (*Anwyk*), 10s;
probate of John Walton, 13s 4d; r. of Bigby, 8s; price of one cow for mortuary
of r. of Careby, 6s 8d.   Total: £21 4s

b.   Archdeaconry of Leicester:
Probate of Henry Borough, 20s; Thomas Kyrkeman, 10s; William Osborne,
12d; John Leek, 12d; John Grey, 8d; John Wild, 12d; William Large, 8d;
William Polle, 12d; John Straker, 12d; Mr Thomas Bedford, r. of
Lubbenham, 20s; John Smyth, 12d; Edmund Crofte, 20d; John Sele, 5s;
Thomas Yacobe, 2s; Thomas Perkyn, 20d; Thomas Gill, 20d; William
Dalman, 2s; Margaret Champyne, 12d; Thomas Dunthorp, 12d; Robert
Harper, 8d; Margaret Cliftone, 12d; Robert Downys, 20d; Ralph Sherard,
12d; Richard Benett, 2s; William Moderby, 12d; William Yoman, 20d;
Isabelle Biglott, 12d; Richard Mariott, 20d; John Carter, 12d; Henry
Chambirlayn, 12d; Robert Aleyn, 8d; Henry Dobilday, 3s 4d; Robert
Markham, 53s 4d; price of one horse for mortuary of v. of Hose (*Howse*), 10s;
price of two volumes of Nicholas de Lyra's *super Bibliam* for mortuary of r. of
Lubbenham, 20s.   Total: £8 14s 4d

c. [fo. 112] Archdeaconry of Stow:
Probate of Robert Fissher, 10s; Roger Colman, 5s; William Shoter, 3s 4d;
William Clement, 5s; Robert Tomlyn, 2s; John Canwik, 12d; John Mason,
2s; Edmund Cawery, 20d; William Wheler, 18d; William Barton, 2s 6d;
Henry Grene, 6s.   Total: 40s

TOTAL RECEIPTS FOR PROBATE IN ARCHDEACONRIES OF LINCOLN, STOW
AND LEICESTER: £31 14s 8d

223.   RECEIPTS FOR VACANCIES OF CHURCHES

a. Archdeaconry of Lincoln, Li.:
Skinnand (*Skynnand*), 9s 10d; Careby, 6s 1d; vic. of Ulceby, 4s 5d; Toft (*Tofte*), 2s 7½d; Greatford (*Gretford*), 19d; Bassingbourn (*Bassingborne*), 14d.

b. Archdeaconry of Leicester, Lei.:
Vic. of Hose (*Howes*), 14d; Lubbenham (*Lubenham*), 20d.

TOTAL: 26s 5½d

224.   RECEIPTS FOR LICENCES IN ARCHDEACONRY OF LINCOLN
Licence to Sir Thomas Fitzwilliam for the celebration of his marriage in the chapel of his manor, 6s 8d; licence for non-residence of r. of Linwood (*Linwoode*), 13s 4d.

TOTAL: 20s

225.   RECEIPTS FOR COMMISSIONS TO RECEIVE PURGATIONS IN ARCHDEACONRY OF LINCOLN
Commission to receive purgation of r. of Stenigot (*Stanygoode*), r. of Gayton le Marsh (*Gayton*), v. of Wrangle, v. of Honington (*Honyngton*), r. of Welby, *dominus* Henry Colom, v. of Stapleford (*Stapilford*), v. of Somerby [*unid.*], 6s 8d each.

TOTAL: 50s

226.   CORRECTIONS IN ARCHDEACONRIES OF LINCOLN, STOW AND LEICESTER
For the correction of v. of Thorpe [*unid.*], 5s; Agnes Esmonde, 10s; r. of Panton (*Paunton*), Li., 20s; William Elys, chap., 2s; r. of Dalderby, Li., 16s 8d; John Hewys, 10s; r. of Well (*Wellie*), Li., 10s; Roger Howton, chap., 20s; *dominus* John Caddall, 40s; *dominus* Thomas Bouchife, 10s; *dominus* John Byllynghey, 6s 8d; v. of Langtoft (*Langtofte*), Li., 13s 4d; Mr Richard Warmouth, r. of St George, Stamford, 40s; v. of Lavington (*Lavyngton*), Li., 25s; v. of Corby, Li., 10s; r. of Dunsby (*Dunnesby*), Li., 10s; v. of Scopwick (*Skaupewik*), Li., 13s 4d; r. of Thoresway (*Thoreswey*), Li., 10s; r. of Stainton [le Vale], Li., 10s.

TOTAL: £14 2s

227.   [fo. 112v] RECEIPTS FROM CHURCHES APPROPRIATED TO THE EPISCOPAL MENSA IN THE ARCHDEACONRY OF LINCOLN
Ch. of Holbeach (*Holbeche*), farmed to Thomas Welby, esq., for annual payment of £46 13s 4d; ch. of Munby, farmed to John Somerby for annual payment of £21.

TOTAL: £67 13s 4d

228.   RECEIPTS FOR PROCURATIONS IN ARCHDEACONRIES OF LINCOLN, STOW AND LEICESTER, DUE TO THE ARCHBISHOP FOR VISITATION

a. Monasteries in archdeaconry of Lincoln:
Elsham (*Ellesham*), 40s; Thornton, Wellow (*Wellowe*), Bardney (*Bardenay*), Stixwould (*Stikkiswold*), Tattershall (*Tatteshall*) coll. ch., 66s 8d each; Nun

Cotham (*Nuncoton*), 40s; Legbourne (*Legburn*), 26s 8d; Greenfield (*Grenefeld*), 40s; Spalding (*Spaldyng*), Croyland (*Croiland*), 66s 8d each; nuns of Stamford, 33s 4d; Newstead by Stamford (*de novo loco*), 40s; Bourne (*Burne*), 66s 8d; Kyme, 53s 4d; Nocton Park (*Nokton*), 40s. Total: £42 6s 8d

229. RECEIPTS FOR TESTAMENTS PROVED BEFORE MR RALPH HANYES, BY AUTHORITY OF THE COMMISSION ISSUED BY MR WALLIS

a. Archdeaconries of Lincoln and Stow:
For probate of [*blank*] Ratheby of North Reston (*Northrestone*), 5s; *dominus* William Chery 6s 8d; William Shoter, 13s 4d; Hugh Williot, 10s; Alan Jeffrey, 10s; John Westwoode, 6s 8d; Thomas Downaby, 6s 8d; Robert Palmer, 6s 8d; William Niker, 3s 4d; John Wyrley, 6s 8d; William Hall, 10s; John Wymeswold, 5s; *dominus* Robert Warwik, 6s 8d; Richard Harleston, 12d; John Naunby, 12d; Thomas de Rasen, 12d; William Barett, 5s; William Grauntham, 5s; John Mower, 3s 4d; Robert Pacy, 33s 4d; price of one gown as mortuary of v. of Saleby, 2s 4d. Total: £7 8s 8d

b. Archdeaconry of Leicester:
For probate of John Dutton, 6s 8d; John Dene, 3s 4d; Robert Hyrnyng, chap., r. of Peatling Parva (*Petlyng Parva*), 10s; price of one portas as his mortuary, 5s; probate of John Warde, 20d. Total: 26s 8d

TOTAL RECEIPTS FOR PROBATE BY MR HANYES IN SAID ARCHDEACONRIES:
£8 15s 4d

230. PROCURATIONS IN ARCHDEACONRY OF NORTHAMPTON
From monastery of Peterborough (*Petisburgh*), which is in archdeaconry of Northampton, 66s 8d; for visitation of dy. of Peterborough, 66s 8d.
TOTAL: £6 13s 4d

231. LETTERS QUESTUARY ISSUED BY MR HANNYES
For hospital of Burton Lazars (*Burton sancti Lazari*), 2s; for hospital of St Anthony, 6s 8d.
TOTAL: 8s 8d

TOTAL OF ALL THE PRECEDING SUMS RECEIVED BY MR WALLYS AND MR HANYES, HIS COMMISSARY, FROM 12 JANUARY TO FEAST OF ALL SAINTS [1 Nov.]: £453 18s 9d

[fo. 113v] ACCOUNT RENDERED BY MR JOHN VEYSEY, D.C.L., COMMISSARY OF THE OFFICIAL *SEDE VACANTE*, AND BY MR WILLIAM IMBROKE, NOTARY PUBLIC, HIS SCRIBE, FOR ARCHDEACONRIES OF BUCKINGHAM, BEDFORD AND HUNTINGDON FROM 12 JANUARY TO 1 NOVEMBER 1495.

232. PROCURATIONS FROM ARCHDEACONRY OF BUCKINGHAM

a. Monasteries:
Notley, Bradwell, Missenden (*Myssenden*), Ankerwyke (*Ankyrwyk*), Burnham (*Burneham*), Little Marlow (*Parva Marlow*), Snelshall (*Snelsale*), Ravenstone (*Ravistone*), 66s 8d each; Eton coll., 40s. Total £28 13s 4d

b. Deaneries

Waddesdon (*Woddestone*), Mursley (*Murseley*), Buckingham (*Bukkyngham*), Newport Pagnell (*Newport*), Wendover, Burnham (*Burneham*), Wycombe, 66s 8d each.   Total £23 6s 8d

TOTAL PROCURATIONS IN ARCHDEACONRY OF BUCKINGHAM: £52

233.   PAYMENTS FROM ARCHDEACON OF BUCKINGHAM
At Easter, £10; at Michaelmas, £10.   TOTAL: £20

234.   PENSIONS IN ARCHDEACONRY OF BUCKINGHAM

a. At various feasts:
From prior of Bisham (*Burstelesham*) for ch. of East Claydon at Purification of B.V.M. [2 Feb.], 6s 8d; r. of Walton for annexed mediety, at Purification of B.V.M., 12d; r. of Saunderton for annexed mediety, at Purification of B.V.M., 3s; abbot of Notley for ch. of Chetwode (*Chatewoode*) at Annunciation of B.V.M. [25 Mar.], 6s; dean and chapter of St Stephen's, Westminster, for ch. of Bledlow (*Bedlowe*), at Easter, 20s; prior of Bradwell for vic. of Padbury at Nativity of St John the Baptist [24 June], 2s.

b. At Michaelmas:
Dean and chapter of St Stephen's, Westminster, for ch. of Bledlow, 20s; prior of Bisham for ch. of West Wycombe (*Westwicombe*), 6s 8d; prioress of Marlow for ch. of Little Marlow (*Merlow*), 20s; r. of Ashbridge for Pitstone (*Potesden*), Chesterton, Ox., and Ivinghoe (*Ivynge*), 20s; r. of Beachampton (*Bechampton*) for mediety there, 2s.

TOTAL PENSIONS IN ARCHDEACONRY OF BUCKINGHAM: £5 7s 4d

235.   [fo. 114] INSTITUTIONS OF RECTORS AND VICARS IN ARCH-
DEACONRY OF BUCKINGHAM
R. of Horwood Magna (*Horwoode Magna*), v. of Caversfield (*Caversfelde*), r. of Addington (*Aldingtone*), r. of *Swynestone* [unid., possibly Swyncombe, Ox.], 6s 8d each.   TOTAL: 26s 8d

236.   RECEIPTS FOR PROBATE OF TESTAMENTS IN ARCHDEACONRY OF
BUCKINGHAM
For probate of Ralph Newton, 12d; John Cotesford, chap., 6s 8d; John Grene, 12d; Isabelle Hosier, 12d; Edith Countas, 2s; William Peerse, 6s 8d; William Reynesford, 16d; Matilda Travelowe, 12d; John Kirnell, 6s 8d; John Carter, 6s 8d.   TOTAL: 34s

237.   CHURCHES APPROPRIATED TO THE EPISCOPAL MENSA
For the fruits and other emoluments of ch. of Wooburn (*Woburne*) for one whole year, £9.

TOTAL OF ALL PROCURATIONS, PAYMENTS, PENSIONS AND OTHER EMOLU-
MENTS IN ARCHDEACONRY OF BUCKINGHAM: £87 8s

PROCURATIONS, PAYMENTS AND OTHER SPIRITUAL DUES AND EMOLU-
MENTS IN ARCHDEACONRY OF BEDFORD

238.   PROCURATIONS

a. Monasteries:
Markyate (*Markeyate*), Dunstable (*Dunstaple*), Northill (*Northale*), coll., Elstow
(*Elmestowe*), Caldwell (*Caldewell*), Newnham (*Newenham*), 66s 8d each.
                                                                Total: £20

b. Deaneries:
Dunstable, Fleete (*Flytte*), Shefford, Bedford (*Bedfordie*), Clapham (*Clopham*),
Eaton (*Etone*), 66s 8d each.   Total: £20

        TOTAL PROCURATIONS IN ARCHDEACONRY OF BEDFORD: £40

239.   PAYMENTS OF ARCHDEACON OF BEDFORD
At Easter, £7; at Michaelmas, £7.   TOTAL: £14

240.   PENSIONS IN ARCHDEACONRY OF BEDFORD

a. At feast of the Annunciation of B.V.M. [25 Mar.]:
From r. of St Peter's, Dunstable, for ch. of St Mary's, Bedford, 10s.

b. [fo. 114v] At Easter:
From prior of Dunstable for manor of Shortgrave, 26s 8d; from abbess of
Barking (*Berkyng*) for ch. of Lidlington (*Litlyngton*), 10s; from provost and
fellows of King's Hall, Cambridge, for ch. of Felmersham, 20s; from prior of
Newnham for chs. of All Saints and St Paul, Bedford, 3s 4d. Total: 60s

c. At Nativity of St John the Baptist [24 June]:
From prioress of St Helen's, London, for ch. of Eyworth, 20s.

d. At Michaelmas [29 Sept.]:
From warden and chaps. of chantry of Chalgrave for ch. of Offley (*Feley*),
Hrt., 20s; from abbot and conv. of Wardon (*Verdone*) for Wardon ch., 3s 4d.
                                                                Total 23s 4d

    TOTAL OF ALL PENSIONS IN ARCHDEACONRY OF BEDFORD: £5 13s 4d

241.   RECEIPTS FOR INSTITUTIONS IN ARCHDEACONRY OF BEDFORD
R. of Marston Moretaine (*Merston*), v. of Sundon (*Sundonne*), v. of
Felmersham, v. of Willington (*Wyllyngtonne*), 6s 8d each. TOTAL: 26s 8d

242.   RECEIPTS FOR PROBATE IN ARCHDEACONRY OF BEDFORD
For probate of Henry Wales, 10s; John Waltershire, 8d; Alice Bither, 6s 8d;
William Fresby, 20d; Thomas Wawton, 40s; John Pedder, 6s 8d.
                                                            TOTAL: 65s 8d

243.   RECEIPTS FOR MORTUARIES OF RECTORS AND VICARS
From r. of Marston Mortaine (*Morston*), a book called *Lira super Bibliam*, value
40s; from v. of Sundon, a sheep estimated at 20d; from v. of Felmersham, a
horse, value 7s; from r. of Edworth, a psalter, value 6s 8d. TOTAL: 50s 4d

SUM TOTAL OF ALL PROCURATIONS, PAYMENTS, PENSIONS, INSTITUTIONS, PROBATE FEES, MORTUARIES AND OTHER RECEIPTS IN THE ARCHDEACONRY OF BEDFORD: £67 12d

RECEIPTS FROM PROCURATIONS, PAYMENTS, PENSIONS AND OTHER DUES IN ARCHDEACONRY OF HUNTINGDON

244.   PROCURATIONS

a. Monasteries
St Neots, Stonely (*Stonley*), Ramsey, Huntingdon (*Huntyngdon*), 66s 8d each.
TOTAL: £13 6s 8d

b. Deaneries
St Neots, Leightonstone (*Leitamstone*), Yaxley (*Yakesley*), St Ives, Huntingdon, Baldock (*Baldok*), Hitchin (*Hichen*), Hertford, Berkhampstead (*Berkhampstede*), 66s 8d each.
TOTAL: £30

245.   PAYMENTS OF ARCHDEACON OF HUNTINGDON
At Easter, £14; at Michaelmas, £14.
TOTAL: £28

246.   RECEIPTS FOR PENSIONS IN ARCHDEACONRY OF HUNTINGDON

a. At Christmas:
From abbot of Thorney for chs. of Yaxley, Hu., and Stanground (*Stangrounde*), Hu., 6s 8d; r. of Coppingford, Hu., for ch. of Upton, Hu., 2s.

b. [fo. 115] At Purification of B.V.M. [2 Feb.]:
From abbot of Westminster for ch. of Aldenham, Hrt., 6s 8d.

c. At Annunciation of B.V.M. [25 Mar.]:
From r. of St John's, Huntingdon, for annexed chantry, 16d.

d. At Easter:
From master and scholars of Clare Hall, Cambridge, for ch. of Great Gransden (*Magna Grandesden*), Hu., 10s; from prior of Stonely for ch. of Kimbolton (*Kymbalton*), Hu., 40s.

e   At Nativity of St John the Baptist [24 June]:
From abbot of Thorney for chs. of Yaxley (*Kesley*) and Stanground (*Stangre*), 6s 8d; from abbot of Westminster for Aldenham, 6s 8d; from v. of Waresley (*Weresley*), Hu., for annexed chantry, 3s 4d.

f. At Assumption of B.V.M. [15 Aug.]:
From prior of the London Charterhouse for chs. of Great Staughton (*Stokton*), Hu., Edlesborough (*Edelesburg*), Bk., and North Mimms (*Mymmes*), Hrt., 40s; from r. of Gravely, Hrt., for ch. of Chivesfield (*Chevesfeld*), Hrt., 2s; from master and scholars of Clare Hall, Cambridge, for ch. of Great Gransden, 10s; from prior of Huntingdon for ch. of Southoe (*Southo*), Hu., 20s.

TOTAL PENSIONS IN ARCHDEACONRY OF HUNTINGDON: £7 15s 4d

SUM TOTAL OF ALL RECEIPTS IN ARCHDEACONRY OF HUNTINGDON:
£79 2s

SUM TOTAL OF ALL RECEIPTS IN THE ARCHDEACONRIES OF BUCKINGHAM, BEDFORD AND HUNTINGDON COLLECTED BY MR JOHN VEYSEY AND WILLIAM IMBROKE, AS ITEMISED ABOVE: [*blank*, £233 11s]

ACCOUNT RENDERED BY MR ROGER CHURCH, DECR. D., COMMISSARY OF THE OFFICIAL *SEDE VACANTE*, IN ARCHDEACONRIES OF OXFORD AND NORTH-AMPTON, FROM 12 JANUARY TO 1 NOVEMBER 1495.

247.   PROCURATIONS IN ARCHDEACONRY OF OXFORD

a. Religious houses:
St Frideswide's, Oxford (*in Oxonia*), Osney (*Osseney*), Godstow (*Godstowe*), Wroxton, Goring (*Goryng*), Littlemore (*Litelmore*), Studley (*Stodeley*), Lincoln coll., Oxford, Oriel coll. (*collegio regali*), Oxford, 66s 8d each. TOTAL: £30

b. Deaneries
Henley, Ashton (*Astone*), Oxford, Woodstock (*Woodestoke*), Witney, Chipping Norton (*Chiping Nortone*), Cuddesdon, Deddington (*Deddyngton*), Bicester (*Byssetur*), 66s 8d each.   TOTAL: £30

c. Note that the monasteries of Dorchester, Eynsham (*Eynesham*), Cold Norton and Bicester (*Byssetyr*) were visited by the dean of Lincoln.

248.   [fo. 115v] RECEIPTS FOR PENSIONS IN ARCHDEACONRY OF OXFORD
From r. of Ashridge (*Ashrigge*) [Bk.] for chs. of Pitstone (*Patesdoune*), Bk., Chesterton and Ivinghoe (*Ivynhoo*), Bk., 20s; from abbot of Osney for chs. of Cowley, Steeple Barton (*Barton*) and South Weston (*Weston*), 6s 8d; from dean and chapter of the chapel royal, Windsor, for chs. of Datchet (*Dachett*), Bk., Wraysbury (*Wyardisbury*), Bk., and Deddington (*Dadyngtone*), 67s 4d; from abbot of Eynsham for chs. [*not named*], 40s; from prior of Cold Norton for ch. of [*blank*], 6s 8d; from prioress of Studley (*Stodeley*) for ch. of Beckley (*Brekyll*), 10s.   TOTAL: £8 14s

249.   PAYMENTS OF ARCHDEACON OF OXFORD
At Purification of B.V.M. [2 Feb.], £10; at Michaelmas [29 Sept.], £10
                                                            TOTAL: £20

250   RECEIPTS FOR PROBATE IN ARCHDEACONRY OF OXFORD
For probate of Robert Smyth of Great Tew (*Tewe*), 3s 4d; John Trad of Well, Li., 13s 4d.   TOTAL: 16s 8d

251.   PROCURATIONS IN ARCHDEACONRY OF NORTHAMPTON

a. Religious houses:
Chacombe, Catesby *alias* Shopes (*Shopis*), Daventry (*Daventre*), St James Northampton, Delapré (*de Pratis*), Fotheringhay (*Fodringay*) coll., Irthling-borough (*Irtlingbourgh*) coll., 66s 8d each.
No payment was made by Fineshade (*Fynsherd*), since the abp, has remitted the procuration for this vacancy.
                                          Total: £21 6s 8d

b. Deaneries:
Brackley (*Berkeley*), Daventry, Northampton, Preston (*Prestone*), Haddon (*Haddone*), Rothwell (*Rowell*), Welton (*Weldone*), Rutland (*Rutlond*), Oundle (*Owndell*), Higham Ferrers, 66s 8d each.   Total: £33 6s 8d

TOTAL   PROCURATIONS   IN   ARCHDEACONRY   OF   NORTHAMPTON:
£54 13s 4d

Note that the procurations of the monastery and dy. of Peterborough are in the account of Mr Wallys.

252.   RECEIPTS FOR PENSIONS FROM APPROPRIATED CHURCHES IN ARCHDEACONRY OF NORTHAMPTON

a. At unspecified dates:
From chs. of Stanford on Avon (*Stanford*), 5s; Cotterstock (*Coterstoke*), 40s; Great Doddington (*Dadington*) and Earls Barton (*Bartone*), 13s 4d; Naseby, 5s; Badby, 66s 8d; Ashby [*unid.*] (*Asshby*), 11s;[1] Boddington (*Bodyngton*), 6s 8d; Grendon (*Grendone*), 13s 4d; Woodford (*Woodeford*), 100s.   TOTAL: £13 12d

> [1] The chs. of Ashby Folville and Ashby St Ledgers were appropriated to Launde priory.

b. At Michaelmas:
From abbot of Lavendon (*Lawneden*) for ch. of Easton Maudit (*Estone iuxta Higham*), 6s 8d; abbot of Peterborough (*Borogh*) for ch. of Oundle (*Ownedell*), 20s; ch. of Lilford, 3s 4d; ch. of Thornhaugh (*Thornehoo*), 3s; ch. of Easton-on-the-Hill (*Estone iuxta Stanford*), 8d; ch. of Moulton (*Mauton*), 6s 8d; ch. of Blatherwycke (*Bladerwik*), 3s 4d; prior of Fineshade (*Fynneshede*), for ch. of Laxton, 16d; abbot of Pipewell (*Pipwell*), 43s 4d; prioress of Rothwell (*Rothewell*) for ch. of Desborough, 6s 8d; abbot of Sulby, 40s; abbess of Delapré (*de Pratis*), 13s 4d; abbot of Combe for ch. of Naseby, 5s; prior of Daventry (*Daventre*), 8s; prior of Chacombe, 40s; prior of Canons Ashby (*Asshby*), 6s 8d; ch. of Boddington (*Bodingtone*), 3s 4d; prioress of Sewardsley (*Swerasley*), 10s; abbot of Peterborough for ch. of Great Easton (*Burghest*), 13s 4d.   TOTAL: £11 14s 8d

253.   [fo. 116] PAYMENTS FROM ARCHDEACON OF NORTHAMPTON
At Annunciation of B.V.M. [25 Mar.], £27 5s; at Michaelmas [29 Sept.], £27 5s.   TOTAL: £54 10s

254.   RECEIPTS FOR PROBATE OF TESTAMENTS IN ARCHDEACONRY OF NORTHAMPTON
For probate of Elizabeth Tuke, widow, whose inventory extends to £55 8s: 13s 4d; Mr John Morrcok, r. of Cottesbrooke (*Cotisbroke*), inventory £182 19s 4d: 40s; William Yoman of Oundle (*Ownedell*), 3s 4d; John Browne, 4s; William Osewestyr, 2s.   TOTAL: £8 2s 8d

ACCOUNT RENDERED BY MR JOHN WALLYS AND WILLIAM MILLER FOR
VARIOUS RECEIPTS FROM 1 NOVEMBER 1495 TO 1 JANUARY 1496.

255.   RECEIPTS FOR INSTITUTIONS
a. Archdeaconry of Lincoln:
All Saints, Wainfleet, 28 Oct., by d.; Tetford, by d.; St Peter's, Ingoldmells
(*Ingolmellys*); vic. of Sixhills (*Sixhill*), by d.; Skinnand (*Skynnand*), 17 Jan., by
res.; Corby (*Coreby*), by d.; vic. of Edlington (*Edlyngton*), 26 Jan., by d.; vic. of
Burgh le Marsh (*Burgh*), by d.; Fleet (*Flete*), 5 Feb., by d., 6s 8d each.
                                                          TOTAL: 60s

b. Archdeaconry of Stow, Li.:
Waddingham St Mary (*Wadyngham*), 15 Dec., by d., 6s 8d.

c. [fo. 116v] Archdeaconry of Leicester:
Ashby Parva (*Asshby Parva*), by res.; Withcote (*Wythcoke*), by res.;
Frowlesworth (*Frolesworth*), by d., 6s 8d each.   TOTAL: 20s

d. Archdeaconry of Northampton:[1]
Holcot (*Holcottes*); Kelshall (*Kelsall*), Hrt.; Ashwell (*Asshwell*), Hrt.; Wood
Walton, Hu.; Alwalton, Hu.; vic. of St Neots, Hu.; 6s 8d each.
                                                          TOTAL: 40s

> [1] *Sic*; five of these institutions refer to the archdeaconry of Huntingdon,
> while one Northamptonshire institution is included in no. 255e.

e. Archdeaconry of Huntingdon:
Buckworth (*Bukworth*), Hu.; Kelshall (*Kelsall*), Hrt. [cf. no. 255d]; collation of
chap. of Sponne's chantry, Towcester, Np., vac. by d.; 6s 8d each.
                                                          TOTAL: 20s

256.   RECEIPTS FOR PROBATE IN ARCHDEACONRY OF LINCOLN
For probate of Richard White, 13s 4d; William Skipwit, 6s 8d; r. of
Ingoldmells, 6s 8d; v. of Friskney (*Friskeney*), 20s, and price of one cow as his
mortuary, 9s 9d; for probate of r. of Wainfleet, 19s, and as his mortuary a
book called *Januensis* (James of Genoa) *in opere quadragesimale*, value 7s; price of
one mazer as mortuary of v. of Edlington, 8s.   TOTAL: £6 15s 10d

257.   RECEIPTS FOR VACANCY
From vacancy of ch. of Stroxton (*Strawston*), Li., 22d.

258.   PENSIONS DUE AT CHRISTMAS
a. Archdeaconries of Lincoln and Stow:
Ch. of Wigtoft (*Wigtofte*), 66s 8d; ch. of Frampton, 13s 4d; ch. of Ewerby
(*Iwardby*), 6s 8d; vic. of Barkston (*Berkeston*) and Plumgar (*Plumgarth*), 6s 8d;
ch. of St Helen, Helmswell (*Helmeswell*), 2s.   TOTAL: £4 15s 4d

b. Archdeaconry of Leicester:
Ch. of Shackerstone (*Shakreston*), 13s 4d; ch. of Ouneby (*Oundeby*), 6s 8d.
                                                          TOTAL: 20s

TOTAL PAYMENTS BY MR JOHN WALLIS AND WILLIAM MYLLER FROM FEAST
           OF ALL SAINTS TO 1 JANUARY: £19 19s 8d

259.   ACCOUNT OF MR ROGER CHURCH FOR ARCHDEACONRY OF NORTH-AMPTON FROM 1 NOVEMBER 1495 TO 1 JANUARY 1496, PAYMENT BEING MADE BY MR ROBERT KNYGHT, OFFICIAL OF THE ARCHDEACON.

a. Moiety of the probate of testaments proved before Mr Robert Knyght, 77s 9d.

b. Moiety of the corrections of various persons corrected by Mr Knyght after the abp.'s visitation, 12s 2d.

c. Two parts of the vacancies of the chs. of Easton [*unid.*] and Thrapston, the third part being payable to the archd., 38s 8d.

TOTAL SUM RECEIVED BY THE HANDS OF MR ROBERT KNYGHT:
£6 8s 7d

260.   PENSIONS IN ARCHDEACONRY OF OXFORD FROM MICHAELMAS 1495 TO 1 JANUARY 1496 RECEIVED BY MR JOHN VEYSEY.
No details entered. There is gap of approx. 90 mm. at foot of folio.

261.   [fo. 117] Bull of Pope Alexander VI directed to the abp, of Canterbury, notifying him of the translation of William Smith from the see of Coventry and Lichfield to that of Lincoln. St Peter's Rome, [6 Nov.][1] 1495.
     [1] Cf. *Fasti Ecclesiae Anglicanae 1300–1540: Lincoln Diocese*, ed. H. P. F. King, 1962, 3.

262.   Mandate of the abp. to Mr John Wallys, can. of Lincoln cath. and Official *sede vacante*, ordering him to surrender to the new bp. all registers and muniments concerning the spiritualities of the see, except the register of the vacancy, which is to be transmitted to the abp., and to permit the bp. and his officials free administration of the dioc., reserving to the abp. correction of faults detected during visitation, confirmation or rejection of the election of Denise Akworth as prioress of Markyate, presented by the subprioress and conv. but not yet confirmed, and collection of all revenues due to the abp. by virtue of the vacancy of the see. Lambeth, 31 Jan. 1496.

263.   Commission to Mr Robert Smyth, S.T.P., the abp.'s commissary in Oxford, and to Mr John Veysey, D.C.L. jointly and singly. It has been brought to the abp.'s attention by reliable reports and confirmed by the recent visitation conducted in the vacancy of the see of Lincoln that Richard Walker, prior of the priory of St Frideswide in Oxford, does not providently and fruitfully collect, administer and expend the revenues of that house, but rather unscrupulously and improvidently squanders, consumes and wastes them, so that by his carelessness and negligence he has burdened the priory with debts of £400 or more, which were not contracted to the advantage of the house. He has allowed the cloisters, houses and other buildings to fall into ruin, and he is so remiss that observance of the Rule, the divine office and those acts of piety customarily performed in accordance with the foundation ordinance are neglected and daily decrease, so that the pious intentions of the founders are set at naught. A few of the brethren commit scandalous and criminal acts in church and both within and without the bounds of the priory, and their access

to brothels and prostitutes goes unpunished, to the peril of the souls of prior and brethren, to the disgrace of religion and the Divine Majesty, and to the bad example and scandal of the multitude. The abp., therefore, wishing as befits his pastoral office to destroy evil and to implant virtue, and being bound to provide for the reformation of the priory, commissions Mr Smith and Mr Veysey to enquire into the crimes, excesses and defects of the prior and his brethren, to correct, punish and reform them, and also to enquire into the nature and extent of the dilapidation, consumption and dissipation of the goods of the house, that is, how, why and by whose agency this situation has occurred, and to what extent the priory is indebted at the present time, with the names of creditors. They are to certify the abp. of the action taken or to be taken by them. Definitive sentence or final decree, if such is required, is reserved to the abp. himself. Lambeth, 24 Aug. 1495.

[fo. 118] PROCEEDINGS AND ACTS OF THE WORTHY MASTER ROBERT SHIRBORNE, TREASURER OF THE CATHEDRAL CHURCH OF HEREFORD, OFFICIAL, COMMISSARY AND GUARDIAN OF THE SPIRITUALITY OF THE CITY AND DIOCESE OF EXETER BY AUTHORITY OF THE VERY REVEREND FATHER IN CHRIST AND LORD JOHN, ARCHBISHOP OF CANTERBURY, PRIMATE OF ALL ENGLAND AND LEGATE OF THE APOSTOLIC SEE, DURING THE VACANCY OF THE SEE OF EXETER FOLLOWING THE TRANSLATION BY APOSTOLIC AUTHORITY OF THE REVEREND FATHER AND LORD RICHARD, LATELY BISHOP, TO THE CATHEDRAL CHURCHES OF BATH AND WELLS, FROM 8 MAY 1492 TO 1 MARCH FOLLOWING.

> *Note*: the see became vacant by the translation of Richard Fox to Bath and Wells on 8 Feb. 1492, and was filled by the provision of Oliver King on 1 Oct. 1492.

264.   Commission, with powers of canonical coercion, to Mr Robert Shirborne and Mr James Adam, B.C.L., as commissaries of the abp. and guardians of the spirituality of the dioc. of Exeter in the vacancy of the see following the translation of bp. Richard Fox, with the powers specified in no. 1. Lambeth, 8 May 1492.

265.   [fo. 118v] Mandate addressed by Mr Shirborne to the archd. of Exeter or his Official ordering the citation of clergy and people to appear before him during the impending visitation of the archdeaconry, with an attached schedule detailing the visitor's itinerary. 21 May 1492.
Itinerary:
Friday 1 June, visitation of cath. ch. of Exeter in the chapter house; Saturday 2 June, visitation of dy. of Christianity, Exeter, in ch. of St Mary Major; Monday 4 June, visitation of priory of St Nicholas, Exeter, where the morning meal will be taken; Tuesday 5 June, visitation of priory of St John, Exeter, where the morning meal will be taken, and of Polsloe (*Polslo*) priory; Wednesday 6 June, visitation of dys. of Kenn and Dunsford in ch. of St Thomas, Exeter; the morning meal will be taken in Exeter; Thursday 7 June, visitation of dy. of Aylesbeare (*Aillesberre*) in coll. ch. of Ottery St Mary (*Otterey beate Marie*), where the morning meal and dinner will be taken and the visitor will spend the night; Friday 8 June, visitation of coll. ch. of Ottery St Mary, where the morning meal will be taken; the night will be spent at Honiton (*Honyton*); Saturday 9 June, visitation of dys. of Honiton and Dunkeswell (*Dunkiswill*) in chapel of Honiton; the morning meal will be taken at Honiton and the night spent at Exeter; Thursday 14 June, visitation of dy. of Plymtree (*Plymptre*) in ch. of Collumpton (*Columpton*), where both morning meal and dinner will be taken and the visitor will spend the night; Friday 15 June, visitation of Canonsleigh (*Canonlegh*) abbey, where the morning meal will be taken; the night will be spent at Tiverton (*Tuverton*); Saturday 16 June, visitation of dy. of Tiverton in Tiverton ch., where the night will be spent; Monday 18 June, visitation of dy. of Cadbury (*Cadburye*) in coll. ch. of Crediton

(*Cryditon*), where the morning meal will be taken with the precentor before visitation of the coll.; dinner will also be taken and the night spent there.

266.   [fo. 119] Certificate of the mandate of citation, which he had received on 24 May, by John Tyak, Official of the archd. of Exeter, with a schedule of the names of those cited to appear before the visitor. 31 May 1492.

267.   Deanery of Christianity, Exeter:

Chapel of St Sidwell (*sancte Satimole*) without Eastgate
Dean and chapter of Exeter, prop.; John Hernbroke, cur.; John Lake, John Symon, Christopher Cressy, pns.

St Laurence
Prior and conv. of hospital of St John the Baptist, Exeter, prop.; John Hancock, cur.; Richard Duke, John Wynter, Richard Carter, pns.

St Stephen
Richard Nakes, r.; William Beamond, cur.; Thomas Erle, John Sayer, William Whitelok, John Aysshton, pns.

St Martin
Walter Bonavise, r.; John Crayes and William Rosell, chaps.; Richard Cliff, Walter Coffere, William Pascowe, John Snelle, pns.

All Hallows, Goldsmith Street (*in Aurifabria*)
John Dormond, r.; William Robyn, Thomas Oliver, Peter Herewood, William Goodiere, pns.

St Paul
Thomas Merifeld, r.; Richard Germyn, Stephen Frende, Walter Woode, William Haiward, pns.

St Pancras
Thomas Benebowe, r.; Simon Carrowe, Peter Fabry, Stephen Elowe, pns.

St Kerian
John Waty, r.; Thomas Cutteler, John Brownyscombe, John Furse, pns.

St Mary Major
Mr Walter Cost, r.; [*blank*] Underhill, Walter Bray and John Stowman, chaps.; Richard Clerk, Robert Russell, John Gibbys, William Baker, John Whitfeld, Nicholas Sandy, pns.

St Petrock
Thomas Aclom, r.; Robert Newton, John Collishill, William Nordon, John Bruyaunt, pns.

St John
Marinus Upjohn, r.; John Mylton, cur.; John Trencher, chap.; William Oblegh, Richard Unday, John Doowne, pns.

Holy Trinity
Robert Yonge, r.; Thomas Horwill, cur.; John Leche, John Hogge, Philip Baker, Stephen Barteram, pns.

St John Arches (*de Arcubus*)
William Hoo, r.; John Peke, Henry Faryer, John William, Gilbert Waryn, pns.

St Olave
Mr John Philip, r.; Richard John, cur.; Nicholas Hamelyn, Matthew Alyngton, Robert Colton, William Trote, pns.

All Hallows-on-the-Walls (*omnium sanctorum super muros*)
Thomas Weryn, r.; John Clyston, John Wyswill, William Cope, John Bery, pns.

St Mary Steps (*de gradibus*)
John Neucomb, r.; William Farewill, William Crugge, John Lewes, Simon Andrew, pns.

St Edmund-on-Exe-Bridge (*super pontem de Exe*)
William Mountegue, r.; John Berde, John Torring, John Ayscote, John Honywill, William Clyff, pns.

Chapel of St Mary-on-Exe-Bridge
Walter Will, chap.

St Leonard
Mr Walter Northoryn, r.; John Davy, chap. of Sir William Courtenay; Richard Thomas, Edward William, Robert Aisshton, pns.

Chapel of St David
Dean and chapter of Exeter, prop.; Mr John Burton, v.; Richard Elyngham, chap.

Also cited:
William Torre and Thomas Clerk, chaps. celebrating in Exeter; Richard Wirth, chap. of chapel of St Mary in parish of St John Arches.

268.   Deanery of Kenn (*Kenne*), De.:

St Thomas the Martyr, Cowick
Abbot and conv. of Tavistock (*Tavistok*), prop.; Walter Wyll, v.; John Vicary, Robert Lanecroft, Richard Sherlond, Richard Wrayford, pns. All well.

Kenn
Mr John Tyok, r.; Otto Thomkyn, cur.; John Borowe, David Dyer, William Colyn, pns. All well.

Alphington (*Alphyngton*)
Robert Wise, r.; John Goodeman, cur.; Martin Elyett, Thomas Salter, John Pleye, Richard Skerbourd, John Cotell, Thomas Fefe, pns. All well.

Exminster (*Exmyster*)
Mr William Fowell, r.; Simon Weke, cur.; John West snr., Stephen Hurdyng, John Bohay, Thomas Croke, pns. All well.

Powderham
William Caslegh, r.; William Elyott, cur.; John Lokes, William Trewlofe, Robert Edwood, Thomas Merssh, pns. All well.

Kenton
Dean and chapter of Salisbury, prop.; John Trewola, v.; Robert Yeateman and John Yere, chaps.; Thomas Hurslo, John Grene, Thomas Trygge, John Wawtard, pns. All well.

Mamhead (*Mamhede*)
Henry Oblegh, r.; John Lerkeber, Roger Waye, pns. All well.

Ashcombe (*Ayscomb*)
Matthew Michell, r.; John Downe, John Rigeway, pns. All well.

Stoke-in-Teignhead (*Stokyntenehed*)
John Simon, r.; John Lawry and William Selman, chaps.; John Payne, John Seward, Nicholas Vaysy, pns. All well.

Combe-in-Teignhead (*Comyntenehed*)
Nicholas Knyght, r.; Richard Skynner, chap.; William Fynymore, William Seward, William Bekeford, Edward Worthy, pns. All well.

West Ogwell (*Weste Ogwill*)
John Yonge, r. All well.

East Ogwell (*Est Ogwill*)
William Antonye, r.; Robert Moge, chap.; Thomas Lyndon, Stephen Torre, pns. All well.

Chudleigh (*Chudlegh*)
Stephen Cowlyng, r.; John Marshall, John Dunkyswill, pns. All well.

Trusham (*Trysham*)
Robert Kyntishall, r.; Robert Conant, John Hamond, pns. All well.

Dunchideock (*Dunsydyok*)
Thomas Jamys, r.; Geoffrey Jericot, William Woode, John Serell, pns. All well.

Shillingford (*Shelyngford*)
William Shank, r.; Ralph Serell, pn. All well.

Bishopsteighton (*Teygnton Episcopi*)
Robert Betty, v.; John Suddon, William Eston, Robert Sooper, pns. All well.

Haccombe
Thomas Rympyn, r.

269.   [fo. 119v] Deanery of Dunsford

Dunsford
Abbess and conv. of Canonsleigh (*Canonlegh*), prop.; Mr James Adam, v.; William Sewell, John Estbroke, John Stabak, pns. All well.

Christow (*Cristawe*)
Abbot and conv. of Tavistock, prop.; John Osborne, v.; Robert Dayman, Alexander Pethebridge, William Trende, pns. All well.

Throwleigh (*Throwlegh*)
Mr Robert Batishill, r.; John Langeman, John White snr., John Wonston, pns. All well.

Drewsteignton (*Teyngtownedrewe*)
Thomas Amodas, r.; William Tolle, cur.; William Hilman, Edward Hayne, John Deker, pns. All well.

Chagford
Mr Henry Grymston, r.; William Kympe, cur.; John Ebbesworthy, William Potter, Simon Aisshe, pns. All well.

Hittisleigh (*Hytteslegh*)
William Chepe, r.; Stephen Northway, pn.

Doddiscombsleigh (*Legh*)
John Clerk, r.; Robert Cotlegh, cur.; Robert Holbeine, Robert Shyre, pns. All well.

Ashton (*Aisshton*)
William Blackhay, r.; Richard Archer, John Dudenay, Stephen Grene, pns. All well.

Cheriton Bishop (*Cheryton*)
William Radway, r.; John Bowde, Thomas Egler, Henry Floode, pns. All well.

Whitestone (*Whitstone*)
Richard Adam, r.; John Terlake, John Simon, John Atway, pns. All well.

Spreyton (*Sprayton*)
Abbot and conv. of Tavistock, prop.; John Aller, v.; Richard Cokyll, Robert Atcombe, pns. All well.

Bridford
Richard Foorde, r.; Roger Benet, chap.; John Swawynston, Richard Farewell, William Stoke, pns. All well.

South Tawton (*Southtawnton*)
Dean and chapter of the royal chapel of Windsor, prop.; Walter Rondelle, v.; John Wonston, Robert atte Woode, pns. All well.

Holcombe Burnell (*Holcombe*)
Dean and chapter of Wells, prop.; Laurence Rime, v.; John Madrige, William Fowkener, pns. All well.

Tedburn St Mary (*Tedborne*)
Mr Richard Beamond, r.; Richard Wryford, cur.; Thomas Mortyn, Richard Pantisford, Robert Parre, pns. All well.

Gidleigh (*Gydlegh*)
John Denys, r.; John Grene, John Todewle, pns. All well.

270.   Deanery of Aylesbeare (*Aill'*), De.

Ottery St Mary (*Oterey beate Marie*)
David Thirk, minister,; Thomas Strode, cur.; William Slade and John Westcombe, chaps.; John Underdon, Thomas Clode, Thomas Hewe, John Baret, William Furnyse, Henry Whiting, pns. All well.

Pinhoe (*Pynhoo*)
Prior and conv. of St Nicholas, Exeter, prop.; John Westlake, v.; John Germyn, William Raynold, John Page, pns. All well.

Clyst-St Mary (*Cliste beate Marie*)
Philip Long, r.; Walter Colwill, John Potter, pns. All well.

Clyst-St George (*Cliste sancti Georgii*)
William Uppehome, r.; William Hunte, Thomas Prouse, pns. All well.

Lympstone (*Lympston*)
Mr Thomas Appelford, r.; Robert Whetecomb, cur.; Thomas Hopkin, Richard Basse, William Frank, Thomas Brooke, Thomas Pawlyn, pns. All well.

Budleigh (*Budlegh*)
Prioress and conv. of Polsloe (*Polsloo*), prop.; John Raynold, v.; John Seward, cur.; Walter Yonge, Richard Duke, John Elys, John Basse, pns. All well.

Chapel of Withycombe Raleigh (*Wethycombe*)
Nicholas Pawlyn, cur.; John Coole, Richard Scorch, pns. All well.

Otterton (*Oterton*)
Abbess and conv. of Syon, prop.; John Smyth, v.; John Crokhay, cur.; William Rawe, Richard Denys, John Drake, Thomas Veneman, Philip Cooke, William Brasy, pns. All well.

Colaton Raleigh (*Coleton Ralegh*)
Dean and chapter of Exeter, prop.; John Champion, v.; Richard Jule, cur.; John Chanon, Robert Herth, pns. All well.

Bicton (*Buketon*)
John Treman, r.; William Webber, John Gilham, John Skynner, pns. All well.

Harpford (*Harford*)
Abbess and conv. of Syon, prop.; John Frye, v.; William Cok, John Peke, John Gegge, John Plympton, pns. All well.

Huxham
John Brymmesgrove, r.; John Courtnay, Robert Hoggeland, pns. All well.

Rockbeare (*Rokebear*)
Abbess and conv. of Canonsleigh, prop.; Henry German, v.; John Lake, John Fylmore, John Archeboll snr., pns. All well.

Whimple (*Whympell*)
Mr John Burton, r.; John Bright, cur.; William Roche, John Coppe, Richard Martyn, Thomas Hayman, pns. All well.

Poltimore (*Poltymore*)
John Rawlyn, r.; Walter Grete, cur.; John Beere, Thomas Beere, John Clerke, pns. All well.

Broadclyst (*Clyston alias Brodeclyste*)
Prior and conv. of Totnes (*Totton'*), prop.; Nicholas Helyare, cur.; John Clement, chap.; William Wylle, John Chanon, Henry Northleche, John Crockhay, Richard Pyle, Alan Pomeray, pns. All well.

Aylesbeare (*Aillisbeare*)
Prioress and conv. of Polsloe, prop.; Elias Walsshe, v.; John Bagcary, chap.; Nicholas Profford, Thomas Herdyng, William Sampford, John Rugge, pns. All well.

Farringdon (*Faryngdon*)
Henry Chambryur, r.; Mr John Faryngdon, William Holman, pns. All well.

Sidmouth (*Sydmouth*)
Abbess and conv. of Syon, prop.; John Hooper, v.; William Cowle, John Clerk, Nicholas Cowle, Henry Dadeney, pns. All well.

Woodbury (*Woodebyri*)
Vicars choral of Exeter cath., prop.; Thomas Potell, cur.; Richard Westcote, John Smyth, John Moore, Maurice John, pns.

271. [fo. 120] Deanery of Honiton (*Honyton*), De.

Axminster (*Axmystre*)
Dean and chapter of York, prop.; John Wacy, v.; Thomas Andrewe, Nicholas Were, John Cooke, John Kyng, pns.

Chapel of Membury (*Memby*)
Thomas Lowe, cur.; Thomas Mere, Roger Kate, William Bokey, pns.

Thorncombe (*Thornecombe*)
Abbot and conv. of Forde (*Ford*), prop.; Robert John, v.; Richard Hayball, Richard Bragge, pns.

Combepyne (*Combpyne*)
German Frensh, r.; Robert Abbot, Thomas Lugge, pns.

Uplyme
Richard Sause, r.; Thomas Hawkin, John Morecok, John Hawkyn, pns.

Chapel of Kilmington (*Kylmyngton*)
Thomas Gylle, chap.

Musbury (*Musbyri*)
Richard Watson, r.; John Walrond, Roger Perrok, John Hooper, pns.

Southleigh
John Longe, r.; John Kyngedon, Robert Hengley, John Badstone, pns.

Farway (*Fareway*)
Robert Cornewale, r.; John Cheseman, chap.; Robert Durke, Thomas Hatdon, Peter Haydon, pns.

Honiton (*Honyton*)
John Meldy, r.; Philip John, chap.; John Pope, William Bonythyn, John Takyll, John Andrew, pns.

Gittisham (*Gyddisham*)
Richard Nakys, r.; John Shordych, cur.; Nicholas Whiting, Michael Evely, John Wylkyn, pns.

Cotleigh (*Cotlegh*)
Nicholas Harnewill, r.; John Woode, William Molter, John Tepe, pns.

Combe-Raleigh (*Combralegh*)
Thomas Combdorowe, r.; John Clerk, Robert Menesye, Thomas Loman, pns.
    Marginal note: in dy. of Dunkeswell.

Northleigh (*Northley*)
John Smyth, r.; John Gerveys, John Clapp, William Parson, pns.

Seaton (*Seton*)
Abbot and conv. of Sherborne, prop.; John Williams, v.; Richard Churchway, William Hechin, pns.

Offwell (*Ofwill*)
John More, r.; William Millys, John Hanne, Roger Clappe, pns.

Widworthy (*Wydeworthy*)
Mr William Cothay, r.; John Tegan, cur.; John Cuckefild, Robert Sarger, John Parrok, pns.

Axmouth
Abbess and conv. of Syon, prop.; John Capell, v.; John Gage, John Trapnell, pns. All well.

272.   Deanery of Dunkeswell (*Dunkeswyll*), De.

Churchstanton (*Sheristaunton*), So.
Robert Cornewall, r.; John Belle snr., John Belle jnr., John Hawell, pns.

Awliscombe (*Aulescomb*)
Abbot and conv. of Dunkeswell, prop.; John Don, v.; John Bysshop, John Norhampton, William Serle, John Burton, pns.

Luppit (*Lovepit*)
Abbot and conv. of Newenham (*Nuham*), prop.; John Kenier, v.; John Hacche, Richard Avery, John Grounger, pns.

Dunkeswell
Abbot and conv. of Dunkeswell, prop.; John Ylmyster, cur.; Thomas Nicoll, John Philip, pns.

Sheldon (*Shildon*)
Abbot and conv. of Dunkeswell, prop.; Thomas Calow, cur.; John Walrond, John Knyght, pns.

Clayhidon (*Hydon*)
John Norys, r.; John Jenyn, John Hauke, John Holway, pns.

Hemyock
John Wyndovere, r.; John Clayford and Mr John Boreman, chaps.; Peter
Potter, Thomas Stokeman, Nicholas Tytway, John Scadyn, pns.

Upottery (*Uptery*)
Dean and chapter of Exeter, prop.; Mr William Swan, v.; William Coker,
John Spreke, pns.

Yarcombe (*Yartecombe*)
Abbess and conv. of Syon, prop.; Roger Whiler, v.; Robert Grenelefe, cur.;
Thomas Vyncent, John Walter, William Whyttum, pns.

Combe-Raleigh (*Combralegh*), see above under dy. of Honiton.

273.   [fo. 120v] Deanery of Plymtree (*Plymptre*), De.

Collumpton (*Columpton*)
Prior and conv. of St Nicholas, Exeter, prop.; Mr John Coryngdon, v.; Mr
John Foorde, cur.; Philip Lynke, William Stokeman and John Alisaunder,
chaps.; John Prescote, William Tye, John Chace, John Broke snr., John
William, Richard Alway, pns. All well.

Silverton (*Sylverton*)
Mr William Summaster, r.; John Cookes, cur.; William Walrond, chap.;
Thomas Smyth, Thomas Brodemede, Thomas Ayssh, Andrew Richard, pns.

Butterleigh (*Boterlegh*)
John Cookes, r.; John Basse, cur.; Walter Walryn, William Prous, William
Wyett, pns.

Rewe
Mr William Summaster, r.; John Vicarie, cur.; William Swysmore,
Alexander Elyot, John Hake, pns. All well.

Broadhembury (*Brodehemby*)
Dean and chapter of Exeter, prop.; Mr Laurence Mortymer, v.; John Potter,
Walter Smyth, John Smyth, John Webber, pns. All well.

Payhembury (*Payhemby*)
Abbot and conv. of Forde, prop.; William Bykcomb, v.; Richard Robyn,
John Salter, John Thorowe, Henry Salter, pns. All well.

Buckerell (*Bokerell*)
Dean and chapter of Exeter, prop.; John Knyf, v.; John Strebe, Christopher
Salter, John Bisshop, John Floye, pns. All well.

Feniton (*Fenyton*)
Thomas Hoye, r.; John Rawlyn, cur.; John Salter jnr., Thomas Pomery,
Henry Skynner, Henry Adam, pns.

Talaton (*Taleton*)
John Carnyk, r.; Richard Gooldesworthy, Henry Cooke, John Borowe, Thomas Hurdyng, pns. All well.

Kentisbeare (*Kentisbere*)
John Haryson, r.; Richard Coterell, cur.; John Butteston, John Grene, Thomas Hille, John Trugge, pns.

Clyst St Lawrence (*Clyste Laurencii*)
John Waryn, r.; Michael Evelegh, chap.; Richard Hitte, Michael Moore, Thomas Comb, pns. All well.

Clyst Hydon (*Clystyhidon*)
Edmund Halse, r.; Peter Longe, cur.; John Ferent, Robert Parker, Roger Fordes, John Perydon, pns.

Plymtree (*Plymptre*)
Mr William Rayny, r.; Richard Mogrige, chap.; John Drewe, John Pounde, William Salter, John Tye, pns. All well.

Bradninch (*Bradnynche*)
Mr Robert Froste, r.; John Wylle, cur.; Henry [*blank*], chap.; Thomas Clerk, Thomas Torre, William Denner, Thomas Dunne, Robert Butte, pns. All well.

Blackborough (*Blakburgh*)
Pascavius Davy, r.

274.   Deanery of Tiverton (*Tuverton*), De.

Tiverton
Mr John Bower, r. of Pitt (*Pitte*) portion; Mr John Crugge, r. of Tydecombe (*Tethercum*) portion; Mr Ralph [*blank*], r. of Clare portion; prior of St James in the ch. of Tiverton; Humphrey Orton, Richard London, William Houghton and Robert Jamys, chaps.; William Grey, John Talond, Walter Tailor, Thomas Skynner, John Parkehowe, William Bustell, Richard Wanter, Thomas Rede, pns.

Holcombe Rogus (*Holcomb Rogus*)
[*Blank*] [prior and conv. of Montacute], prop.; William Sanyng, v.; Robert Wise, Thomas Legh, John Joys, Robert Thacher, pns.

Hockworthy (*Hockeworthy*)
[*Blank*] [abbess and conv. of Canonsleigh], prop.; John Aisshford, v.; Robert Atthoole, William Graunt, William Colman, pns.

Huntsham (*Hunseham*)
John Vicary, r.; John Dixton, cur.; John Kersewill, William Atkyn, Edmund Sherlond, pns.

Clayhanger
Mr John Bedman, r.; Stephen [*blank*], cur.; John Tanner, John Crosse, John Adam, pns.

Morebath (*Morepath*)
Richard Bowdyn, r.; William Robyn, Geoffrey More, pns.

Bampton
Abbot and conv. of Buckland (*Bokeland*), prop.; Mr Thomas Desedall, cur.; John Gerynge, Robert Longman and Thomas Sengere, chaps.; William Hundaler, Thomas Chapillayn, James Halwell, pns.

Burlescombe (*Burlyscombe*)
Abbess and conv. of Canonsleigh, prop.; Richard Beryman, v.; John Forswild, can.; John Paynter, chap.; John Hadlond, William Deneam, Thomas Gene, pns.

Washfield (*Waisshfeld*)
Laurence London, r.; Thomas Hervy, cur.; John Hok, Stephen Kyng, John Bylhoose, pns.

Calverleigh (*Cadwoodlegh*)
John Turner, r.; John Taylor, William Smyth, John Crugge, pns.

Halberton
Abbot and conv. of St Augustine, Bristol, prop.; Mr Thomas Harper, v.; *dominus* Ralph Style, William Hooper, pns.

Sampford Peverell
John Hake, r.; Christopher Thomson, cur.; John Hillyng, Thomas Crosse, John Clement, pns.

Uffculme (*Ufculme*)
Mr John Halliswill, r.; John [*blank*], cur.; John Browne, John Hays, John Snaydon, John Atwood, John Leyman, Elias Gooderige, pns.

Willand (*Willond*)
John Deverlond, r.; John Toborowe, Robert Bynforde, pns.

Canonsleigh (*Connanlegh*)
Dominus John Woode; William and Richard, cans. at Canonsleigh.

Uploman (*Uplumpne*)
John Bromefeld, r.; John Churley, Richard Tanner, Ralph Pasure, pns.

275.   [fo. 121] Deanery of Cadbury (*Cadbery*), De.

Newton St Cyres (*Newton sancti Cyriaci*)
Prior and conv. of Plympton, prop.; Laurence Treway, v.; William Wealford, William Knyston, John Pedisbech, John Bidwill, Walter Seman, pns. All well.

Shobrooke (*Shogbroke*)
Mr John Crugge, r.; Thomas William, cur.; Richard Warde, Nicholas Bidwill, Michael Bremerugge, pns. All well.

Down St Mary (*Downe beate Marie*)
John Clement, r.; Richard Galor, Thomas Squyer, William Spetill, pns.

Upton Hellions (*Uptonhelyon*)
John Harry, r.; John Rawly, John Northcote, pns.

Stockleigh English (*Stokeleghenglys*)
John Sherowe, r.; Robert Mortymer, Christopher Dert, Edward Wallkyn, pns. All well.

Poughill (*Poghill*)
Thomas Austyn, r.; Thomas Dert, Hugh Quik, Thomas Hooper, pns.

Cheriton Fitzpaine (*Cheryton Phitpayne*)
Mr Thomas Austell, r.; John Poole, cur.; John Beare, Robert Rympeland, Robert Hancok, John Hurd, pns.

Stockleigh Pomeroy (*Stokelegh Pomery*)
Richard Legh, r.; William Tunthewe, cur.; John Stronge, William Hurde, Robert Stronge, pns. All well.

Cadeleigh (*Cadlegh*)
Mr Walter Watson, r.; Robert Byrcheman, John Godbehere, pns. All well.

Cadbury
Prior and conv. of St Nicholas, Exeter, prop.; John John, v.; John Fursedon, John Werth, pns. All well.

Thorverton
Dean and chapter of Exeter, prop.; Simon White, v.; John Gloviere, chap.; William Atholme, John Drake snr., Thomas Paynston, William Grede, pns. All well.

Brampford Speke (*Brampford*)
Prior and conv. of St Nicholas, Exeter, prop.; Walter Hurdyng, v.; Nicholas Sowdon, John Sowdon, Wiliam Knollyng, John Wheton, pns. All well.

Upton Pyne
Mr Robert Wylliford, r.; John Holme, Richard Coker, William Moore, pns. All well.

Crediton (*Credyton*)
Mr John Phillip, dean; John Sutton and Richard Scholemaister, chaps.; John Ganett, Giles Legh, Edward Fishere, John Walle snr., John Rymond, Richard Byrche, William Canne, Peter Blisse, pns. All well.

Morchard Bishop (*Morteherd Episcopi*)
John Cooke, r.; John Byrday, chap.; Robert Trobrigge, [*blank*] Coker, Walter Fullford, John Rushell, pns. All well.

Kennerleigh (*Kenerlegh*)
John Jobe, pr.; Robert Downe, John Kene, John Gower, pns. All well.

276. Clergy of the cath. ch. of Exeter:

a. Canons.

Mr John Arundell, dean, did not appear because he was with the prince [of Wales].
Mr John Comb, precentor, appeared and stated that all was well.
Mr John Taylor, chancellor, did not appear because he was at Rome.
Mr Thomas Austell, treasurer, appeared and stated that the dean did not reside and that the sheriff conducted secular business in the chapterhouse.
Mr Thomas [*recte* William] Silke, archd. of Cornwall, appeared and stated that all was well.
Mr Richard Nyck, archd. of Exeter, did not appear because he was with the bp. of Winchester.
Mr John Burton, can., appeared and stated that the annuellars did not usually celebrate mass daily.
Mr John Coryngdon, can., did not appear because he was with the bp. of Winchester.
Mr Patrick Holyburton, Mr John Pascowe and Mr Richard Mayow, cans., and Mr William Sumaister, subdean, appeared and stated that all was well.
Mr Philip Devenold, can., did not appear.
Mr Thomas Harryes appeared in the person of his proctor, Mr Patrick Holyburton.
Mr Thomas Fraunces, can., did not appear.
Mr Walter Oudebre, can., appeared.
Mr John Rise and Mr John Beeke, cans., appeared in the person of their proctor, Peter William.
Mr Walter Catisbye did not appear.
Mr Christopher Urswik appeared in the person of his proctor, Peter William.
Mr Oliver Kyng did not appear because he was with the king.
Mr Thomas Tomyowe, can., appeared in the person of his proctor, Peter William.
Mr Esward Wyllybie, can., did not appear.

b. Holders of dignities in the cth. ch.

Mr Edmund Chaderton, archd, of Totnes, and Mr William Elyott, archd. of Barnstaple, appeared in the person of their proctor, Mr Peter William.

c. [fo. 121v] Vicars of the cath. ch.

Mr Stephen Edwards, succentor, appeared and stated that all was well.
John Clerk, Thomas Webber, John Baron, John Kendale, John Wytt, Richard Beare, John Baynard, John Borow, Richard Way, William Dunnyng, John Beane, Nicholas Byllowe, John Fychet, Thomas Hay, John Honywell and Richard Skybury appeared and exhibited their letters of ordination.

d. Annuellars of the cath. ch.

Thomas Pak appeared and stated that the organ was exceedingly difficult to play; he did the best he could.
Thomas Warderoper, John Pygman, John Dayman, Michael Perkyn, John

Nicchol, John Plynmouth, John Selle, John Yeott, John Tancrett, Benedict Carwynek and William Frensch stated that all was well.

e. Secondaries of the cath. ch.

John Maior stated that John Trigis and John Davy, secondaries, wandered the country without licence.
Thomas Whitewood, John Drewe and John Wylliam agreed with his testimony.

277.   Citation directed by Mr Shirborne to the prior and conv. of St Nicholas, Exeter [O.S.B.] to submit to visitation on Monday 4 June. Sealed with seal of the Official of the archd. of Totnes. 21 May 1492.
Citation received on 22 May. Certificate of the prior dated 3 June, with schedule of those cited:
Henry White, William Wye, Thomas Lymmesfeld, Richard Hastyng, Robert Fane.

John Herford, prior, stated that his brethren failed to have a decent tonsure befitting honest monks; some of them had smaller crowns and longer hair than secular priests. They were negligent in various matters and paid scant regard to his frequent monitions.
Richard [sic] White, subprior, William Way, Thomas Limsford [sic] and Richard [sic] Fane appeared, recognised the jurisdiction of the abp. of Canterbury *sede vacante* and submitted to the visitation conducted by Mr Shirborne on 4 June.
Richard White admitted that one of the brethren had been professed at Battle (*Batell*) and afterwards had been sent to Brecon (*Brekenok*) in Wales, where his insolent manner of life so disturbed the brethren that they obtained from the abbot of Battle his transfer to another house, that is, St Nicholas at Exeter, and now he disturbed the peace here, breaking down doors, threatening the brethren and annoying the servants, to the anger of the prior and the constant disquiet of the brethren. He complained also of the smallness of his crown and the length of his hair.
William May [sic] stated that some of the brethren did not treat the prior with due reverence and sometimes called him disparagingly in English 'syr pryour'.

278.   [fo. 122] Citation of the prior and brethren of the hospital of St John the Baptist, Exeter, to submit to visitation on Tuesday 5 June. 21 May 1492.
Br John Oliver, prior, stated that the number of brethren was complete, except for one who had taken flight after he had stolen various goods. The number of poor persons and boys was also complete. He said that the financial state of the house was good and that it was not burdened by debt. Mr William Elyott, archd. of Barnstaple, had withheld for the past eight years 16d *per annum* due for his tenement. The bp. of Winchester, formerly bp. of Exeter, held to this day, contrary to the will of the brethren and without any recompense, £46 13s 4d of the goods of the house.
Br John Pete, Br Richard Hille and Br John Lugge testified as above.
The visitor thereupon concluded his visitation.

279.   Citation of the prioress and conv. of Polsloe (*Polsloo*) O.S.B. to submit to visitation on Tuesday 5 June after the morning meal. 21 May 1492.
Citation received on 23 May. Certificate of prioress Isabelle Trevranok dated 3 June, with schedule of those cited:
Isabelle Trebranok, Joan Germyn, Cecily Militon, subprioress; Elizabeth Cotterell, Julia Michehals, Joan Notherton, Joan Columppe, Joan Kelly, Matilda Clerk, Margaret Trot, Edith Skott.
All stated that all was well, and the visitor thereupon concluded the visitation.

280.   [fo. 122v] Citation of the warden and brethren of the coll. ch. of Ottery St Mary (*beate marie de Otery*) to submit to visitation on Friday 8 June. 21 May 1492.
Thomas Cornish, bp. of Tenos (*Tinen'*), warden of the coll. ch.
Mr David Chirke, minister, stated that the warden and precentor each held three acres and paid for them. The sacrist also held three acres, but paid nothing for them. He stated that he should receive some profit (*beneficio*) from the four dignitaries, as was prescribed in the first chapter of the statutes. At the end of the year, moreover, injury was done to the office of minister, in that he received nothing for the portion of his residence.
Mr William Holcomb, precentor, stated that the secondaries should have an exemplification of the statutes, but that this was not the case.
Mr William Hillyng, sacrist, stated that it had occurred to him that he was infringing the statutes, in that he received in the division a portion for the times of his absence.
Mr Fenne, prebendary, did not appear.
Mr John Ryse, prebendary, appeared in the person of his proctor, Peter William.
Mr John Hyde, prebendary, appeared in person.

Vicars.
John Flete, Henry Lowe, John Hockere, John Londe, John Greder, Thomas Hutt, Thomas Hunt, Richard Lane, William Smith and William Perott all stated that all was well.

Secondaries and clerks.
The secondaries and clerks stated that all was well, but were ordered to provide a copy of the statutes of the coll. newly written by the feast of St Peter *ad Vincula* [1 Aug.], on pain of sequestration of their salaries. They also stated that their pension was withheld long after the appointed term, and that the vicars and secondaries ought from now on to have suitable robes. The sacrist was ordered to pay their salaries at the due time, on pain of sequestration of his revenues.

281. [fo. 123] Citation of the abbess and conv. of Canonsleigh (*Canonlegh*) [O. S. A.] to submit to visitation on Friday 15 June. 21 May 1492.
Citation received on 5 June. Certificate of the abbess, Joan Stabba, dated 6 June, with schedule of those cited:
Agnes Stone, prioress; Florence Carowh, subprioress; Amicia Clyfton, Thomasina Sweton, Joan Cruyssh, Elizabeth Powell, Sabina Copelston, Joan George, Elizabeth Jhobre, Alice Bonde, Joan Pappam, Philippa Forsthew.

Joan Stabba, abbess, deposed that Nicholas Bluett of Ashbrittle (*Aisshbritell*), So., unjustly withheld 2s for a certain farm *de la Torr* and had done so for three years, although it had been the abbey's property from time immemorial. She also requested licence for the celebration in perpetuity of the mass of St Mary in the chapel of St Mary and St John the Baptist in the south part of the chancel, for as often as a mass of St Mary is celebrated there.

Agnes Stone, prioress, deposed that Joan Conyssh [*sic*] was not obedient in religion and was shameless in disposition. She also said that they were short of their complete number by three persons.

Florence Carow, subprioress, Joan George and Amicia Clifton said that all was well.

Joan Ornis [*sic*] said that in time past she had been disobedient, but she had been corrected for this fault. She also said that the prior of Barlinch (*Barlegh*) retained the ring of her profession, which was valued at 13s 4d.

Elizabeth Jhope and Alice Bonde said that all was well.

Joan Poppam and Philippa Fortescu stated that they were not professed.

The visitor thereupon concluded his visitation.

282.   Citation of the precentor and brethren of the coll. ch. of Holy Cross, Crediton, to submit to visitation on Monday 18 June. 21 May 1492.
Citation received on 21 July [*sic*]. Certificate of the precentor dated 3 June.

Mr John Bower, precentor, appeared and was ordered to present a financial statement concerning those things which pertained to his office and cure at 5 p.m. the same day, and to exhibit his letters of collation at Exeter or wherever else in the dioc. the commissary happened to be. He was also to exhibit the letters of appropriation of the ch. of Coleridge (*Colrigge*), De., and all other appropriations conceded to his ch. He was asked how often the statutes of the ch. were publicly read, and stated that they were not read publicly, but sometimes privately among the canons when they pleased. He stated that they should have sixteen vicars, but at the present time had only six. Asked if he knew that the vicars wandered about the town in a suspicious manner at night and other unseemly times, he stated that he was not aware of this. The commissary instructed that within a fortnight he should demonstrate any reason why he should not be declared a perjurer for his failure to obey the statutes of the ch.

Thomas Cook, treasurer, appeared and did not have his institution according to the statutes. He was instructed to produce his letters of institution before the abp. of Canterbury or his commissary by 24 June and to demonstrate why the office of treasurer should not be declared vacant. Asked whether he had ever heard the statutes read publicly, he declared that from the time that he was assigned his benefice he had never heard them so read; of the other evils he could not testify.

Mr John Phillip, dean, appeared and stated that to his knowledge the statutes of the ch. had not been read publicly since his induction.

Stephen Clement, Elias Dayman and John Carvanell, vicars of the ch., stated that they had never heard the statutes publicly read in the chapterhouse, and they did not know to what they were bound.

283.   [fo. 123v] Citation of the prior and conv. of Frithelstock (*Fridelstok*) [O.S.A.] to submit to visitation on Saturday 30 June. 21 May 1492.

John Osborn, prior, appeared and stated that he did not have any statutes, ordinances, compositions or documents concerning the foundation of the priory.
John Bromeford, Thomas Parre and Thomas Jacob, cans., said that all was well.
The visitor thereupon concluded his visitation.

284.   [fo. 124] Citation of the prior and conv. of Pilton (*Pylton*) [O.S.B.] to submit to visitation on 21 June. 21 May 1492.

John Oke, prior, [cf. no. 301] stated that he did not have any statutes, ordinances, compositions or documents relating to the foundation, nor the appropriations of any chs. He said that he had not found any of the brethren to be contumacious. He stated that Peter, formerly bp. of Exeter, had two silver-gilt salt-cellars belonging to the priory and worth 20 marks in pledge for 10 marks to be paid by the prior to King Edward, as was confirmed by the indenture between them; these royal tenths the bp. should receive from the collector of the tenth, and this was to the great prejudice and injury of the priory. The bp. had promised to return the two salt-cellars to the prior, but they still remained in his hands.
John Russhel and William Malmesbury, ms., stated that all was well.
The visitor thereupon concluded his visitation.

285.   Citation of the abbot and conv. of St Nectan, Hartland (*Hertlond*) [O.S.A.] to submit to visitation on Monday 25 June. 21 May 1492.
Citation received on 16 June. Certificate of the abbot dated 25 June.

Richard Lorymer, abbot, did not render the visitor due obedience or submission in his reception in the abbey.
Walter Pernecotte said that the house was not bound to a specified number of cans., but there used normally to be nine.
Roger Bonde, precentor, John the sacrist, John Parson the succentor, John Prist, deacon, and Thomas Hamond said that all was well.
The commissary requested the procurations payable by ancient custom to the bp. of Exeter for visitation. The abbot replied that he had never paid any procurations to the bp. of Exeter for visitation. He was ordered to demonstrate at Exeter before the feast of St Peter *ad Vincula* [1 Aug.] why he should not pay procurations to the abp. of Canterbury.

286.   [fo. 124v] Citation of the prior and conv. of Launceston [O.S.A.] to submit to visitation on 28 June. 21 May 1492.
Citation received on 15 June. Certificate of the prior dated 28 June.

William Hopkyn, prior, stated that he had nothing to say of the evil disposition of his brethren, because to his knowledge they behaved decently and well.
John Carlyon, subprior, stated that all was well. Asked how many cans. there were at present, he replied that there were ten but should be thirteen.

Richard Lille, can., said that all was well.

John Kent stated that two years ago there was in the priory a can. named Walter Bent, who left without the licence of the prior, and where he went nobody knew. The prior had been commanded to search him out as quicky as possible and to produce him in the priory.

William Raylin and Thomas Hikke, cans., said that all was well.

William Symon, can., stated that the subprior had lately sold a gold chalice worth £4 at Exeter and had given a law book worth 10 marks to Mr Thomyowe; he had squandered very many other goods and ornaments of the house and had put various ornaments in pledge to various persons, notably a bed with all its trappings to a certain man at Tavistock.

[Blank] Kettowe, Robert Fott and Thomas Sok, cans., said that all was well.

The prior was instructed to certify that he had reformed and repaired all these defects at Exeter by 1 Aug., and by the same date to show reason why he should not pay the procuration which had been demanded and which he denied was due.

287.   [fo. 125] Citation of the prior and conv. of Bodmin (*Bodmine*) [O. S. A.] to submit to visitation on Sunday after the feast of St Peter and St Paul [1 July]. 21 May 1492.
Citation received on 16 June. Certificate of the prior dated 1 July.

William John, prior, appeared and stated . . . [*blank*].

John Huchyn, subprior, appeared and stated that the conv. was not at full strength according to ancient custom, for there used to be ten brethren. He said that John Richard refused to carry a lantern as he was appointed to do, or to observe the ceremonies or obey the precepts of the prior and subprior according to the rule of St Augustine, as he was bound to do by oath. The subprior was ordered to render an account to his prior of the goods in his hands by 1 Aug.

John Richard appeared and was similarly ordered to render an account to the prior.

John Walty appeared and stated that certain alms used in the past to be distributed in the cloister, but they were now distributed in the porch of the hall; they also used to be distributed by an almoner appointed for the task.

David Broker appeared and stated that they used to have a clerk serving continually in the chapel of St Mary, but now they did not have such a clerk. He also was ordered to render account to the prior.

William Stafford appeared and stated that they used to have a clerk in the chapel of St Mary and also a candle burning before the image of St Mary. He also was ordered to render account to the prior.

Richard Lywer was ordered to render account to the prior.

The commissary instructed the prior to remedy the foresaid defects by 1 Aug.

288.   Citation of the dean and chapter of the coll. ch. of Crantock (*sancti Carentoci*) to submit to visitation on Wednesday 4 July. 21 May 1492.
Citation received on 18 June. Certificate of the dean dated 4 July.

Mr John Edmund, dean, was sworn to continual personal residence according to the statutes, on pain of deprivation.

All the prebendaries should be in deacon's orders at the time of their collation, according to the statutes, on pain of deprivation.
Prebendaries: Mr William Sylk, Mr Richard Nix, Mr Robert Wooderof, Mr John Symon, Mr Hugh Emelyn, Mr John Burton, Mr Walter Hyngdon, Mr William Elyott.
Vicars: John Benett, Peter Tanner, Richard Prelett, Philip Harry.
The vicars were four in number according to the statutes, and were so at present. According to the statutes they should have two or three boys continually present there, and one clerk at the charge of the prebendaries. These they did not have at present, and they were instructed to procure them by Michaelmas.

289.   [fo. 125v] Citation of the provost and chapter of the coll. ch. of St Thomas the Martyr, Glasney (*Glaseney*) [Penrhyn] to submit to visitation on 7 July. 21 May 1492.
Citation received on 11 June and certified by the provost.

Mr John Obye, provost, appeared and stated that they did not say matins in the middle of the night according to the statutes of the coll., nor were they dispensed from so doing.
Mr William Nicholl, sacrist, appeared and stated that according to the statutes they ought to have thirteen vicars, but at the present they had only seven. The provost was ordered to provide for the full number by the feast of [*blank*]. He also stated that Mr John Pascow, lately provost, had erased the statutes concerning divine service where they dealt with the office of provost, so that nobody knew the duties of the provost as regards divine service.
Mr Robert Tresuthen, Mr John Edmond and Mr Benedict Kelligrewe, prebendaries, appeared.
Mr John Carew, prebendary, appeared and stated that divine office was not performed at night as it should be according to the statutes.
Non-residents: William Cokkys and John Luke did not appear. Thomas Achumppe, Mr William Sylk, archd. of Cornwall, and Mr Hugh Lynk appeared in the person of their proctor, Peter William.
The houses of William Cokkes, Thomas Achumppe and John Luke were in poor repair, in fact almost in ruins. The fruits of their prebends were therefore sequestrated and committed to the custody of the provost and Mr William Pers.
Mr William Pers, prebendary, appeared and stated that they were bound to distribute 40s among the poor each year, according to the statutes, and they did not distribute a penny. This distribution should be made by the sacrist. They all stated that the resources of the church nowadays did not extend to the distribution of such alms.

Vicars:
John Anger, v., stated that the statutes of the coll. were not publicly read and that the vicars' steward did not pay the vs. from his receipts.
John Luky, v. there and v. of St [*blank*], stated that they did not have written statutes. They were ordered to provide new copies by Michaelmas.
John [*blank*], John Hygar and Richard Fowy, vs.

William Breberveth, v., who is also v. of Gwinear (*Wynnyer*) nearby, was ordered to reside in his own vic.
John Chynnowe, v.

Presbiteri de ponte:
Stephen Nicholl and Odo Roby, cans., appeared.

Annuellars:
John Mens and Ralph Harry, cans., appeared.

The visitor thereupon concluded his visitation.

290.   [fo. 126] Citation of the prior and conv. of Tywardreath (*Tre-wardreith*) [O.S.B.] to submit to visitation on Tuesday 10 July. 21 May 1492. Certificate of the prior dated 22 June.

Walter Barnecoll, prior, stated that Richard Haringdon of Lanreath (*Lanrethow*), Co., had unjustly detained for four years, against the will of the prior and conv., a tenement called *Garghinyll* worth more than 20s.
Richard Clerton, subprior, Henry Porch, John Thom, Richard Martyn, John Pyk and John Austell, ms., stated that all was well.
The visitor thereupon concluded his visitation.

291.   Citation of the prior and conv. of St Germans [O.S.A.] to submit to visitation on Friday 13 July. 21 May 1492.
Citation received on 15 June. Certificate of the prior, with schedule of those cited:
Walter Wilshman, subprior; Richard Beare, William Colbeare, William Rowe, Robert Gillowe and John Adam.

John Serle, prior, stated that a certain John Jamys, lately professed there and in the order of St Benedict [*sic*], had left the priory and his religious observance without seeking or obtaining licence, and he had gone to regions unknown to the prior and his brethren.
The other canons cited stated that all was well. The visitor thereupon concluded his visitation.

292.   [fo. 126v] Citation of the abbot and conv. of Tavistock (*Tavestok*) [O.S.B.] to submit to visitation on Saturday 14 July. 21 May 1492. Certificate of the abbot [undated].

Richard Banham, abbot, appeared and stated that all was well.
William Toryton, prior, appeared and stated that Robert Binles, the bell-ringer, was continually negligent in his office.
John Gylle, precentor, Ralph Penson, seneschal, and Thomas Rewe, m., appeared and stated that all was well.
John Clement, m., stated that all was well.
Nicholas Rewe, m., residing in the Isles of Scilly (*insula de Sillegh*), did not appear, nor could he because of the peril of the sea and the distance and because of other business essential to the house.
Nicholas Hille, m. of Cowick (*Carik*), did not appear because, it was said, he served the cure of *Walrage* [*unid.*].

Henry Denham, prior of the cell of Cowick (*Cowyk*), appeared and stated that all was well.

Thomas Crokkere, m., appeared and stated that all was well.

Thomas Cooke, m., appeared and stated that he was professed before Thomas Crokker but had been ejected from his place and seniority, contrary to the statutes of the house and the order. Later in the day the commissary rectified the injury done to him and restored him to his due place, according to the statutes of the order.

Robert Berdon, Andrew Thomas and Stephen Gewe, ms., stated that all was well.

The visitor thereupon concluded his visitation, saving the accustomed rights due to the abp.

293.   Citation of the prior and conv. of Plympton [O.S.A.] to submit to visitation on Tuesday 17 July. 21 May 1492.
Citation received on 22 May. Certificate of the prior dated 8 June.

David Berklegh, prior, appeared and stated that the pension from the ch. of Bridestowe (*Bridstowe*), De., due to the priory and amounting to 20 nobles *per annum* had been subtracted and detained by Mr John Fulford, the present r., for a year and a half.

Philip Bawdyn, subprior, appeared.

William Howe, prior of Marsh Barton (*Merssh*), appeared and stated that John Sayer of Exeter had for ten years unjustly detained 7s *per annum* due to the priory from a certain tenement which he now held in Exeter, adjoining the guildhall.

John Gwyn, can., appeared.

John Austyn, prior of St Anthony's in Cornwall, appeared at Penrhyn.

John Davison, William Muddyn and Ralph Lovecroft, cans., appeared.

James Davy, can. of St Anthony's, appeared at Penrhyn.

Henry Derk and Gilbert William, cans., appeared.

Henry Tancrett, can., did not appear and was not cited, because he was wandering in apostasy on the borders of Wales, under sentence of excommunication because he had left the priory without licence.

Richard Kyrton, John Rys and William Cooke, cans., appeared.

William Blower, can., was absent because he was at Marsh Barton.

Philip Stephen, can., appeared.

John Pollard, can., was on vacation from his study in the university of Oxford.

The visitor thereupon concluded his visitation.

294.   [fo. 127] Citation of the rector and fellows of the coll. ch. of St Mary, Slapton, to submit to visitation on Thursday 19 July. 21 May 1492.

Vincent Cooke, r. of the coll.

Andrew Top, minister, Robert Colyn, sacrist, and Peter Scriche, fellow, appeared.

The books and desks were not in good repair, the wood of the lecterns was not properly repaired and the glass in the windows was broken. They were instructed to repair these defects by Easter. They were also ordered to produce

a written inventory of all the ornaments, books and valuables of the house by Michaelmas. They were to produce a newly-written copy of the statutes and a complete account by the next archidiaconal visitation.
Secondaries: John Elryn and John Philip.
Choristers: John Toppe and Robert Stirche.
The commissary adjourned his visitation.

295.   Citation of the prioress and conv. of Cornworthy [O.S.A.] to submit to visitation on Thursday 26 July. 21 May 1492.

Thomasina Dynham, prioress, appeared.
Christina Avey, Joan Germyn and Isabelle Malerbe, nuns.

296.   Citation of the prior and conv. of Totnes (*Totton'*) [O.S.B.] to submit to visitation on Friday 27 July. 21 May 1492.

William Cooke, prior, stated that Roger Newnant was the first founder, but now the king of England had succeeded as patron by the forfeiture of Lord de la Souch,[1] who was still living. According to the foundation the house should contain thirteen brethren, and now there were only four. The prior was ordered to make up the number of twelve monks as quickly as he could. He testified also of a certain William Frank, lately a monk of the house, who through the prior's negligence had misappropriated various goods and robes which were stored in a certain chest, together with the common seal of the conv., with which he had sealed blank charters and also a charter granting him an annual pension of six marks for the duration of his life; he was now in the prison of the bp. of Bath and Wells.
William Hooper and Henry Gune, professed ms.
William Lamborn, not professed.
The visitor adjourned his visitation, saving all rights of the abp.

    [1] *CPR 1485–94*, p. 93.

297.   [fo. 127v] Mandate to the archd. of Cornwall and his Official to issue citations for the impending visitation of the archdeaconry. 30 May 1492.
Certificate of the archd.'s Official, dated 16 June.

REGISTER OF INSTITUTIONS TO PARISH CHURCHES IN THE DIOCESE OF EXETER *SEDE VACANTE* PERFORMED BY MR JAMES ADAM, B.C.L., DEPUTED BY THE ARCHBISHOP, FROM 1 JUNE 1492.

298.   [fo. 128] Inst. of William Denys, chap., to vic. of St-Mary-Church (*Seintmarychurch*), De., vac. by d. of John Feygon. P. dean and chapter of Exeter. I. official of the peculiar jurisdiction. 2 June 1492.

299.   Inst. of Laurence Hoskyn, chap., to vic. of Wendron (*sancte Wendrone*), Co., vac. by d. of John John. P. abbot and conv. of Rewley (*regali loco prope Oxon'*), O. Cist., Lincoln dioc. I. archd. of Exeter [*sic*]. 6 July 1492.

300.   Inst. of James Nutcomb to vic. of Pinhoe (*Pynhoo*), De., vac. by res. of John Westlake. P. prior and conv. of St Nicholas, Exeter. I. archd. of Exeter. 15 July 1492.

301.   Inst. of William Kyngeswoode to office of prior of Pilton (*Pylton*), vac. by d. of Br John Cooke. P. abbot and conv. of Malmesbury, O.S.B., Salisbury dioc. I. archd. of Barnstaple. 26 July 1492.

302.   Inst. of John Dixton, chap., to ch. of Huntsham (*Hunsham*), De., vac. by res. of John Vyckrye. P. Mr John Bere. I. archd. of Exeter. 27 July 1492.

303.   Inst. of John Forde, chap., to vic. of Dawlish (*Dawlissh*), De., vac. by d. of Roger Sydall. P. dean and chapter of Exeter. I. Official of the peculiar jurisdiction. 29 Aug. 1492.

304.   Inst. of John Mylmett, chap., to ch. of Halwill (*alias Haywill*), De., vac. by res. of John Poole. P. John Kendale, prior of the hospital of St John of Jerusalem in England. I. archd. of Totnes. 13 Sept. 1492.

305.   Inst. of John Boleyn, chap., to ch. of Whitstone (*Whitestone*), Co., vac. by d. of Roger Sare. P. John Arundell, esq., son and heir of Sir Thomas Arundell, lately deceased; John Dynham, lord Dynham; Joan Dynham, widow of Sir John Dynham, kt.; Sir William Huddesfeld, kt.; Sir John Byconell, kt.; Sir John Sabcote, kt.; Charles Dynham, esq.; and Thomas Tregarthen snr. and Stephen Calmady, *generosi*, on this occasion. 18 Sept. 1492.

306.   [fo. 128v] Inst. of Mr Robert Holcote, chap., to ch. of Goodleigh (*Goodlegh*), De., vac. by d. of Hugh Lynke. P. Thomas Kyrkham, esq., on this occasion. I. archd. of Barnstaple. 22 Sept. 1492.

307.   Inst. of Mr Robert Barbour, chap., to ch. of St Paul, Exeter, vac. by d. of Thomas Meryfeld. P. dean and chapter of Exeter. I. archd. of Exeter. 26 Sept. 1492.

308.   Inst. of Mr Edmund Ynge, chap., to vic. of Cadbury, De., vac. by res of John John [cf. no. 299]. P. prior and conv. of St Nicholas, Exeter, I. archd. of Exeter. 27 Sept. 1492.

309.   Inst. of John Boleyn, chap., to ch. of Shirwell (*Shirwill*), De., vac. by d. of Hugh Lynke. P. Hugh Beaumond. I. archd. of Barnstaple. 4 Oct. 1492.

310.   Inst. of Mr John Cooke, chap., to ch. of Ashbury (*Aisshbury*), De., vac. by res. of John Trenethall. P. prior and conv. of St Stephen, Launceston. I. archd. of Totnes. 11 Oct. 1492.

311. Inst. by the abp. of John Kneboon, chap., in the person of his proctor William Potkyn, notary public, to vic. of St Merryn (*Meryn*), Co., vac. by d. of Benedict Chenell, and in his collation due to the vacancy of the see of Exeter. I. archd. of Cornwall. 20 Nov. 1492.

312.   Inst. of John Cheper, chap., to ch. of Georgenympton (*Nymet sancti Georgii*), De., vac. by d. of John Wykes. P. Thomas Hache, esq. I. archd. of Barnstaple. 22 Nov. 1492.

313.   Inst. of John Edmond, chap., to vic. of Perranzabulo (*sancti Pierani*), Co., vac. by d. of Samson Bloyow. P. dean and chapter of Exeter. I. Official of the peculiar jurisdiction in Cornwall. 4 Dec. 1492.

314.   Inst. of Edward Mayowe, chap., to vic. of Landrake (*Lanrak*), Co., vac. by res. of Richard Waryn. P. prior and conv. of St German's. I. Official of the peculiar jurisdiction. 9 Dec. 1492.

315.   [fo. 129] Inst. of John Casse, chap., to ch. of Cruwys Morchard (*Cruys Morchard*), De., vac. by d. of Alexander Cruys. P. John Cruys, esq. I archd. of Barnstaple. 17 Dec. 1492.

316.   Inst of John Aller, chap., to ch. of East Allington (*Alyngton*), De., vac. by d. of Thomas Barett. P. Richard Coffyn. I. archd. of Barnstaple. 17 Dec. 1492.

317.   Inst. of Robert Martyn, chap., to ch. of Ladock (*sancte Ladoce*), Co., vac. by res. of Ralph Hynkys. P. Halnatheus Maliverer, esq., Joan his wife, and Thomas Carmyow, esq. I. archd. of Cornwall. 17 Dec. 1492.

318.   Inst. of William Menwynnyk, chap., to ch. of Southhill (*Southhyll*), Co., vac. by res. of Robert Oliver. P. Sir John Byconell, kt., and Robert Stowell, esq. I. archd. of Cornwall. 20 Dec. 1492.

319.   Inst. of John Teak, chap., to vic. of Littleham (*Lytilham*) [in East Budleigh hundred], De., vac. by d. of Mr Thomas Wormeswell. P. dean and chapter of Exeter. I. archd. of Exeter. 1 Jan. 1493.

320.   Inst. of Richard Wrayford, chap., to vic. of Spreyton (*Sprayton*), De., vac. by res. of John Allere. P. abbot and conv. of Tavistock. I. archd. of Exeter. 2 Jan. 1493.

321.   Inst. of John Alegh, chap., to ch. of Harford (*Hardford*), De., vac. by res. of John Teack. P. John Gylle, John Woode, Robert Stowell, William Poughill and William Founteyne. I. archd. of Totnes. 28 Jan. 1493.

322.   Inst. of John Gylle, chap., to ch. of Rakenford (*Rakerneford*), De., vac. by d. of Alexander Ornys. P. John Cruys of Morchard. I. archd. of Barnstaple. 1 Feb. 1492.

323.   [fo. 129v] Ordinations celebrated in the coll. ch. of Ottery St Mary by Thomas bp. of Tenos, according to the commission issued to him by Mr James Adam, on 22 Dec. 1492.

a. *Accolites*

Thomas Colman, Henry Redelake, Thomas Trebnyth, Thomas Bragge, John Adam, John Herytt; John Wykam of Worcester dioc.; John Smyth, John Broke.

b. *Subdeacons*

Baldwin Preston, to t. of Tavistock abbey.

Richard Conner, to t. of Torre abbey.

Nicholas Bolter, to t. of priory of St Nicholas, Exeter.

William Spoltte, accolite, to t. of Dunkeswell abbey, O. Cist.

John Aynell of Bath and Wells dioc., by l.d., to t. of Taunton priory.

John Pewe of Bath and Wells dioc., by l.d., to t. of hospital of St John the Baptist, Wells.

Thomas Straunge, accolite of Worcester dioc., by l.d. for ordination to holy orders, to t. of master and brethren of hospital of St John, Bristol.

Roger Richard of Bath and Wells dioc., by l.d., to t. of Dunkeswell abbey, O. Cist.

Philip Gay, to t. of Frithelstock priory.

Br Robert Cogan, m. of Newenham, O. Cist.

Robert Constapill, accolite, to t. of Tavistock abbey.

William Aissh, accolite, to t. of Totnes priory.

John Frye, accolite, to t. of Canonsleigh abbey.

John Evan, to t. of hospital of St John the Baptist, Wells.

William Lane, accolite, to t. of coll. of Ottery St Mary.

John Baker, to t. of St German's priory.

c. *Deacons*

Br Richard Hoore of Sutton, O. Carm.

Richard Davy of St Davids dioc., by l.d., to t. of priory of St Mary Magdalene, Barnstaple.

Br Henry Gunne, subdeacon, m. of Totnes, O.S.B.

d *Priests*

Stephen Langston, deacon, to t. of Launceston priory.

Geoffrey Geffe, to t. of Taunton priory, Bath and Wells dioc.

John Gowle of Salisbury dioc., by l.d., to t. of Abbotsbury abbey.

Br John Thorney, m. of Muchelney, O.S.B., Bath and Wells dioc.

Br William Upton, deacon, m. of Muchelney, O.S.B., Bath and Wells dioc.

Br John Adam, can. of St German's priory.

Roger Worthing, deacon, to t. of St German's priory.

Thomas Key of Hereford dioc., by l.d., to t. of Wigmore abbey.

REGISTER OF TESTAMENTS PERTAINING TO THE PREROGATIVE JURISDICTION OF THE ARCHBISHOP PROVED IN THE DIOCESE OF EXETER FROM THE FEAST OF ST PETER AD VINCULA.

324.   Last testament of the lady Margaret Courtenay, 1487.
IN THE NAME of God, Amen. The moneth of July the yere of oure Lord God mcccclxxxvii I Dame Margaret Courtenay, being in my right mynde, make my testament and last will in the maner and forme folowing. First I bequeth my soule to almyghti God and my body to be buried in the parisshe chirch of Powderham where my hushand was buried, for my husband and I made there the newe ile and also the body of the chirch att oure owen cost and charge,

except that I had of the parissh there to the help of the said bilding .viii. d. Item I wil myne executours bringe me worshipfully on erth and kepe my moneth mynde and the yeris mynde, as I have specialle put my trust on theym. And I wil sette of my goodes to helpe bilde the body of the said chirch of Powderham .x. l. Also I wil there be disposid by myne executours to .v. parissh chirches in Devonshire by the discretioun of myne executours .v. l, that is to every chirch .xx. s. Also I wil there be songe in as goodly hast aftre my decesse for my housband and me by prestis and freres in Excester or elshere by the discretioun of myne executours a .m.[1] masses, every prest taking for a masse .ii. d. Item I bequeth to John Pyle and Richard Wakeham every of theim .xl. s, and to every man that is in my covenant with me at this day, except my botteller and cooke which cam but late to me, .xx. s. And I bequethe to Margery my servant .iii. s .iiii. d. Also I wil that William Martyn have his evidence that I have that perteneth to him, payingh for theim .xx. s, for so paied I. Also I will that all writingges or any other evidences that I have that longith to my son Sir William Courtnay or to any other person be deliveryd to him that they longith unto. AND THE RESIDUE of alle my goodes not bequethid I geve and bequeth to Maister David Hopton archidiacon of Excestre, Edward Pers frere, my sonnes, and to John More of Colunton, and theyme I make myn executours, and I wil that everiche of the said Maister David Hopton and other have for there laboures .xx. s. to execute this my wil.

Probate granted 22 Sept. 1492. Administration granted to Edward and Peter, sons of the deceased.

325.   [fo. 130] Last testament of John Gyffard [Latin], 9 Nov. 1487.
I bequeath my soul to Almighty God, the B.V.M. and all the saints of heaven, and my body to be buried in the cath. ch. of St Peter, Exeter. I bequeath to the high altar of the ch. of St George, Exeter, my black silken gown, and to the parish ch. of St John the Baptist, Withycombe Raleigh (*Wythecombe*), De., for my tithes forgotten 3s 4d, and to the high altar of the same ch. my checkered silken robe and 6s 8d. I will that my wife shall have the third part of all my lands and tenements as her dower. I will that my brother Leonard shall have my gold chain and all my rings. I bequeath to my brother John Cooke my great horse, and to my sister Elizabeth a bowl with a lid, which is called 'Sunspotte'. I will that William Coole shall have for his maintenance for three years five marks *per annum*. I bequeath to Margaret Cole a black gilded belt. I bequeath to John Coole senior all the clothes which I normally wear. I bequeath to John Frigon, John Alyn and William Pathase over and above their stipends 40s each, and to William Snellyng my servant 20s. I give and bequeath to the daughters of Thomas Denys three silver bowls with their lids. I bequeath to Richard Northeren, my host, over and above his expenses, 26s 8d. I bequeath to Alice Score, serving-girl of the house, 20d, and to the serving-boy 12d. I bequeath to Thomas Denbawe, chap., 6s 8d. I leave to the two orders of friars 3s 4d each. I bequeath to John Alyn for the duration of his life an annuity of four marks to be drawn on my lands and to be received at the free assignation of my executors and feoffees. I will that immediately after the fulfilment of my will and the payment of my debts and their expenses, my executors should retain all my goods and the residue of my plate, together with

all my utensils, in their hands for a term of six years, and if my brother Leonard dies within this term without heirs, I will that my sister Elizabeth and her heirs shall receive the residue of my plate and all my goods otherwise left to my brother Leonard, with the exceptions detailed above and the exception of those things disposed by my executors for the health of my soul. I appoint as the executors of this my testament or last will Thomas Denys, Robert Holbaine, John Coole and Richard Melhuysh, and I will that each of my executors shall have 40s for the execution of my will without fraud, which I trust they will do. I owe to my brother John Cooke £26 10s, which he shall receive at the rate of £10 *per annum* from my lands. I owe to Richard Melhuyssh £20, which I will that he should receive from my lands.

Probate granted 3 Nov. 1492. Administration granted to Thomas Denys and Robert Holbeine, with reservation of the right to commit administration to the other executors named.

326.   Last testament of Henry Roper [Latin], 12 Dec. 1491.
I bequeath my body to Almighty God and my body to be buried in the ch. of St Peter and St Paul, Taunton, before the image of St Botulph. I bequeath to the parish ch. of Yarcombe (*Yercumb*), De., 6s 8d, to the vicar there 3s 4d, and to the holy-water-clerk, 12d. I bequeath to John, my eldest son, 6s 8d, to Wilma my daughter £20, and to Richard my son who is with the vicar of Stogumber (*Stokegumer*), So., £6 13s 4d. The residue of my goods I bequeath to Wilma my wife, that she may dispose of them as her own for the health of my soul, and I ordain her my executrix that she may faithfully implement my testament, of which I ordain as supervisors John and Robert Roper, to help and counsel her in its execution.

Probate gratned 2 Aug. 1492. Administration granted to his widow as executrix, who was to render account by the Monday before Michaelmas [24 Sept.].

327.   Last testament of Richard Woode, esq. [Latin], 27 Oct. 1492.
I bequeath my soul to Almighty God, the B.V.M. and all saints, and my body to be buried in the aisle of St Mary in the south part of the parish ch. of North Tawton, De., beside my father's body. I bequeath to the stock of St Mary of Crooke (*Croke*), De., an heifer. I bequeath to the parish ch. of St Peter the Apostle in North Tawton 10s. I bequeath to my daughters Mary, Ivott and Dorothy each twenty nobles when they shall come to marriageable age, provided they be well governed; and if one or two of them die before that age, then I will that the surviving one or two shall have that sum; and if they all die before that age, I will that the sum shall be at the disposition of my executors. The residue of my goods I bequeath to Thomasina Wood my mother and Emmotte my wife, whom I ordain my executors, to dispose for the health of my soul as they think best.

Probate granted 16 Nov. 1492. Administration granted to the executrices, who were to render account by the feast of St Andrew [30 Nov.].

328.   [fo. 130v] Last testament of Alexander Carewe, esq. [Latin], 20 Sept. 1492.
I bequeath my body to Almighty God, the B.V.M. and all saints, and my body to holy burial. I bequeath to the parish ch. of Sheviock (*Shebik*), Co., 6s 8d. I bequeath to the chs. of Maker, Rame, St Germans, St Stephen [*unid.*] and the chapel of St Nicholas at Saltash (*Saltaissh*), Co., 6s 8d each. I leave to the v. of St Anthony (*Anton'*) [*unid.*] for my tithes forgotten 6s 8d. I bequeath to Thomas Crese 20s, and to John Spiller, chap., 3s 4d. I bequeath to the ch. of Shobrooke (*Shodbroke*), De., 13s 4d, and to the ch. of Luppitt (*Lovepit*), De., 6s 8d. I bequeath to each of my stepchildren one sheep. The residue of all my goods I bequeath to John my son and Isabelle my wife, whom I ordain my executors to dispose for the health of my soul.

Probate granted at Plymouth, 12 Nov. 1492. Administration granted to John, son of the deceased. Subsequently the v. of St Anthony was commissioned to commit administration to Elizabeth [*sic*], widow of the deceased, who was to render account by the feast of the Purification of the B.V.M. [2 Feb.].

329.   Last testament of Henry Hanforth of the parish of St Petroc, Exeter [Latin], 12 Dec. 1492.
I bequeath my soul to Almighty God and my body to be buried in the cemetery of Exeter cath. I bequeath to the r. of St Petroc 53s 4d; to the prior and conv. of St Nicholas, Exeter, 3s 4d; to the prior and brethren of St John by the east gate of Exeter, 3s 4d; to the friars Preacher and the friars Minor of Exeter, 3s 4d each. I bequeath to Juliana my daughter £20 sterling and plate to the value of £4. I bequeath to Henry Hanforth my brother £4, that is, 20s sterling and merchandise to the value of £3. I bequeath to each of my apprentices of either sex 6s 8d, to be delivered to them on the completion of their apprenticeship. I will that my executors hire a suitable priest to celebrate for my soul in the ch. of St Petroc for a whole year. The residue of my goods I bequeath to Elizabeth my wife and Thomas Acclum, clerk, my curate, whom I ordain my executors, to dispose for the health of my soul according to their discretion. I will that Thomas Acclum, clerk, should have for his labour 40s. Given at Exeter.

Probate granted 12 Jan. 1493. Administration granted to Elizabeth, widow of the deceased, who was to render account by Easter.

330.   Last testament of John Balle [Latin], 14 Aug. 1493.[1]
I bequeath my soul to Almighty God, the B.V.M. and all saints, and my body to be buried in the cemetery of the ch. of St Mary, Totnes (*Totton*), De. I will that a suitable chap. should be hired to celebrate in that ch. for a whole year for the souls of all my benefactors and all the faithful departed, taking eight marks *per annum* as his stipend. I bequeath to William my son and Wilma my daughter together twenty marks, two silver cups and two dozen spoons, to be divided equally between them; and if it happens that one of them should die before they come to the age of discretion, then I will that all should remain to the survivor. I bequeath to William my son my best silver standing-cup with its lid, and if William dies before he comes to the age of discretion, I will that it should pass to Wilma my daughter. I will that all my feoffees in all my

messuages, lands and tenements with their appurtenances in the manor and borough of Totnes and in Harberton (*Hurberton*), De., should after my decease deliver estate to Margery my wife for the term of her life; and after her decease all the foresaid messuages, lands and tenements with their appurtenances shall remain to William my son and the legitimate heirs of his body to be held of the capital lords of the fees by the accustomed rents and services; and if it happens that William should die without legitimate heirs of his body, then I will that all the foresaid messuages *etc.* shall remain to Wilma my daughter and the legitimate heirs of her body; and if it happens that Wilma should die without legitimate heirs of her body, then I will that all the foresaid messuages *etc.* shall remain to Nicholas Balle my brother and the legitimate heirs of his body; and if it happens that Nicholas should die without legitimate heirs of his body, I will that all the foresaid messuages *etc.* shall remain to Margery Balle my sister and the legitimate heirs of her body; and if it happens that Margery should die without legitimate heirs of her body, then I will that all my messuages etc. in the manor and borough of Totnes should be granted in perpetuity to the use of the ch. of Totnes, and that all my messuages *etc.* in Harberton should be used to provide a mass of Jesus every Friday in the ch. of Totnes in perpetuity. I bequeath to the prior of Totnes for my tithes forgotten 2s. The residue of my goods I leave to Margery my wife, whom I ordain my executrix, to dispose for the health of my soul as seems best to her. I also ordain John Beworth, clerk, and William Huckmor, snr., to be supervisors of my testament, each of them to receive for his labour 10s.

Probate granted 26 Nov. 1493. Administration granted to Margery, widow of the deceased, who was to render account by the feast of St Nicholas [6 Dec.].

[1] Unless there is a scribal error, both nos 330 and 331 were written, and probate granted, after the end of the vacancy of the see of Exeter. This suggests that the register was not written up until after 26 Nov. 1493.

331. [fo. 131] Last testament of William Martyn of Lostwithiel (*Lost-wythiol*), Co., [Latin], 5 Aug. 1493.
I bequeath my soul to Almighty God, the B.V.M. and all saints, and my body to be buried beneath the ch. of St Bartholomew the Apostle, Lostwithiel. I bequeath to the priory of St Andrew at Tywardreath (*Tylwardreth*) a portion (*doole*) and a half of stannary called *le Quothcoke*. I bequeath to the ch. of St Ciriac, Luxulyan (*Luxawn*), Co., half a portion of stannary called *le Bralrebere*. I bequeath to the ch. of St Bartholomew, Lostwithiel, half a portion of stannary called *le Penprynne*. I bequeath to my mother £4, to my sister Joan 40s and to my brother John 20s. I bequeath to the child in the womb of Alice, widow of John my deceased son, if he attains the age of majority, £20 in money and in merchandise as determined by my executors. I bequeath to Thomas Burnard my curate, for tithes forgotten and negligently detained, 10s. I bequeath to the v. of Lanlivery (*Lanlyvery*), Co., for my tithes forgotten and negligently detained, 3s 4d. I bequeath to Thomas Gybys, chap., 6s 8d. I will that my executrix shall maintain a suitable priest to celebrate for my soul and the souls of all the faithful departed at the altar of the B.V.M. in the ch. of St Bartholomew for two whole years after my decease. I bequeath to Nicholas Kent, clerk, and John Lowre a sum of money to be determined by my

executrix, with the intention that they should aid and counsel her in all legitimate business. The residue of all my goods, after the payment of my debts and the fulfilment of my legacies, I bequeath to Amicia my wife, with the intention that she shall dispose for the health of my soul and the souls of all the faithful departed as seems best to her, and I ordain the foresaid Amicia my executrix.

Probate granted in the cath. at Exeter, 18 Oct. 1493. Administration granted to Amicia, widow of the deceased.

ACCOUNTS OF THE VACANCY OF THE SEE

332.   Procurations in the archdeaconry of Exeter.

a. Dy. of Kenn (*Kenne*), De.:
Cowick (*Cowik*), Alphington (*Alphyngton*), 6s 8d each; Exminster (*Exmynstre*), Kenn, 8s each; Powderham, 4s; Kenton, 10s; Mamhead (*Mamhed*), 2s; Ashcombe (*Aisshcomb*), 5s 8d; Dunhideock (*Dunshidiok*), 4s; Stoke-in-Teignhead (*Stokeyntynhide*), 8s; East Ogwell (*Estwogwill*), 5s 4d; Trusham (*Trisma*), 2s 8d; Combe-in-Teignhead (*Combyntynhede*), 8s; Shillingford (*Shilyngford*), West Ogwell (*Westwogwill*), Horridge (*Holrigge*) and Haccombe (*Haccomb*), nil.   Total: £3 19s

b. [fo. 131v] Dy. of Dunsford, De.:
Whitestone (*Whitstone*), Doddiscombsleigh (*Legh*), Ashton (*Aisshton*), Christow (*Cristowe*), Bridford (*Brideford*), 5s each; Dunsford, Drewsteignton (*Teyngton*), Chagford (*Chageford*), 6s 8d each; Throwleigh (*Throwlegh*), 5s; Gidleigh (*Gidlegh*), 3s; South Tawton, 8s; Spreyton (*Sprayton*), 5s; Hittisleigh (*Hitteres-legh*), 4s; Cheriton Bishop (*Churyton*), Tedburn St. Mary (*Tetteborn*), 6s 8d each; Holcombe Burnell (*Holecomb*), 4s.   Total: £4 7s 4d

c. Dy. of Cadbury, De.:
Newton-St Cyres (*Newton*), Shobrooke (*Shogbroke*), Down-St Mary (*Downe*), 6s 8d each; Stockleigh-English (*Stokeleghinglish*), 4s; Poughill (*Poghill*), 5s; Cheriton-Fitzpaine (*Churiton*), 6s 8d; Stockleigh-Pomeroy (*Stokeleghpomeray*), 4s; Cadeleigh (*Cadlegh*), Cadbury (*Cadburye*), 5s each; Thorveton, Brampford-Speke (*Brampford*), Upton-Pyne, 6s 8d each; Upton-Helions (*Uptonhilion*), nil.
Total: £3 9s 8d

d. Dy. of Tiverton (*Tuverton*), De.:
Bickleigh (*Bikelegh*), 6s 8d; Tiverton – Pitte, Tydecombe, Clare and St James portions, 2s each; Huntsham (*Hunsham*), Washfield (*Wasshefeld*), 3s 4d each; Bampton (*Baumton*), 8s; Morebath, 6s 8d; Clayhanger, 3s 4d; Holcombe-Rogus (*Holcomb*), 6s 8d; Hockworthy (*Hokworthy*), Burlescombe (*Burlecombe*), 3s 4d each; Halberton, 8s; Willand (*Wyllond*), 20d; Uploman (*Lumpne*), Sampford Peverell (*Sampford*), 4s each; Uffculme (*Uffecolumpp*), 8s; *Herterlond* [*unid.*], nil.   Total: £3 18s 4d

e. Dy. of Plumtree (*Plymptre*), De.:
Buckerell (*Bokerall*), Feniton (*Fynaton*), Broadhembury (*Brodehemburye*), Payhembury (*Payhemburye*), Talaton (*Taleton*), Kentisbeare (*Kentisbere*),

91

Collumpton (*Columpton*), Plymtree, Clyst-Hydon (*Clisthidon*), Clyst-St Lawrence (*Clist Laurencii*), Bradninch (*Bradenynch*), Silverton, 6s 8d each; Rewe, 3s 4d; Butterleigh (*Botislegh*), Blackborough (*Blakbourgh*) nil.

Total: £4 3s 4d

f. Dy. of Duneswell (*Dunkiswill*), De.:
Hemyock (*Hemyok*), Churchstanton (*Cherestaunton*), Clayhidon (*Hydon*), 6s 8d each; Sheldon (*Shildon*), 2s 6d; Dunkeswell, 5s; Luppitt (*Lovepitt*), Uppottery (*Upotery*), Yarcombe (*Yarnekomb*), Combe-Raleigh (*Combralegh*), Awliscombe (*Awlescomb*), 6s 8d each.

Total: £3 0s 10d

g. Dy. of Honiton (*Honyton*), De.:
Honiton, Gittisham (*Gydesham*), Cotleigh (*Cotelegh*), Offwell(*Uffewill*), Widworthy (*Wydeworthy*), 6s 8d each; Axminster (*Axmynstre*), 8s; Thorncombe (*Thorncomb*), Uplyme, Combepyne (*Combpyne*), Musbury (*Musberye*), Axmouth, Seaton (*Seton*), Southleigh (*Southlegh*), 6s 8d each; Northleigh (*Northlegh*), 3s; Farway (*Fareway*), 6s 8d; Rousdon St Pancras (*sancti Pancratii*), 2s 8d; Colyton, 18d; Membury, Kilmington (*Kilmyngton*), nil. Total: £5 22d

h. [fo. 132] Dy. of Aylesbeare (*Aillisbeare*), De.:
Ottery St Mary (*Otery Marie*), Harpford (*Herpford*), Sidmouth (*Sydmouth*), Otterton (*Ottirton*), Colaton-Raleigh (Colaton), 6s 8d each; Bicton (*Bukyngton*), 10s; Lympstone (*Lympston*), Aylesbeare (*Allesbeare*), Whimple (*Whympell*), Rockbeare (*Rokebeare*), 6s 8d each; Clyst-St Mary, 4s; Sowton (*Cliste Famison*), Broadclyst (*Cliston*), Poltimore (*Poltemoure*), Farrington (*Faryngdon*), Pinhoe (*Pynhoo*), 6s 8d each; Huxham, 4s; Clyst-St George (*sancti Georgii de Cliste*), Woodbury (*Woodebury*), Littleham (*Lytilham*), Dotton (*Dadyngton*), nil.

Total: £5 14s 8d

j. Dy. of Christianity, Exeter:
St Mary Major, St Mary Arches, St Mary Steps, St Martin, St Petrock, St Stephen, St Paul, All Hallows Goldsmith Street, All Hallows-on-the-Wall, St Kerian, Holy Trinity, St Leonard, St Olave, St George, St Edmund-on-Exe-Bridge [no figures given]. Total: [*blank*]

TOTAL PROCURATIONS IN ARCHDEACONRY OF EXETER: £33 15s

333. Procurations in the archdeaconry of Barnstaple.

a. Dy. of Chulmleigh (*Chulmelegh*), De.:
Chulmleigh, Chawleigh (*Chalvelegh*), Lapford (*Lapworth*), Zeal-Monachorum (*Sele Monachorum*), 6s 8d each; Clannaborough (*Clinnebourgh*), Nymet-Rowland, 3s 4d each; Nymet-Tracy, North Tawton (*Tawton*), Bondleigh (*Bonelegh*), Coleridge (*Colrigge*), 6s 8d each; Brushford (*Brusshford*), 3s 4d; Wembworthy (*Wemmeworthi*), 6s 8d; Eggesford (*Egesford*), 3s 4d; Burrington (*Borington*), 6s 8d.

Total: £4

b. Dy. of Torrington (*Toryton*), De.:
Great Torrington, Roborough (*Roburg*), Beaford (*Beauford*), Ashreigney (*Esse Regni*), Winkleigh (*Wynkelegh*), Dolton (*Douelton*), 6s 8d each; Dowland (Doulond), 3s 4d; Iddesleigh (*Ideslegh*), Meeth (*Methe*), Petrockstow (*Pedrok*), 6s 8d each; Buckland Filleigh (*Bokelond Fillegh*), 4s 6d; Newton St Petrock

(*Newton*), 2s 2d; Shebbear (*Shebbeare*), Langtree (*Langtre*), Peter's Marland (*Merlond*), 6s 8d; Merton, 4s 6d; Little Torrington (*Toryton Parva*), 6s 8d; Huish (*Huissh*), 3s 2d. Total: £4 4s 4d

c. Dy. of Hartland (*Hertlond*), De.:
Hartland, Clovelly (*Clovely*), Parkham, Alwington (*Alvyngton*), Abbotsham (*Abbatisham*), Northam, Bideford (*Bydeford*), 6s 8d each; Alverdiscott (*Alverdiscote*), Weare Giffard (*Weare*), 3s 4d; Frithelstock (*Frithelstok*), 6s 8d; Monkleigh (*Monklegh*), 4s 6d; Littleham (*Lytilham*), 2s 2d; Buckland Brewer (*Bokelond Brewer*), Woolfardisworthy (*Wolfradisworthi*), 6s 8d each; Landcross (*Lancras*), nil. Total: £4

d. Dy. of Barnstaple (*Baron'*), De.:
Barnstaple (*Barnastapell*), Pilton, 6s 8d each; Filleigh (*Fillegh*), 3s 4d; Chidelhampton (*Chedilhampton*), High Bickington (*Bukington*), Atherington, Yarnscombe (*Ernyscomb*), Huntshaw (*Hunshaue*), Westleigh (*Westlegh*), 6s 8d each; Instow (*Instowe*), 3s 4d; Fremington (*Fremyngton*), Tawstock, (*Tawstok*), 6s 8d each; Newton Tracey (*Newton*), Horwood (*Horewoode*), nil.
Total: £3 13s 4d

e. [fo. 132v] Dy. of Shirwell (*Shirwill*), De.:
Shirwell, Marwood (*Merewood*), Heanton Punchardon (*Heghampton*), Georgeham (*Ham sancti Georgii*), Morthoe (*Morthoo*), West Down (*Westdowne*), 6s 8d each; Bittadon (*Bittedene*), 2s 2½d; Ilfracombe (*Ilfradecombe*), Berrynarbor (*Bury*), East Down (*Estdowne*), Arlington (*Alryngton*), Kentisbury, Combe Martin (*Combmartyn*), 6s 8d each; Trentishoe (*Trenshoo*), 2s 2d; Martinhoe (*Martynghoo*), 4s 5d; Brendon, Parracombe (*Pawracomb*), Challacombe (*Chaudecomb*), High Bray (*Bray*), 6s 8d each; Charles (*Charlys*), 3s 4d; Stoke Rivers (*Stokeryvers*), Bratton Fleming (*Bratton*), 6s 8d each; Loxhore (*Lokishare*), 3s 4d; Lynton, 6s 8d; Countisbury (*Conttesbury*), West Rackenford (*Westrakerneford*), 3s 4d each; Goodleigh (*Godelegh*), Ashford (*Aisshford*), nil. Total: £7 13s 0½d

f. Dy. of Molton, De.:
South Molton, Roseash (*Esse Rauff*), Knowstone (*Knoudeston*), 6s 8d each; Rackenford (*Rakinford*), 2s 2½d; Molland (*Malland*), 6s 8d; West Anstey (*Westansty*), 3s 4d; East Anstey (*Anstansty*), 20d; Oakford (*Okeford*), 4s 2d; Studley (*Stodelegh*), Cruwys-Morchard (*Crusmorchard*), 6s 8d each; Woolfardisworthy (*Wolfradesworthy*), 3s 4d; Puddington (*Potyngdon*), 20d; Thelbridge (*Thelbrigge*), East Worlington (*Estwolrington*), West Worlington (*West Wolryngton*), Cheldon (*Chedelton*), Meshaw (*Meshaue*), Romansleigh (*Romondesley*), 2s 2½d each; King's Nympton (*Nymet Regis*), 6s 8d; Warkleigh (*Warkelegh*), 2s 2½d; George Nympton (*Nymet Georgii*), 3s 2½d; North Molton, 6s 8d; Satterleigh (*Saterlegh*), Affeton Barton (*Affeton*), Creacombe (*Crewcomb*), Mariansleigh (*Marlegh*), nil; Washford Pyne (*Waisfeld*), 20d; Witheridge (*Witherigge*), 6s 8d. Total: £5 12s 4d

TOTAL PROCURATIONS IN ARCHDEACONRY OF BARNSTAPLE:
£30 3s 0½d

334.   Procurations in the archdeaconry of Cornwall.

a. Dy. of Eastwyvelshire (*Est'*), Co.:
Lewannick (*Lawanak*), Northill, Linkinhorne (*Lankinhorne*), Southill, Stoke
Climsland (*Stoke*), Calstock (*Calstoke*), St Dominick (*Dompnek*), St Mellion
(*Melane*), 7s 5½d each; Pillaton (*Pylaton*), 6s; Landulph (*Landulpe*), 6s 5d; Botus
Fleming (*Boteflemyng*), 3s; Antony (*Anton*), 7s 5½d; St John by Antony (*sancti
Johannis*), 3s; Maker, Rame, 7s 5½d each; Sheviock (*Shevioke*), 4s; Menheniot
(*Mahynyet*), Quethiock (*Quedek*), St Ives (*Iva*), 7s 5½d each.   Total: £6 10s

b. Dy. of Westwyvelshire (*West'*), Co.:
St Cleer (*Clare*), Liskeard (*Leskerd*), Duloe (*Dulo*), Morval (*Morvall*), St Martin
by Looe (*Martyn*), Talland (*Tallan*), Pelynt (*Plenynt*), Lanteglos by Fowey
(*Lanteglos*), Lansallos (*Lansalwis*), St Veep (*Wepe*), Lanreath (*Lanrathowe*),
7s 5½d each; St Pinnock (*Pynnok*), 5s; St Neot (*Nyott*), 7s 5½d; Warleggan
(*Walregan*), 2s; Cardinham (*Cardynan*), 7s 5½d.   Total: £5 3s 11½d

c. Dy. of Powder:
Fowey (*Fowy*), 2s 6½d; Tywardreath (*Trewardeith*), 19s 2½d; St Austell
(*Austell*), 7s 5½d; St Mewan (*Mewan*), 6s; St Ewe (*Ewa*), 7s 5½d; Mevagissey
(*Mevagisby*), 4s; Goran, 6s 8d; Caryhays *alias* St Stephen in Brannel (*Caryhoes*),
Creed (*Crede*), 7s 5½d each; Ladock (*Ladok*), 6s 8d; Probus, Tregoney
(*Tregonye*), 7s 5½d each; St Just in Roseland (*St Just*), 4s; Veryan (*Elerky*),
Philleigh (*Eglosros*), Ruan Lanihorne (*Lanyhorne*), 7s 5½d each; Lamorran
(*Lamoren*), 3s 4d; St Michael Penkivel (*Penkevell*), 5s; *Krive* (*unid.*), 6s 8d; St
Allen (*Alune*), 5s; St Clement (*Moreske*), 7s 5½d; Legh (*Lee*) and Kenwyn
(*Kenewyn*), 10s 8d; Feock (*Feok*), 6s 8d; Roche, 7s 5½d; Truro (*Truru*), 4s.
                                                Total: £8 11s 5½d

d. [fo. 133] Dy. of Kerier (*Ker'*), Co.:
Gwennap (*Weneppe*), 7s 5½d; Stythians (*Stedyans*), 6s 8d; Mawnan, 3s 4d;
Constantine (*Constantyne*), 7s 4d; Mawgan, 7s 5½d; Manaccan, 5s; St Antony
in Meneage (*Antony*), 3s 4d; St Keverne (*Kewryn*), 7s 5½d; Grade (*Grada*),
3s 4d; Landewednack (*Landewynnek*), 6s 8d; Mullion (*Melian*), 7s 5½d; Ruan
Major (*Rumon Major*), 5s; Cury (*Corantyn*), Breage (*Breki*), Wendron, Helston,
Sithney (*Sithny*), 7s 5½d each.   Total: £5 2s 9½d

e. Dy. of Penwith, Co.:
Perranuthnoe (*Uthno*), 4s; St Hillary (*Hillary*), Gulval (*Lanyskelegh*), Paul
(*Paule*), Sancreed (*Sancrede*), St Just (*Juste*), Madron (*Madren*), Ludgvan (*Lud-
van*), St Erth (*Ergh*), Lelant (*Lananta*), Gwinear (*Wynnyer*), Crowan (*Crewen*),
Camborn (*Cambron*), Illogan (*Illogans*), 7s 5½d each; Redruth (*Redruyth*), 5s;
Phillack and Gwithian (*Felys et Conor*), 12s; Zennor (*Senar*), 7s 5½d.
                                                Total: £6 5s 5d

f. Dy. of Pyder (*Pider*), Co.:
Cubert (*Cuthbert*), Newlyn, St Enoder (*Ennoder*), 7s 5½d each; Colan, 4s;
Mawgan, St Columb Major (*Columba Major*), St Wenn (*Wenna*), 7s 5½d;
Withiel, 5s; Lanivet (*Lanyvet*), 7s 5½d.   Total: 56s 2½d

g. Dy. of Trigg Minor (*Minoris Trigge*), Co.:
Bodmin (*Bodmyn*), 4s; Helland (*Hellond*), 5s; Blisland (*Bliston*), St Breward

(*Breward*), 7s 5½d each; Michaelstow, 5s; St Mabyn (*Mabyn*), St Tudy (*Tudi*), St Kew (*Kewa*), Minster (*Mynstre*), St Teath (*Tetha*), Lanteglos by Camelford (*Lanteglos*), Tintagel (*Tyndagill*), 7s 5½d each; Trevalga, Forrabury (*Forebury*), 11½d each; Minster [*sic*, repeated], 7s 5½d; Lesnewth, 5s; Endellion (*Endelyvent*) and prebends therein of St Nicholas Melaneak, of Peter Tregose and of John Myles, 22½d each.   Total: £4 19s 10d

h. Dy. of Trigg Major (*Majoris Trigge*), Co.:
St Juliot (*Julyt*), Otterham (*Oterham*), 5s each; St Gennys (*Genys*), Poundstock (*Poundistok*), Jacobstow (*Jacobistow*), Week St Mary (*Weke sancte Marie*), Marhamchurch, Launcells (*Launcels*), Stratton, Poughill (*Poghill*), Kilkhampton (*Kylkhampton*), Morwenstow (*Morestow*), Whitstone (*Whitton*), North Petherwin (*Northpederwyn*), Treviglas (*Treweglis*), Warbstow (*Warbistow*), Davidstow (*Dewstow*), St Clether (*Cleder*), Egloskerry (*Egliskery*), Altarnum (*Alternon*), 7s 5½d each.   Total: £8 13s 4½d

TOTAL PROCURATIONS IN ARCHDEACONRY OF CORNWALL:
                                                  £46 17s 9½d

335.   Procurations in the archdeaconry of Totnes (*Totton'*), De.:

a. Dy. of Moretonhampstead (*Morton'*), De.:
Ilsington (*Ilsyngton*), Bovey Tracey (*Boveytracy*), Widecombe in the Moor (*Widecomb*), 6s 8d each; Manaton, North Bovey (*Northbovy*), 5s each; Moretonhampstead, Lustleigh (*Lustlegh*), 6s 8d each; Hennock (*Heanok*), 5s; Ideford, 4s; Kingsteignton (*Teyngton Regis*), 6s 8d; Highweek (*Hewike*), 5s.
                                                  [Total: £3 4s]

b. [fo. 133v] Dy. of Ipplepen (*Ippl'*), De.:
Berry Pomeroy (*Birypomeray*), Brixham, 6s 8d each; Abbotskerswell (*Carshwill Abbatis*), 4s; Denbury (*Denebury*), 3s; Torbryan (*Torrebrian*), 5s; Broadhempston (*Hempston Magna*), 3s; Ipplepen, 6s 8d; Torre (*Torre Abbatis*), Wolborough (*Wolburgh*), Little Hempston (*Hempston Parva*), nil.   [Total: £1 15s]

c. Dy. of Totnes (*Totton'*), De.:
Ashprington (*Aishpryngton*), 6s 8d; Cornworthy, 5s; Townstal (*Townestall*), Stoke Fleming (*Stokeflemyng*), Blackawton (*Blakaueton*), Diptford (*Depeford*), South Brent (*Brent*), 6s 8d each; Dean Prior (*Deneprior*), 5s; Rattery (*Rattre*), 6s 8d; Dartington (*Dertyngton*), 5s; Totnes, 6s 8d; Holne (*Hall*), 4s; Harberton (*Hurberton*), Dittisham (Diddeham), 6s 8d; Buckfastleigh (*Bucfastlegh*), nil.
                                                  [Total: £4 5s 8d]

d. Dy. of Woodleigh (*Wodelegh*), De.:
Stokenham (*Stokyngham*), 6s 8d; South Pool (*Poole*), Portlemouth (*Portelemouth*), Charleston, 5s each; West Alvington (*Alvyngton*), Malborough (*Malburgh*), 6s 8d each; South Milton (*Milton*), nil; Thurlestone (*Thurleston*), Churchstow (*Churstow*), 5s each; Kingsbridge (*Kyngisbrige*), nil; Bigbury, 6s 8d; Ringmore (*Ridmore*), 4s; Aveton Giffard, Loddiswell (*Lodiswill*), 6s 8d each; Woodleigh (*Wodelegh*), 5s; Moreleigh (*Morlegh*), 3s; East Allington (*Alyngton*), Slapton, 6s 8d each; Dodbrooke (*Dodbroke*), nil.   [Total: £4 10s 4d]

e. Dy. of Plympton, De.:
Cornwood (*Cornwode*), 6s 8d; Harford (*Herpforde*), Huish (*Hiwish*), 4s each; Modbury, Ugborough (*Ugburgh*), Ermington (*Ermynton*), Holbeton, Yealmpton (*Yalmpton*), Newton Ferrers, 6s 8d each; Plymouth (*Sutton*), 5s.

[Total: £2 19s 8d]

f. Dy. of Tamerton, De.:
Egg Buckland (*Egebokelond*), 5s; Stoke Damarel (*Stokedamerell*), 4s; Tamerton Foliot (*Tamerton*), 5s; Buckland Monachorum (*Bokelond Monachorum*), 6s 8d; Marytavy (*Tavy Marie*), 4s; Petertavy (*Tavy Petri*), 5s; Whitchurch, Bere Ferrers, 6s 8d each; Walkhampton, 5s; Meavy (*Mewy*), 6s; Bickleigh (*Bikelegh*), 4s; Sheepstor (*Shittister*), nil.   [Total: £2 18s]

g. Dy. of Tavistock (*Tavistok*), De.:
Bridestowe (*Bristow*), 6s 8d; Sourton, nil; Lydford, Coryton, 3s each; Marystow (*Stow Marie*), 6s 8d; Sydenham Damarel (*Siddeham*), nil; Milton Abbot (*Milton Abbatis*), 6s 8d; Dunterton, Bradstone (*Bratston*), Kelly, 3s each; Lifton (*Lyfton*), 6s 8d; Virginstow (*Virgynstow*), nil. Broadwoodwidger (*Brodewodewiger*), 6s 8d; Stowford, 4s; Lewtrenchard, 3s; Tavistock, nil.

[Total: £3 2s]

h. Dy. of Holsworthy (*Hall'*), De.:
Milton Damarel (*Milton Damerell*), 6s 8d; Cookbury (*Cokebury*), Abbots Bickington (*Bukyngton*), Luffincott (*Lofyngcote*), nil; Bridgerule (*Brigruell*), 5s; Holsworthy (*Hallisworthy*), Bradworthy (*Brodeworthy*), 6s 8d each; Sutcombe (*Suttecombe*), Putford, Thornbury, Bradford, 5s each; Black Torrington (*Blaktoriton*), 6s 8d; Halwill, 5s; Ashwater, 6s 8d; Clawton, Tetcott (*Tettecote*), 5s each; Pyworthy (*Piworthy*), 6s; Hollacombe (*Holcombe*), nil.

Total: £3 19s 4d

j. [fo. 134] Dy. of Okhampton (*Okhampton*), De.:
Germansweek (*Weke sancti Germani*), 3s; Bratton Clovelly (*Bratton*), 6s 8d; Beaworthy, 5s; Northlew, 6s 8d; Highampton (*Heghampton*), Monk Okehampton (*Monkokhampton*), 4s each; Hetherlegh (*Hatherlegh*), 6s 8d; Broadwood Kelly (*Brodewodekelly*), 4s; Sampford Courtenay, 6s 8d; Belstone (*Belton*), Exbourne (*Ekisborn*), Jacobstow (*Stow sancti Jacobi*), Inwardleigh (*Inwardelegh*), Okehampton, 5s each; Honeychurch (*Honychurch*), Ashbury (*Aishbury*), nil.   3 11s 8d

TOTAL PROCURATIONS IN ARCHDEACONRY OF TOTNES: £30 4s 8d

TOTAL PROCURATIONS OF PARISH CHURCHES IN EXETER DIOC.:
£141 18d

336.   Procurations of religious houses and collegiate churches.
a. Archdeaconry of Exeter:
Prior of St Nicholas, Exeter, and coll. ch. of Ottery St Mary, 26s 8d each; coll. ch. of Crediton, 67s 10d; abbess of Canonsleigh and prioress of Polsloe, 26s 8d each.

b. Archdeaconry of Barnstaple:
Prior of Pilton, 20s; ch. of Hartland (*Hartlond*), [*blank*]; ch. of Launceston, 13s 8d; ch. of Bodmin (*Bodmian*), 13s; ch. of Tywardreath, [*blank*]; prior of St Germans, 8s.[1]

> [1] Launceston, Bodmin, Tywardreath and St Germans were in fact in the archdeaconry of Cornwall.

c. Archdeaconry of Totnes:
Ch. of Tavistock, [*blank*]; ch. of Plympton, 20s; r. of Slapton coll., [*blank*]; prior of Totnes, [*blank*].

d. [Archdeaconry of Cornwall:]
Coll. of Crantock, [*blank*]; coll. of St Thomas of Penryn, [*blank*]; coll. of St Thomas of Penryn, [*blank*].

337.   Pensions due to the bps. of Exeter annually from churches:
Coll. of Slapton at Michaelmas, 40s; ch. of South Tawton, De., at Easter, 13s 4d; abbot of Rewley (*de regali loco*), Ox., for ch. of Stithians (*Stediane*), Co., at Easter, 26s 8d; coll. of Windsor, Brk., for ch. of Saltash (*Saltaish*), Co., at [*blank*], 26s 8d; ch. of Stokenham (*Stokynham*), De. [appropriated to and conv. of Bisham], [*blank*]; ch. of Bampton (*Baunton*). De. [appropriated to abbot and conv. of Buckland], 20s.

338.   Account of Peter Williams, notary public by apostolic and imperial authority, appointed by Mr Robert Shirborn as scribe of his acts and collector of the spiritual revenues of the dioc. of Exeter *sede vacante*, from 4 May 1492 to 20 Jan. 1493.

Procurations of the parish chs. of the dioc. as detailed in list for each archdeaconry above: £147 14s 2d
Procurations of religious houses and coll. chs., as detailed in account of Mr Thomas Elyot lately rendered to Peter Courtenay, formerly bp. of Exeter, and signed by his own hand: £2 6s 8d[1]
Annual pension payable to bp. of Exeter for the indemnity of Slapton: £2
Probate of testaments before the feast of St Peter *ad Vincula*, as detailed in the register [*sic*]:[2]   £11 6s 4d
Probate of testaments after the feast of St Peter *ad Vincula*, as detailed in the register [*sic*]:   £16 18s 10d
Testaments pertaining to the prerogative of the abp. of Canterbury, as detailed in the register: £19 7s 6d
Fees of the rural deans of the whole dioc.:[3]   £2 17s
Fees for inst. to parish chs. after the feast of St Peter, as detailed in the register of insts.:   £5 6s 8d
Received from the vacancies of chs.:   £4 6s 8d

TOTAL RECEIPTS BY PETER WILLIAM: £212 3s 9d

Allowance for the fees of the rural deans[4] that year, *viz.* 42s to the eight deans of the archdeaconry of Exeter, 30s 8d to the six deans of the archdeaconry of Barnstaple, 56s 8d to the eight deans of the archdeaconry of Cornwall and

30s 8d to the nine deans of the archdeaconry of Totnes, as detailed in the list for this year above this account: £7 19s 6d

Allowance for procurations not paid: allowance is sought for procurations of Mr James Babbe for his chs. of Ashprington (*Aishprynton*), De., 6s 8d, and Woodleigh (*Wodelegh*), De., 5s; of Mr John Burton for his ch. of Whimple (*Whympell*), De., 6s 8d; of the prioress of Cornworthy for her ch. of Cornworthy, De., 5s; of Nicholas Melconek for his prebend in ch. of Endellion (*sancte Endeliente*), Co., 22½d; for the procuration of Colaton Raleigh (*Coliton*), De., 18d; for the archidiaconal [*sic*] procuration of Ottery St Mary, 6s 8d; of the conv. ch. of Canonsleigh, 26s 8d; of the ch. of Payhembury, De., 5s 4d, as is detailed in the list for this year above this account: £3 5s 4½d

Allowance for various expenses paid to various persons in the course of the commissary's itinerary, according to the account-book thereof, £8 5s 2d, and for various other expenses according to the schedule, £5 13s 2d.

Total: £13 19s 4d

Allowance for the sum of £185 5s 7d paid to the abp. and to Mr Robert Shirborn, his commissary in Exeter dioc., at various times in cash:

£185 5s 7d

TOTAL OF ALL ALLOWANCES, EXPENSES AND PAYMENTS MADE BY PETER WILLIAM: £210 9s 9½d

[1] This sum is smaller than that expected, according to no. 336. Nos. 285–6 provide evidence of resistance to procurations. In the vacancy of 1519 procurations were received from the coll. chs. of Crediton and Ottery St Mary and from the monasteries of St Nicholas Exeter, Polsloe and Pilton; the total then was £7 10s 11d (Reg. Warham, fo. 275v).

[2] The only testaments transcribed or listed above are those pertaining to the abp.'s prerogative.

[3] This entry is expanded in 1519: fees paid by the thirty-one rural deans of the dioc. at the time of their admission at the rate of 2s each, total 57s (Reg. Warham, fo. 275).

[4] This is expanded in the 1503 vacancy as fees for their service during the visitation; in that year only 57s 4d was paid (Reg. Warham, fo. 212v).

[fo. 135] PROCEEDINGS AND ACTS DONE BY THE WORTHY MASTER ROGER CHURCH, DECR. D., OFFICIAL, COMMISSARY *SEDE VACANTE* AND GUARDIAN OF THE SPIRITUALITY OF THE CITIES AND DIOCESE OF BATH AND WELLS BY AUTHORITY OF THE VERY REVEREND FATHER IN CHRIST AND LORD JOHN, BY DIVINE MERCY CARDINAL PRIEST OF ST ANASTASIA IN THE HOLY ROMAN CHURCH, ARCHBISHOP OF CANTERBURY, PRIMATE OF ALL ENGLAND AND LEGATE OF THE APOSTOLIC SEE, THE SEE OF BATH AND WELLS BEING VACANT BY THE TRANSLATION OF THE REVEREND FATHER AND LORD RICHARD FROM THOSE CHURCHES TO THAT OF DURHAM IN THE PROVINCE OF YORK, THESE PROCEEDINGS BEING CONDUCTED FROM 1 JANUARY 1495 AND ENREGISTERED IN THE FOLLOWING FORM.

> *Note*: the see became vacant by the translation of Richard Fox to the see of Durham on 30 July 1494, but the temporalities of Durham were not restored to him until 8 Dec. 1494. The see was filled by the translation of Oliver King from Exeter on 6 Nov. 1495.

339.   In the chapter house of the cath. ch. in the presence of the prior and chapter Mr John Barett, notary public by apostolic authority, appeared before Mr Church and presented a commission from the abp., requesting him on the abp.'s behalf to proceed according to its tenor. Mr Church, because of his reverence for the abp., accepted the commission, which was read publicly by Mr Barett. Bath, 8 Jan, 1495.

340.   Commission with powers of canonical coercion to Mr Roger Church, Decr.D., as vicar-general and guardian of the spiritualities of the see of Bath and Wells in the vacancy following the translation of bp. Richard to the see of Durham, with the powers specified in no. 1 above. Lambeth, 12 Dec. 1494.

341.   [fo. 135v] Mandate directed to the archd. of Bath or his Official inhibiting the exercise of any inferior jurisdiction during the visitation of the archdeaconry. Wells, 12 Jan. 1495.

342.   Citation directed to the archd. of Bath or his Official for the visitation of the religious houses, clergy and people of the archdeaconry, the dates and locations being listed in an attached schedule [not transcribed]. Citation received on 13 Jan. Certificate of the Official dated 20 Jan. Wells, 12 Jan. 1495.

343.   [fo. 136] Similar inhibition directed to the archd. of Wells or his Official. Wells, 12 Jan. 1495.

344.   Similar citation directed to the archd. of Wells or his Official. Wells, 12 Jan. 1495.

345.   Similar inhibition directed to the archd. of Taunton or his Official. Wells, 12 Jan. 1495.

346.   Similar citation directed to the archd. of Taunton or his Official. Wells, 12 Jan. 1495.

347.   [fo. 136v] Citation of the prior and conv. of Bath (*Bathon'*), O.S.B., to submit to visitation on Friday 30 Jan. Bath, 20 Jan. 1495.
Citation received 20 Jan. Certificate of the prior dated 30. Jan., with a schedule of the names of those bound to attend:
Mr John Cantlowe, prior; David Pensforde, subprior; John Norton, precentor; John Abyndon; Richard Forde, chamberlain; John Swaynyswyke; William Eyles, prior of Dunster; Richard Wydycombe; Thomas Brystowe; William Byrde, scholar at Oxford; Thomas Browne; Thomas Gregory and Richard Pestell, at Dunster; William Royall; Thomas Bath; John Wyke, at Dunster; John Wurcetur; John Compton, John Keynysham; Robert Pavy and John Cowper, accolites; Thomas Bekyngton, not professed.

348.   Citation of the abbot and conv. of Glastonbury (*Glaston'*), O.S.B., to submit to visitation on 6 Feb. Bath, 20 Jan. 1495.
Certificate of the abbot dated 4 Feb., with a schedule of the names of those bound to attend:
Richard Bere, abbot; Thomas Mason, prior; John Wolyngton, William Pedurton, Thomas Excetur, Thomas Worspring, Robert Camell, John Barington, William Wiche, John Dultyng, Roger Andrewe, John Scovyld, Richard Flynte, Richard Felde, Nicholas Barkelay, Peter Weston, William Cheddur, John Bayly, William Forde, John Lymsam, William Water, John Marke, John Shepton, John Barnarde, Thomas Dunster, John Wynchcombe, Richard Wylton, Alexander Colyns, William Newton, William Stowell, Edward Coker, John Mylton, Richard Mylbourne, John Shelton, John Marten, John Brent, William Axbrigge, Richard Wynterburne, Henry Colmer, William Newporte, Nicholas Wedmore, Robert Clerke, Thomas Bonerant, John Frome, Nicholas London, Thomas Sutton, Robert Strete, John Taunton, John Davyngton, John Glastonbury, John Bevynge, Thomas Dunston.
On 6 Feb. the commissary sat judicially in the chapter house and canonically visited the abbey in head and members, and the abbot and all the brethren humbly submitted to visitation. After he had reformed those things which according to law should be reformed, he dissolved the visitation.

349.   [fo. 137] The commissary canonically visited the abbey of Keynsham (*Keynysham*), O.S.A., in head and members, and abbot John Gylmyn and all the brethren humbly submitted to visitation. Keynsham, 31 Jan. 1495.

350.   The commissary canonically visited the priory of Bruton, O.S.A., in head and members, and prior John Henton and all the brethren humbly submitted to visitation. Bruton, 10 Feb. 1495.

351.   The commissary canonically visited the abbey of Muchelney, O.S.B., in head and members, and abbot William Wyke and all the brethren humbly submitted to visitation. Muchelney, 14 Feb. 1495.

352.   The commissary canonically visited the priory of Taunton, O.S.A., in head and members, and prior John Prowce and all the brethren humbly submitted to visitation. Taunton, 17 Feb. 1495.

353.   The commissary canonically visited the priory of Barlinch (*Berlinch*), O.S.A., in head and members, and prior Thomas Lyrd and all the brethren humbly submitted to visitation. Barlinch, 19 Feb. 1495.

354.   The commissary canonically visited the abbey of Athelney, O.S.B., in head and members, and abbot John George and all the brethren humbly submitted to visitation. Athelney, 25 Feb. 1495.

355.   [fo. 137v] The commissary canonically visited the priory of Worspring, O.S.A., in head and members, and the prior and all the brethren humbly submitted to visitation. Worspring, 26 Feb. 1495.

356.   Citation of the dean and chapter of Wells to submit to visitation on Saturday 27 Feb. Bath, 20 Jan. 1495.
Citation received 23 Jan. Certificate of William Bokett, subdean, dated 26 Feb., with the names of those cited listed in an attached schedule [not transcribed].
    On 27 Feb. the commissary canonically visited the cath. ch. of Wells in head and members, and the canons, vicars choral and annivellars humbly submitted to visitation.

357.   Ordinations celebrated in the conventual ch. of the hospital of St John the Baptist, Wells, on the abp.'s authority, by Thomas bp. of Tenos (*Tinen'*) on 13 Mar. 1495.

a. *Accolites*

Henry Turnour, William Gaucyny, Robert Venaunce, Richard Walter, John Philip, John Denham, William Ferseman.
Thomas ap Ryce, John David, of Llandaff dioc.
Thomas ap John of St Davids dioc.
James Serle of Exeter dioc.
John Byggys of Salisbury dioc.

b. [fo. 138] *Subdeacons*

John Wade, to t. of Bath (*Bathon'*) priory.
William Macy, to t. of Milton (*Mydleton*) abbey, Salisbury dioc.
Richard Olyver of Exeter dioc., by l.d., to t. of Glasney (*Glasneya in Cornubia*) coll.
Alexander Meryfild of Exeter dioc., by l.d., to t. of Launceston (*Lancastre, sic*) priory.
John Coxdon, to t. of Forde (*Forde*) abbey, Exeter dioc.
Thomas Payne, to t. of Keynsham (*Keynyssham*) abbey.
William Pyers of Exeter dioc., by l.d., to t. of Hartland (*Hertlonde*) abbey.
Robert Clerke, m. of Glastonbury (*Glaston'*).

c. *Deacons*

John Maiour of Exeter dioc., by l.d., to t. of dean and chapter of Exeter cath.
Robert Richman of Winchester dioc., by l.d., to t. of Monkton Farleigh (*Farlegh*) priory, Salisbury dioc.
Germanus Dawe of Exeter dioc., by l.d., to t. of Tywardreath (*Tydworthe*) priory.
David Lange of Salisbury dioc., by l.d., to t. of Abbotsbury (*Abbatisbury*) abbey.
Robert Chaper of Salisbury dioc., by l.d., to t. of Cerne abbey.
Richard Volvell, John Jamett, cans. of Bruton.
Thomas Broke, m. of Glastonbury.
John Burford, William Gregory, cans. of Taunton.
John Chamberleyn, m. of Hinton (*Henton*) charterhouse.
Thomas Bomaunt, m. of Glastonbury.

d. *Priests*

Thomas Redbert, to t. of Montacute (*Montagewe*) priory.
William Canyngton, m. of Muchelney.
John Cove, can. of Barlinch (*Berliche*).
John Lewys, m. of Witham (*Wytham*).
John Peke, John Austen, ms. of Tywardreath (*Tydewardreth*) priory.
William Morepathe, m. of Glastonbury.

[fo. 138v blank]

[fo. 139] ACCOUNTS OF THE VACANCY OF THE SEE FROM CHRISTMAS 1494 to CHRISTMAS 1495.

358.   PROCURATIONS OF RELIGIOUS HOUSES:
Dean and chapter of Wells (*Wellen'*), prior of Bath (*Bathon'*), abbots of Keynsham (*Keynessham*), Glastonbury, Muchelney, priors of Taunton and Barlinch (*Berlinche*), abbot of Athelney, priors of Bruton and Worspring (*Wospring*), 66s 8d each.   Total: £33 6s 8d

359.   PROCURATIONS OF RURAL DEANERIES:

a. Archdeaconry of Bath
Dys. of Stalls (*Stallys*) and Redcliffe (*Radcliff*), 66s 8d each. Total: £6 13s 4d

b. Archdeaconry of Wells
Dys. of Frome, Cary, Marston (*Merston*), Pawlett (*Paulet*), Axbridge (*Axbrigge*), Ilchester (*Yllcestre*), 66s 8d each.   Total: £20

c. Archdeaconry of Taunton
Dys. of Crewkerne (*Crockhorne*), Taunton, Dunster and Bridgewater (*Brigwater*), 66s 8d each.   Total: £13 6s 8d

TOTAL PROCURATIONS: £73 6s 8d

360.   RECEIPTS FOR INSTITUTIONS TO BENEFICES AND INQUISITIONS INTO THE RIGHT OF PATRONAGE:
For inst. to chs. of Thorne Falcon (*Thorne Fawkyn*), Bathealton (*Bathiolton*), Somerton, Muchelney, Norton, [*blank*] and inquisition into same, Nettle-combe (*Netilcombe*) and inquisition into same, [*blank*] and inquisition into same, 6s 8d each.   Total: 73s 4d

361. RECEIPTS FOR THE PROBATE OF TESTAMENTS:
For probate of William Mey of Chard (*Sherde*), 12d; Richard Colyar of Curry Mallet (*Corymalett*), 10s; John Wylcombe, 23s 4d; Ralph Turner of Hill Farraunce (*Hilferons*), 2s; r. of Treborough (*Trebourgh*), 20d; Thomas Dunkyn of Nettlecombe (*Netilcombe*), 12d; Catherine Harrys of Dunster, 3s 4d; John Luker of Withycombe (*Withicombe*), 9s; John Chilcote of Monksilver, 12d; Nicholas Slyme of Minehead (*Mynehede*), 16d; John Towker of *Hewiche* (*unid.*) 12d; John Tyrrel of Chillington, 3s; Patrick Smarte of Minehead (*Mynhed*), 12d; John Ever, 8s; John Lathwell of Wootton (*Wotton*), 3s; Robert Hancoke of Brompton, 5s; Philip Boydon, 18d; John Wylcoke of *Chirch* [? Church Hill], 11s; John Burlond of Staplegrove (*Stapulgrove*), 5s; Richard Slappe of Kingston (*Kyngiston*), 3s; William Gore of Selworthy, 2s; Robert Huyssh of Brushford (*Busshford*), 2s 8d; Thomas Brice of Kingston, 2s; Richard Frere of Stogursey (*Stowegurcy*), 12d; John Bartelett, 3s 4d; Walter Morys of Kingston, 12d; Richard Colbronde of Pitminster (*Pitmystre*), 15s; John Petigrue of Pensford, 10s; William Knyght of Congresbury (*Congarisby*), 10s; John Radnare, v. of Wellow (*Wellowe*), 50s; John Barton of Redcliffe (*Radclif*), 12d; John Crosse of Nempnett Thrubwell (*Nempnet*), 2s 6d; Thomas Levemore, 5s; John Frenssh of Castle Cary (*Cary*), 6s 8d; Isabelle Horsley, 20d; John Kynsham of Keynsham, 16d; Richard Hooker of Taunton, 6s 8d; John Crosse of Exton, 6s 8d; Agnes Kyrse of Wells, 20d; Robert Warderoper of Bridgewater (*Brigwater*), 3s 4d; John of the city of Wells, 6s 8d; Henry Harding of Chew [Magna *or* Stoke], 8s; John Robyns of Chewton Mendip (*Chewton*), 20d; Lewis Wever, 12d; John Grenefeld, 2s; Thomas Gardyner, 5s; John Hubbow, 12d; John Keynysham, 20d.   Total: £13 10s 10d

362.   [fo. 139v] RECEIPTS FOR THE RECONCILIATION OF CHURCHES AND CEMETERIES:
Ch. of St Cuthbert, Wells (*Wellie*), and cemeteries of St Andrew, Wells, and Compton Dundon (*Cumptondunden*), 66s 8d each.   Total: £10

363.   For the confirmation of Mr Gilbert, can. and prior-elect of Bruton, £10.

364.   PENSIONS DUE AT MICHAELMAS:
From ch. of Butleigh (*Butley*), 6s 8d; from chs. of Curry Rivel (*Corywell*) and Yeovil (*Yevill*), 3s 4d each.   Total: 13s 4d

365.   TOTAL RECEIPTS FROM PROCURATIONS, PROBATE, INSTITUTIONS, RECONCILIATION AND OTHER SPIRITUAL REVENUES: £110 4s 2d

From which:

Paid to Mr Richard Esmond for his labours in preaching the word of God for one week, 6s 8d; to Mr Walter Morys for the same task, 40s; paid to Mr John Baret on 7 Apr. by William Potkyn, £60; paid to Mr John Baret on 25 July by William Potkyn, £11 3s 4d; paid to Mr John Barett by William Potkyn, £8 4s; paid to Mr Baret on 12 Dec. by William Potkyn, £8 16s 10d; paid to Mr Baret on 31 Dec. by William Potkyn for reconciliation of Compton Dundon (*Comptondandon*), 66s 8d; paid to Mr Baret by Mr John Botley for inst. to ch. of Norton, 6s 8d; paid by Mr Thomas Mades for procurations of cath. ch. of Wells, 66s 8d; for the expenses of Mr Church in his visitation, £12.

TOTAL OF ALL PAYMENTS AND EXPENSES: £109 10s 10d

[fo. 142] ACTS AND PROCEEDINGS CONDUCTED BY THE WORTHY MASTER ROGER CHIRCHE, DECR. D., COMMISSARY AND GUARDIAN OF THE SPIRITUALITY OF THE CITY (*sic*) AND DIOCESE OF COVENTRY AND LICHFIELD BY AUTHORITY OF THE VERY REVEREND FATHER IN CHRIST AND LORD JOHN, BY DIVINE MERCY CARDINAL PRIEST OF ST ANASTASIA IN THE HOLY ROMAN CHURCH, ARCHBISHOP OF CANTERBURY, PRIMATE OF ALL ENGLAND AND LEGATE OF THE APOSTOLIC SEE, THE SEE OF COVENTRY AND LICHFIELD BEING VACANT BY THE TRANSLATION OF THE REVEREND FATHER AND LORD WILLIAM, LATELY BISHOP OF THESE CATHEDRAL CHURCHES, TO THAT OF LINCOLN, TO WHICH HE WAS PREFERRED BY APOSTOLIC AUTHORITY: THESE PROCEEDINGS BEING CONDUCTED FROM THE LAST DAY OF FEBURARY 1496 UNTIL 8 NOVEMBER 1496.

> *Note*: the see became vacant by the translation of William Smith to Lincoln on 30 Jan. 1496 and was filled by the provision of John Arundel on 3 Aug. 1496.

366.   In the chapter house of the cath. priory in the presence of the prior and conv. Mr William Potkyn, notary public by apostolic authority, delivered to Mr Roger Chirch, Decr. D., letters of commission from the abp., and requested him to act according to their tenor. Mr Chirch, out of reverence for the abp., accepted the commission which was then publicly read by Mr Potkyn. Coventry (*Coventren'*), 29 Feb. 1496.

367.   Commission with powers of canonical coercion to Mr Roger Church, Decr. D., as vicar-general and guardian of the spirituality of the see of Coventry and Lichfield in the vacancy following the translation of bp. William to the see of Lincoln, with the powers specified in no. 1 above. Lambeth (*Lamehith'*), 31 Jan. 1496.

368.   [fo. 142v] Commission with powers of canonical coercion to Mr Roger Chirch, Decr. D., and Mr Richard Salter, Decr. D., jointly or severally to proceed in the episcopal consistory during the vacancy of the see in all ecclesiastical causes, both *ex officio* and instance, including matrimonial causes, to terminate such causes, to correct and punish the excesses, crimes and faults of any of the abp.'s subjects in the cities and dioc. who are delinquent or who by reason of crime or contract come under ecclesiastical jurisdiction, and to do all else necessary or expedient which pertains to the office of Official of the consistory. Lambeth, 1 Feb. 1496.

369.   Mandate directed to the archb. of Coventry and his Official, inhibiting them and those subject to them from any action prejudicial to the visitation of archdeaconry about to be conducted by Mr Chirch or his commissaries in the abp.'s name. They are to announce that by authority of the vicar-general, or rather of the abp., any licences granted by bp. William or

on his authority concerning parish chs. and cemeteries unconsecrated or polluted or other places which have not received the necessary consecration, licences for the celebration of mass in oratories and chapels, dispensations and licences for non-residence and for the farming of benefices, are suspended and revoked. Lichfield (*Lich'*), 2 Mar. 1496.

[fo. 143 wanting.]

370.   [fo. 144] Similar mandate to the archd. of Stafford and his Official. Lichfield, 2 Mar. 1496.

371.   Similar mandate to the archd. of Derby and his Official. Lichfield, 2 Mar. 1496.

372.   Similar mandate to the archd. of Shrewsbury and his Official. Lichfield, 2 Mar. 1496.

373.   [fo. 144v] Similar mandate to the archd. of Chester and his Official. Lichfield, 2 Mar. 1496.

374.   Citation of the prior and conv. of the cath. priory of Coventry (*Coven'*) [O.S.B.] to submit to visitation and the correction of any faults discovered on 8 Mar. The prior is to certify by letters patent the names of those bound to be present. Coventry, 1 Mar. 1496.
Citation received 6 Mar. Certificate of the prior dated 8 Mar., with a schedule of names of those cited:
Richard Share,[1] prior; William Pollesworth, subprior; Robert Grene, penitencer; Richard Drowthe, steward; John Hewood; Thomas Southam, precentor; Henry Wellys, succentor; Robert Colman, cellarer; John Warde, John Pope, John Belle, William Trowthe, John Bristowe, Robert Derby, Robert Barnesley, ms.; John Weedon, novice; William Wynde, novice.
On 8 Mar. the commissary sat judicially in the chapter house of the priory, and having received the prior's certificate, which was read aloud, he canonically visited the priory in head and members in the name of the abp., and the prior and all the brethren humbly submitted to visitation. After he had reformed those things which in accordance with law should be reformed, he dissolved the visitation.
     [1] Cf. *Fasti 1300–1541, Coventry and Lichfield*, p. 5, where the name of the prior is given, from governmental records, as Richard Coventry.

375.   [fo. 145] Citation of the abbot and conv. of Kenilworth (*Kenelworth*) [O.S.A.] to submit to visitation on Friday 11 Mar. [Undated].
Citation received 5 Mar. Certificate of the abbot dated 10 Mar., with a schedule of names of those cited:
Ralph Maxstoke, abbot; Thomas Mogge, prior; William Curtlyngton, subprior; Philip Walter, precentor; Robert Bromeall, cellarer; Hugh Gleve; Henry Rolston, kitchener; Richard Colshill, almoner; John Balsale, sacrist; John Rogers, John Hasebery, Richard Warewick, professed cans.; Nicholas Smyth, Robert Hervy, John Lyster.

The visitation was duly conducted on 11 Mar.

376.   Citation of the prior and conv. of Maxstoke (*Machestok*) [O.S.A.]
[Undated].
Citation received and certificate of the prior dated 7 Mar., with a schedule of
names of those cited:
John Freman, prior; William Blake, subprior; John Hoyton, William
Ellesmere, Henry Elyett, Robert Hillary, William Noland, Roger Harryson,
Robert Boseworth, Richard Perkyns, professed cans.
The visitation was duly conducted on 14 Mar.

377.   [fo. 145v] Citation of the prior and conv. of Arbury (*Eardbury*)
[O.S.A.] to submit to visitation on Thursday 17 Mar. [Undated].
Citation received 7 Mar. Certificate of the prior with a schedule of names of
those cited:
William Cockes, prior; William Clement, subprior; John Coventre, William
Lynde, William Hynkley, John Byrd, William Rampton, professed cans.
John Burton, professed can. of the house, has been in apostasy for 24 years.
The visitation was duly conducted on 18 [*sic*] Mar.

378.   Citation of the abbess and conv. of Polesworth (*Pollesworth*) [O.S.A.]
to submit to visitation on Saturday 19 Mar. [Undated].
Citation received 7 Mar. Certificate of the abbess with a schedule of names of
those cited:
Margaret Ruskyn, abbess; Ann Fitzherberd, prioress; Elizabeth Foxmore,
subprioress; Elizabeth Fraunces, Edith Lynde, Cecilia Walker, Margaret
Motton, Susan Harecourt, Alice Draper, Margaret Totty, Catherine Ruskyn,
Margaret Casewall, Benedicta Burton, Ann Bothe.
The visitation was duly conducted on 19 Mar.

379.   [fo. 146] Citation of the prior and conv. of Church Gresley (*Greseley*)
[O.S.A.] to submit to visitation on Monday 21 Mar. [Undated].
Citation received 7 Mar. Certificate of the prior with a schedule of the names
of those cited:
Robert Mogge, prior; John Manchestre, subprior; John Tuder, John Selly,
novices.
The visitation was duly conducted on 21 Mar.

380.   Citation of the prior and conv. of Repton (*Rypingdon*) [O.S.A.] to
submit to visitation on Tuesday 22 Mar. [Undated].
Citation received 7 Mar. Certificate of the prior with a schedule of the names
of those cited:
Henry Preiste, prior; John Steyne, subprior; Richard Burton, cellarer;
Richard Clerke, John Welford; William Derby, cellarer of Calke; William
Tutburye, Henry Belton, John Rolton; John Hyntes, subcellarer; William
Machyn, Thomas Daws; Richard Mordock, sacrist; John Wyrkesworth,
novice; Richard Newhall, novice.
The visitation was duly conducted on 22 Mar., and the following injunctions
were issued:

[fo. 146v] First, the prior and each of his brethren was ordered to observe diligently the rule, observances, ordinances and institutes of St Augustine, especially with regard to the observance of the divine office, the refectory, the cloister and the dormitory. The prior was instructed to draw up a full and accurate inventory of all the goods and debts of his house, specifying the name of each creditor, old or new, and to exhibit the written inventory before the commissary at Lichfield by Pentecost, on pain of excommunication.

The prior was instructed to draw up a full and accurate account of the financial state of the house, detailing receipts, payments, expenses and the disposal of goods by himself and his brethren, and to exhibit the account to the commissary at Lichfield by Pentecost, on pain of payment of £5.

The prior was ordered that he should not grant licence to go beyond the bounds of the priory to any of the brethren, nor should they be permitted to go out with a companion save for a specified and honourable reason, under pain of the same penalty.

The canons were ordered not to go out alone into any of their fields, even those within the bounds of the priory, nor should they go out with a companion or companions if there was any female in the field. They should never henceforth have open or clandestine conversation with any woman within the bounds of the house, unless they had previously obtained express licence from the prior, on pain of incarceration for seven days for the first offence, twenty days for the second offence, one month for the third offence, three months for the fourth offence, the penalty thereafter increasing at the prior's discretion. The prior was ordered, by virtue of the demands of canonical obedience and on pain of deprivation of office in perpetuity, that laying aside all excuses he should inflict, or cause to be inflicted, the above-specified penalties whenever one of his brethren was culpable.

The prior was ordered that by Pentecost he should obtain from each of the officials of the house an accurate account of all the possessions of the priory received or disbursed by them by virtue of their office, such accounts to be rendered to the prior and his brethren, or the greater part of them. Henceforth he should demand such accounts at least twice a year, on pain of 40s payable to the fabric of Christ Church, Canterbury, whenever by the connivance, guilt or negligence of the prior such an account is not rendered.

381.   Citation of the abbot and conv. of Darley (*Derley*) [O.S.A.] to submit to visitation on Saturday 26 Mar. [Undated].
Citation received 7 Mar. Certificate of the abbot, with a schedule of names of those cited:
John Aissby, abbot; Ralph Penyston, subprior; Thomas London, cellarer; John Chester, Richard Hegge, William Stewall, Thomas Cannesby, Henry Derby, John Alton, Henry Wyndeley, Thomas Beston, Robert Yeldersley, Thomas Wirksworth, Adam Derby; Richard Callow, novice; Henry Hervy, novice.
The visitation was duly conducted on 26 Mar.

382.   [fo. 147] Citation of the prioress and conv. of Derby [King's Mead, O.S.B.] to submit to visitation on Monday 28 Mar. [Undated].

Citation received 7 Mar. Certificate of the prioress with a schedule of names of those cited:
Margaret Chaundele, prioress; Joan Brewd, Joan Longford, Bryde de Poole, Catherine Bagott, Alice Knolles.
The visitation was duly conducted on 28 Mar.

383.   Citation of the prior and conv. of Tutbury (*Tuttbury*) [O.S.B.] to submit to visitation on 29 Mar. [Undated].
Citation received 7 Mar. Certificate of the prior with a schedule of names of those cited:
William Whalley, prior; Thomas Bradbourne, subprior; Thomas Bermycham, John Barton, Thomas Rolston, John Tuttbury, John Etwall, John Madely, Thomas Brassyngton, Thomas Stone; John Belyngton, novice; Roger Stafford, novice; Thomas Hamburye, novice.
The visitation was duly conducted on 29 Mar.

384.   [fo. 147v] Citation of the abbot and conv. of Burton-on-Trent (*Burton super Trent*) [O.S.B.] to submit to visitation on Monday 11 Apr. [Undated].
Citation received 9 Apr. Certificate of the abbot with a schedule of names of those cited:
William Fligh, abbot; John Burton, prior; John Norton, subprior; William Kenesall, cellarer; John Reptan, succentor; Robert Elyott, John Blount, Thomas Moyott, Christopher Townesley, Christopher Alton, William Bayne, Robert Busbe, Thomas Swayne, Thomas Tutburye, John Poole, Thomas Pyrre, John Harvye, John Poope.
The visitation was duly conducted on 11 Apr.

385.   Citation of the abbot and conv. of Rocester (*Rowcetter*) [O.S.A.] to submit to visitation on Saturday 16 Apr. [Undated].
Citation received 9 Apr. Certificate of the abbot with a schedule of names of those cited:
George Caldon, abbot; William Butlere, prior; John Ensawere, William Horpe, Richard Shenton, William Jhon, John Todde; Roger Rolston, novice; Thomas Taylour, novice.
The visitation was duly conducted on 16 Apr.

386.   [fo. 148] Citation of the prior and conv. of Stone [O.S.A.] to submit to visitation on Tuesday 19 Apr. [Undated].
Citation received 9 Apr. Certificate of the prior with a schedule of names of those cited:
Thomas Forth, bp. of Achonry (*Acaden'*), prior; William Duddisbury, John Reyneford, Robert Atkyn, William Blant, Thomas Barbery, Thomas Matson, Richard Dodycote.
The visitation was duly conducted on 19 Apr.

387.   Citation of the prior and conv. of Trentham [O.S.A.] to submit to visitation on Thursday 21 Apr. [Undated].
Citation received 4 Apr. Certificate of the prior with a schedule of names of those cited:

Thomas Williams, prior; Robert Stringer, subprior. Henry Johnson, Thomas Dakyn, John Deyne; Alexander Foxe, novice; Ralph Thikkyns, novice. The visitation was duly conducted on 21 Apr.

388.   Citation of the prior and conv. of Ranton (*Ronton*) [O.S.A.] to submit to visitation on 21 Apr. [Undated].
Citation received 4 Apr. Certificate of the prior with a schedule of names of those cited:
Richard Smyth, prior; Thomas Ecculsall, Henry Slawton; William Bradgate, novice; Thomas Alton, novice; Richard Thunster, novice.
The visitation was duly conducted on 21 Apr.

389.   [fo. 148v] Citation of the abbot and conv. of Haughmond (*Hagmond*) [O.S.A.] to submit to visitation on Wednesday 27 Apr. [Undated].
Citation received 11 Apr. Certificate of the abbot with a schedule of names of those cited:
Richard Pontisbury, abbot; John Meykin, prior; George Hagiston; William Peers, chamberlain; William Rann; Hugh Mynton, cellarer; John Ferrour, precentor; John Colfox, chap.; William Rolf, novice; Richard Pontisbury, novice; Thomas Gryme, novice.
The visitation was duly conducted on 27 Apr.

390.   Citation of the abbot and conv. of St Peter, Shrewsbury (*Salop*) [O.S.B.] to submit to visitation on Saturday 30 Apr. [Undated].
Citation received 11 Apr. Certificate of the abbot with a schedule of names of those cited:
Thomas Mynde, abbot; Thomas Wynnys, prior and warden of St Winifred's shrine; John Coly, subprior, sacrist and warden of chapel of B.V.M.; John Chesshire, warden of St Catherine's chapel; William Castell, treasurer; Roger Chapman, prior of Morville (*Morefeld*); David Alscote, precentor; Richard Porter, infirmarer, pittancer and master of the works; John Shrousbury, abbot's steward; Laurence Grenelefe, third prior; Irianus Fisshere, Thomas Appary, William Gough; Richard Broughton, chap. and cellarer; Richard Lye, scholar at Oxford; Roger Wright, subsacrist; Thomas Butler, novice.
The visitation was duly conducted on 30 Apr.

391.   [fo. 149] Citation of the prior and conv. of Wombridge (*Wombrigge*) [O.S.A.] to submit to visitation on Monday 2 May. [Undated].
Certificate of the prior with a schedule of names of those cited:
Thomas Forster, prior; William Boydon, William Stacy, William Whyliford, William White.
The visitation was duly conducted on 2 May.

392.   Citation of the abbot and conv. of Lilleshall (*Lylleshull*) [O.S.A.] to submit to visitation on Tuesday 3 May. [Undated].
Citation received 11 Apr. Certificate of the abbot with a schedule of names of those cited:
Robert Fitzjon, abbot; John Smyth, prior; John Danson, John Ofley, Geoffrey Barton, Richard Newport, John Rollys, John Halle, John Hatton,

Christopher Ledis;[1] Thomas Darynton, novice; John Pontisbury, novice; Thomas Butler.[2]
The visitation was duly conducted on 3 May.

[1, 2] It is not clear from MS whether Ledis and Butler are included among novices.

393.   [fo. 149v] Citation of the prioress and conv. of Brewood White Ladies (*monialium albarum de Brewoode*) [O.S.A.] to submit to visitation on Friday 6 May. [Undated].
Citation received 31 Mar. Certificate of the prioress with a schedule of names of those cited:
Alice Wood, prioress; Margaret Cowper, Agnes Vyes, Margaret Sandford, Cecilia Croston.
The visitation was duly conducted on 8 May.

394.   Citation of the prior and conv. of St Thomas the Martyr near Stafford [Baswich, O.S.A.] to submit to visitation on Monday 9 May. [Undated].
Certificate of the prior with a schedule of names of those cited:
William Chedull, prior; John Pirle, subprior; Thomas Hollam, precentor; Ralph Davison; William Stiche, sacrist; Christopher Sympson, Thomas Weynne, John Messingham; Richard Whitell, novice.
The visitation was duly conducted on 9 May.

395.   [fo. 150] Citation of the dean and chapter of the cath. ch. of Lichfield (*Lich'*) to submit to visitation on Monday 16 May, with inhibition of any action prejudicial to the visitation. [Undated].
Certificate of the dean, Mr John Yotton, S.T.P., with a schedule of names of those cited:
Personally apprehended by the dean in the cath.: Mr Richard Salter, preb. of Hansacre (*Handesaker*); Mr Hugh Lehee, preb. of Whittington (*Whitington*).
Cited by means of citations left in their stalls, so that they might be found by their vs. or acquaintances: Mr Charles Both, treasurer and preb. of Sawley (*Sallow*); Mr Robert Slimbridge, precentor and preb. of Bishop's Itchingdon (*Ichynton Episcopi*); Mr Hugh Holdom, preb. of Colwich (*Colwicke*); Mr Henry Ediall; preb. of Gaia Minor; Mr John Moorton, preb. of Bishopshull (*Bishopshill*); Mr John Hervy, preb. of one moiety of Oloughton (*Ufton Cantoris*); Mr Edmund Chadirton, preb. of Bolton; Mr Ralph Hethcote, preb. of Offley (*Offeley*); Mr George Downe, preb. of Freeford (*Freyford*); Mr Oliver Denham, preb. of Wolvey (*Wolvay*); Mr Thomas Worseley, preb. of Tachbrooke (*Tachebroke*); Mr William Pykinham, preb. of Gaia Major; Mr Thomas Neleson, preb. of Longdon; Mr Humphrey Hawardyn, preb. of Tervin (*Tervyn*); Mr William Johns, preb. of other moiety of Oloughton (*Ufton Decani*); Mr Robert Mome, preb. of Sandiacre (*Sandeacre*); Mr John Moore, preb. of Flixton; Mr Thomas Barowe, preb. of Culborough (*Culborowe*); Mr William Smith, preb. of Ryton (*Ruyton*); Mr Richard Delves, preb. of Pipa Parva (*Parva Pipa*); Mr John Argentyne, preb. of Dernford (*Derneford*); Mr John Rawcliff, preb. of Bovenhull (*Bohenhull*).
The forementioned prebs. were cited to appear in the chapter house on 16

111

May, with notification that the visitation would proceed whether or not they were present. The dean also cited the vicars, chaplains and ministers of the church. He made protestation in the name of the cath. ch. of Lichfield, of himself and of his co-residents, that according to long-established custom of the church, its privileges and statutes and compositions with former bps. of Coventry and Lichfield, confirmed by authority of Pope Martin V, the vicars-choral, cantarists and other ministers of the ch. and all the servants of the cans. living within the close are considered to be free and immune from the jurisdiction of the bp. of Coventry and Lichfield and should not be cited, nor are they bound to attend the visitation.[1] If anything, therefore, of the foregoing is found to be contrary or prejudicial to the privileges, statutes, compositions and customs to which he is bound in law, the dean hereby revokes and retracts the same.

[1] For episcopal visitation at Lichfield, see K. Edwards, *The English Secular Cathedrals in the Middle Ages* (2nd edn., Manchester 1967), p. 132. There is no indication in the register that the visitation was conducted in 1496.

396.   [fo. 150v] Citation of the prior and conv. of Burscough (*Burscogh*) [O.S.A.] to submit to visitation on Wednesday 8 June. [Undated].
Certificate of the prior, with a schedule of names of those cited:
Hector Scarisbroke, prior; Hugh Hulme, subprior.
The visitation was duly conducted on 8 June.

397.   Citation of the abbot and conv. of Norton [O.S.A.] to submit to visitation on Monday 13 June. Lichfield, 21 Feb. 1496.
Certificate of the abbot with a schedule of names of those cited:
John Malbone, abbot; William Merton, prior; Robert Wyse, Richard Kynnesley, John Christemas, William Peynketh, John Peynketh, William Norton, Roger Halle.
The visitation was duly conducted on 13 June.

398.   Citation of the prior and conv. of Calwich [O.S.A.] to submit to visitation on Saturday 16 April. Lichfield, 29 Feb. 1496.
Certificate of the prior with a schedule of names of those cited:
Robert Elderbeke, prior; William Kyrkby.
The visitation was duly conducted on 16 Apr.

399.   [fo. 151] Citation of the warden of coll. of Tong (*Tonge*) to submit to visitation on 5 May. [Undated].
Certificate of the warden with a schedule of names of those cited:
Thomas Brown, warden; William Smyth, Ralph Elcocke, John Morys *alias* Pardener.
The visitation was duly conducted on 5 May.

400.   Citation of the prior and conv. of Upholland (*Holond*) [O.S.B.] to submit to visitation on 9 June. [Undated].
Certificate of the prior with a schedule of names of those cited:
Thomas Ecgleston, prior; James Roby, Richard Wuswald, John Smalshefe, Hugh Fayreclof.

The visitation was duly conducted on 9 June.

401. Citation of the prioress and conv. of St Mary, Chester (*Cestr'*) [O.S.B.] to submit to visitation on 16 June. [Undated].
Certificate of the prioress with a schedule of names of those cited:
Margaret Pasmych, prioress; Elizabeth Savage, subprioress; Eleanor Norys, Elizabeth Bekinsall, Florence Waughan, Catherine Asshowe, Joan Aderton, Catherine Tatton, Margery Taylour, Margaret Tatton; Margaret Woodward, not yet professed; Catherine Gawyn, not yet professed.
The visitation was duly conducted on 16 June.

402. [fo. 151v] Citation of the prior and conv. of Birkenhead (*Byrkinhed*) [O.S.B.] to submit to visitation on 18 June. [Undated].
Certificate of the prior with a schedule of names of those cited:
Thomas Chestir, prior; Thomas Meldrom, subprior; Richard Ruthdale, Nicholas Tassye, Roger Rawlyn.
The visitation was duly conducted on 18 June.

403. Citation of the warden of the coll. ch. of Gnosall (*Gnavesall*) to submit to visitation on 23 June. [Undated].
Certificate of the warden with a schedule of the names of those cited:
Mr Edmund Halse, preb. of Chilternhall (*Chiltenhall*); Mr Robert Nonne, preb. of Beverlehall (*Bevlehall*); Mr Henry Best, preb. of Morehall; Richard Ardune, preb. of Seturhall; William Tailour, John Thomasson, Thomas Turelehall, Humphrey Eton, vicars-choral.
The visitation was duly conducted on 23 June.

404. [fo. 152] Mandate directed to the archd. of Coventry and his Official, announcing the intention of the vicar-general to visit the archdeaconry on the days and at the places detailed in the attached schedule [not transcribed in register]. They are to cite or cause to be cited all abbots, priors, rs. and vs. holding any office or ecclesiastical benefice, par. and stip. chaps., and especially those claiming to have the ordinances or foundations of chantries within the archdeaconry. They are also to cite from each parish eight, six or four trustworthy men, according to the size of the parish, who have sound knowledge of the matters into which enquiry will be made. The archd. or his Official, together with those cited, shall appear before the vicar-general or his commissaries to swear an oath of canonical obedience to the abp.; they shall exhibit titles to their dignities and benefices, the foundations and ordinances of their chantries and their letters of ordination, so that they may be enregistered, and shall pay the procurations due to the abp. by virtue of his visitation, and the jurors shall render true testimony in the matters into which enquiry is to be made. The archd. and his Official are to cite all those who do not reside in their benefices as they are bound to do, or who let their benefices to farm, and also those religious or any others who hold appropriated benefices within the archdeaconry or who claim the right to receive pensions, portions or part of the tithe from chs., that they should appear on the day ordained to exhibit their dispensations, licences or graces by virtue of which they make such claim. The archd. and his Official are inhibited, as also are rural deans

113

and other ministers, from any attempt prejudicial to the visitation, and if anything is done in public or in secret to the prejudice of the visitation, the vicar-general hereby revokes such action and declares it void. The archd. or his Official is to certify the vicar-general or his commissary of the date of receipt of this mandate and the names of those cited in each dy., with the reason for their citation. Coventry, 29 Feb. 1496.

405. Certificate of John Parkys, Official of the archd. of Coventry. In accordance with the above mandate, he has cited the dy. of Coventry to appear in the ch. of St Michael, Coventry, on Wednesday 9 Mar., the dy. of Marton (*Merton*) in Southam ch. on Thursday 10 Mar., the dy. of Stoneleigh (*Stoneley*) in Kenilworth (*Kenely*) ch. on Saturday 12 Mar., and the dy. of Arden (*Ardena*) in Coleshill (*Collsul*) ch. on Tuesday 15 Mar., as appears more fully in the attached schedule. 8 Mar. 1496.

406. [fo. 152v] Certificate of similar mandate directed to the archd. of Stafford and his Official, returned by Mr John Cowper, Decr.B., archd.'s Official. By virtue of the mandate which he received on 11 Mar. he has, by the agency of Malus Bate, literate of Stafford, archd.'s apparitor, cited clergy and parishioners to the requisite number to appear on the days and at the places specified. The names of those cited are detailed in an attached schedule. Alveston (*Alveton*), Wa., 18 Apr. 1496.

407. Certificate of a similar mandate by the Official of the archd. of Derby. 20 Mar. 1496.

408. [fo. 153] Certificate of a similar mandate by John Lye, Official of the archd. of Shrewsbury. Shrewsbury, 26 Apr. 1496.

409. Certificate of similar mandate by Mr Thomas Twemlowe, Decr. B., Official of the archd. of Chester. The mandate had been received by him on 10 Mar. 14 May 1496.

INSTITUTIONS

> *Note:* mandates for induction were normally addressed to the appropriate archd. or his Official.

410. [fo. 153v] Inst. of Hugh Grene, pr., to ch. of Wistaston (*Wystaston*), Chs., vac. by res. of Robert Taverner. P. Hugh Egerton, esq., and John Peshale, *generosus*. I. Official of the peculiar jurisdiction of Wybunbury. Lichfield, 7 Apr. 1496.

411. Inst. of Robert Banes, pr., to ch. of Swarkestone (*Swerkeston*), Db., vac. by d. of Thomas Fiddelere. P. Thomas Babington, guardian of Roger Rolleston, minor, heir of Henry Rolleston, deceased, late of Swarkeston. I. archd. of Derby. Lichfield, 7 Apr. 1496.

412. Inst. of Thomas Janyns, pr., to ch. of Norbury, St., vac. by d. of Richard Turnour, P. John Botiller, esq., of Herefordshire. I. archd. of Stafford, Newport, Sa., 24 Apr. 1496.

413.   Inst. of Mr Edmund Aisshton, Decr. B., to ch. of Middleton (*Mydulton*), La., vac. by d. of John Barton, P. Richard Asshton, esq. I. archd. of Chester. Lichfield, 5 May 1496.

414.   Inst. of Mr Robert Canlayn, B.C.L., to perpetual vic. of the altar of St Oswald, king and martyr, in conv. ch. of St Werburgh, Chester (*Cestr'*), vac. by res. of Mr Henry Reynford, Decr. B. P. abbot and conv. of St Werburgh, Chester. I. archd. of Chester. Brewood, St., 7 May 1496.

415.   Inst. of Ralph Sheppard, chap., to ch. of Kirk Langley (*Kyrklangley*), Db., vac. by res. of Richard Rolleston. P. Thomas Twyford, esq. I. archd. of Chester [*sic*]. Assignment of an annual pension of 4 marks from the fruits of the ch. to Richard Rolleston for his food and clothing. Lichfield, 29 May 1496.

416.   Inst. of John Dicon, chap., to the altar of St Michael in the chantry of St Mary Magdalene in parish ch. of Chesterfield (*Chestirfeld*), Db., vac. by d. of John Verdon. P. Thomas Duraunt. I. archd. of Derby. Lichfield, 27 June 1496.

417.   Inst. of John Burman, pr., to ch. of Radbourn (*Rodburne*), Wa., vac. by d. of John Atkyns. P. Sir John Ryssley, kt. of the king's body. I. archd. of Coventry. London, 12 July 1496.

418.   [fo. 154] Inst. of Henry Dixwell, chap., to vic. of Clifton (*Clyfton*), Wa., vac. by res. of Geoffrey Clerk. P. abbot and conv. of St Mary de Pratis, Leicester. I. archd. of Coventry. Assignation of an annual pension of 40s from the fruits of the ch. to Geoffrey Clerk for his food and clothing. Lichfield, 12 Aug. 1496.

419.   Inst. of William Schawe, chap., to ch. of Baxterley, Wa., vac. by res. of Thomas Sowderne. P. abbot and conv. of Merevale, O. Cist. I. archd. of Coventry. Assignment of an annual pension of 13s 8d from the fruits of the ch. to Thomas Sowderne for his food and clothing. Lichfield, 28 Aug. 1496.

420.   Inst. of Robert Bradshawe, chap., to ch. of Aighton (*Aghton*), La., vac. by d. of William Bradshawe. P. Thomas Bradshawe, esq., of Upholland (*Uplitherlond*), La. I. archd. of Chester. Lichfield, 5 Sept. 1496.

421.   Inst. of William Toples, chap., to perpetual chantries of St Mary and St Michael in ch. of Melbourne (*Melborn*), Db., vac. by d. of John Cantevell. P. Robert Shurley, esq., and William Sandes, chap. I. archd. of Derby. Lichfield, 20 Sept. 1496.

422.   Inst. of Thomas Eyre to vic. of Hathersage (*Hathersag*), Db., vac. by d. of Thurstan Eyer. P. prior and conv. of Launde, O.S.A., Lincoln dioc. I. archd. of Derby. Stone priory, 20 Sept. 1496.

423.   Inst. of Roger Eyer, junior, chap., to the altar of St Michael in the perpetual chantry of St Mary Magdalene in the parish ch. of Chesterfield,

Db., vac. by d. of Richard Arwek. P. Thomas Durant of Chesterfield. I. archd. of Derby. Stone priory, 28 Sept. 1496.

424.   Inst. of Mr John Potter, S.T.B., to vic. of Spondon, Db., vac. by res. of Henry Dudlyn. P. master and brethren of Burton Lazars. I. archd. of Coventry. Assignment of an annual pension of 5 marks from the fruits of the ch. to Henry Dudlyn. Priory ot St Thomas near Stafford, 5 Oct. 1496.

425.   Inst. of Richard Dunn, chap., to vic. of Dronfield (*Dronfeld*), Db., vac. by res. of William Byngley. P. abbot and conv. of Beauchief. I. archd. of Derby. Lichfield, 10 Oct. 1496.

426.   [fo. 154v] Inst. of Thomas Rydley, clerk, in the person of his proctor Richard Wybynbury, literate, to prebend and canonry in coll. ch. of St John, Chester, vac. by d. of Mr John Atkyns. P. the king, by virtue of vacancy of the see. I. dean of the coll. ch. or his deputy. Coventry, 16 Oct. 1496.

427.   Inst. of the abp. of Henry Hyckes, chap., to vic. of the prebendal ch. of Tachbrook (*Tuchebroke*), Wa., vac. by d. of Richard Walker, and in the abp.'s collation by virtue of the vacancy of the see. I. dean and chapter of the cath. ch. of Coventry and Lichfield [*sic*]. Lambeth, 4 Nov. 1496.

428.   Ordination celebrated in the cath. ch. of Lichfield on the abp.'s authority by Thomas bp. of Achonry (*Achaden'*) on 28 May 1496.

> *Note*: all ordinands are from the dioc. of Coventry and Lichfield, unless otherwise stated.

a. Accolites:

Secular

Thomas Robyns, Robert Fychett, Thomas Twyford, Robert Tadursall, Ralph Bardow, Henry Cowper, Seth Lighgo, Elias Tay, Edmund Fleccher, Robert Smyth, Thomas Hunt, Roger Scott, Richard Halle, William Barett, Ralph Longford, John Balle, Christopher Johnson, William Turnour, William Twys, Ralph Shawe, James Byrom, Hugh Birde, Thomas Hinxley, Humphrey King, Roger Newton, Ralph Ratclif, John Bisshop, Roger Worthington, John Botfeld, John Wright, John Haynes, Thomas Heywood, Robert Whitington, John Turnar, Peter Halle, William Wylkynson, Richard Holand.

Regular

Christopher Ledys, can. regular of Lilleshall (*Lylleshull*) abbey.
John Lynton, can. regular of Church Gresley (*Grissley*) priory.

b. Subdeacons

Secular

Ralph Holand, John Crowder and Roger Shobilworth, to t. of Whalley abbey.
Humphrey Hert, to t. of Holland Bridge (*Holand*) priory.
Nicholas Payne, to t. of Breadsall (*Bradsal park*) priory.
John Wilshawe, to t. of Merevale (*Miravalle*) abbey.
John Herwe, to t. of Canwell (*Canwal*) priory.

Thomas Pynchware, to t. of St Mary's priory, Chester.
Seth Houghton, to t. of Holland Bridge priory.
William Seyffe, to t. of Farewell (*Ferwall*) priory.
Thomas Stryngare, to t. of hospital of St John the Baptist, Chester (*Cestr'*).
Hugh Yardeley, to t. of Combermere (*Cumbermere*) abbey.
William Bradshay, to t. of Holland Bridge priory.
Richard Sutton, to t. of Darley abbey.
John Beel, to t. of Croxden (*Crokisden*) abbey.
Hugh Columbele, to t. of Darley abbey.
Henry Roper, to t. of Dieulacres (*Dieulenacres*) abbey.
George Blakwall, to t. of Dale abbey.
Edward Pontisbury, to t. of Haughmond (*Hagmond*) abbey.
Robert Barefote, to t. of Dieulacres abbey.
Ralph Hichinson, to t. of Breadsall priory.
Regular
John Anyon, O.P. of Chester.
William Lynse and William Knightley, cans. of Arbury (*Erdbury*) priory,
O.S.A.
Thomas Alton and Richard Tunstall, cans. of Ranton (*Ronton*) priory, O.S.A.

c. [fo. 155] *Deacons*

Secular
John Bancroft, to t. of Combermere (*Cumbermere*) abbey.
Roger Smith, to t. of St Mary's priory, Chester.
John Crewe and Ralph Madok, to t. of Trentham priory.
Otvel Halle, to t. of Norton abbey.
Charles Mynshull, to t. of Vale Royal (*Valle Regali*) abbey.
Nicholas Smith, to t. of St Mary's priory, Chester.
Robert Frene, to t. of Holland Bridge priory.
Humphrey Hassall, to t. of Combermere abbey.
Thomas Ekles, to t. of St Mary's priory, Chester.
Thomas Tonge, to t. of Buildwas (*Bildewas*) abbey.
Henry Forde, to t. of Daventry (*Daventre*) priory.
Thomas Hurste, to t. of Croxden (*Crokisden*) abbey.
Richard Feyrefeld, to t. of Dieulacres (*Dieuleneacres*) abbey.
Otvel Rigeway, to t. of Beauvale (*Belle Vallis*) priory.
William Wyrall, to t. of Combermere abbey.
Henry Alkoke, to t. of Birkenhead (*Byrkinhed*) priory.
Thomas Moston, to t. of Combermere abbey.
Thomas Grene, to t. of Canwell (*Canwall*) priory.
Richard Atkynson, to t. of Church Gresley priory.
John Lancashire, to t. of Whalley abbey.
Thomas Bushell, to t. of Vale Royal abbey.
Edward Champen and Oliver Fleccher, to t. of Dieulacres abbey.
James Aystowe, to t. of Holland Bridge priory.
John Barnys, to t. of Wroxton priory.
John Woode, to t. of hospital of St Giles by Shrewsbury (*Salop'*).
William Buguley, to t. of St Mary's priory, Chester.
John Crosse, to t. of hospital of St Giles by Shrewsbury.

Regulars
John Hycoke, O.P. of Chester.
John Swepston, can. regular of Church Gresley priory.
John Todde, can. regular of Rocester (*Rowcestre*).
William Hatton and William Alben, ms. of Dieulacres, O.Cist.

d. *Priests*

Secular
Humphrey Rugge, to t. of Halesowen abbey.
Laurence Browne, to t. of Whalley abbey.
Simon Acson, to t. of Vale Royal abbey.
Henry Longforth, to t. of Calwich (*Calwick*) priory.
Richard Madok, to t. of St Mary's priory, Chester (*Cestrie*).
Robert Rigby, to t. of Holland Bridge priory.
John Wright, to t. of hospital of St Giles by Shrewsbury.
John Smith, to t. of Tong (*Tonge*) coll.
Richard Whiteaker, to t. of Combermere abbey.
Hugh Laksell, to t. of Whalley abbey.
William Wrightinton, to t. of Birkenhead (*Byrkinhed*) priory.
Ralph Sheparde, to t. of Tutbury priory.
Oliver Rage, to t. of Dale abbey.
Richard Dutton, to t. of Combermere abbey.
Roger Cumbrebache, to t. of Dieulacres abbey.
William Massy, to t. of Combermere abbey.
Robert Cokkes, to t. of Derby [King's Mead] priory.
William Trevenande, to t. of hospital of St Giles by Shrewsbury.
Peter Warde, to t. of Dieulacres abbey.
Thomas Hervy, to t. of Newstead (*de Novo Loco*) priory.
Richard Manson, to t. of Combermere (*Cumbremere*) abbey.
Robert Gundys, to t. of Ranton (*Rannton*) priory.
Richard Huntyngton, to t. of Birkenhead priory.
John Snape, to t. of Basingwerk (*Basingwark*) priory.
Thomas Randoll, to t. of Trentham priory.
John Homfrey, to t. of St Mary's priory, Chester.
John Trafort, to t. of Croxden abbey.
William Gorway, to t. of Halesowen abbey.
Ralph Rage, to t. of Darley (*Derlegh*) abbey.
Robert Eyton, to t. of his prebend of *Langarmewe* and *Dynmerchiant* [*unid.*].[1]
William Southford, to t. of Ranton priory.
Richard Mason, to t. of Halesowen abbey.
Edmund Turnur, to t. of Farewell (*Ferwall*) priory.
Thomas Maderer, to t. of Stone priory.
Laurence Holiwell, to t. of Holland Bridge (*Holande*) priory.
John Hudson, to t. of Dale abbey.
Thomas Newbold, to t. of St Anne's priory, Coventry (*iuxta Coventr'*).
John Lewis, to t. of hospital of St Giles by Shrewsbury.
John Dutton, to t. of St Mary's priory, Chester.
Thomas Holyns, to t. of Dieulacres priory.
Robert Wright, to t. of Burton abbey.

Roger Sumnour, to t. of Arbury (*Erdbury*) priory.
John Cowper and Oliver Ledsham, to t. of St Mary's priory, Chester.
Alexander Birkbeke of Carlise dioc., by l.d., to t. of Lambley (*Lamble*) priory.
Lewis ap Ievan ap Tudur of Bangor dioc., by l.d., to t. of abbey of St Seiriol
[Penmon, Anglesey].
Regular
Robert Capnest, m. of St Werburgh's abbey, Chester.
John Colfoxe, can. regular of Haughmond, O.S.A.

> [1] This prebend has not been identified, but *Dynmerchian* is probably
> Dymmerghion, the older form of Tremeirchion, Flints. This ch. formed part
> of the prebend of Faenol, held by the precentor of St Asaph (John Le Neve,
> *Fasti Ecclesiae Anglicanae* xi: *Welsh Dioceses 1300–1541*, 42n.]

ACCOUNT OF SUMS RECEIVED DURING THE VACANCY OF THE SEE BY MR
ROGER CHURCH, DECR. D., AND WILLIAM POTKYN, NOTARY PUBLIC, HIS
SCRIBE, FROM 29 FEBRUARY TO 8 NOVEMBER 1496.

429.   PROCURATIONS.

a. Archdeaconry of Coventry:
Dys. of Coventry, Marton, Stoneleigh (*Stoneley*), Arden (*Ardena*), 66s 8d each;
prior of Coventry, £6 13s 4d; abbot of Kenilworth (*Kenelworth*), 66s 8d; prior
of Maxstoke, 40s; dean of Astley coll., 20s; prior of Arbury (*Eardbury*), 66s 8d.
Total: £29 13s 4d

b. [fo. 155v] Archdeaconry of Stafford:
Dys. of Lapley and Trysull (*Lappley et Trisill*), Alton and Leek (*Leke*), Stafford
and Newcastle-under-Lyme (*Novo Castro*), Tamworth (*Tameworth*) and
Tutbury, Tamworth coll., abbot of Burton, prior of Tutbury, 66s 8d each;
prior of Sandwell (*Saundwell*), 20s; Gnosall (*Gnovesall*) coll., 26s 8d; cath. ch. of
Lichfield, 53s 4d.   Total: £27 6s 8d

c. Archdeaconry of Derby:
Dys. of Castellar, Repton, Derby (*Derbei*), Ashbourne (*Aisshborne*), High Peak
(*Alto Pecco*), Scarsdale (*Scarisdale*), 66s 8d each; prior of Repton (*Repingdon*),
40s; abbot of Darley, 66s 8d.   Total: £24 6s 8d

d. Archdeaconry of Shrewsbury:
Dys. of Shrewsbury, Newport (*Newporte*), master of St Chad's coll.,
Shrewsbury, 66s 8d each; master of Battlefield (*Batilfeld*) coll., 26s 8d; abbot of
St Peter's, Shrewsbury, 66s 8d.   Total: £12 13s 4d

e. Archdeaconry of Chester:
Dys. of Middlewich (*Medii Wici*), Macclesfield (*Mayfild*), Manchester
(*Manchestre*), Blackburn (*Blakborne*), Leyland (*Leylond*), Warrington (*Wer-
ington*), Frodsham (*Frawesham*), Chester (*Cestr'*), Wirral (*Wyrall*), Malpas,
Nantwich (*Vici Malpani*), 66s 8d each; coll. of St John, Chester, 26s 8d.
Total: £38

TOTAL PROCURATIONS: £132

430. SYNODALS DUE AT EASTER.

a. Archdeaconry of Coventry:
Deans of Coventry, 8s; Marton, 16s; Stoneleigh (*Stonley*), 13s 4d; Arden, 20s.
Total: 57s 4d

b. Archdeaconry of Stafford:
Deans of Lapley and Trysull, 13s 4d; Alton (*Alneton*) and Leek (*Leeke*), 10s. Stafford and Newcastle-under-Lyme, 13s 4d; Tamworth and Tutbury, 8s; prebends of Colwich, 10s; Brewood, 8s, Eccleshall, 20s, Longdon, 10s; Baswich (*Barkiswiche*), 3s.
Total: £4 16s 4d

c. Archdeaconry of Derby:
Deans of Scarsdale and Derby, 62s each; Ashbourne (*Aissheburne*), 42s 4d; Repton and Castellar, 56s 8d.
Total: £11 3s

d. Archdeaconry of Shrewsbury:
From the Official of the archd. for synodals and Peter's Pence at Easter, £4 13s 4.

TOTAL SYNODALS DUE AT EASTER: £23 10s

431. [fo. 156] PETER'S PENCE DUE AT MICHAELMAS.
From archd. of Coventry and his Official, £12 10s 8d; from Official of Derby, £12 7s 8d; from archd. of Shrewsbury, £4 13s 4d; from archd. of Stafford, £9 17s 4d.
Total: £39 9s

432. RECEIPTS FROM INSTITUTIONS AND VACANCIES OF CHURCHES.
Inst. to ch. of Radbourn (*Radbourne*), Wa., 6s 8d; vacancy of same ch., 20s; inst. to vic. of Clifton (*Cliftone*), Wa.; ch. of Baxterley (*Baxtarley*), Wa.; chantries of St Mary and St Michael in ch. of Melbourne, Db.; chs. of Aighton (*Aighton*), La.; Hathersage (*Hathersege*), Db.; prebend in coll. ch. of St John, Chester; altar of St Michael in chantry of St Mary Magdalene in ch. of Chesterfield (*Chestirfeld*), Db.; vics. of Spondon, Db., and Dronfield (*Dronefeld*), Db., 6s 8d each; confirmation of prior of Stone, £5; inst. to ch. of Wistaston (*Wistauston*), Chs., 6s 8d; induction to same, which is in the jurisdiction of Wybunbury (*Wybonbury*), 6s 8d; inst. to chs. of Swarkeston (*Swerkeston*), Db.; Norbury, St.; Middleton (*Middylton*), La.; vic. of St Oswald, Chester, 6s 8d each; vacancy of vic. of St Oswald, Chester, 3s 4d; inst. to ch. of Kirk Langley, Db. and to chantry of St Mary Magdalene in ch. of Chesterfield (*Chestirfeld*), Db., 6s 8d each.
Total: £12 3s 4d

433. RECEIPTS FROM BENEFICES APPROPRIATED TO THE EPISCOPAL MENSA.
From Robert Quaryare, farmer of ch. of Wybunbury (*Wybonburye*), Chs., £18; from farmer of ch. of Denford (*Droneford*), Np., £15; for the farm of various fields in the city of Coventry, 34s.
Total: £34 14s

434. PENSIONS DUE AT EASTER AND OTHER DATES.

a. Archdeaconry of Coventry:
From Warwick coll. for ch. of Wolfhamcote (*Willfancote*), Wa., 13s 4d; prior of Maxstoke for chs. of Bishop's Itchingdon (*Echington*), Wa., Maxstoke, Wa.,

and Shustoke, Wa., at the feast of the Annunciation of the B.V.M. [25 Mar.], 20s; master of coll. of St Lawrence Poultney (*Pulteney*), London, for ch. of Napton, Wa., at Corpus Christi [2 June], 3s 4d; prior of St Anne's, Coventry, for ch. of Wolverton (*Wolecheston*), Wa., at Easter, 13s 4d.   Total: 50s

b. Archdeaconry of Stafford:
Prior of Stone for ch. of Madely, St., at Easter, 13s 4d; abbot of Hulton for chs. of Audley, St., and Biddulph (*Bedulphe*), St., at feast of the Invention of the Holy Cross [3 May], 33s 4d.   Total: 46s 8d

c. Archdeaconry of Derby:
Prior of Tutbury for ch. of West Broughton (*Broughton*), Db., at Michaelmas [29 Sept.] and Nativity of St John the Baptist [24 June], 13s 4d; abbot of Beauchief (*Bucheff*) for ch. of Dronfield (*Dronfeld*), Db., at Nativity of St John the Baptist, 13s 4d; r. of Eckington (*Ekynton*), Db., for that ch. at Annunciation of B.V.M., 13s 4d.   Total: 40s.

d. Archdeaconry of Chester:
Warden of ch. of Stoke in Wirral (*Wyrall*), 6s 8d; dean of coll. ch. of St John, Chester, for ch. of Plemonstall (*Pleymystowe*), Chs., at Nativity of St John the Baptist, 13s 4d.   Total: 20s

435. [fo. 156v] PENSIONS DUE AT MICHAELMAS AND AT OTHER DATES.

a. Archdeaconry of Coventry:
Dean of Astley (*Aistley*) for ch. of Hillmorton (*Hylmorton*), Wa., 13s 4d; abbot of Lavendon (*Lavenden*) for ch. of Shotteswell (*Shoteswell*), Wa., 3s 4d; prior of Clattercote (*Chatircote*) for ch. of Ratley (*Roteley*), Wa., 6s 8d; abbot of Burton for ch. of Austrey (*Aldestre*), St., 20s; prioress of Markyate (*Markeyate*) for ch. of Kingsbury (*Kynnesbury*), Wa., 6s 8d; abbot of Sulby for ch. of Wappenbury (*Wapynbury*), Wa., at All Saints [1 Nov.], 6s 8d; prior of Arbury for ch. of Leigh, Chs., at Michaelmas, 6s 8d; abbot of Merevale (*Meryvall*) for ch. of Mancetter (*Mancestre*), Wa., at Michaelmas, 13s 4d.   Total: 76s 8d

b. Archdeaconry of Derby:
Coll. of Leicester for ch. of Duffield (*Duffeld*), Db., at feast of St Andrew [30 Nov.], 40s; abbot of Dale for chs. of Ilkeston ((*Illeston*), Db., and Heanor (*Henor*), Db., at Michaelmas, 6s 8d; rs. of ch. of Darley in the Peak at Michaelmas, 6s 8d; prior of Mount Grace (*Monte Gre*) for ch. of Beighton (*Boghton*), Db., 3s 4d.   Total: 63s. 4d

c. Archdeaconry of Shrewsbury:
Abbot of Haughmond (*Hamond*) for chs. of Hanmer (*Hannemere*), Sa., Stanton (*Staundon*), Sa., and Ryton (*Ruyton*), Sa., at Michaelmas, 36s 8d; master of Battlefield (*Batilfeld*) coll. for ch. of Idsall (*Edishale*), Sa., at Michaelmas, 13s 4d; master of Tong (*Tonge*) coll. for ch. of Lapley, St., at Michaelmas, 4s; abbot of St Peter's, Shrewsbury, for ch. of Great Ness (*Nissestrange*), Sa., at Michaelmas, 13s 4d.   Total: 67s 4d

d. Archdeaconry of Stafford:
Abbot of Bordesley for ch. of Kinver (*Kynsare*), St., at Michaelmas, 6s 8d; dean of Windsor for ch. of Uttoxeter (*Uttoxhater*), St., at Michaelmas, 10s;

prior of St Thomas by Stafford for chs. of Bushbury (*Bysshbury*), St., Weston-upon-Trent (*Weston*), St., and Baswich (*Berkiswich*), St. at Michaelmas, 13s 4d.   Total: 60s 8d.

e.   Archdeaconry of Chester:
Master of Manchester (*Mancestr'*) coll. for same coll. at Michaelmas, 40s; master of Bunbury coll. for the same at feast of St Martin [11 Nov.], 10s; prior of Penwortham (*Penthwortham*) for ch. of Leyland (*Leylond*), La., at Michaelmas, 40s; v. of Croston for ch. of Croston, La., at Michaelmas, 6s 8d; v. of Prescot (*Prescote*) for ch. of Prescot, La., at Michaelmas, 13s 4d.
                                                                          Total: £5 10s

436. Received from Mr Edmund Chaterton, archd. of Chester, for various revenues, that is for the vacancies of benefices, synodals and probate of testaments due to the abp. from the archdeaconry of Chester during the vacancy of the see.   Total: £12 13s 4d

437. RECEIPTS FOR PROBATE OF TESTAMENTS.
For probate of John Jakes of Coleshill (*Colshill*), Wa., 5s; William Normanton of Burton, St., 3s 4d; Ralph Chaunterell, chap., of Tutbury, St., 10s; Thomas Storere of Wirksworth (*Worsworth*), Db., 20s; Richard Woode of Hodnet (*Hudnett*), Sa., 5s; William Merydene of Shrewsbury (*Shroisbury*), 6s 8d; Roger Coly of Hodnet (*Hodnett*), Sa., 20d; William Fer of Walsall (*Walshall*), St., 5s; Elizabeth Fleccher of Walsall, 5s; Richard Turnour, r. of Norbury, St., 6s 8d; Simon Bricebridge of Kingsbury (*Kynnesbury*), Wa., 10s; Robert Sprote of Walsall (*Walshale*), St., 12d; William Scott of Great Barr (*Barre*), St., 3s 4d; Robert Smyth of Marchington, St., 12d; Ralph Tyddiswall of Alton (*Alneton*), St., 16d; Thomas Leke of Cheddleton (*Chedulton*), St., 12d; Thomas Frere of Biddulph (*Bedulphe*), St., 12d; Peter Knyght of Biddulph, St., 2s 4d; Thomas Lokwoode of Leek (*Leke*), St., 16d; John Checkley (*Chekeley*), St., 14d; William Cattister of Worfield (*Worfild*), Sa., 3s 4d; Margaret Barow, widow of Chester, 20s; Henry Gardiner, chap. of Coventry, 6s 8d; Richard Dycon of Newton [*unid.*], 20d; William Bradley of Ladbrooke (*Lodbroke*), Wa., 12d; Clement Wilkes of Coventry, 10d; John Hobeson of Coventry, 20d; William Forster of Coventry, 6s 8d; John Allewton of Coventry, 10d; Robert Clerk of Coventry, 5s 8d; John Prymerhose of Coventry, 8d; John Bateman of Coventry, 3s 4d; John Truflove of Hapton, La., 3s 4d; John Amyth of Harbury (*Harburburye*), Wa., 2s; Thomas Cadington of Packington (*Pakington*) [*unid.*], 12d; William Prentosle of Cotton, Db., 16d; John Gefferey of Exhall (*Exale*), Wa., 6s 8d; Nicholas Gawsell, esq., of Barlborough (*Barlebourgh*), Db., 40s; William Bowdon of Acton [*unid.*], 2s 4d; William Tetryngton of *Astonfeld* [? Aston Heath, Chs.], 4s; Roger Stonys of Tottington (*Tetryngton*), La., 4s; John Salte of Weston [*unid.*], 12d; James Salte of Weston [*unid.*], 12d; William Bagshawe of Weston [*unid.*], 5s; William Ely of Youlgreave (*Yolgrave*), Db., 2s; Thomas Berde of Glossop (*Glossope*), Db., 12d; William Handeley of Stoke [*unid.*], 12d; John Henshawe of Wolstanton, St., 2s; Roger Colborne of Biddulph (*Bedull*), St., 12d; William Walker of Handsworth (*Handisworth*), St., 12d; Thomas Archer of Tutbury (*Tudbury*), St., 3s 4d; Richard Barwell of Ranton (*Ronstone*), St., 20s; Margaret Pultney

of Coventry, 3s 4d; Henry Smyth of Horsley, Db., 13s 4d.
Total: £13 13s 10d

438. [fo. 157] RECEIPTS FOR PROBATE OF TESTAMENTS OF TESTATORS
HAVING GOODS IN VARIOUS DIOCESES.
For probate of Thomas Walker of Coventry, whose inventory extends to
£31 3s 2d, 8s 4d; Simon Haryngton of Bicton (*Bysshton*), Sa., whose inventory
extends to £53 8s 4d and whose debts are £29 3s 2d, 10s; William Mytton,
esq., of Weston under Lizard (*Lusyard*), Sa., whose inventory extends to
£107 23s 4d, 23s 4d; Richard Wentnor of Shrewsbury (*Shroysburye*), whose
inventory extends to £239 6s 8d, 53s 4d; Hugh Hunt of Burbage on the Wye
(*Burbage*), Db., whose inventory extends to £123 5s 11d, 26s 8d; Robert
Thirkhill of *Sharsford* [*unid.*],[1] whose inventory extends to £11 9s, 3s 4d; Henry
Frenshe of Onneley (*Only*), St., whose inventory extends to £42 16s 11d, 8s;
William Walding, whose inventory extends to £51, 20s; for letters of
administration for Sir Henry Boold of Bold, La., 6s 8d; probate of Sir Henry
Boold, whose inventory extends to £123 6s 9d and whose debts are £147 5s 5d,
16s 8d; Thomas Cabe of Stanford on Avon (*Staunford super Haven*), Np., whose
inventory extends to £353 3s 4d and whose debts are £28 7s 4·d, £4; Robert
Lambard of Nuneaton (*Nuneton*), Wa., whose inventory extends to £51 8s 2d,
13s 4d   Total: £13 9s 8d

  [1] Possibly Sharnford, Lei., or Charford, Ha.

TOTAL OF PROCURATIONS, SYNODALS, VACANCIES OF CHURCHES, INSTITU-
TIONS, PENSIONS, FRUITS OF CHURCHES APPROPRIATED TO EPISCOPAL
MENSA AND OTHER ECCLESIASTICAL REVENUES: £307 17s 10d.[1]

    [1] Correct total for subtotals is £308 7s 10d, and from individual figures £309
    11s 6d.

[fo. 159] ACTS AND PROCEEDINGS CONDUCTED BY THE WORTHY MASTER ROGER CHIRCHE. DECR. D., OFFICIAL, COMMISSARY AND GUARDIAN OF THE SPIRITUALITY IN THE CITY AND DIOCESE OF ROCHESTER BY AUTHORITY OF THE VERY REVEREND FATHER IN CHRIST AND LORD JOHN, BY DIVINE MERCY CARDINAL PRIEST OF ST ANASTASIA IN THE HOLY ROMAN CHURCH, ARCHBISHOP OF CANTERBURY, PRIMATE OF ALL ENGLAND AND LEGATE OF THE APOSTOLIC SEE, THE SEE OF ROCHESTER BEING VACANT BY THE TRANSLATION OF THE REVEREND FATHER AND LORD THOMAS FROM THAT CHURCH TO THE CHURCH OF LONDON, TO WHICH HE WAS LATELY PREFERRED BY APOSTOLIC AUTHORITY, THESE PROCEEDINGS BEING CONDUCTED FROM 4 NOVEMBER 1496 A.D.

> *Note*: the see became vacant by the translation of Thomas Savage to London on 3 Aug. 1496 and was filled by the provision of Richard Fitzjames on 18 Feb. 1497.

439. In the chapter house of the cath. priory, in the presence of the prior and chapter, Mr William Potkyn, notary public by apostolic authority, delivered to Mr Roger Chirch, Decr. D., letters of commission from the abp., and requested him to act according to their tenor. Mr Chirch, out of reverence for the abp., accepted the commission, which was then read publicly by Mr Potkyn. Rochester, 4 Nov. 1496.

440. Commission with powers of canonical coercion to Mr Roger Church, Decr. D., as vicar-general and guardian of the spiritualities of the see of Rochester in the vacancy following the translation of bp. Thomas to the see of London, with the powers specified in no. 1. Lambeth, 4 Nov. 1496.

441. [fo. 159v] Mandate directed to the archd. of Rochester and his Official inhibiting them and those subject to them from any action prejudicial to the visitation of the archdeaconry to be conducted by Mr Church or his commissaries on behalf of the abp. Rochester, 4 Nov. 1496.

442. [fo. 160] Citation of the abbot and conv. of Lesnes (*Lesunnes*) [O.S.A.] to submit to visitation on Monday 14 Nov. Rochester, 4 Nov. 1496. Certificate of the abbot dated 10 Nov., with a schedule of the names of those cited:
William Bright, abbot; John Cope, subprior; Richard Abell, cellarer; William Basse, Thomas Fermerk, John Makyn, professed cans.
The visitation was duly conducted on 14 Nov.

443. Citation of the warden of Cobham college to submit to visitation on 17 Nov. Rochester, 4 Nov. 1496.
Certificate of the warden, with a schedule of the names of those cited:
John Sprot, warden. Richard Walker, chap.; John Baker, M.A., fellow.
The visitation was duly conducted on 17 Nov.

444.   [fo. 160v] Citation of the master of the hospital of B.V.M. of the New Work, Strood (*Strode*), to submit to visitation on Friday 18 Nov. Rochester, 4 Nov. 1496.
Certificate of William Barber, master.
The visitation was duly conducted on 18 Nov., the master alone appearing.

445.   Citation of the prioress and conv. of Higham (*Lillechurch*) [O.S.B.] to submit to visitation on Saturday 19 Nov. Rochester, 4 Nov. 1496.
Certificate of the prioress dated 15 Nov., with a schedule of the names of those cited:
Elizabeth Bradfeld, prioress; Alice Herne, Agnes Water, Agnes Swayne, Helen Ormuston, Joan Longe.
The visitation was duly conducted on 19 Nov.

446.   [fo. 161] Citation of the prior and conv. of the cath, priory of Rochester [O.S.B.] to submit to visitation on Monday 21 Nov. Rochester, 4 Nov. 1496.
Certificate of the prior dated 21 Nov., with a schedule of the names of those cited:
William Bisshop, prior; John Annoell, subprior; William Annoell, precentor; John Nodyn, Edmund Hertfeld, William Watford, William Caynok, John Dertford, John Pecham, John Quyntlok, John Gynnett, Thomas Hemisby, John Page, John Noble, William Lunt, Roger Smyth; Thomas Comlyne, sick; Robert Pylton, at Oxford. William Nicoll lives as an apostate.
The visitation was duly conducted on 21 Nov.

447.   [fo. 161v] Citation of the abbess and conv. of Malling (*Mallyng*) [O.S.B.] to submit to visitation on Saturday 26 Nov. Rochester, 4 Nov. 1496.
Certificate of the abbess dated 23 Nov., with a schedule of the names of those cited:
Elizabeth Hulle, abbess; Joan Knyght, prioress; Joan Dygges, subprioress and precentress; Margery Hilgerden, sacristan; Elizabeth Wath, Agnes Digges, Joan Norton, Ermenilda George, Anne Appulton; Catherine Merden and Alice Jamys, not professed; Felicity Kolte, refectorer.
The visitation was duly conducted on 26 Nov.

448.   Citation directed to the archd. of Rochester or his Official for the visitation of the archdeaconry. Rochester, 4 Nov. 1496.

ACCOUNT OF MR ROGER CHURCH, DECR. D., AND WILLIAM POTKYN, NOTARY PUBLIC, HIS SCRIBE.

449.   [fo. 162] PROCURATIONS.

a. [Deaneries]:
Dys. of Rochester (*Roffen'*), £10 0s 2d; Dartford (*Dertford*), £9 3s 4d; Malling (*Mallyng*), £9 4s 10d.   Total: £28 8s 3d

b. [Religious houses]:
Prior and conv. of Rochester, 66s 8d; abbess of Lesnes (*Lesnys*), 53s 4d; abbess and conv. of Malling, 40s; master of Strood hospital, 40s; master of Cobham coll., 46s 8d.   Total: £12 6s 8d

TOTAL PROCURATIONS: £40 14s 9d

450.   PENSIONS DUE AT VARIOUS FEASTS.
From prior and conv. of Rochester for the *exennium*,[1] £10; from abbot and conv. of Bermondsey (*Bardmonsey*) for chs. of Shorne, Cobham, Birling (*Birlyng*) and Kemsing (*Keamsyng*), at the Annunciation of the B.V.M. [25 Mar.], £4; from r. of Lambeth (*Lamehith*), Sy., for pension due at Easter, 33s 4d; from r. of Nettlestead (*Netilstede*) for pension for East Barming (*Barmyngest*) ch. due at feast of St Andrew [30 Nov.], 20d; from master of Cobham coll. for chs. of Horton Kirby (*Horton*) and Chalk due at feast of St Andrew, 13s 4d; from master of St Lawrence Poultney (*Pulteney*), London, for ch. of Spelhurst at Purification of B.V.M. [2 Feb.], 7s. Total: £16 15s 4d

[1] The *exennium* was paid by the prior and conv. to the bp. of Rochester on the feast of St Andrew as recompense for the separation of the *mensa conventualis* from the *mensa episcopalis*; see R.A.L. Smith, 'The Financial System of Rochester Cathedral Priory' in *Collected Papers* (1947), p. 43.

451.   RECEIPTS FOR INSTITUTIONS.
For inst. of v. of Higham, 6s 8d; for inst. to [*blank*], 6s 8d; for inst. to [*blank*], 6s 8d.   Total: 20s

TOTAL OF PROCURATIONS, PENSIONS AND INSTITUTIONS: £58 10s 1d

Fos. 163–6 are blank.

VACANCY OF THE SEE OF WORCESTER, 1498

[fo. 167] VACANCY OF THE EPISCOPAL SEE OF WORCESTER THROUGH THE
DEATH OF JOHN DE GIGLIS OF GOOD MEMORY, LATELY BISHOP OF WORCES-
TER, WHICH VACANCY BEGAN ON 25 AUGUST 1498 A.D. AND IN THE TWELFTH
YEAR FROM THE TRANSLATION OF THE VERY REVEREND FATHER IN GOD
AND LORD JOHN, BY DIVINE MERCY CARDINAL PRIEST OF ST ANASTASIA IN
THE HOLY ROMAN CHURCH, ARCHBISHOP OF CANTERBURY, PRIMATE OF
ALL ENGLAND AND LEGATE OF THE APOSTOLIC SEE.

> *Note*: the see became vacant by the death of John de Giglis on 25 Aug. 1498
> and was filled by the provision of Silvester de Giglis on 24 Dec. 1498.

452. In the chapter house of the cath. ch., in the presence of the subprior
and conv. gathered in chapter, Mr Roger Church, Decr. D., appeared before
William prior of Worcester bearing a commission from the abp. directed to
the prior, and on the abp.'s behalf requested the prior to act according to its
tenor. The letter was read aloud by Mr William Potkyn, notary public, and
the prior, out of reverence for the abp., accepted the commission and decreed
that proceedings should be conducted in accordance with it. Worcester
(*Wigorn'*), 22 Sept. 1498.

453. Commission, with powers of canonical coercion, to the prior of
Worcester as Official in the vacancy of the see following the d. of bp. John,
which commission had been requested by the prior and conv.[1] The prior is to
exercise the duties of Official in person or by suitable deputy and is to account
to the abp. for all spiritual revenues due to him and to the ch. of Canterbury
by virtue of the vacancy of the see. Lambeth, 1 Sept. 1498.

> [1] In accordance with the composition between the prior and conv. and abp.
> Boniface; see I. J. Churchill, *Canterbury Administration* (1933), ii, 59–61.

454. In the chapter house of the cath. ch., in the presence of the monks
gathered in chapter, the prior of Worcester appeared before Mr Roger
Church, Decr.D., presented to him letters of commission and requested him
to accept them and act according to their tenor. After the letters had been read
publicly by Mr William Potkyn, Mr Church reverently accepted the
commission and decreed that proceedings should be conducted in accordance
with it. Worcester, 24 Sept. 1498.

455. Commission of William prior of Worcester and Official of the abp. of
Canterbury in the vacancy of the see of Worcester to Mr Roger Church,
Decr.D. Rehearsal of the abp.'s commission to the prior [no. 453].[1] Since the
prior is burdened by various arduous business so that he probably will not be
able to conduct a visitation and fulfil the other duties of Official, he has issued
a commission, irrevocable during the vacancy of the see, to Mr Roger Church
to act as his deputy, to conduct a visitation of the dioc., inquire into crimes
etc., sequestrate benefices, receive oaths of obedience, examine and approve
exchanges, grant probate of testaments, inquire into appropriations, compel

residence, receive revenues, issue letters of acquittance, account for those revenues and do all else necessary and opportune in this office. Worcester, 22 Sept. 1498.

      [1] The abp.'s commission is dated at Knole, 1 Sept. 1498; cf. no. 453. No. 456 also emanated from Knole on the same day.

456.   [fo. 168] Commission of the abp., with powers of canonical coercion, to Mr Roger Church, Decr. D., to proceed in the episcopal consistory during the vacancy of the see of Worcester in all cases, *ex officio*, promoted and at the instance of parties, including matrimonial causes, to terminate such cases, to correct and punish the excesses, crimes and faults of any of the abp.'s subjects in the city and dioc. who are delinquent or who by virtue of debt or contract fall under ecclesiastical jurisdiction, to impose salutary penance and to do all else which pertains to the office of Official of the consistory. Knole (*Knoll'*), 1 Sept. 1498.

457.   In the consistory in the cath. ch. Mr Church accepted the abp.'s commission as Official of the consistory, and in the presence of Mr Robert Inkebarough and Mr Nicholas Gooldwyn, notaries public, he appointed Mr William Potkyn, notary public, as scribe of his acts. Worcester, 24 Sept. 1498.

458.   Citation of the prior and conv. of the cath. ch. of St Mary, Worcester, to submit to visitation on Thursday 25 Oct. Worcester, 1 Oct. 1498.
Citation received 20 Oct. Certificate of the prior dated 25 Oct., with schedule of those cited:
William Wenlok, prior; John Weddisbury, subprior; William Dene, John Ombersley, Richard Bromysgruve; Richard Myton, infirmarer; John Stafford, almoner; William Lemyster, *maior*; William Clifton, Thomas Croxthorn, Robert Lyndesey; Thomas Myldenham, sacrist; John Halys; William Worcetter, precentor; William Hodyngton, refectorer; John Sylsetter; John Hardewyk, pittancer; John Stookes, keeper of the tomb; John Duddeley; Edmund Ledbury, chaplain; Laurence Clifford; Robert Alchurch, master of the chapel; John Lechifeld, chaplain; Thomas Stafford, third prior; Humphrey Grafton, kitchener; Henry Chestre, cellarer; John Webbeley, subchamberlain; John Sudbury, William Lynsill; John Lemystre, subcellarer; John Kedirmyster, subalmoner; William Moore, fourth prior; William Barmisley, scholar; William Alston, scholar; Clement Hartillesbury, infirmarer; Randolph Helyngton; Thomas Asteley, subsacrist; Thomas Moorton, William Borton, John Wellys, John Ewysham, Thomas Glowcetter, William Upton, Roger Stanford.
On 25 Oct.[1] Mr Church commenced his visitation and, after he had received the prior's certificate, which was read by Mr Potkyn, he enjoined the prior to produce a true account of the finances of the house and a true inventory and to present them to him, wherever he might be in the dioc., before Christmas, on pain of suspension from office for one whole year. He then adjourned his visitation to the feast of the Purification of the B.V.M. [2 Feb.] or any day before that which might seem best to him for the reformation of those things which required reform.

      [1] MS: 20 Oct.

459.   [fo. 168v] Citation of the abbot and conv. of Tewkesbury [O.S.B.] to submit to visitation on Tuesday 30 Oct. Worcester, 1 Oct. 1498.
Citation received 18 Oct. Certificate of the abbot dated 24 Oct., with schedule of those cited:
Richard Cheltynham, abbot; Brs William Preston, prior; John Stokes, John Evesham, Thomas Wroston; John Teynton, precentor and chamberlain; Robert Prestbury, prior of Deerhurst (*Derhurst*); John Worcetter, infirmarer; William Hanley, *magister specierum*; Thomas Lychefeld; John Derhurst, sacrist; John Kyrdiff, S.T.B., almoner and master of the chapel of St Mary; John Alston, hosteler; John Sucley, subprior; Thomas Salisbury; John Appurley, succentor; William Compton, cellarer; Henry Beley, kitchener; Thomas Stourton; William Cheltynham, subcellarer; Roger Bodynton; Robert Cheltynham, third prior; Hugh Kyngiston, Nicholas Pollard, Thomas Lemynton; Thomas Wynchecombe, subsacristan; Thomas Cheltynham, chaplain; Andrew Tewkisbury, Thomas Wolston, Edmund Stanley, George Kyngeston, William Dydicote, Thomas Marlowe.
The visitation was duly conducted on 30 Oct.

460.   [fo. 169] Citation of the abbot and conv. of St Peter, Gloucester (*Gloucestrie*) [O.S.B.] to submit to visitation on Tuesday 20 Nov. Worcester, 1 Oct. 1498.
Citation received 4 Oct. Certificate of the abbot dated 10 Oct., with schedule of those cited:
John Malverne, abbot; John Chedworth, subprior and president; Richard Clyve; William Elmeley, prior of Leonard Stanely (*Stanley*); Walter Forest, infirmarer; John Walden, chaplain; Thomas Froucetter, precentor; Thomas Oldebury, sacrist; Thomas Braunche, S.T.B., cellarer; John Arundell, Thomas Rose; John Harland, master of the works; Thomas Gloucetter, subcellarer; Anthony London; John Berkeley, master of the churches; William Arthure, John Martyn, Thomas Newent; Edmund Hanley, *monachus ville*; Thomas Bulley; John Lempster, subalmoner; Richard Russell; William Sutton, chamberlain; William Notyngham, kitchener; John Huntley, John Hoope; William Monyngton, refectorer; Richard Wulruge, subsacristan; Richard Standissh; Thomas Staunton, master of the chapel; Thomas Hereford, third prior; John Whitby, hosteler; Roger Compton, succentor; John Grafton, Robert Asplyn, John Ley, Andrew Tewkysbury, John Graswell, John Moore, Edmund Wotton, Richard Ledbury, John Poole, Walter Tutbury, William Thornbury, John Cisceter, Thomas Bisley, William Chedwell, Thomas Exetter, Thomas Bewdeley, Robert Dursley. Scholars at Oxford: John Newton, S.T.B., William Motlowe, S.T.B., John Arundell, Hugh Bowles.
The visitation was duly conducted on 20 Nov.

461.   [fo. 169v] Citation of the prior and conv. of Llanthony (*Lanthon'*) [O.S.A.] to submit to visitation on Thursday 8 Nov. Worcester, 1 Oct. 1498. Citation received 8 Oct. Certificate of prior Henry [Deane] dated 25 Oct., with schedule of those cited:
Brs John Mersfeld, subprior; John Sodbury, *custos ordinis*; Thomas Alford; John Brown, sacrist; Walter Keylok and Thomas Sistestre, proctors in

Ireland; John Gloucestre, John Chestre; William de Aune, infirmarer; William Notingham, almoner; Richard Newent, precentor; Richard Deene, subcellarer; John Combe, Philip Bristowe; Edmund Forest, scholar; Thomas Hale, refectorer; John Halynton, Thomas Lylliston, Robert Cone.
The visitation was duly conducted on 8 Nov. A sermon was preached by Mr Edmund Frowcettre, S.T.P., on the text: *Vita mea reddam coram domino pro omni populo*.[1]

  [1] *Psalms*, 115 14.

462.   [fo. 170] Citation of the master and fellows of the coll. of Westbury upon Trym (*Westbury*) to submit to visitation on Saturday 10 Nov. Worcester, 1 Oct. 1498.
Certificate of the dean dated 3 Nov., with schedule of those cited:
William Cretyng, dean; John More, preb. of Goodringhill (*Goderinghill*); Richard Carpenter, preb. of Laurensweston; Roger Braggis, preb. of Henbury; Hugh Inge, preb. of Aust; Richard Nykke, preb. of Halley; John Wellywe, subdean; Nicholas Barbur, grammar master; Thomas Dainkys, treasurer; Robert Woode, perpetual fellow; William Lulle, second treasurer; John Janyns, Adam Wynhall, Philip Morys, John Carpenter, William West, perpetual fellows: Henry Jakes, John Mylton, Thomas Floude, William Mylyn, John Hulle, Richard Cooke, John Collys, Ralph Whitfare, Henry Massingham, William Wrangeford.
The visitation was duly conducted on 10 Nov.

463.   [fo. 170v] Citation of the abbot and conv. of St Augustine, Bristol (*Bristollie*) [O.S.A.] to submit to visitation on Monday 12 Nov. Worcester, 1 Oct. 1498.
Citation received 20 Oct. Certificate of the abbot dated 10 Nov., with schedule of those cited:
John Newland, abbot; Thomas Grene, subprior; John Martyn; John Denham, precentor; Thomas Clerk, refectorer; William Hobbis, infirmarer; William Crekelade, almoner, *anniversarius*, keeper of the vestry and novice-master; Robert Elyott, sacrist and cellarer; John Howell, kitchener and hosteler; John Gylis, William Oswald; Nicholas Chapell, subsacrist; William Wynter, John Westcott,, John Whetnoll, Richard Norton, Henry Pavye, John Smert, William Burton, John Harman, William Phille.
The visitation was duly conducted on 12 Nov.

464.   [fo. 171] Citation of the master and fellows of Gaunt's hospital (*domus sancti Marci de Gauntes*), Bristol, to submit to visitation on Thursday 15 Nov. Worcester, 1 Oct. 1498.
Citation received 11 Oct. Certificate of the minister dated 10 Nov., with schedule of those cited:
Thomas Tyler, minister; John Randolf, John Colman, Thomas Stalleworth, William Halle.
The visitation was duly conducted on 15 Nov.

465.   Citation of the abbot and conv. of St Mary, Cirencester (*Cirencestre*) [O.S.A.] to submit to visitation on Friday 23 Nov. Worcester, 1 Oct. 1498.

Citation received 16 Nov. Certificate of the abbot dated 22 Nov., with schedule of those cited:
The abbot; the prior and first treasurer; *domini* Thomas Sawnders; John Malvern, subprior, warden of ch. of St John the Baptist and novice-master; John Bristowe, warden of the refectory; John Okeborn; Richard Taunton, pittancer, sacrist, warden of chapel of St Mary, warden of the infirmary and *magister ordinis*; John Wyke, subsacristan; Richard Castelcombe, chaplain, hosteler and succentor; John Dursley, chamberlain, kitchener and warden of Cheltenham (*Cheltynham*) ch.; William Wynterworth, succentor; Thomas Atherbury, scholar at Oxford; Thomas Brymsfeld, Thomas Payneswik; Brs John Aston, John Blake, Walter Ameney, Richard Cistetur, William Burford, Walter Tewxbury, John Saxton, William Sarney.
The visitation was duly conducted on 23 Nov.

466.   [fo. 171v] Citation of the abbot and conv. of St Mary and St Kenelm, Winchcombe (*Wynchecombe*) [O.S.B.] to submit to visitation on Thursday 29 Nov. Worcester, 1 Oct. 1498.
Citation received 20 Oct. Certificate of the abbot dated 27 Nov., with schedule of those cited:
Richard Kedymyster, S.T.D., abbot, kitchener, hosteler and chamberlain; Brs William Quyvhill, prior, sacrist and master of chapel of St Mary; William Colarde; John Fekenham, subprior; Thomas Wynchecombe; [*blank*] Lenche, almoner and penitentiary; Thomas Ekynton, infirmarer; Richard Upton, Robert Henley, John Cheltnam; John Moorton, subsacrist; Thomas Snodeley, precentor; Richard Malvern, third prior and subchamberlain; John Cissetter; John Worcetter, subprecentor; Edmund Aisshby, S.T.B., scholar; Thomas Cheltnam, cellarer; Thomas Lewkisbury, William Shoreborn, William Omursley, Robert Enworth, Robert Burton, John Wynnyng, William Kenelme, Robert Benett.
The visitation was duly conducted on 29 Nov.

467.   [fo. 172] Citation of the abbot and conv. of Pershore [O.S.B.] to submit to visitation on Tuesday 4 Dec. Worcester, 1 Oct. 1498.
Citation received 5 Oct. Certificate of abbot John dated 4 Dec., with schedule of those cited:
The abbot; John Walcote, prior; Stephen Cradway, hosteler; Richard Powyk, chamberlain; William Evesham, infirmarer; Richard Lemster; Benedict Everton, sacrist; William Aldemerston, warden and kitchener; Walter Lee, seneschal and subcellarer; Stephen Bronnesgrove is in prison; Robert Cowley, refectorer; William Befford, almoner and warden of chapel of St Mary; Thomas Pershore, subprior and precentor; Thomas Aburton; Robert Cheltenham, scholar; Richard Hawkisbury, Richard Newland, Richard Langney; John Wardbarowe, subsacristan; William Nawton, third prior; Thomas Upton; John Cambeden, succentor; Thomas Dudley, Thomas Stratford.
The visitation was duly conducted on 4 Dec.

468.   Citation of the master and fellows of the coll. ch. of Stratford to submit to visitation on Thursday 13 Dec. Worcester, 1 Oct. 1498.

Citation received 11 Oct. Certificate of the subwarden dated 12 Dec., with schedule of those cited:
Chaplains of the coll.: Mr John Stoke, warden; William Purdun, subwarden; Robert Nicollys, parish pr.; John Powys, Thomas Higges, Richard Bogy, Walter Baker, John Grene; John Bloke, v. of Luddington (*Lodington*), Wa.
Chaplains of the chapel: Henry Barons, John Somor, Robert Stonys, Thomas Maryns, William Shardeley.
Stip. chaplains: Henry Shyrive, Alexander Motton, Thomas Barons.
Churchwardens (*gardiani ecclesie*): John Elys, John Barbour, William Horsman, Robert Gardiner.
Yconomi: Richard Bogy, John Bedill, William Jeffes, Richard Bentley, Robert Pagett, Thomas Tasker, William Body, Thomas Mychaell, John Brightwell, Thomas Lampett.
The visitation was duly conducted on 13 Dec.

469. [fo. 172v] Citation of the prior and conv. of St Sepulchre, Warwick [O.S.A.], to submit to visitation on Tuesday 18 Dec. Worcester, 1 Oct. 1498. Certificate of the prior dated 16 Dec., with schedule of those cited:
Robert Echington, prior; *domini* John Lambe and Hugh Ellismore, Br Richard Warwick, professed cans.
The visitation was duly conducted on 18 Dec.

470. [fo. 173] Citation of the master and fellows of the coll. ch. of St Mary, Warwick, to submit to visitation on Friday 14 Dec. Worcester, 1 Oct. 1498. Citation received 14 Oct.[1] Certificate of the dean dated 6 Dec., with schedule of those cited:
Richard Brakinburgh, dean.
Canons, residentiary and non-residentiary: Mr Roger Lupton, Decr. D., Mr John Gylbert, Mr Clement Smyth, Mr Robert Benley, Mr John Alestre.
Vicars and chaplains: Oliver Grecson, parish pr.; William Clerk, George Mede, William Sherard, John Turle, John Fichepole, Humphrey Taylor, John Kay, Robert Horsey, Edmund Wotton, John Webbe.
The visitation was duly conducted on 14 Dec.

[1] MS: Dec.

471. Citation of the prioress and conv. of Wroxall (*Wrexhale*) [O.S.B.] to submit to visitation on Monday 17 Dec. Worcester, 1 Oct. 1498.
Certificate of the prioress, with schedule of those cited:
Elizabeth Shacsper, prioress; Isota Lee, lately prioress; Josa Browne, Juliana Toky, Matilda Sheldisley; Agnes Pawton, not professed.
The visitation was duly conducted on 17 Dec.

472. [fo. 173v] Citation of the prior and conv. of Alcester (*Allyncestre*) [O.S.B.] to submit to visitation on Thursday 20 Dec. Worcester, 1 Oct. 1498. Citation received 30 Nov. Certificate of the prior dated 8 Dec., with schedule of those cited:
William Whitechurch, prior, then absent at the will of the abbot of Evesham; Henry Collesdon, Walter Bewdeley.
The visitation was duly conducted on 20 Dec.

473.   Citation of the prior and conv. of Studley (*Stodeley*) [O.S.A.] to submit to visitation on Friday 21 Dec. Worcester, 1 Oct. 1498.
Citation received 14 Nov. Certificate of the prior, with schedule of those cited: Thomas Att Woode, prior; Brs William Tutbury, subprior; William Stafford, John Eton, William Alcetter, William Fraunceys.
The visitation was duly conducted on 21 Dec.

VISITATIONS OF RURAL DEANERIES

> *Note*: For the rural dys. of Powick, Gloucester and Dursley (nos. 479–81) no indication is given in the register as to whether the parochial clergy answered the citation and appeared before the visitor, although occasionally an incumbent was noted as non-resident. For the other dys. (nos. 482–87) clergy are normally noted to have appeared and exhibited their letter of ordination and, in the case of incumbents, of institution. In nos. 482–87 where appearance is not recorded in the MS, a note to this effect has been added in this calendar.

474.   [fo. 174] Mandate directed to the archd. of Worcester and his Official inhibiting the exercise of any inferior jurisdiction during the visitation of the archdeaconry. Worcester, 1 Oct. 1498.

475.   Similar mandate directed to the archd. of Gloucester and his Official. Worcester, 1 Oct. 1498.

      [Fo. 174v blank.]

476.   [fo. 175] Citation directed to the archd. of Worcester and his Official for the visitation of the archdeaconry at the places and times specified in the attached schedule. Worcester, 1 Oct. 1498.
The ch. of Powick (*Powyck*), Wo., on Friday 26 Oct.; dy. of Powick in ch. of Little Malvern (*Malverne Minor*), Wo., on Saturday 27 Oct.; dy. of Pershore in ch. of Pershore, Wo., on Monday 3 Dec.; dy. of Blockley in ch. of Blockley, Gl., on Friday 7 Dec.; ch. of Great Wolford (*Wulford*), Wa., on Monday 10 Dec.; dy. of Kineton (*Kington*) in ch. of Stratford upon Avon, Wa., on Wednesday 12 Dec.; ch. of Wootton Wawen, Wa., on Tuesday 18 Dec.; dy. of Christianity, Warwick, in ch. of Alcester, Wa., on Wednesday 19 Dec.; ch. of Tardebigge (*Terbycke*), Wo., on Saturday 22 Dec.; ch. of Astley (*Asteley*), Wa., on Monday 10 Dec.; dy. of Kidderminster in ch. of Kidderminster, Wo., on Tuesday 11 Dec.; ch. of Halesowen, Wo., on Wednesday 12 Dec.; dy. of Droitwich (*Wich*) in ch. of Bromsgrove, Wo., on Thursday 13 Dec.; dy. of Worcester in St Helen's ch., Worcester, on Friday 14 Dec.
Certificate of Robert Enkbarough, Official of the archd. of Worcester, dated 3 Dec. 1498.

477.   [fo. 175v] Similar citation directed to the archd. of Gloucester and his Official. Worcester, 1 Oct. 1498.
The ch. of Deerhurt (*Durherst*), Gl., on Wednesday 31 Oct.; dy. of Gloucester in St Michael's ch., Gloucester, on Wednesday 7 Nov.; dy. of Dursley in St

James's ch., Dursley, Gl., on Friday 9 November; dy. of Bristol in All Saints ch., Bristol, on Wednesday 14 Nov.; St Bartholomew's hospital, Bristol, on Saturday 17 Nov.; dy. of Hawkesbury in ch. of Sodbury (*Sobbury*), Gl., on Monday 19 Nov.; dy. of Stonehouse in ch. of Tetbury, Gl., on Tuesday 20 Nov.; dy. of Cirenchester in ch. of Cirencester, Gl., on Thursday 22 Nov.; dy. of Fairford in ch. of Fairford, Gl., on Monday 26 Nov.; dy. of Stow (*Stowe*) in ch. of [blank] on Tuesday 27 Nov.; dy. of Winchcombe in ch. of Winchcombe, Gl., on Wednesday 28 Nov.; ch. of Didbrook (*Dudbroke*), Gl., on Saturday 1 Dec.; ch. of Beckford, Gl., on Saturday 1 Dec.; ch. of Childswickham (*Wyckwan*), Gl., on Wednesday 5 Dec.; ch. of Longborough (*Langbarough*), Gl., on Monday 10 Dec.; dy. of Campden in ch. of Campden, Gl., on Tuesday 11 Dec.
Certificate of Mr Thomas Holforde, Decr.B., Official of the archd. of Gloucester, dated at Tetbury, Gl., 27 Oct. 1498.

478.   [fo. 176] On 26 Oct. 1498 Mr Roger Church, sitting judicially in the parish ch. of Powick (*Powycke*), Wo., canonically visited the clergy and people of that parish, and afterwards adjourned his visitation until the feast of the Purification of the B.V.M. [2 Feb.] or any day before then which might seem best to him for the reformation of those things which required reform.
Prior Maculinus Ledbury and the conv. of Great Malvern (*Magna Malverne*), prop., appeared in the person of Edward Hill, chap.; Edward Hill, v., appeared and exhibited his letters of inst.; John Broke and Henry Colwyck, chws., and Richard Shyrkyll, Robert Savage, Robert Starke, Henry Bucheham, William Hale, pns., deposed that all was well.

479.   On 27 Oct. 1498 in the conv. ch. of Little Malvern (*Malverne Minoris*) Mr Church canonically visited the clergy and people of the dy. of Powick, Wo., and adjourned his visitation until the feast of the Purification, *etc.*

Upton on Severn (*Upton super Sabrinam*)
Mr George Savage, r., does not reside; Barnaby Kere, chap.; John Smyth, Richard Catley, John Geffereys, pns., deposed that all was well.

Redmarley d'Abitot (*Rydmerley*)
Mr George Savage, r., does not reside; George Muckeley, par. ch.; Thomas Baldwin, chap. of chantry; John Jonys, Richard Stevyns, William Holford, Nicholas Thornycrofte, pns.

Suckley
Matthew Clerk, r.; Richard Hall, chap. of chantry; Henry Turnour, chap. of Lulsley chapel; John Hall, chw.

Mathon (*Mathom*)
William Hill, r.; Thomas Hyde and William Motlow, chws., deposed that all was well.

Cherkenhill (*Chocknell*)
Mr John Locke, r., does not reside; John Hey, chap.

Leigh (*Lygh*)
Mr Nicholas Barbur, r.; John Bagnyll, chap.

Acton Beauchamp (*Acton Becham*)
Richard Wolf, r.; John Hall, John Wever, pns.

Pendock (*Pendocke*)
Richard King, r.; Richard Ede, chap.; Thomas Cane, Richard Grenewey, John Barnard, pns.

Hanley Castle (*Hanley*)
Prior and conv. of Little Malvern, prop.; John Kyton, v.; Mr John Falows, chap.; Edward Hawkys, chap. of chantry; Richard Tele and John Rugge, chws.

Staunton
William Restell, r.; Richard Wyttington, Henry Davies, pns.

Birtsmorton (Byrtismorton)
Thomas Langley, r.; Henry Woodward, William Clerke, pns.

Eldersfield (*Ellisfeld*)
John Cowper, v.; John Burwold, John Snede, pns.

Madresfield (*Mattysfeld*)
Robert Walley, r.; Robert Peynter, William Rede, pns.

Great Malvern (*Malverne Magna*)
Prior and conv. of Great Malvern, prop.; John More, v.; Humphrey Bagnyll, chap.; William Baxter, Richard Wyler, chws.

Longdon
Abbot and conv. of Westminster, prop.; Henry Woldy, v.; Thomas Bodylache, chap. of chantry; John Shawe, Robert Smyth, Richard Pynnocke, pns.

Castle Morton (*Castelmorton*)
William Bysshop, chap.; Thomas Roose, John Russell, Robert Weston, pns.

Chaddersley Corbett (*Chattisley*)
John Otter, chap.; William Beele, John Holdship, chws.

Welland (*Wellond*)
John Storre, chap.

Berrow (*Berowe*)
Prior and conv. of Worcester, prop.; John Botterton, chap.; John Clerke, William Woodley, chws.

Clevelode (*Cloveloode*)
John Cumbregge, chap. of the chapel.

480.   [fo. 176v] On 7 Nov. 1498 in the parish ch. of St Michael, Gloucester, Mr Church canonically visited the clergy and people of the dy. of Gloucester, and adjourned his visitation to the feast of the Purification, *etc.*

St Michael, Gloucester
Mr David Clune, r.; Maurice Mores, stip.; Thomas Hunte, Robert Frances, James Ivy, John Leyson, pns.

St John, Gloucester
Mr Edmund Froucetter, r.; Walter Lane, par. chap.; Henry Hopkyns, John
Hopkins, John Payne, Richard Barnard, stips.; John Grenowe, John Litill,
John Bayly, Thomas Hopkyns, pns., deposed that all was well.

St Nicholas, Gloucester
Prior and conv. of St Bartholomew, Gloucester, prop.; John Byrdsey, William
Cooke, William Seyffe, Thomas Hervey, stips.

St Mary before the Abbey Gate, Gloucester
Abbot and conv. of St Peter, Gloucester, prop.; Mr John Osborne, v.;
Thomas Walker, Thomas Wood, stips.; John Branche, John Wyche, Thomas
Walker, John Cockys, pns.

St Owen, Gloucester
Prior and conv. of Llanthony, prop.; Mr Maurice Bartram, v.; Robert
Walker, chap.; Hugh Clerke, William Grete, pns.

St Mary in the South, Gloucester
Thomas Dyer, r.; John Peke, chap.; Richard Colens, Richard Davies, pns.

Holy Trinity, Gloucester
Abbot and conv. of St Peter, Gloucester, prop.; Robert Cove, v.; William
Webbe, Richard Pers, stips.; Richard Peynter, William Baker, pns.

All Saints, Gloucester
Thomas Woodward, r.; Richard Pooton, John Taunton, chws.

Grace Lane (*Gracelond*), Gloucester
Henry Farley, chap.; John Wyche, Nicholas Tele, stips.; Robert Vuet,
Richard Wooke, pns.

St Aldate, Gloucester
Nicholas Kemyll, r.; William Sheldon, chap.; Thomas Humfrey, Thomas
Elkyns, chws.

Ashelworth (*Asshelworth*)
Abbot and conv. of St Augustine, Bristol, prop.; Mr John Osborne, v.;
William Longe, William Marsfeld, pns.

Hartpury (*Harpbury*)
Abbot and conv. of St Peter, Gloucester, prop.; Nicholas Farley, v.; Richard
Forty, William Gelis, pns.

Brookthorpe (*Brokethorp*)
Abbot and conv. of St Peter, Gloucester, prop.; Richard Scaltocke, v.;
William Nybbelet, Robert Nybbelet, pns.

Chapel of Maisemore
John Bonde, cur.; William Elkyns, William Reede, chws.

Standish
Abbot and conv. of St Peter, Gloucester, prop.; Mr William Blome, v.;
William Chewe, Henry Watkins, chws.

Haresfield (*Harsfeld*)
Prior and conv. of Llanthony, prop.; Geoffrey Jonys, v.; Richard Hunteley, chap.; John Harrys, John Byrte, John Gardyner, John Bewmond, pns.

Frocester (*Frowcetter*)
Abbot and conv. of St Peter, Gloucester, prop.; David Harres, v.; William Warner, John Dycke, pns.

Arlingham (*Erlingham*)
Abbot and conv. of St Peter, Gloucester, prop.; Walter Longney, v.; Walter Cordy, chap.; Walter Walle, Robert Corde, chws.

Fretherne (*Frethorn*)
John Kemyll, r.; John Ithell, chw.

Longney
Prior and conv. of Great Malvern, prop.; Robert Bryther, v.; John Bullocke, William Asplyn, Richard Trotter, John Howe, pns.

Chapel of Elmore
John Horne, chap.; John Bullocke, Robert Cooke, chws.

Chapel of Saul (*Salle*)
Thomas Meburne, chap.; Robert Bullocke, Thomas Harres, pns.

Moreton in Marsh (*Moreton*)
Dean and chapter of Hereford, prop.; Thomas Harper, chap.; Robert Hanowe, Thomas Broker, chws.

Chapel of Quedgeley (*Quaddisley*)
Henry Mynet, chap.; Thomas Barne, William Harries, chws.

Chapel of Hardwicke (*Hardwyke*)
John Walowfeld, cur.; Thomas Skreven, John Sous, chws.

Matson (*Matstone*)
Thomas Tyler, r.; Richard Barne, William Okey, pns.

Chapel of Upton St Leonard (*Upton*)
Hugh Lytill, Richard Broke, chaps.; Thomas Edward, John Harebard, chws.

Chapel of Whaddon (*Waddon*)
John Griffyth, chap.; Richard Carter, William Harreys, chws.

Chapel of Barnwood (*Burnewood*)
Robert Barton, chap.; John Steward, stip.; Walter Wey, proctor of the chapel.

Chapel of Randwick (*Renwyke*)
Christopher Wynship, chap.; William Shypman, William Wele, chws.

Chapel of Hempstead (*Hempstede*)
Geoffrey Jonys, chap.; William Smythe, Robert Mynet, chws.

Harescombe with Pitchcombe (*Harshcombe et Pethnichcombe*)
The rectory has been vac. for more than forty years; Thomas Pynchbecke, cur.; John Gardyner, William Hill, chws.

481.   [fo. 177] On 9 Nov. 1498 in the parish ch. of St James, Dursley, Gl., Mr Church canonically visited the clergy and people of the dy. of Dursley and adjourned his visitation to the feast of the Purification, *etc.*

Coaley (*Cowley*)
Abbot. and conv. of St Peter, Gloucester, prop., appeared by their proctor, Mr Stakesley; Richard Davies, v.; John Forde, John Webbe, Richard Flower, Nicholas Fordes, pns.

Dursley
Archd. of Gloucester, prop.; Matthew Saunder, par. chap.; Edward Davies, stip.; Edmund Gybby and John Wynnyng, chws., stated that the fencing of the cemetery was in need of repair. The commissary ordered the chws. to repair it by Christmas, on pain of 6s 8d payable to the fabric of Christ Church, Canterbury.

Thornbury (*Thornebury*)
Abbot and conv. of Tewkesbury, prop.; Mr John Fortey, v.; John Harptre, par. chap.; Walter Bussher and John Man, cantarists; William Body, John Wytfeld, John King, John Adams, pns.

Rockhampton (*Rochampton*)
Mr Robert Burton, r.; Richard Wood, chap.

Beverstone
Mr Thomas Morton, r., resides; John Levet, chap.; Richard Unwyn, Thomas Unwyn, chws.

Kingscote (*Kyngscote*)
William Clerke, chap.; John Turnour, William Ricardis, pns., deposed that all was well.

Free chapel of Lasborough (*Lasshbarogh*)
Mr Roger Church, r.

Newington Bagpath (*Nawnton*)
John Unwyn, r.; Richard Cutler, chap.; Thomas Nycollys, John Clerke, chws.

Wotton under Edge (*Wotton*)
Robert Loge, r.; Thomas Peresall, chap.; Edward Nevell, stip.; Mr John Chylcote, master of the school; John Tyler, Edward Nevill, chws.

North Nibley (*Nybley*)
John Smyth, par. chap.; John Hoskyns, stip.; John Jobbyns, John Byrt, chws.

Ozleworth (*Oselworth*)
John Maunce, r.; Nicholas Higgys, chw.

Berkeley
Abbot and conv. of St Augustine, Bristol, prop.; Mr John Awstell, v.; John Hyll, John Brown, John Towker, Richard Hawlet, John Bower, chaps.; Thomas Tyler, jnr., William Mylward, John Wynter, William Smyth, Richard Lacy, Thomas Turnocke, pns., deposed that all was well.

Mr William Wall, prior of Longbridge (*Longbregge*); Thomas Haldman, cantarist of Newport; William Hechyns, warden of Breadstone (*Bredstone*) chantry.

Stone
John Somerford, par. chap.; Hugh [*blank*], cantarist; William Smyth, John Benet, chws.

Hill
Thomas Bower, par. chap.; John Hyckyns, John Whetely, chws.

Slimbridge (*Slymbregg*)
Mr David Iya, r.; Richard Wellys, chap.; John Halling, John Horne, chws., deposed that all was well. Simon Byrne, cantarist of Cambridge chantry.

Frampton on Severn (*super Sabrinam*)
Prior and conv. of Clifford, prop.; Willliam Heydon, v.; William Calton, chap.; John Frier, John Crome, chws.

Cam (*Camme*)
Abbot and conv. of St Peter, Gloucester, prop.; Richard Knyght, v.; Henry Oswold, Richard Chapman, chws.

Stinchcombe (*Stynchcombe*)
Mr John Lucas, chap.; William Hickys, Thomas Knyght, chws.

Uley
Mr William Braggys, r.; John Higgys, chap.; John Sanders, Thomas Cowley, pns., deposed that all was well.

482.   [fo. 177v] On 14 Nov. 1498 in the parish ch. of All Saints, Bristol, Mr Church canonically visited the clergy and people of the dy. of Bristol and adjourned his visitation to the feast of the Purification *etc.*

All Saints, Bristol
Abbot and conv. of St Augustine, Bristol, prop., appeared by their proctor Mr John Griffiths; Mr John Thomas, v.; Mr John Burton, prior of the Kalends; Thomas Meryfeld, Thomas Furberer, cantarists of the Kalends; David Feyrcastell and John Ferthmores, stips.; Paul Jamis, Walter Coke, Thomas Snygg, Thomas Parvaunt, pns.

St Nicholas, Bristol
Abbot and conv. of St Augustine, Bristol, prop., appeared by proctor; Mr John Burton, v., appeared by Thomas Furborer; Eliseus Gens, par. chap.; Thomas Carter, Thomas Fychet, John Townkys, John Dyer, William Carpynter, Robert Walker, John Hurdman and John Frend, stips.; William Easby, William Thorne, chws.

St Stephen, Bristol
Mr John Esterfeld, r., appeared by Richard Brian; Henry Witney, par. chap.; Thomas Wynter, Robert Warner, Thomas Tapiscote, Robert Venaunce, John Boton and Richard Vale, stips.; John Ley, John Walsh, Richard Stephyns, pns.

Holy Trinity, Bristol
Mr William Jonys, r., appeared by John Lorymer; John Lorymer, par. chap.;
Thomas Lynckhall, William More, John Chewe and David Croley, stips.;
John Myles and Robert Capper, chws.

St Peter, Bristol
Mr Thomas Wodington, r., appeared by Mr Nicholas Stokisley; Thomas
Shaffespere, par. chap.; Richard Briant and John Doune, stips.; Robert
Yonge, William Doe, John Jonson, Matthew Cooton, pns.

St John, Bristol
Mr William Thomas, r.; John Marchall, Thomas Huchyns, William
Brightwyn and Richard ap Rice, stips.; Richard Crosse, Hugh Barker, chws.

St Werburgh, Bristol
Richard Wood, r.; William Hawkys, John Dier, Robert Smyth and Thomas
Harford, chaps.; Andrew Glosse, John Dee, chws.

St Leonard, Bristol
Abbot and conv. of St Augustine, Bristol, prop.; Mr William Cloffe, v.;
William Sare, chap.; Henry Whoper, William Geffery, chws.

St Mary in the Market Place (*in foro*)
Mr John Hawley, r.; Mr Maurice Walker, chap.; Thomas Pyggyn, Robert
Rusell, chws.

St James, Bristol
Abbot and conv. of Tewkesbury, prop.; Alexander Oberton, par. chap.;
Matthew Rowe and Robert Belamy, stips.; Robert Richardies, Richard
Baker, chws.

St Ewen, Bristol
Mr John Venymecum, r.; Ralph Hickys, chap., appeared *etc.*

St Lawrence, Bristol
Mr John Newton, r.; Mr John Ball, Richard Wheler and Edward Kenwall,
stips.; William Pille, John Stokys, chws.

St Philip, Bristol
Abbot and conv. of Tewkesbury, prop.; Robert Brown, v.; John Griffith and
John Knottysford, chaps.; Robert Forthey, John Hawkyns, chws.

St Augustine, Bristol
Abbot and conv. of St Augustine, Bristol, prop.; Mr John Griffith, v.; John
Harper, Simon Tailour, chws.

St Michael, Bristol
Edmund Moreys, r.; Robert Pendulton, chap.; William Eyvolin, William
Cradoke, chws.

Winterbourne Downe (*Wynterborne*), Gl.
Mr Thomas Palmer, r.; *dominus* William Doding, warden (*gardianus*); Richard
Hewes, chap.; William Hassul, John Geydde, pns.

Olveston, Gl.
Prior and conv. of Bath, prop., appeared by their proctor John Chaunceler; Mr John Forthey, v.; Thomas Davies, John Baker and Mr John Parsons, stips.; Thomas Hanyes, Thomas West, chws.

Almondsbury (*Almondesbury*), Gl.
Abbot and conv. of St Augustine, Bristol, prop.; Mr John London, v.; Mr Henry Scurlock and John More, stips.; Thomas Haynes, Thomas West, William Dyer and William Mody, pns., deposed that all was well.

Henbury (*Hembury*), Gl.
John Landaff, v.; Edmund Oryall, Peter Manby and John de Northwycke, stips.; George Willington, Richard Erle, pns.

Littleton-on-Severn (*Lytilton*)
John Bovet, r.; John Orchard, John Boyse, chws.

Stoke Giffard (*Stoke Gefford*), Gl.
Prior and conv. of Little Malvern, prop.; William Bromysfeld, v.; John Robyns, Thomas Lyende, chws.

Filton Fishponds (*Fylton*), Gl.
William Meredith, r.; John Wade, Thomas Symons, chws.

Chapel of Ellerton (*Eylberton*)
John Pycheley, chap.; Maurice Baker, Richard Clerke, chws.

Chapel of Stapleton (*Stapulton*), Gl.
John Davy, chap.; John Goodwyn, P. Wynhill, chws.

Chapel of Mangotsfield (*Mangarsfeld*), Gl.
David Walsh, chap.; Edmund Underhill, chw.

Clifton (*Cliffeton*), Gl.
Dean and chapter of Westbury, prop.; Henry Cater, Nicholas Whoper, chws.

483.   [fo. 178] On 19 Nov. 1498 in the parish ch. of Great Sodbury Mr Church canonically visited the clergy and people of the dy. of Hawkesbury, Gl., and adjourned his visitation to the feast of the Purification *etc.*

Great Sodbury (*Sobbury*)
Prior and conv. of Worcester, prop.; Mr John Paynter, dean of the dy., v.; John Tailour, Edward Adams and John King, stips.; Robert Boys, Robert Hill, chws.

Cold Ashton (*Coldaston*)
Mr [*blank*] Russell, r.; Maurice Gold, chap.; John at Mill, John Ymbers, chws.

Boxwell
Mr Richard Draper, r.; Richard Byddill, chap.; William Myllward, Robert Ford, chws.

Marshfield (*Mershfeld*)
Abbot and conv. of Tewkesbury, prop.; Mr Thomas Pyltys, v.; Thomas Edwardes and John Olyver, stip.; William Typper, Thomas Reede, chws.

Iron Acton (*Ureacton*)
Mr Richard Boket, r.; John Dey, chap.; John Barkeyley, John Webbe, chws.

Wickwar (*Wykesguare*)
Mr Robert Woodward, r.; John Tom, chw.

Cromhall (*Cromall*)
Hugh Walborne, r.; Mr Richard Power, chap.; Robert Pycher, Thomas Hyckys, chws.

Pucklechurch (*Poculchurche*)
Dean and chapter of Wells, prop.; John Pyryman, v.; Henry Kydd, John Taylour, chws.

Frampton Cotterell (*Frampton Coterel*)
George Blackbarough, r.; William Hoper, Thomas Royall, stips.; William Croke, John Rawlyn, chws.

Tytherington (*Tyderton*)
Prior and conv. of Llanthony, prop.; Thomas Draper, v.; William Camborne, Thomas Colymore, chws.

Tortworth (*Torteworth*)
William Poleyn, r.; William Serney, Henry Mabson, chws.

Charfield (*Charfild*)
Thomas Wolworth, r.; John Knollys, William Hyckys, chws.

Tormarton (*Thormorton*)
Mr Walter Saintlowe, r.; Thomas Taylour, chap.; John Olyver, John West, chws.

Hawkesbury (*Hawkisbury*)
Abbot and conv. of Pershore, prop.; Mr John Wilcokys, v.; Thomas Bray, chap.; Thomas Wycam, Nicholas Longdene, chws.

Siston (*Syseton*)
Edward Geynard, r.; Matthew Syllys, chap.; Richard Clerke, John Clerke, chws.

Wapley (*Wapeley*)
Abbot and conv. of St Augustine, Bristol, prop.; Robert Lewellen, v.; William Bradford, chap.

Yate
John Beneham, r.; Thomas Dymer, chap.; William Walker, Walter Brown, chws.

Alderley
Robert Higgys, r.; Thomas Mason, John Wever, chws.

Doynton (*Dyneton*)
Richard Harreys, r.; John Brewer, Thomas Hobbys, chws.

Dyrham (*Dyrram*)
Robert Burnell, r.; William Were, Thomas Newbere, chws.

Bitton (*Bytton*)
Dean and chapter of Wells, prop.; John Tyler, v.; Richard Compton, chap. of Hanham; John Warne, John Reede, chws.

Oldbury-upon-Severn (*Woldbery*)
William Synton, r.; Maurice Kyngkiscote, John Wales, chws.

Weston Birt (*Weston Byrte*)
Mr William Bowment, r.; John Unwyn, chap.

Great Badminton (*Badmonton Magna*)
Abbot and conv. of Lilleshall, prop.; Mr John Vikaries, v.; John Gurdfild, John Brownyng, chws.

Acton Turville (*Acton Tyrfild*)
Lewis Apparell, v.; John White, John Hopkyns, chws.

Little Sodbury (*Sobbury Parva*)
John Notbroke, r.; John Halyer, Thomas Pavy, chws.

Westerleigh (*Westurley*)
John Skay, chap.; John Strete, Thomas Rogers, chws.

Abson (*Abbotston*)
Boniface [*blank*], chap.; Richard Hoddys, William Morthesird, chws.

484.   [fo. 178v] On 20 Nov. 1498 in the parish ch. of Tetbury, Gl., Mr Church canonically visited the clergy and people of the dy. of Stonehouse, Gl., and adjourned his visitation to the feast of the Purification *etc.*

Tetbury
Abbot and conv. of Evesham, prop.; Mr Thomas Holford, v.; Richard Jonys, John Pynnocke, John Lane, Robert Wylcockes and John Yonge, stips.; John Harding, William Bydill, William Wattys and John Hale, pns.

Minchinhampton (*Hampton*)
Mr Richard Gyam, r.; Richard Broke, John Tofte, chaps.; Richard Willat, John Branwood, chws.

Sapperton (*Sapurton*)
Mr John Wythington, r.; John Monden, John Man, chws.

Avening (*Avenyng*)
Mr Edward Vaghan, r.; John Whithede, chap.; Richard Ball, Thomas Hathwey, chws.

Shipton Moyne (*Shepton Moyne*)
Mr Roger Braggys, r.; Richard Smyth, chap.; Nicholas Hall, Robert Hiller, chws.

Cherrington (*Cherington*)
Mr John Gobbys, r.; William Leche, chap.

Rodmarton (*Rodmorton*)
Mr Thomas Holford, r.; Richard Curtes, chap.; John Andrews, Walter Barnard, chws.

Eastington (*Estington*)
Mr William Blowmer, r.; Richard Baly, chap.; William Cloterboke, Thomas Dryver, chws.

Elkstone (*Elkeston*)
Mr Robert Woodward, r.; William Prowt, chap.; Hugh Cogill, Maurice Churchey, chws.

Nympsfield (*Nymifeld*)
Mr Richard Gossage, r.; John Adams, Robert Newman, chws.

Painswick (*Payniswyck*)
Prior and conv. of Llanthony, prop.; Mr Richard Skey, v.; Thomas King, chap.; Richard Quaddisley, John King, chws.

King's Stanley (*Stanley Regis*)
Richard Bellmore, r.; Geoffrey Jonys, chap.; Thomas Harmore, Edward Spenser, chws.

Stonehouse (*Stanhouse*)
Prioress [*recte* abbess] and conv. of Elstow, prop.; Mr Richard Petyde, v.; William Mylle, John Clerke, chws.

Leonard Stanley (*Stanley Leonarde*)
Abbot and conv. of St Peter, Gloucester, prop.; Thomas Goodson, chap.; Thomas Mabbe, Thomas Harmer, chws.

Woodchester (*Woodchestr'*)
Robert Dalton, r.; Richard Davies, chap.; John Brownyng, Hugh Witnan, chws.

Coberley (*Coburley*)
Thomas Wever, r.; William Hill, John Asshby, chaps.; Richard Tryptrap, John Scuven, chws.

Cowley
Thomas Bershyn, r.; Thomas Wever, chap.; John Blowmer, John White, chws.

Bisley (*Bysseley*)
Dean and chapter of Stoke by Clare, Sf., prop.; John Rogers, v.; Maurice Unwyn, cantarist; John West, John Kent, chws.

Edgeworth (*Eggisworthy*)
John Salle, r.; John Petet, Thomas Reve, chws.

Winstone (*Wynston*)
John Tomlynson, r.; Thomas Starncorn, Thomas Elys, chws.

Miserden (*Myserdene*)
John Catell, r.; Alan Edwardes, chap.; John Ockwold, John Chedworth, chws.

Horsley (*Horseley*)
Prior and conv. of Bruton, prop. William Cornysh, v.; Nicholas Mylle, stip.; John Cheltnam, William Stevyns, chws.

Wheatenhurst (*Whetynhurst*)
Prior and conv. of Bruton, prop.; William Nycolson, v.

Cranham (*Croneham*)
Walter Bydfeld, r.; John Churchys, John Davys, chws.

Brimpsfield (*Brymysfeld*)
Mr William Pedder, r.; Richard Sadeler, John Hastmede, chws.

Chapel of Stroud (*Strode*)
John Archbold, chap.

Chapel of Rodborough
Thomas Jonys, chap.

485.   [fo. 179] On 22 Nov. 1498 in the parish ch. of Cirencester Mr Church canonically visited the clergy and people of the dy. of Cirencester, Gl., and adjourned his visitation to the feast of the Purification *etc*.

Cirencester (*Cirencestrie*)
Abbot and conv. of Cirencester, prop.; Richard Cateson, dean of the dy.; John Glover, William Brownwiche, Mr William Amyson, Mr Thomas Devoras, William Mannyng, William Hunte, Thomas Walker, Thomas Cornysh, Richard Thurleman, John Cusshe and Richard Hadowe, stips.; Thomas Gyfford, John Gylbet, chws.

South Cerney (*Sowthcerney*)
Abbot and conv. of St Peter, Gloucester, prop.; John Sevenacre, v.; John Gye, Richard Tryndar, chws.

Driffield (*Driffeld*)
Abbot and conv. of Cirencester, prop.; Robert Drake, v.; Richard Tryndare, Richard Parsons, chws.

The parishioners of the town of Cirencester made presentation that John Clerke of Cirencester had impregnated Alice Cantell, daughter of Robert Cantell. The commissary ordered him to be cited to appear in the conv. ch. on 26 Nov., when he appeared and confessed. The commissary ordered that next Sunday he should go before the cross in the procession around the parish ch., barelegged, barefoot and bareheaded, clad in a short gown with a lighted candle in his hand, as was customary, and the following Sunday he should do similar penance in the conv. ch. The woman has fled the area.

Harnhill
John Palmer, r.; Mr [*blank*] Hall, William Brayne, chws. [*sic*].

Ampney St Mary (*Ampney Marie*)
Abbot and conv. of Cirencester, prop.; Henry Gerveys, chap.; William Brown, William May, chws.

Bibury (*Bybery*)
Abbot and conv. of Osney, prop.; Thomas Walle, John Marshall, chaps.; William Dewe, Richard Norys, chws.

Coln Rogers (*Culme Rogers*)
Reginald Grene, r.; James Tymerel, Thomas Curtes, chws.

Coln St Denis (*Culme Denyes*)
Walter Devoras, r.; James Tymerell, William Curtes, chws.

Farmington (*Thormerton*)
John Bray, chap.; John Taylor, William Tailour, chws.

Northleach (*Northlache*)
Abbot and conv. of St Peter, Gloucester, prop.; William Sawnder, v.; William Tyknall, William Smyth, chaps.; William Mydwynter, William Bekinhill, chws.

Hampnett (*Hampnet*)
William Derby, r.; Richard Baker, chap.; Richard Slayde, Richard Grene, chws.

Chedworth
Abbess and conv. of Syon, prop.; John Longge, v.; Robert Taylour, Robert Mason, chws.

Rendcombe (*Rencombe*)
Mr Richard Triesham, r.; Robert Freman, John Prydon, chws.

North Cerney
Mr William Nele, r. [appearance not noted]; William Whitechurche, chap. [appearance not noted].
William Freman and Henry Hall, pns., made presentation that *dominus* William White [*sic*] kept and still keeps Agnes Wilkins in his house as his concubine, and that he had often been detected and had abjured her before the bp. of Worcester. The commissary ordered them to be cited to appear in the conv. ch. of Cirencester on 26 Nov., when they appeared and admitted their guilt. He suspended William from the celebration of mass for the next six months and ordered Agnes to remove herself within ten days from the dioc. of Worcester, and never to return, on pain of major excommunication which he now promulgated against her in writing should she contumaciously disobey this mandate.

Daglingworth
William Strange, r.; Thomas Geffreys, Thomas Page, chws.

Bagendon (*Bagyndene*)
William Lewes, chap. [appearance not noted]; John Marchald, John Foxley, chws.

Duntisbourne Rous (*Duntisburn Militis*)
John Jonys, r. [appearance not noted]; Richard Elys, Thomas Maskall, pns.

Duntisbourne Abbots (*Duntisburn Abbatis*)
John White, r.; Thomas Malpas, chap.; Simon Foxley, John Geyle, chws.

Stretton
John Reede, chap.; William Freman, Robert Blackwell, chws.

Coates (*Cotes*)
Richard Pachy, r.; Richard Hall, William Snowe, chws.

Siddington Mary (*Syddington*)
Rectory is vacant; John Lancastre, chap.; William Hay, Thomas Pynbury, chws.

Siddington Peter (*Sadington Petre*)
George Webee, r.; Thomas Reynoldis, John White, chws.

486.   [fo. 179v] On 26 Nov. 1498 in the parish ch. of Fairford (*Fayreford*) Mr Church canonically visited the clergy and people of the dy. of Fairford, Gl., and adjourned his visitation to the feast of the Purification *etc.*

Kempsford (*Kemysforde*)
Abbot and conv. of St Peter, Gloucester, prop.; John Dursley, v.; Walter Hychman, William Inner, chws.

Lechlade (*Lychelade*)
Mr Clement Brown, v.; George Stary, par. chap.; Mr John Mason, Mr Thomas Caproun, Mr John Brown and Nicholas Chirke, cantarists; John Webster, stip. Robert Hychman and Robert Grene, pns., made presentation that Thomas Stone publicly keeps Elizabeth Doding as his concubine and has fathered four children by her. The woman was cited and appeared, and she admitted the charge. The commissary imposed public penance, that is, that the next Sunday she should go before the cross in procession around the churchyard at Lechlade, barelegged, barefoot and bareheaded, with a lighted candle in her hand, and should do similar penance on a feast day before Christmas in the churchyard of the parish ch. of Cirencester. The man has fled the area.

Meysey Hampton (*Hampton*)
Mr Robert Isham, r.; Richard Wheler, chap.; John Taskare, Robert Smarte, chws.

Eastleach (*Estlache*)
John Saunders, r.; William Palmer, Robert Lyffeley, chws.

Sherborne (*Shurborne*)
Abbot and conv. of Winchcombe, prop.; Laurence Wykylwurth, v.; Richard Meryck, John Lambarte, chws.

Fairford (*Faireforde*)
Abbot and conv. of Tewkesbury, prop.; Mr William Skynner, v. [appearance not noted]; John Marner, chw.

Quenington (*Quenynton*)
Thomas Petyr, r.; John Russell, chap.; Thomas Tucket, Thomas Perkyns, chws.

Down Ampney (*Downeampney*)
Preceptor of Quenington, prop.; John Hacket, v.; Richard Hogges, Thomas Hewe, chws.

Ampney Crucis (*Holyrode Ampney*)
Abbot and conv. of Tewkesbury, prop.; Thomas Forthey, v.; Richard Curteys, Richard Brigfeild, pns.

Coln St Aldwyn (*Culne Aylwyn*)
Abbot and conv. of St Peter, Gloucester, prop.; John Yonge, v.; John Maior, John Tasker, chws.

Southrop (*Southtrup*)
Preceptor of Quenington, prop.; Robert Strete, v.; Robert Perkyns, John Thownysend, chws.

Hatherop (*Evrthrup*)
John Stephyns, r.; Christopher Welson, chap.; Robert Hathewey, John Grene, chws.

487.   [fo. 180] On 27 Nov. 1498 in the parish ch. of Stow on the Wold Mr Church canonically visited the clergy and people of the dy. of Stow (*Stowe*), Gl., and adjourned his visitation to the feast of the Purification *etc*.

Stow on the Wold (*Stowe*)
Mr John More, r.; John Shawe, chap.; Thomas Woodhouse, stip.; John Dowe, John Smyth, chws.

Bourton on the Water (*Burton*)
Mr Thomas Grevile, r.; Richard Swynerton, chap.; Richard Perott, Thomas Symondys, chws.

Oddington
Mr Thomas Cotys, r.; John Peyrson, chap.; Thomas Worwell, Richard Tailor, chws.

Great Rissington (*Resington Magna*)
Mr John Hanchurche, r.; John Goone, Richard Lumbert, chws.

Broadwell (*Bradwell*)
George [*blank*], r.; Robert Pyket, John Profit, chws.

Rissington Wick (*Wycke Resingdon*)
Thomas Leche, r.; Richard Lenche, Richard Hyllys, chws.

Windrush (*Wynregge*)
Prior and conv. of Llanthony, prop.; John Hicheman, v.; John Pynchepole, John Bogg, pns.

Little Barrington (*Barington Parva*)
Prior and conv. of Llanthony, prop.; William Becher, v.; Richard Scalter, William Fabyan, chws.

Great Barrington (*Barington Magna*)
Prior and conv. of Llanthony, prop.; John Johnys, v.; William Brown, William Saunders, chws.

Little Rissington (*Resington Parva*)
David Johannys, r.; John Jonson, chap.
Robert Bale, Thomas Veysy, William Aikyll and John Aylewyn, pns., stated that Joan Gararde had borne two children by *dominus* John Jonson and that he had abjured her before Mr Holford, Official of the archd. of Gloucester, but he still kept her in the r.'s house and had a relationship with her. They were cited and appeared in person before the commissary at Broadway (*Bradwey*), where they admitted the charge. The commissary suspended John from the celebration of mass for the next twelve months and also ordered him to remove himself within twelve days from this dioc. to any other dioc. he wished, and not to reside in this dioc. for the next ten years; if he failed to remove himself within twelve days, or if within the next ten years he stayed in the dioc. for more than three days, he should be excommunicated, as the commissary now certified in writing. He ordered that Joan Garrard next Sunday should go before the cross in procession around the churchyard of Rissington, with a lighted candle in her hand.

Shipton Sellars (*Shipton Solas*)
Thomas Wever, r.; John Cawthryn, chap.; William Seneker, John Malle, chws.

Salperton (*Salvyrton*)
Prior and conv. of Studley, prop.; William Halle, chap.; Robert Rove, John Fyfild, chws.

Hawling (*Halling*)
John Sylwyn, r.; Richard Everton, William Hyet, chws.

Hazleton (*Halsitton*)
Mr John Harold, r.; Thomas Bedyll, chap.; John Seynton, John Fox, chws.

Turkdean (*Thurkdene*)
Abbot and conv. of Osney, prop.; John Jeffys, v.; John Humfrey, John Collys, chws.

Notgrove (*Note Greve*)
John Grenewood, r.; John Nycollys, chw.

Aston Blank (*Aston*)
Prior and conv. of Little Malvern, prop.; John Wheler, v.; Thomas Blockeley, John Edwardys, Thomas Turnour, Richard Lorde, pns.

Upper Slaughter (*Sloucestrie Superior*)
Thomas Rogers, r.; John Fysscher, John Ankys, chws.

Sutton-by-Brailes (*Sutton*)
Mr Richard Dudley, r.; John Preston, chap.; Thomas Stowte, Richard Eddon, chws.

Little Compton (*Compton*)
Abbot and conv. of Tewkesbury, prop.; Walter [*blank*], chap.; John Lambarte, Richard Brayles, chws.

Chapel of Adlestrop (*Tadistrop*)
Mr John Scanyngton, chap.; Richard Frethorne, John Frethorne, pns.

Bledington (*Bladington*)
Abbot and conv. of Winchcombe, prop.; William Packer, v.; Robert Bedowe, John Riche, chws.

Westcote
Robert Walker, r.; John Godfray, John Distling, chws.

Upper Swell (*Swell Superior*)
John Buswell, r.; John Flecher, Thomas Hawkys, chws.

Lower Swell (*Swell Inferior*)
Abbot and conv. of Notley, prop.; Robert Colwyn, v.; John Alen, Robert Arle, chws.

Temple Guiting (*Gayting Temple*)
Preceptor of Quenington, prop.; John Smyth, chap.; John Pole, John Compton, chws.

Lower Guiting (*Gayton Inferior*)
Preceptor of Quenington, prop.; Gilbert Ferror, v.; Henry Garret, Robert Smyth, chws.

Naunton (*Newyngton*)
Mr William Plomer, r.; John Wadynton, chap.; Richard Jonys, Robert Godyn, chws.

488.   [fo. 180v] On 28 Nov. 1498 in the parish ch. of Winchcombe, Gl., Mr Church canonically visited the clergy and people of the dy. of Winchcombe and adjourned his visitation to the feast of the Purification *etc*.

        [Fos. 181–3 blank.]

INSTITUTIONS

489.   [fo. 184] Inst. of Ralph Strete, chap., to vic. of Southrop (*Sothrop*), Gl., vac. by res. of William Scounide. P. John Kendall, prior of the Hospital of St John of Jerusalem in England. I. archd. of Gloucester. Hospital of St Wulfstan, Worcester, 28 Oct. 1498.

490.   Inst. of Mr Robert Colman, M.A., to vic. of Lower Swell (*Swellys*), Gl., vac. by res. of Mr John Altherton. P. abbot and conv. of Notley (*Notteley*), Lincoln dioc. I. archd. of Gloucester. Worcester, 3 Oct. 1498.

491.	Inst. of Maurice Westbury, clerk, to ch. of Stanton (*Staunton*), Gl., vac. by d. of Thomas Williams, chap. P. abbot and conv. of Winchcombe. I. archd. of Gloucester. Worcester, 7 Oct. 1498.

492.	Inst. of Mr Thomas Holes, clerk, to prebend of Bitton (*Bytton*), Gl., vac. by d. of Mr John Gunthorp, clerk, and in the collation of the bp. of Salisbury. I. dean of Sodbury. Worcester, 20 Oct. 1498.

493.	Inst. of Hugh Turnour, chap., to perpetual chantry of B.V.M. in chapel of Stone in the parish of Berkeley, Gl., vac. by d. of Thomas Dyryet. P. John Serjaunt and Christine his wife. I. archd. of Gloucester. Worcester, 22 Oct. 1498.

494.	Inst. of Mr Thomas Holford, clerk, in the person of his proctor Mr John Osborne, clerk, to ch. of Rodmarton (*Rodmerton*), Gl., vac. by res. of Mr Thomas Byrchold, clerk. P. William Grevyle and William Wye, by virtue of enfeofment by Thomas Whitington, lord of Rodmarton. I. archd. of Gloucester. There appeared before the commissary as he sat judicially in St Wulfstan's hospital Mr Robert Enkbarough, notary public, Byrchold's proctor, who requested the commissary to assign to Byrchold for his livelihood an annual pension from the fruits of the ch. The commissary assigned to him for the duration of his life an annual pension of 10 marks, to be paid in equal instalments at the feast of the Annunciation of the B.V.M. and at Michaelmas. Worcester, 24 Oct. 1498.

495.	[fo. 184v] Inst. of Mr Roger Lupton, clerk, to prebend or canonry of St Michael in the coll. ch. of St Mary, Warwick, vac. by res. of Mr Peter Greves. P. the king. I. archd. of Worcester. Winchcombe, 29 Nov. 1498.

496.	Inst. of Thomas Clerke, chap., to hospital or leperhouse of St Michael, Warwick (*Warwik'*), vac. by res. of Mr Thomas Clerke *alias* Wyckwan. P. the king. I. archd. of Worcester. Gloucester, 29 Nov. 1498.

497.	Inst. of Mr Thomas Strange, clerk, to vic. of St Philip and St James in the suburbs of Bristol, vac. by res. of Robert Brown, chap. P. abbot and conv. of Tewkesbury. I. archd. of Gloucester. Winchcombe, 30 Nov. 1498.

498.	Inst. of Robert Hunte, chap., to ch. of Siddington by Cirencester (*Sudington*), Gl., vac. by d. of Thomas ap Morgan. P. prior and conv. of Monmouth (*Monemouth*). I. archd. of Gloucester. Worcester, 22 Dec. 1498.

499.	Inst. of Ralph Heyfond, chap., to vic. of Studley (*Stodeley*), Wa., vac. by d. of Thomas Dawby. P. prior and conv. of Studley. I. archd. of Worcester. Worcester, 24 Dec. 1498.

500.	Inst. of Mr Edward Derby, M.A., to ch. of Little Rissington (*Resingdon*), Gl., vac. by res. of Mr David Jonys. P. abbot and conv. of Osney, Lincoln dioc. I. archd. of Gloucester. An oath was taken to pay the retiring incumbent an annual pension of 46s 8d. 2 Feb. 1499.

501.   Inst. of Mr Harper, clerk, to vic. of St Nicholas, Bristol, vac. by d. of Mr John Burton, clerk. P. abbot and convent of St Augustine, Bristol. I. archd. of Gloucester. 3 Feb. 1499.

502.   [fo. 185] Inst. of Mr John Vaughan, clerk, to perpetual chantry known as the first chantry of the priory of the fraternity of the Kalends in the ch. of All Saints, Bristol, vac. by d. of Mr John Burton, clerk. P. Philip Ryngstone, mayor of Bristol. I. archd. of Gloucester. 8 Feb. 1499.

[Fo. 185v blank.]

ACCOUNTS OF THE VACANCY OF THE SEE

503.   [fo. 186] Procurations due from the archdeaconry of Worcester:
From clergy of dy. of Worcester (*Wigorn'*), 66s 8d; preceptor of St Wulfstan's hospital, Worcester, 66s 8d; r. of Astley (Asteley), Wo., 53s 4d; prior of Great Malvern for ch. of Powick (*Powycke*), Wo., 66s 8d; prior of Little Malvern, 20s; clergy of dy. of Droitwich (*Wiche*), 66s 8d; abbot of Bordesley for ch. of Tardebigge (*Terbick*), Wo., 53s 4d; clergy of dy. of Kidderminster (*Kyddermyster*), 66s 8d; abbot of Halesowen for Halesowen ch., 53s 4d; clergy of dy. of Christianity, Warwick (*Warwici*), 66s 8d; prioress of Wroxall for ch. of Wroxhall (*Wrexhale*), Wa., 53s 4d; prior of Alcestre (*Alincestre*), 53s 4d; prior of Wootton Wawen (*Wotton Wawen*) for ch. of Wootton (*Wotton*), Wa., 53s 4d; dean and chapter of coll. ch. of St Mary, Warwick, 53s 4d; prior of St Sepulchre, Warwick, 53s 4d; clergy of dy. of Kineton (*Kington*), 66s 8d; ch. of Wolford, Wa., 53s 4d; coll. ch. of Stratford upon Avon, Wa., 53s 4d; clergy of dy. of Pershore, 66s 8d; abbot of Pershore, 66s 8d; clergy of dy. of Blockley, 40s.   Total: £64 6s 8d

504.   Procurations due from the archdeaconry of Gloucester:
From clergy of dy. of Campden (*Campdene*), 66s 8d; chs. of Campden, Didbrook (*Dudbroke*), Childswickham (*Wyckwan*) and Beckford (*Beckforde*), 53s 4d each; clergy of dy. of Stow (*Stowe*), 66s 8d; Longborough (*Langbarough*) ch., 40s; clergy of dy. of Fairford (*Faireford*), 66s 8d; Fairford ch., 53s 4d; clergy of dy. of Cirencester (*Cirencestrie*), 66s 8d; abbot of Cirencester, 66s 8d; clergy of dys. of Stonehouse, Dursley, Hawkesbury (*Hawkysbury*) and Bristol, 66s 8d each; abbot of St Augustine's, Bristol, 66s 8d; St Mark's hospital (*sancti Marci de Gauntes*), Bristol, 26s 8d; coll. ch. of Westbury on Trym, 53s 4d; clergy of dy. of Gloucester, 66s 8d; abbot of St Peter's, Gloucester, 66s 8d; prior of Llanthony, 53s 4d; clergy of dy. of Winchcombe (*Wynchcombe*), 66s 8d; abbots of Winchcombe and Tewkesbury (*Tewkysbury*), 66s 8d each; ch. of Deerhurst (*Durhurste*), 53s 4d.   Total: £74

TOTAL PROCURATIONS: £138 6s 8d

505.   Synodals due in the archdeaconry of Gloucester at Michaelmas:
Dean of dy. of Bristol (*Bristollie*), 10s 4d; deans of Dursley, 11s 8d; Cirencester, 13s 4d; Winchcombe, 8s; Campden, 16s 8d; Blockley, 3s 6d;

Stonehouse, 15s 4d; Fairford, 8s; Stow, 14s; Gloucester, 12s 8d; Hawkesbury, 16s 8d.   Total: £6 9s 10d

506.   Benefices appropriated to the episcopal *mensa*:
For tithes of grain of Blockley, Gl., £23 15s; tithes of grain of Hillingdon, Mx., £33 6s 8d.   Total: £57 20d

507.   [fo. 186v] Peter's Pence:
Deans of Bristol, 10s 2d; Dursley, 47s 4d; Cirencester, 30s; Winchcombe, 55s; Campden, 37s; Blockley, 6s 1d; Hawkesbury, 34s; Stonehouse, 39s; Fairford, 23s 6d; Stow, 36s 6d; Gloucester, 28s 5d; dean of Christianity, Warwick, 57s 6d; treasurer of Warwick, 7s 5d; deans of Kidderminster, 26s 6d; Kineton, 53s 4d; Powick, 29s; Droitwich, 24s 10d; Pershore, 24s 4½d; Worcester, 40s.   Total: £30 9s 2½d

508.   Pensions due at Michaelmas:
Abbot of Tewkesbury for ch. of Thornbury (*Thornebury*), Gl., 26s 8d; same for priory of Deerhurst (*Durhurst*), 20s; same for ch. of Little Compton (*Compton*), Wa., 6s 8d; provost and fellows of the Queen's College (*Aule Regine*), Oxford, for ch. of Newbold Pacey (*Newbold*), Wa., 6s 8d; abbot of Westminster for ch. of Longdon, Wo., 20s; v. of Kidderminster (*Kyddermystr'*), Wo., for ch. of the same, 13s 4d; master of St John's hospital, Warwick, for ch. of Moreton Morell (*Morton Morell*), Wa., 3s 4d; abbot of Evesham for ch. of Mickleton (*Mekylton*), Gl., 13s 4d; abbot of Halesowen for ch. of Clent (*Clente*), Wo., 26s 8d; same for ch. of Dodford (*Dudford*), Wo., 6s 8d; prior of Coventry for ch. of Honington (*Hunynton*), Wa., 20s; prioress of Cook Hill (*Cokhill*) for ch. of Bishampton (*Bysshampton*), Wo., 13s 4d; abbot of Evesham for ch. of Ombursley (*Umbursley*), Wo., 30s; same for priory of Alcester (*Alincestre*), 13s 4d; same for ch. of Eyford, Gl., 10d; abbot of Lilleshall (*Lyllishill*), 6s 8d; prior of Great Malvern for ch. of Upper Snodsbury (*Snodsbury*), Wo., 6s 8d; same for chapel of Woodsfield (*Wordefeld*), Wo., 6s 8d; abbot of Chester for ch. of Campden, Gl., 10s; abbot of Biddlesden for ch. of Ebrington, Gl., 13s 4d; abbot of Hailes for ch. of Avening (*Avynnyng*), Gl., 20s; abbot of Winchcombe for ch. of Bledington (*Bladington*), Gl., 3s 4d; prior of Worcester for ch. of Stoke Prior (*Stoke*), Wo., 6s 8d; abbot of Pershore for ch. of Broadway (*Bradwey*), Wo., 3s 4d; same for ch. of Eckington (*Ekington*), Wo., 3s 4d; same for ch. of St Peter, Worcester, 3s 4d; dean and chapter of Warwick [St Mary's] for ch. of Chaddesley Corbett (*Chaddesley*), Wo., 6s 8d; same for ch. of Heathcote (*Haselosa*), Wa., 3s 4d; same for ch. of Pillerton (*Pyllarton*), Wa., 6s 8d; same for ch. of St Peter, Warwick, 3s 4d; same for ch. of St Nicholas, Warwick, 13s 4d; same for ch. of Dudbrook (*Dudbroke*), Gl., 6s 8d; abbot of Gloucester for ch. of Holy Trinity, Gloucester, 5s; same for ch. of St Mary before the Abbey Gate, 6s 8d; prior of St James, Bristol, for ch. of St Philip, Bristol, 6s 8d; dean and chapter of Westbury upon Trym for ch. of Clifton (*Clyfton*), Gl., 12d; same for ch. of Kempsey (*Keamsey*), Wo., 6s 8d; v. of Pucklechurch (*Pokulchurch*), Gl., for church of same, 6s 8d; chantry of Lechlade (*Lichlade*), Gl., for Lechlade priory, 6s 8d; dean and chapter of Stoke by Clare for ch. of Bisley (*Bysseley*), Gl., 26s 8d; archd. of Gloucester for ch. of

Dursley (*Durseley*), Gl., 2s; abbot of Kenilworth for triennial pension for ch. of Bidford-on-Avon (*Bydforde*), Gl., 53s 4d.   Total: £24 12d

509.   Receipts for institutions to benefices:
Vic. of Southrop (*Sothrop*), Gl.; prebend of Bitton, Gl.; chantry of St Mary in chapel of Stone, Gl.; vic. of Lower Swell (*Swellys*), Gl.; ch. of Stanton (*Staunton*), Gl.; ch. of Rodmarton (*Rodmerton*), Gl.; hospital of St Michael, Warwick; prebend of St Michael in coll. ch. of Warwick; ch. of St Philip and St James, Bristol; ch. of *Chesyncote*; ch. of Siddington (*Sudington*), Gl.; vic. of Studley (*Stodeley*), Wa.; vic. of St Nicholas, Bristol; ch. of Little Rissington (*Resingdon Parva*), Gl.; chantry of the fraternity of the Kalends, Bristol, 6s 8d each.   Total: £5

510.   [fo. 187] Receipts for probate of testaments.
John Mylys of Gloucester, 3s 4d; Nicholas Jonys of Horsley (*Horseley*), Gl., 10s; John Meysy of Eycote, Gl., 20s; Ralph Garret of Stourbridge (*Sturbregge*), Wo., 10s; Agnes Langford, wife of John Lanford of Worcester, 20s; John Payne of Tewkesbury, Gl., 6s 8d.   Total: 76s 8d

[Total revenue *sede vacante* here listed: £265 5s 0½d.]

[Fo. 187v blank, fos. 188–9 wanting, fo. 190 blank.]

[fo. 191] VACANCY OF THE EPISCOPAL SEE OF SALISBURY THROUGH THE DEATH OF JOHN BLYTHE OF GOOD MEMORY, LATELY BISHOP OF SALISBURY WHICH VACANCY BEGAN ON THE [blank] DAY OF AUGUST 1499 A.D. IN THE THIRTEENTH YEAR FROM THE TRANSLATION OF THE VERY REVEREND FATHER IN CHRIST AND LORD JOHN, BY DIVINE MERCY CARDINAL PRIEST OF ST ANASTASIA IN THE HOLY ROMAN CHURCH, ARCHBISHOP OF CANTERBURY, PRIMATE OF ALL ENGLAND AND LEGATE OF THE APOSTOLIC SEE, AND LASTED UNTIL THE FOLLOWING 19 MARCH.

Note: the see became vacant by the death of John Blythe on 23 Aug. 1499 and was filled by the translation from Bangor of Henry Deane on 8 Jan. 1500.

511.   Commission with powers of canonical coercion to Mr Laurence Cockys, Decr. D., canon-residentiary of the cath. ch. of Salisbury (*Sar'*), nominated with Mr William Russell and Mr William Elyott, also canons-residentiary, by the dean and chapter of Salisbury according to the composition between their predecessors and abp. Boniface,[1] as Official in the city and dioc. of Salisbury in the vacancy of the see following the d. of bp. John, with power to exercise episcopal jurisdiction and the obligation to account to the abp. for all revenues due by virtue of the vacancy to the abp. and to the ch. of Canterbury. Knole, 19 Sept. 1499.

    [1] I. J. Churchill, *Canterbury Administration* (1933), ii, 55-9.

512.   [fo. 191v] Inst. of Mr Christopher Bainbrige, J.U.D., to ch. of Elington (*Elyngdon*) alias Wroughton, Wlt., vac. by d. of Mr Edmund Chaterton. P. Thomas bp. of Winchester. I. archd. of Wiltshire. Salisbury, 28 Sept. 1499.

513.   Inst. of Richard Lee to free chapel of St Michael the Archangel, Norridge (*Norrige*), Wlt., vac. by d. of Gervase Beteel. P. John Lee, esq. I. archd. of Salisbury. Salisbury, 30 Sept. 1499.

514.   Inst. of Thomas Cowley, chap., to ch. of Corscombe, Do., vac. by d. of Mr John Husee. P. abbot and conv. of Sherborne. I. archd. of Dorset. Salisbury, 28 Sept. 1499.

515.   Inst. of John Aisshe, chap., to ch. of Sutton Veny (*Venney Sutton*), Wlt., vac. by d. of Mr Thomas Pray. P. Robert Baynard, esq. I. archd. of Salisbury. Salisbury, 2 Oct. 1499.

516.   Inst. of Thomas Everard, chap., to ch. of St Michael, Wareham (*Warham*), Do., vac. by d. of Mr David Mylis. P. prior and conv. of the Charterhouse of Sheen. I. archd. of Dorset. Salisbury, 5 Oct. 1499.

517.   Inst. of Edmund Worthynton, chap., to wardenship of the hospital of St Bartholomew, Newbury, Brk., vac. by d. of William Bray. P. Sir William

Noys, kt., and Sir Robert Harecourt, kt. I. archd. of Berkshire. Salisbury, 5 Oct. 1499.

518.   Inst. of Mr Thomas Martyn, Decr. D., pr., to vic. of Tilshead (*Tydilside*), Wlt., vac. by d. of William Okey. P. prior and conv. of Ivychurch (*Ederos'*). I. archd. of Salisbury. Salisbury, 10 Oct. 1499.

519.   [fo. 192] Inst. of John Pope, chap., to vic. of Windsor (*Wyndesore*), Brk., vac. by d. of Richard Reynford. P. abbot and conv. of Waltham Holy Cross. I. archd. of Berkshire. Salisbury, 10 Oct. 1499.

520.   Inst. of William Foster, chap., to perpetual chantry of St Mary in the north part of the parish ch. of All Saints, North Wraxall (*North Wraxhale*), Wlt., vac. by d. of William Straunge. P. Thomas Yonge, esq. I. archd. of Wiltshire. Salisbury, 10 Oct. 1499.

521.   Inst. of Mr William Thornebourgh, D.C.L., to ch. of St Mary, Steeple Langford (*Stepillangford*), Wlt., vac. by d. of Mr Edmund Martyn. P. Sir John Huddelston, kt., and Joan his wife. I. archd. of Salisbury. Salisbury, 11 Oct. 1499.

522.   Inst. of Mr William Vowell, Decr. B., to ch. of Stoke Abbot (*Stoke Abbatis*), Do., vac. by res. of John Loscombe. P. abbot and conv. of Sherborne. I. archd. of Dorset. Sherborne, 16 Nov. 1499.

523.   Inst. of Robert Knoddy, B.A., chap., to vic. of East Hagbourne (*Hakeborne*), Brk., vac. by d. of Mr Edward Overton. P. abbot and conv. of Cirencester in Worcester dioc. I. archd. of Berkshire. Salisbury, 22 Nov. 1499.

524.   Inst. of William Chichestre, B.C.L., clerk, to free chapel in the manor of Athelhampton (*Athelhamstone*), Do., vac. by d. of Mr Edmund Martyn, J.U.D. P. William Martyn, esq. I. archd. of Dorset. Salisbury, 27 Nov. 1499.

525.   Inst. of William Dadyng, chap., to ch. of West Kington (*Westkynton*), Wlt., vac. by res. of Mr Richard Berde. P. the king. I. archd. of Wiltshire. Salisbury, 2 Dec. 1499.

526.   Inst. of William Coventre, chap., to ch. of Manningford Abbots (*Mannyngford Abbatis*), Wlt., vac. by res. of John Clerk. P. abbot and conv. of Hyde, Winchester dioc. I. archd. of Wiltshire. Salisbury, 3 Dec. 1499.

527.   [fo. 192v] Inst. of John Stratton *alias* London to ch. of Holy Trinity, Wareham (*Warham*), Do., vac. by res. of Mr William Vowell, Decr. B. P. abbot and conv. of Sherborne. I. archd. of Dorset. Salisbury, 5 Dec. 1499.

528.   Inst. of Hugh Palmer, chap., to ch. of St Peter, Everley, Wlt., vac. by res. of Mr William Palmer. P. abbess and conv. of Wherwell, Winchester dioc. I. archd. of Wiltshire. Salisbury, 11 Dec. 1499.

529.   Inst. of John Crosse, chap., to ch. of St Michael South Street, Wilton (*Wylton*), Wlt., vac. by res. of John Stratton. P. prioress and conv. of Dartford, Kent. I. archd. of Salisbury. Salisbury, 11 Dec. 1499.

530.   Inst. of John Chapman, chap., to ch. of Batcombe, Do., vac. by res. of William Bachell. P. Robert Willoughby, lord Broke. I. archd. of Salisbury. Salisbury, 11 Dec. 1499.

531.   Inst. of Mr Thomas Alphyn, B.C.L., pr., to vic. of Gussage (*Gyssage*) All Saints, Do., vac. by res. of Elias Banester. P. Robert Langton, J.U.D., archd. of Dorset. I. archd. of Dorset. 14 Dec. 1499.

532.   Inst. of Roger Kyrlagh, B.A., pr., to vic. of North Morton, Brk., vac. by res. of Mr Thomas Martyn, Decr. D. P. Mr Stephen Berworth, M.D., archd. of Berkshire.[1] I. archd. of Berkshire. 16 Dec. 1499.

   [1] MS Dorset; cf. *Fasti 1300–1540, Salisbury*, p. 10.

533.   Inst. of John Paytrell, chap, to ch. of Babstoke, Wlt., vac. by d. of William Horsman. P. abbess and conv. of Wilton. I. archd. of Salisbury. 3 Dec. 1499.

534.   [fo. 193] Inst. of John Elys, chap., to ch. of Wimborne Minster (*Wymborn Mynstre*), Do., vac. by d. of Hugh Shoore. P. Mr Hugh Oldom, dean of the royal free chapel of Wimborne Minster and patron of the parish ch. of Stanbridge (*Stanbrigge*), Do., true patron *hac vice* of the parish ch. of Wimborne Minster, at the nomination to him of Elys by Richard Willoughby, esq. I. archd. of Dorset. Salisbury, 23 Dec. 1499.

535.   Inst. of Richard Okus, chap., to ch. of St Andrew, West Chelborough (*Chalebury*), Do., vac. by res. of John Paytrell. P. abbess and conv. of Wilton, I. archd. of Dorset. 23 Dec. 1499.

536.   Inst. of William Foxcote, chap., to vic. of Seagry (*Segre*), Wlt., vac. by d. of Thomas Raffeson. P. prior and conv. of Bradenstoke. I. archd. of Wiltshire. Salisbury, 3 Jan. 1499.

537.   Inst. of Mr Thomas Martyn, Decr. D., to ch. of Semley (*Semely*), Wlt., vac. by res. of Mr Edward Willoughby. P. abbess and conv. of Wilton. I. archd. of Salisbury. Salisbury, 4 Jan. 1500.

538.   Inst. of Mr John Toppyng, br. of the Trinitarian house of Easton Royal (*Eston*), Wlt., as minister of the same house. P. William Ryngebourne, esq., *hac vice*. I. archd. of Wiltshire. Salisbury, 7 Jan. 1500.

539.   Inst. of Thomas Pendilton, chap., to vic. of Eisey (*Eysy*), Wlt., vac. by d. of David Philip *alias* Jonys. P. abbot and conv. of Cirencester, Worcester dioc. I. archd. of Wiltshire. Salisbury, 14 Jan. 1500.

540.   Inst. of Mr Robert Parker, Decr. B., chap., to rectory of Bradford Peverell, Do., vac. by d. of William Pers. P. warden and scholars of Winchester coll. I. archd. of Dorset. 17 Jan. 1500.

541. [fo. 193v] Inst. of Henry Russell, clerk, student of Oxford University, to ch. of East Stoke (*Est Stoke*), Do., vac. by d. of Thomas Symmes. P. Roger Cherevell, *generosus*. I. archd. of Dorset. Salisbury, 24 Jan. 1500.

542. Inst. of James Stretbarell, chap., to prebend or canonry of Alton Borealis in cath. ch. of Salisbury, vac. by res. of Mr Hugh Oldham. P. the king. I. dean and chapter of Salisbury. Salisbury, 1 Feb. 1500.

543. Inst. of Richard Parson *alias* Willys to vic. of Tilshead (*Tyleshede*), Wlt., vac. by res. of Mr Thomas Martyn. P. prior and convent of Ivychurch. I. archd. of Salisbury. Salisbury, 13 Feb. 1500.

544. Inst. of John Rewstone, chap., to ch. of St Peter, Wareham, Do., vac. by d. of William Jagons. P. prior and conv. of the Charterhouse of Sheen, Winchester dioc. I. archd. of Dorset. Salisbury, 4 Mar. 1500.

545. Inst. of Thomas Robynson, chap., to ch. of Draycot Cerne (*Draycote Cerne*), Do., vac. by d. of Richard Baldewyn. P. Thomas Longe, esq. I. archd. of Wiltshire. Salisbury, 16 Mar. 1500.

546. Inst. of John Aphewell, chap., to ch. of Easthampstead (*Esthamstede*), Brk., vac. by d. of John Downe. P. prior and conv. of Hurley. I. archd. of Berkshire. Salisbury, 16 Mar. 1500.

547. Inst. of William Kent, chap., to vic. of Box, Wlt., vac. by res. of Edward Betrich. P. prior and conv. of Monkton Farleigh. I. archd. of Wiltshire. Salisbury, 18 Mar. 1500.

548. Inst. of Thomas Lecher, chap., to vic. of Waltham St Lawrence, Brk., vac. by d. of Nicholas Hendlowe. P. prior and conv. of Hurley. I. archd. of Berkshire. Salisbury, 19 Mar. 1500.

549. [fo. 194] On 29 June 1499 there had appeared in person before the Official in the consistory court in the cath. John Whitehorne, r. of Letcombe Bassett (*Letombasset*), Brk., and John Lydtister, chap., of Sparsholt (*Sparsold*), Brk., who admitted all the charges against them, as detailed in their abjurations below. On 2 Nov. 1499 they appeared before the Official in his residence, and he ordered that on the following Sunday they should proceed before the cross in the cath. ch., bareheaded and barefoot, a faggot on their left shoulders and a torch in their right hands, Whitehorne in addition having certain of his books openly suspended around his neck, and that when the procession was concluded they should publicly abjure their heresies and errors before the people in the accustomed form; and that on the following Tuesday they should go from the cath. through the busiest streets of the city, followed by the curates of the chs. of St Thomas and St Edmund, who should discipline them with rods at certain stations, and they should proceed thus to the cross in the market place where they should abjure their heresies and errors as before. There Whitehorne should give up the books around his neck to the fire. They should then return to the cath., praying to God as they went.

550.   Abjuration of John Whitehorne.

In the name of the Trinite, Fader, Sonne and Holy Gost, His blissid moder and all the holy companye of hevin, I, Sir John Whitehorne, parson of the parissh chirch of Lettcombassett in the diocese of Sarum, gretely noted, defamed, detect, unto the reverend fader in God John by the grace of God late bisshop of Sarum, my juge and ordinary, denounced for an untrewbeleving man, and also that I shuld holde, afferme, teche and defende opinly and prively heresies, errours and singuler opinions and fals doctrines contrarie to the common doctrine of oure moder Hooly Chirch with fals sotilteis evilsounding and dissaiveable to the erys of trew symple-understandyng Cristin people, whiche be to me nowe by the auctorite of myn ordynarie proceding to office promoted iudicyally obiect.

Articuli obiecti contra dictum Whithorne.

Fyrst, that in the sacrament of the aulter is not the verry body of Crist that was borne of a virgin, that was crucified and died to redeem mankynd, that arose from deth to lyef and that stied into hevinn, but there is pure brede and nowght els, saying that Crist assendid into hevin in His verry body, so that He con, myght not nor shall not come ayenn here in erth untyll the day of dome, whenne He shall juge all the world; and that Crist saying to His dissiples at His mawndy: 'Take and ete, this ys My body etc.', mente nat of brede that He brak ther but of Goddes word, as in the begynnyng of Saint Johns gospell, and therefore whoo so ever resceive devoutly Goddis word, he resceyvith the verrye body of Criste.

Item, that it is of no nede to be shrevin to a prest or to any other mynestre of the Chirch, but that it is inowgh to be aknowyng to God and to be sory for the synne, being in wil to returne no more to the sinne.

Item, that imagis of the crucifix, of oure lady and other saintes shuld not be worshipped nor noo lightes shuld be sett afore theim, for they be but stokkes and stonys.

Item, that thise pilgremagis usid of good Cristin people unto the hooly saintes be not availeable nor lefull, and that the money spent in suche cause is but wastid and lost, for the saintes have noe nede thereof.

Item, that the Pope is Antecrist and other ministres of the Chirch be his disciples, for like as it hath be said that Antecrist shuld turne all upp and downe at his commyng, so that the Pope be his lawes and dispensaciouns turneth upp and downe the lawes that Crist lefte to the people.

Item, whenne Crist shulde ascende into hevin He left His power with His appostylles, and from theim the same power remayneth with every goode trewe Cristin mann and womann lyving virtuously as the appostelles did, so that prestes and bysshoppes have no more auctorite thenne another laymann that folowith the teching and the good conversacioun of the appostolles.

Item, that the curses and other sentences of the Chirch be of noone effect and nowght to be sett by, for no curse is to be sette by ne dred but only the curse of God, which the bisshoppis and prestes have not in ther power.

Thise articules and every of theim afore rehersid and to me by mynn ordynarie iudicially obiectid I, Sir John Whitehorne afore said, opinly knowliche my silf and confesse of my fre will to have hold, lernyd and belyvid, and so have tought and affermed to other, which alle and every of theim I undrestond and belyve herisies and contrary to the common doctrine and determinacioun of the universall Chirch of Crist, and confesse me here to have be an heretik lerner and techer of heresies, errors, opinions and fals doctrinis contrary to the Cristin faith. And for as moche that it is so that the lawes of the Chirch of Crist and holy canouns of saintes be grounded in mercy, and God wil not the deth of a synner but that he be convertid and live, and also the Chirch closith not hir lappe to theym that wil returne, I therefore, willing to be partyner of this foresaid mercy, foresake and renownce also thise articulis afore rehersid and confess theim to be heresies, errors and prohibite doctrine, and nowe being contrite and fully repentyng theym alle and every of theim iudicially and solemnely do theim forsake, abiure and wilfully renunce for evermore, and not only theim but alle other heresies, errors and dampnable doctrinis contrary to the determination of the universall Church of Criste; also that I shall nevir hereaftre be to any suche persones or persone favorour, councelar, mayntener, prively or pertly, but yf I knowe any suche hereaftre I shall denunce and disclose theim to myne ordinarye beyng at that tyme or to his officers or els to sum persones of the Chirch as have iurisdiccioun on thes persones so fawte, so helpe me God and thise Holy Evangelys, submittyng me opinly, not coacte but of my fre will to the payne, regour and sharpenes of the lawe that a man relapsid ought to suffre in such caas yf I ever do or hold contrary to this my present abiuracioun in part or in hoole thereof. In witnesse whereof I subscribe with myne owen hand making a crosse and require all Cristin menn here present to recorde and witnes ayenst me and this my present confessioun and abiuracioun yf I from this day foreward offence or do contrarye to the same.

551.   [fo. 194v] *Abiuracio domini Iohannis Lydtyster.*
In the name of the Trinite, Fader, Sonne and Holigost *etc.* I, Sir John Lydtister, late serving in the parissh chirch of Sparsold in the diocese of Sarum, gretely notid *etc. ut in precedente abiuracione.*
That in the sacrament in the aulter ys not the very body of Crist that was born of a virgin, that was crucified and died to redeme mankynde, that arose from deth to lief and that stied into hevin, but there is pure brede and nought els, affermyng that it is not possible a man made by God shuld make God his maker, and that Crist assendid into hevin in His verry body, so that He comith not nor shall not come agene here in erthe unto the day of dome whenne He shall juge all the world.
   This articule afore rehersid and to me by myne ordinarie *etc. ut in precedente abiuracione.*

552.   [fo. 195] There appeared before the Official in the consistory court on 4 Nov. 1499 William Turwyn of Ufton Robert, Brk., a clerk or reputed as such, who stated that he had been wrongly and maliciously defamed of the serious crime of the theft of various goods, which he denied. The Official ordered him to purge himself on 25 Nov., and so that his compurgation should not be clandestine, he ordered proclamation to be made at time of divine service in the cath. and the parish chs. of Ufton Robert (*Uffon Robert*) and Sulhampstead Bannister (*Selhamstede*), Brk., where the theft was alleged to have been committed. On 25 Nov. Robert Ryson, mandatory in this matter, swore that proclamation had been made and a monition issued according to

160

the tenor of the mandate. Proclamation was then made once more that if any person wished to object to compurgation he should advance his objection in due legal form. Since no legitimate objection was advanced, any person who might object was accused on William's behalf of contumacy in not proposing his objection, and it was requested that he should be admitted to compurgation, to which request the Official acceded. The article, which had previously been shown to William, was now read to him, and he declared himself under oath to be guiltless and innocent of all the charges included within this article. His compurgators also swore on oath that they believed him to be innocent. It was then requested on William's behalf that the Official should declare him innocent of this crime, and the Official declared that in the eyes of the ecclesiastical court William was in this matter guiltless and innocent. The compurgators were: Edward Duke, Richard David, Richard Woodeward and Richard Lane, of the city of Salisbury (*Nove Sar'*). Salisbury, 25 Nov. 1499.

553.   Mandate of Mr Laurence Cokkys to the cur. of Sulhampstead Bannister (*Selhamstede Banaster*), Brk., and to all chaps. and curs. in Salisbury dioc. William Turwyn of Ufton Robert has informed the Official that he has lately been accused of various crimes alleged to have been feloniously committed by him, and specifically that he with others, by force and with arms, viz. with swords and staves etc., on 3 May 1491 at Sulhampstead Bannister in the county of Berkshire broke into and entered the house of Stephen Russell and feloniously took and carried away £6 16s of the goods and chattels of the foresaid Stephen, against the king's peace, and that on the same day he broke into the same house and took and carried away a chalice worth 15 marks of the goods and chattels of the parishioners of Sulhampstead Bannister which were in the custody of the said Stephen, the guardian of their goods and chattels; for which reason he was taken by the king's servants and placed in custody in the gaol of the liberty of Reading (*Redyng*), and eventually he was convicted of these crimes by a secular judge and as a convicted clerk was delivered by the king's justices to his ordinary for judgement, according to the liberties of the church, and now he requested that the Official should allow him to undertake canonical purgation. The Official therefore orders that proclamation shall be made publicly on a Sunday or feast day in the cath. ch., in the parish ch. of Sulhampstead Bannister and in neighbouring places, that if Stephen Russell or the inhabitants of Sulhampstead Bannister or any other person should wish to accuse William Turwyn of the foresaid crimes or to propose any canonical reason why the Official should not allow him to proceed to compurgation, they should appear in the consistory court in the cath. ch. at the accustomed hour on Monday 25 Nov. before the Official or his specially-deputed commissary to state their interest in this matter. Recipients of this mandate are to certify the Official of action taken. Salisbury, 4 Nov., 1499.

554.   [fo. 195v] Mandate to the incumbent of Stoke Wake (*Stokewake*), Do., all incumbents of the city of Salisbury and Thomas Childe, chap., dean of the rural dy. of Whitechurch, Do. The Official has received a request for admission to compurgation from John Saunders of Stoke Wake, who has been charged that on 17 Feb. 1498 at *Edersley* in Milborne [*unid.*] (*Milborn*), Do., he

lay in ambush on the king's highway and attacked John Suppeley, robbing him of 26s 8d, for which reason he was taken by the lay power, imprisoned and delivered to the bp. of Salisbury. Proclamation is to be made on three Sundays or feast days in the cath. and the parish chs. of Salisbury and Stoke Wake that any who may wish to object to this compurgation should appear in the consistory court on 9 Dec. Salisbury, 28 Oct. 1499.

On 9 Dec. it was certified that this mandate had been executed and, as no legitimate compurgator appeared, John Saunders was admitted to compurgation and released from prison, insofar as this pertained to the ecclesiastical court. The compurgators were: Edward Duke, Richard David, Thomas Barkister, Richard Lane, Richard Wodeward and Thomas Wheler, clerks.

555.   Mandate to the incumbents of Market Lavington (*Estlavington*), Wlt., and of the parish chs. of Salisbury and to William Mylles, the Official's apparitor, to issue proclamations concerning the compurgation of William Jamys of East Lavington, charged that on 14 July 1495 he broke into the house of William Temse, chap. of East Lavington, and stole a rosary worth 40s, a gold ring worth 26s 8d and £10 13s 4d in a purse, for which reason he had been imprisoned by the lay power and delivered to John bp. of Salisbury *etc*. Salisbury, 28 Oct. 1499.

On 9 Dec. it was certified that this mandate had been executed and, as no legitimate objector appeared, William Jamys was admitted to compurgation and released from prison, insofar as this pertained to the ecclesiastical court. Compurgators as no. 554.

556.   [fo. 196] Mandate to the incumbents of Amesbury (*Ambresbury*), Wlt., and of the parish chs. of Salisbury and to William Millys, the Official's apparitor, to issue proclamations concerning the compurgation of *dominus* John Browne of Alton, Wlt., charged that on Monday 27 Aug. 1498 he broke into the house of John Rumsey at Amesbury and stole a dun-coloured gelding worth 18s, 24 yards of blood-red woollen cloth worth £3, 36 yards of tawny-coloured woollen cloth worth 24s, 12 yards of green woollen cloth worth 9s, 12 yards of russet woollen cloth worth 7s 4d, three pairs of sheets worth 6s, 2 lb. pepper worth 2s 4d, 2 oz. saffron worth 2s, and 28 lb. alum worth 2s 4d from the goods of Walter Meraunde in the custody of the said John Rumsey, for which reason he had been imprisoned by the lay power and delivered to the bp. of Salisbury *etc*. Salisbury, 28 Oct. 1499.

On 9 Dec. it was certified that this mandate had been executed and, as no legitimate objector appeared, *dominus* John Browne was admitted to compurgation and released from prison, insofar as this pertained to the ecclesiastical court. Compurgators as no. 554.

557.   [fo. 196v] Mandate to the incumbents of Castle Combe (*Castelcombe*), Wlt., and of the parish chs. of Salisbury and to William Mylles, the Official's apparitor, to issue proclamations concerning the compurgation of Thomas Lambert of Castle Combe, charged that on Monday 5 Nov. 1498 at 10 p.m. at Castle Combe he attacked, beat, wounded and ill-treated Robert Osbourne and then, with a knife called a *London knyffe*, price 4d, stabbed him in the

throat inflicting a mortal wound 2½ inches across and 4½ inches deep, for which reason he had been imprisoned by the lay power and delivered to John bp. of Salisbury *etc*. Salisbury, 28 Oct. 1499.

On 9 Dec. it was certified that this mandate had been executed and, as no legitimate objector appeared, Thomas Lambert was admitted to compurgation and released from prison, insofar as this pertained to the ecclesiastical court. Compurgators as no. 554.

558.　Commission from Mr Laurence Cokkys, Decr. D., to Mr Roger Church, Decr. D.

After rehearsing the abps.'s commission to him as Official *sede vacante* [no. 511 above], Mr Cokkys, because he is and probably will in the future be prevented by various business from visiting the dioc. and fulfilling the obligations of Official, delegates these tasks, specified in the normal terms, to Mr Church, whom he appoints as his commissary-general.

[Fos. 197v–98 are blank.]

INDEX OF PERSONS AND PLACES

In order to prevent this index becoming even larger than it must necessarily be, the names of members of religious houses and of churchwardens and other parishioners cited to appear at visitation, but mentioned in no other context, are not here listed separately.

Abbotsbury (Abbatisbury), Do., abbey, 75b, 323d, 375c
Abbotsham (Abbatisham), De., ch., 333c
Abbotskerswell (Carshwill Abbatis), De., ch., 335b
Abinger (Abyngworth), Sy., ch., 106c
Abson (Abbotston), Gl., ch., 483
Acclum (Aclom), Thomas, r. of St Petroc's, Exeter, 267, 329
Achonry (Achaden'), bp. of, see Forth, Thomas; Welles, Robert
Achumppe, Thomas, prebendary of Glasney coll., 289
Aclom, see Acclum
Acson, Simon, ord., 428d
Acton (unid.), inh. of, see Bowdon, William
Acton Beauchamp (Acton Becham), Wo., ch., 479
Acton Turville, (Acton Tyrfild), Gl., ch., 483
Adam:
  James, Mr:
    Official sede vacante, Exeter dioc., 264, 323
    v. of Dunsford, De., 269
  John:
    can. of St German's, 323
    ord., 323a
  Richard, r of Whitestone, De., 269
Adams, Edward, chap. of Great Sodbury, Gl., 483
Adbaston, St., inh. of, see Sayer, Godfrey
Addington (Aldingtone), Bd., ch., 235
Adlestrop (Tadilstrop), Gl., chapel, 487
Affeton Barton (Affeton), De., ch., 333f
Aighton (Aghton, Aigton), La., ch., 420, 432

Ailby (Aylesby), Li., ch., 216c
Aissby, see Ashby
Aisshe, see Ash
Aisshford, see Ashford
Aisshton, see Ashton; Aston
Akeley (Akle), Lei., dy., 141
Akworth, Denise, prioress-elect of Markyate, 262
Alanson, Thomas, 222a
Alben, William, m. of Dieulacres, 428c
Albone, William, r. of Chilworth, Sy., 65b, 75c
Albury, (Aldbury), Sy., ch., 106c
Alcester (Alincestre, Allyncestre), Wa.:
  ch., 476
  priory, 472, 503, 508
    ms. (named), 472
    prior, see Whitechurch, William
Aldenham, Hrt., ch., 246b, c
Alderley, Gl., ch., 483
Aldford (Aldeforde), Chs., ch., 23
Alegh, see Aller
Alestre, John, Mr, can. of St Mary's, Warwick, 470
Alexander VI, Pope, 261
Aleyn, Robert, 222b
Alford, Li.:
  ch., 138
  inh. of, see Reed, Robert
Alford, John, can. of Bruton, 53d
Algar, John, r. of Christon, So., 51
Algarkirk (Algakyrke, Algerkirk), Li., ch., 198, 219a
Alisaunder, John, chap. of Collumpton, De., 273
Alkoke, Henry, ord., 428c
Aller (Alegh, Allere), John:
  r. of East Allington, De., 316
  r. of Harford, De., 321
  v. of Spreyton, De., 269, 320

Allesley, William de, chantry of, *see* Coventry, Holy Trinity ch.
Allewton, John, 437
Alleyn, Hugh, 43
Allington (Ellyngton), Ha., inh. of, *see* Harris, John; Hyde, Richard
Allington, East (Alyngton), De., ch., 316, 335d
Almondsbury (Almondesbury), Gl., ch., 482
Alphington (Alphyngton), De., ch., 268, 332a
Alphyn, Thomas, B.C.L., v. of Gussage All Saints, Do., 531
Alresford (Alresfourde), Ha., dy., 98b
Altarnum (Alternon), Co., ch., 334h
Altherton, John, Mr, v. of Lower Swell, Gl., 490
Alton (Alneton), St.:
  and Leek (Leeke, Leke), dy., 38h,j; 40d, 429b, 430b
  inh. of, *see* Tyddiswall, Ralph
Alton, Wlt., inh. of, *see* Browne, John
Alton, Thomas, cur. of Ranton, 428b
Alverdiscott (Alverdiscote), De., ch., 333c
Alveston (Alveton), Wa., 406
Alvingham (Allvyngham), Li., ch., 216e
Alvington, West (Alvyngton), De., ch., 335d
Alwalton, Hu., ch., 215
Alwington (Alvyngton), De., ch., 333c
Alyn, John, 325
Amesbury (Ambresbury), Wlt., 556
  inh. of, *see* Meraunde, Walter; Rumsey, John
Amodas, Thomas, r. of Drewsteignton, De., 269
Ampney Crucis (Holyrode Ampney), Gl., ch., 486
Ampney St Mary (Ampney Marie), Gl., ch., 485
Amyson, William, Mr, chap. of Cirencester, 485
Amyth, John, 437
Ancaster (Ancastr'), Li., ch., 138
Andover (Andevere), Ha., dy., 98b
Anell, John, ord., 53a
Anger, John, v. of Glasney coll., 289
Ankerwyke (Ankyrwyk), Bk., priory, 232a
Anstey, East (Estansty), De., ch., 333f

Anstey, West (Westansty), De., ch., 333f
Antony (Anton), Co., ch., 334a
Antoyne, William, r. of East Ogwell, De., 268
Anwick (Anwik, Anwyk), Li., ch., 160, 219a, 222a
Anyon, John, O.P. of Chester, 428b
Aphewell, *see* Hewell
Apjohn, *see* John
Apmorgan, *see* Morgan
Apparell, *see* Parell
Appelford, Thomas, Mr, r. of Lympstone, De., 270
Ap Rice, *see* Rice
Ap Thomas, *see* Thomas
Ap Tudur, *see* Tudor
Ap Wiliam, *see* Wiliam
Arbury (Eardbury, Erdbury, Erderbury), Wa., priory, 39e, 377, 429a, 435a
  apostate from, *see* Burton, John
  cans. (named), 377, 428b, d
  prior, *see* Cockes, William
Archbold, John, chap. of Stroud, Gl., 484
Archer:
  Henry, v. of Milverton stall in Astley coll. ch., 16
  Thomas, 437
Arden (Ardena), Wa., dy., 38b, d; 40a, 405, 429a, 430a
Ardern (Ardune), Richard:
  can. of Gnosall, 403
  r. of Northenden, Chs., 5
Ardyngton, Thomas, kt., and Jocosa, chantry of, see Aston, Wa.
Argentyne, John, Mr, prebendary of Lichfield cath., 395
Arlingham (Erlingham), Gl., ch., 480
Arlington (Alryngton), De., ch., 333e
Arnesby (Ernesby), Lei., ch., 217a
Arnold:
  Robert, 212
  Roger, v. of St Mary's, Derby, 18
Arreton, I.o.W., ch., 99
Arundell:
  John:
    esq., 305
    Mr, dean of Exeter cath., 276a
  Thomas, kt., 305
Arvener, John, ord., 53a

Arwek, Richard, chap. of St Michael's altar in Chesterfield ch., Db., 423

Ash (Asshe), Sy., ch., 106c

Ash (Aissh, Aisshe, Asshe):
John:
ord., 46, 65a
r. of Sutton Veny, Wlt., 515
Thomas, ord, 53c, 65d
William, ord, 323b

Ashbourne (Aisshborne, Aisshborne, Assheborne, Ayssheborne), Db., dy., 38c, e; 40b, 429c, 430c

Ashbrittle (Aisshbritell), De., inh. of, see Bluett, Nicholas

Ashbury (Aisshbury), De., ch., 310, 335j

Ashby (Asseby), Li., ch., 166, 219a

Ashby, Np., see Canons Ashby

Ashby Parva (Asshby Parva), Lei., ch., 192, 255c

Ashby [unid.] (Asshby), Np., ch., 252a

Ashby (Aissby, Asshby), John:
abbot of Darley, 381
chap. of Coberley, Gl., 484

Ashcombe (Aisshcombe, Ayscomb), De., ch., 268, 332a

Ashelworth (Asshelworth), Gl., ch., 480

Ashfield (Asshefeld), John, esq., 71–4

Ashford (Aisshford), De., ch., 333e

Ashford (Aisshford), John, v. of Hockworthy, De., 274

Ashill (Aisshehull), So., prebendal ch., 47

Ashley (Asheley), Ha., ch., 109

Ashprington (Aishpryngton, Aishprynton), De., ch., 335c, 338

Ashreigney (Esse Regni), De., ch., 333b

Ashridge (Ashrigge), Bk., coll. ch. of the Holy Blood, 234b, 248

Ashstead (Asshetede), Sy., ch., 106b

Ashton (Aisshton), De., ch., 269, 332b

Ashton (Astone), Ox., dy., 247b

Ashton, Cold (Coldaston), Gl., ch., 483

Ashurst (Asshehurst), John, 35

Ashwater, De., ch., 335h

Ashwell (Asshewell, Asshwell), Hrt., ch., 210, 255d

Aslacoe (Aslachou), Li., dy., 139

Asshby, see Ashby

Asshe, see Ash

Asshefeld, see Ashfield

Asshehurst, see Ashurst

Asshford, see Ashford

Asshton, see Aston

Astley (Aistley, Asteley), Wa., coll. ch., 16, 39a, 40a, 429a, 435a, 476

Astley (Asteley), Wo., ch., 503

Astley, lord, see Dorset, marquis of

Aston (near Birmingham) (Assyngton), Wa., Ardyngton chantry in ch. of, 33

Aston Blank (Aston), Gl., ch., 487

Aston (Aisshton, Asshton):
Edmund, Decr.B., r. of Middleton, La., 413
Richard, esq., 413

Astonfeld (unid., ? Aston Heath, Chs.), inh. of, see Tetryngton, William

Athelhampton (Athelhamstone), Do., free chapel, 524

Athelney, So., abbey, 76a, 354, 358
abbot, see George, John
ms. (named), 53b, 65c

Atherington, De., ch., 333d

Atkyns, John:
Mr, can. of St John's, Chester, 426
r. of Radbourn, Wa., 417

Atkynson, Richard, ord., 428c

Att Woode, see Woode

Audley, St., ch., 39d, 434b

Austell (Awstell):
John, Mr, v. of Berkeley, Gl., 481
Thomas, Mr:
treasurer of Exeter cath., 276a
v. of Cheriton Fitzpaine, De., 275

Austen (Austyn):
John:
can. of St Anthony's in Cornwall, 293
m. of Tywardreath, 357d
Thomas, r. of Poughill, De., 275

Austrey (Aldestre), St., ch., 39d, 435a

Austyn, see Austen

Aveland (Avelond), Li., dy., 138

Avening (Avenyng, Avynnyng), Gl., ch., 484, 508

Aveton Giffard, De., ch., 335d

Awliscombe (Aulescomb, Awlescomb), De., ch., 272, 332f

Awstell, see Austell

Axebridge (Axbrigge, Axebrige), So., dy., 76b, 359b

Axminster (Axmynstre, Axmystre),
De., ch., 271, 332g
Axmouth, De., ch., 271, 332g
Aylesbeare (Aill', Aillisbeare,
Allesbeare), De.:
ch., 270, 332h
dy., 265, 270, 332h
Aynell, John, ord., 323b
Ayot St Lawrence (Eyate sancti
Laurencii), Hrt., ch., 203, 219h
Aystowe, James, ord., 428c

Babbe, James, Mr, r. of Ashprington
and Woodleigh, De., 338
Babington, Thomas, 411
esq., 17
Babstoke, Wlt., ch., 533
Bachell, William, r. of Batcombe, Do.,
530
Backwell (Bacwell), So.:
ch., 72
inh. of, see Feylond, Robert; Pasty,
John; Vowles, Thomas
lord of, see Rodenay, John
Bacon, John, r. of Swarraton, Ha., 119
Badminton, Great (Badmonton
Magna), Gl., ch., 483
Bagcary, John, chap. of Aylesbeare,
De., 270
Bag Enderby (Bagendirby), Li.:
ch., 151, 219a
inh. of, see Gednay, George
Bagendon (Bagyndene), Gl., ch., 485
Bagnyll:
Humphrey, chap. of Great Malvern,
Wo., 479
John, chap. of Leigh, Wo., 479
Bagshawe, William, 437
Bainbridge (Bainbrige), Christopher,
J.U.D., r. of Elington, Wlt., 512
Bak, Thomas, literate, 88
Baker:
John:
chap. of Olveston, Gl., 482
M.A., fellow of Cobham coll.,
443
ord., 323b
Richard, chap. of Hampnett, Gl.,
485
Walter, chap. of Stratford coll. ch.,
468
Balder, Richard, Mr, prebendary of
Cotton in Tamworth coll. ch., 26

Baldock (Baldok), Hrt., dy., 244b
Baldwin (Baldewyn):
Richard, r. of Draycot Cerne, Do.,
545
Thomas, chantry chap., Redmarley
d'Abitot, Gl., 479
Ball (Balle):
John, 330
Mr, chap. of St Lawrence,
Bristol, 432
ord., 428a
Margery, 330
Nicholas, 330
William, 330
Wilma, 330
Baly, Richard, chap. of Eastington,
Gl., 484
Bampton (Baumton, Baunton), De.,
ch., 274, 332d, 337
Banastre (Banester):
Elias, v. of Gussage All Saints, Do.,
531
Thomas, 105b
Bancroft, John, ord., 428c
Banes, Robert, r. of Swarkeston, Db.,
411
Banester, see Banastre
Bangor dioc., l.d. from, 428d
Banham, Richard, abbot of Tavistock,
292
Banstead (Banstede), Sy., ch., 106b
Barber, William, master of Strood
hospital, 444
Barbour (Barbur):
Nicholas:
grammar-master, Westbury coll.,
462
Mr, r., of Leigh, Wo., 479
Robert, Mr, r. of St Paul's, Exeter,
307
Bardney (Bardenay), Li., abbey, 142,
173, 228
Bardow, Ralph, ord., 428a
Bardys, Adrian de, Mr, 130
prebendary of Hurstbourne Priors,
Ha., 121
r. of Sherborne St John, Ha., 94
r. of Wroughton, Wlt., 94n
Barefote, Robert, ord., 428b
Barett (Baret):
John, Mr, notary public, 88, 339,
365

Thomas, r. of East Allington, De.,
316
William, 229a
ord., 428a
Barford, Thomas, r. of Ashley Parva,
Lei., 192
Barkeley, Thomas, apostate m. of
Hyde, 129
Barker, Robert, ord., 220
Barking (Berkyng), Ess., abbess of, 240b
Barkister, Thomas, clerk, 554-7
Barkston (Berkeston), Li., ch., 258a
Barlborough (Barlebourgh), Db., inh.
of, see Gawsell, Nicholas
Barlinch (Barlegh (sic), Barlinche,
Berlinch, Berlyng), So., priory,
60, 76a, 281, 353, 358
can. of (named), 357d
prior of, see Lyrd, Thomas
Barming, East (Barmyngest), Kent,
ch., 450
Barnard, Richard, chap. of St John's,
Gloucester, 480
Barnecoll, Walter, prior of
Tywardreath, 290
Barnstaple (Barnastapell, Baron'), De.:
archd. of, or Official, 301, 306, 309,
312, 315-6, 322
see also Elyott, William
archdeaconry, 333, 336b
ch., 333d
dy., 333d
priory, 323c
Barnwood (Burnewood), Gl., chapel,
480
Barnys, John, ord., 428c
Baron, John, v. of Exeter cath., 276c
Barons:
Henry, chap. of Stratford coll. ch.,
468
Thomas, chap. of Stratford coll. ch.,
468
Barow (Barowe):
Margaret, 437
Simon, v. of Calceby, Li., 159
Thomas, Mr, prebendary of
Lichfield cath., 395
Barr, Great (Barre), St., inh. of, see
Scott, William
Barrington, Great (Barington Magna),
Gl., ch., 487
Barrington, Little (Barington Parva),
Gl., ch., 487

Barrow Gurney (Barough, Barowe),
So., priory, 60, 67
Barry, William, ord., 65c
Bartelett, John, 361
Bartholomew, John, sub-apparitor,
Bath and Wells dioc., 56
Barton, Earls, Np., ch., 252a
Barton, Steeple, Ox., ch., 248
Barton:
John, 361
r. of Middleton, La., 413
Robert, chap. of Barnwood, Gl.,
480
William, 222c
Bartram, Maurice, Mr, v. of St
Owen's, Gloucester, 480
Barwell, Richard, 437
Basingstoke (Basyngstoke), Ha., 102
dy., 98b
Basse, John, cur. of Butterleigh, De.,
273
Bassingbourn (Bassingborne), Li., ch.,
223a
Baswich (Barkeswyche, Barkiswiche,
Berkeswyche), St.:
ch., 39d, 435d
prebend of Lichfield cath., 38a, 430b
priory, see Stafford, St Thomas the
Martyr
Batcombe, Do., ch., 530
Bate:
Malus, 406
William, 43
Batell, William, 105a
Bateman, John, 437
Bath (Bathon'), So., 339, 347-8, 356
archd. of, or Official, 50, 55, 341-2
archdeaconry, 359a
cath. priory, 76a, 347, 357b, 358,
482
chapter house of, 339
ms. of (named), 65b, d; 347
prior of, see Cantlowe, John
hospital of St John the Baptist, 53b,
75b,c
Bath and Wells:
bp. of, see Fox, Richard;
Shrewsbury, Ralph de;
Stillington, Robert
prison of, 296
dioc., 44-76, 339-65
l.d. from, 323b

sub-apparitor-general of, *see*
   Bartholomew, John
Bathealton (Bathiolton), So., ch., 360
Bathwick, So., prebendal ch. of
   Wherwell abbey, 50
Batishill, Robert, Mr, r. of Throwleigh,
   De., 269
Battersea (Batersey), Sy., ch., 106a
Battle (Batell), Sx., abbey, 277
Battlefield (Batilfeld), Sa., coll. ch.,
   39c, 429d, 435c
Baughurst (Baghurste), Ha., ch., 98c
Baxterley (Baxtarley), Wa., ch., 419,
   432
Bayly, Robert, v.-choral of Wells cath.,
   75d
Baynard:
   John, v. of Exeter cath., 276c
   Robert, esq., 515
Beachampton (Bechampton), Bk., ch.,
   234b
Beaford (Beauford), De., ch., 333b
Beamond:
   Richard, Mr, r. of Tedburn St
      Mary, De., 269
   William, cur. of St Stephen's,
      Exeter, 267
Beane, John, v. of Exeter cath., 276c
Beare, Richard, v. of Exeter cath., 276c
Beauchief (Beauclyffe, Bucheff), Db.,
   abbey, 39b, 425, 434c
Beauvale (Belle Vallis), Nt., priory,
   428c
Beaworthy, De., ch., 335j
Becher, William, v. of Little
   Barrington, Gl., 487
Beckford (Beckforde), Gl., ch., 477,
   504
Beckley (Brekyll), Ox., ch., 248
Beddington (Bedyngton), Sy., ch., 106b
Bedford:
   archd. of, or Official, 213, 239
   archdeaconry, 213, 219e, 238–43
   ch. of All Saints, 240b
   ch. of St Paul, 240b
Bedford, duke of, *see* Tudor, Jasper
Bedford, Thomas, Mr, r. of
   Lubbenham, Lei., 222b
Bedman, John, Mr, r. of Clayhanger,
   De., 274
Bedyll, Thomas, chap. of Hezleton,
   Gl., 487

Beeke, John, Mr, can. of Exeter cath.,
   276a
Beel, John, ord., 428b
Beighton (Boghton, Boughton), Db.,
   ch., 39b, 435b
Belamy, Robert, chap. of St James,
   Bristol, 482
Belenden, John, v. of All Saints,
   Sixhill, Li., 171
Belgrave, Lei., ch., 141
Bell, John, Mr, r. of Ingoldmells, Li.,
   170
Bellmore, Richard, r. of King's
   Stanley, Gl., 484
Belly, Thomas, ord., 75b
Belston (Belton), De., ch., 335j
Beltisloe (Beltislawe), Li., dy., 138
Benebowe, Thomas, r. of St Pancras,
   Exeter, 267
Beneham, John, r. of Yate, Gl., 483
Benett (Benet):
   John, v. of Crantock coll. ch., 288
   Nicholas, ord., 53c
   Richard, 222b
   Roger, chap. of Bridford, De., 269
   William, ord., 65b
Benley, Robert, Mr, can. of St Mary's
   coll. ch., Warwick, 470
Benteley, Nicholas, v. of Shirley, Db.,
   2
Beram, Richard, r. of Pylle, So., 48
Berde:
   Richard, Mr, r. of West Kington,
      Wlt., 525
   Thomas, 437
Bere Ferrers, De., ch., 335f
Bere:
   John, Mr, 302
   Richard, abbot of Glastonbury, 348
   Richard de la, kt., 203
Berkeley, Gl.:
   ch., 481
      Breadstone chantry in, 481
      Newport chantry in, 481
      Longbridge hospital, 481
   Stone in, 481
      chantry of B.V.M. in chapel of,
         493, 509
Berkhampstead (Berkhampstede), Hrt.,
   dy., 244b
Berklegh, David, prior of Plympton,
   293

Berkshire, archd. of, or Official, 517, 519, 523, 532, 546, 548
see also Berworth, Stephen
Bermondsey (Barmonsey, Barmundeseye), Sy.:
ch. of St Mary Magdalene, 78–9, 106a
clergy of (named), 79
abbey, 53b, 450
Berrington (Beryngton), Sa., ch., 9
Berrow (Berowe), Wo., ch., 479
Berrynarbor (Bury), De., ch., 333e
Berry Pomeroy (Birypomeray), De., ch., 335b
Bershyn, Thomas, r. of Cowley, Gl., 484
Berworth, Stephen, M.D., archd. of Berkshire, 532
Beryman, Richard, v. of Burlescombe, De., 274
Best, Henry, Mr, can. of Gnosall coll. ch., 403
Betchworth (Blecgeworth), Sy., ch., 106b
Beteel, Gervase, chap. of St Michael the Archangel, Norridge, Wlt., 513
Betrich, Edward, v. of Box, Wlt., 547
Betty, Robert, v. of Bishopsteignton, De., 268
Beverley, Yk., preceptor of, *see* Eglesfeld, John
Beverley, John, chap. of chantry of B.V.M., Welton, Li., 145
Beverstone, Gl., ch., 481
Beworth, John, clerk, 330
Bibury (Bybery), Gl., ch., 485
Bicester (Byssetur, Byssetyr), Ox.:
dy., 247b
priory, 247c
Bickington, Abbots (Bukyngton), De., ch., 335h
Bickington, High (Bukington), De., ch., 333d
Bickleigh (Bikelegh) (in Exeter archdeaconry), De., ch., 332d
Bickleigh (Bikelegh) (in Totnes archdeaconry), De., ch., 335f
Bicton (Buketon, Bukyngton), De., ch., 270, 332h
Bichton (Bysshton), Sa., inh. of, *see* Haryngton, Simon
Biddlesden, Bk., abbot of, 508

Biddulph (Bedulffe, Bedull, Bedulphe), St.:
ch., 39d, 434b
inh. of, *see* Colborne, Roger; Frere, Thomas; Knyght, Peter
Bideford (Bydeford), De., ch., 333c
Bidford-on-Avon (Bydforde), Gl., ch., 508
Bidworth, Robert, 43
Biford, David, r. of Wilcote, Ox., 197
Bigbury, De., ch., 335d
Bigby, Li., r. of, 222a
Biglott, Isabelle, 222b
Bindon, Do., abbey, 75c
Binles, Robert, bell-ringer at Tavistock, 292
Birde, Hugh, ord., 428a
Birkbeke, Oliver, ord., 428d
Birkenhead (Byrkinhed), Chs., priory, 402, 428c, d
ms. (named), 402
prior of, *see* Chestir, Thomas
Birling (Birlyng), Kent, ch., 450
Birmingham (Brymyngham), Wa., hospital of St Thomas the Martyr, 14
Birport, William, ord., 53a
Birtsmorton (Byrtismorton), Wo., ch., 479
Bisham (Burstelesham), Brk., priory, 234a, b; 337
Bishampton (Bysshampton), ch., 508
Bishopsteignton (Teygnton Episcopi), De., ch., 268
Bishop Stoke (Stoke Episcopi), Ha., ch., 98c
Bisley (Bysseley), Gl., ch., 484, 508
Bisshop (Bysshop):
John, ord., 428a
William:
chap. of Castle Morton, Wo., 479
prior of Rochester, 446
Bitchfield (Bitchefeld), Li., ch., 138
Bither, Alice, 242
Bittadon (Bittedene), De., ch., 333e
Bitton (Bytton), Gl.:
ch., 483
prebend, 492, 509
Blacdon (Blakdon), John, B.A., ord., 65b, 75d
Blackawton (Blakaueton), De., ch., 335c

Blackbarough, George, r. of Frampton
    Cotterell, Gl., 483
Blackborough (Blakbourgh, Blakburgh),
    De., ch., 273, 332e
Blackburn (Blakborne), La., dy., 429e
Blackhay, William, r. of Ashton, De.,
    269
Black Torrington, *see* Torrington
Blakborne, William, r. of Lasham,
    Ha., 126
Blakdon, *see* Blacdon
Blakwall, George, ord., 428b
Blatherwycke (Bladerwik), Np,. ch.,
    252b
Blechingley (Blechingleigh), Sy., ch.,
    106b
Bledington (Bladington), Gl., ch., 487,
    508
Bledlow (Bedlow), Bk., ch., 234a, b
Blisland (Bliston), Co., ch., 334g
Blockley, Gl.:
    ch., 476, 506
    dy., 476, 503, 505-7
Bloke, John, v. of Luddington, Wa.,
    468
Blome, William, Mr, v. of Standish,
    Gl., 480
Blower, William, Mr, r. of Eastington,
    Gl., 484
Bloyow, Samson, v. of Perranzabulo,
    Co., 313
Bluett, Nicholas, 281
Blythe, John, bp. of Salisbury, 511,
    550, 554-7
Boddington (Bodyngtone), Np., ch.,
    252a, b
Bodmin, Bodmian, Bodmine,
    Bodminne, Bodmyn), Co.:
    ch., 334g
    priory, 53c, 65b, c; 75b, c; 287,
        336b
    cans. (named), 287
    prior, *see* John, William
Bodon, William, r. of Stoke-upon-Tern,
    Sa., 3
Bodylache, Thomas, chantry chap.,
    Longdon, Wo., 479
Bogy, Richard, chap., Stratford coll.
    ch., 468
Boket (Bokett):
    Richard, Mr, r. of Iron Acton, Gl.,
        483
    William, Mr:

abp.'s commissary *sede vacante*,
    Bath and Wells dioc., 44
subdean, Wells cath., 356
Boleyn, John:
    r. of Shirwell, De., 309
    r. of Whitstone, Co., 305
Bolingbroke, Li.:
    ch., 138
    dy., 138
Bollis, Ralph, r. of Somerby, Li., 146
Bolston, Thomas, r. of Eggington, Db.,
    17
Bolter, Nicholas, ord., 323b
Bolton, John, 43
Bolyngton, Richard, r. of Normanton,
    Db., 15
Bomaunt, Thomas, m. of Glastonbury,
    357c
Bonavise, Walter, r. of St Martin's,
    Exeter, 267
Bonde:
    John, cur. of Maisemore, Gl., 480
    William, v. of Burgh, Li., 174
Bondleigh (Boneleigh), De., ch., 333a
Boniface, chap. of Abson, Gl., 483
Bonour, Henry, ord., 65b
Bonwey, John, can. of Worspring, 53d
Bookham, Great (Bocam), Sy., ch.,
    106c
Boold, Henry, kt., 438
Bordesley, Wo., abbot of, 39d, 435d,
    503
Boreman, John, Mr, chap. of Henyock,
    De., 272
Borough, Henry, 222b
Borow, John, v. of Exeter cath., 276c
Borste, Henry, S.T.B., prebendary of
    Gnosall coll. ch., 11
Borton, *see* Burton
Boston, Li., 157, 198
    ch., 138, 216c, e
Boston, Richard, 105a
Bosworth (Boseworth), Lei., ch., 141
Botfeld, John, ord., 428a
Bothe (Both):
    Charles, Mr, treasurer of Lichfield
        cath., 395
    Robert, v. of Ulceby, Li., 149
Botiller, *see* Butler
Botley, John, Mr, r. of Norton, So.,
    365
Boton, John, chap. of St Stephen's,
    Bristol, 482

Botterton, John, chap. of Berrow, Wo., 479
Botus Fleming (Boteflemyng), Co., ch., 334a
Bouchife, Thomas, *dominus*, 226
Bourgchier (Bourchier, Burgchyer):
Anne, 201
John, lord Fitzwarren, 48
Thomas, kt., 201
Bourne (Burne), Li.:
abbey, 187–8, 228
ch., 138
Bourton on the Water (Burton), Gl., ch., 487
Bovet, John, r. of Littleton-on-Severn, Gl., 482
Bovey, North (Northbovy), De., ch., 335a
Bovey Tracey (Bovytracy), De., ch., 335a
Bowdon, William, 437
Bowdyn, Richard, r. of Morebath, De., 274
Bower:
John:
chap. of Berkeley, Gl., 481
Mr, precentor of Crediton coll. ch., 282
Mr, r. of Pitt portion in Tiverton ch., De., 274
Thomas, par. chap. of Hill, Gl., 481
Bowge, Richard, can. of Bruton, 53d
Bowment, William, Mr, r. of Weston Birt, Gl., 483
Boxwell, Gl., ch., 483
Boydon, Philip, 361
Braceborough (Brasborogh, Brasbourgh), Li., ch., 163, 219a
Brackley (Berkeley), Np., dy., 251b
Bradcomb, Robert, O.P. of Plymouth, De., 65d
Bradenstoke, Wlt., priory, 536
Bradfeld, Elizabeth, prioress of Higham, 445
Bradford, De., ch., 335h
Bradford Peverell, Do., ch., 540
Bradford, William, chap. of Wapley, Gl., 483
Bradley, William, 437
Bradninch (Bradenynch, Bradnynche), De., ch., 273, 332e
Bradshawe:
Robert, r. of Aighton, La., 420

Thomas, 420
William, r. of Aighton, La., 420
Bradshay, William, ord., 428b
Bradstone (Bratston), De., ch., 335g
Bradwell, Bk., priory, 232a, 234a
Bradworthy (Brodeworthy), De., ch., 335h
Bragge, Thomas, ord., 323a
Braggis (Braggys):
Roger:
Mr, r. of Shipton Moyne, Gl., 484
prebendary of Henbury in Westbury coll. ch., 462
William, Mr, r. of Uley, Gl., 462
Brakinburgh, Richard, dean of St Mary's coll. ch., Warwick, 470
Brampford Speke (Brampford), De., ch., 275, 332c
Bratton Clovelly (Bratton), De., ch., 335j
Bratton Fleming (Bratton), De., ch., 333e
Bray, High (Bray), De., ch., 333e
Bray:
Henry, ord., 65a
John, chap. of Tormarton, Gl., 485
Reginald, kt., 126
Thomas, chap. of Hawkesbury, Gl., 483
Walter, chap. of St Mary Major, Exeter, 267
William, warden of St Bartholomew's hospital, Newbury, Brk., 517
Breadsall (Bradsal park), Db., priory, 428b
Breadstone chantry, *see* Berkeley
Breage (Breki), Co., ch., 334d
Breamore (Brymora, Brymore), Ha., 98a, 134
cans. (named), 134
prior, *see* Harpy, John
Breberveth, William:
v. of Glasney coll., 289
v. of Gwinear, Co., 289
Brecon (Brekenok), priory, 277
Breedon, Lei., priory, 219c
Bremond, William, chap. of Southwark, 79
Brendon, De., ch., 333e
Brent, South (Brent), De., ch., 335c

Brent, John, m. of Glastonbury, 53d
Brewood (Brewode, Brewoode), St, 414
   prebend of Lichfield cath., 38a, 430b
   White Ladies, priory, 393
     nuns (named), 393
     prioress, *see* Woode, Alice
Brian (Bryan), Richard:
   ord., 53b
   proctor, 482
Briant, Richard, chap. of St Peter's,
   Bristol. 482
Brice, Thomas, 361
Bricebridge, Simon, 437
Bridstowe (Bridstow, Bristow), De.,
   ch., 293, 335g
Bridford (Brideford), De., ch., 269,
   332b
Bridgerule (Brigruell), De., ch., 335h
Bridgewater (Briggewater, Brigwater),
   So.:
   dean, 56
   dy., 76b, 359c
   hospital of St John the Baptist, 53c,
     65b, 67
   inh., *see* Vernay, Alexander;
     Warderoper, Robert
Bridgnorth (Brignorth), Sa., inh. of, *see*
   Rolowe, Hugh and Humphrey
Brigeman, William, chap. of St
   Martin's chantry, Wells cath., 59
Brigge, Alexander, 222a
Bright:
   John, cur. of Whimple, De., 270
   William, abbot of Lesnes, 442
Brightwin (Brightwyn), William:
   chap. of St John's, Bristol, 482
Brimpsfield (Brymysfeld), Gl., ch., 484
Bristol (Bristollie), Gl.:
   abbey of St Augustine, 274, 463,
     480–3, 501, 504
     abbot, *see* Newland, John
     cans. (named), 53b, d; 463
   churches in or near:
     All Saints, 477, 482
       chantry or priory of the
       confraternity of the Kalends,
       502, 508–9
     Holy Trinity, 482
     St Augustine's, 482
     St Ewen's, 482
     St James, 482
     St John's, 482
     St Lawrence's, 482

     St Leonard's, 482
     St Mary in the Market Place, 482
     St Michael's, 482
     St Nicholas, 482, 501, 509
     St Peter's, 482
     St Philip and St James, 482, 497,
       508–9
     St Stephen's, 482
     St Werburgh's, 482
   dy., 477, 482, 504–5, 507
   friars:
     O.E.S.A. (named), 53c
     O.P. (named), 53d
   hospitals:
     Gaunt's (St Mark's), 464, 504
       brethren (named), 464
       minister, *see* Tyler, Thomas
     St Bartholomew's, 477
     St John's, 323b
   mayor, *see* Ryngstone, Philip
Bristowe, Thomas, m. of Athelney,
   53b, 65c
Brixham, De., ch., 335b
Broadclyst (Clyston *alias* Brodeclyste),
   De., ch., 270, 332h
Broadhembury (Brodehemby,
   Brodehemburye), De., ch., 273,
   332e
Broadhempston (Hempston Magna),
   De., ch., 335b
Broadway (Bradwey), Wo., 487
   ch., 508
Broadwell (Bradwell), Gl., 487
Broadwood Kelly (Brodewodekelly),
   De., ch., 335j
Broadwoodwidger (Brodewodewiger),
   De., ch., 335g
Brocklesby (Brokelesby), Li., ch., 216e
Brockley, So., ch., 72
Broke:
   Elizabeth, abbess of Romsey, 130
   John, ord., 323a
   Richard:
     chap. of Minchinhampton, Gl.,
       484
     chap. of Upton St Leonard, Gl.,
       480
   Robert Willoughby, lord, 530
   Thomas, m. of Glastonbury, 357c
Brokes, John, 105b
Bromborough (Bromebrogh), chs., inh.
   of, *see* Troutbeke, William

Bromefeld, John, r. of Uploman, De., 274

Brompton, So., inh. of, *see* Hancoke, Robert

Bromsgrove, Wo., ch., 476

Bromysfeld, William, v. of Stoke Giffard, Gl., 482

Brookthorpe (Brokethorp), Gl., ch., 480

Broughing (Broughyng), John, v.-choral of Wells cath., 65b, 75c

Broughton, West (Broughton), Db., ch., 39b, 434b

Brown (Broune, Browne):
   Clement, Mr, v. of Lechlade, Gl., 486
   John, 254
      chap. of Berkeley, Gl., 481
      dominus, 556
      Mr, cantarist of Lechlade, Gl., 486
   Lawrence, ord., 428d
   Robert, v. of St Philip and St James, Bristol. 482, 497
   Thomas:
      r. of Cubley, Db., 4
      warden of Tong coll. ch., 399

Brownwiche, William, chap. of Cirencester, Gl., 485

Brushford (Brusshford), De., ch., 333a

Brushford (Bushford), So., inh. of, *see* Huyssh, Robert

Bruton (Brewton), So., priory, 65b, 76a, 350, 358, 363, 484
   cans. (named), 53d, 357c
   prior, *see* Henton, John
   prior-elect, *see* Gilbert, Mr

Bryan, *see* Brian

Brymmesgrove, John, r. of Huxham, De., 270

Brymyngham, Thomas, esq., 14

Bryther, Robert, v. of Longney, Gl., 480

Buckerell (Bokerall, Bokerell), De., ch., 273, 332e

Buckfast (Bucfast), De., abbey, 53d

Buckfastleigh (Bucfastlegh), De., ch., 335c

Buckingham (Bukyngham):
   archd. of, or Official, 214–5, 233
   archdeaconry, 214–5, 219f, 232–7
   dy., 232b

Buckland (Bokeland), De., abbey, 274, 337

m. (named), 53b

Buckland (Bocland), Sy., ch., 106b

Buckland Brewer (Bokeland Brewer), De., ch., 333c

Buckland Filleigh (Bokelond Fillegh), De., ch., 333b

Buckland Monachorum (Bokelond Monachorum), De., ch., 333f

Buckminster (Bukmynster), Lei., ch., 217b

Buckworth (Bukworth), Hu., ch., 208, 255d

Budleigh (Budlegh), De., ch., 270

Buguley, William, ord., 428c

Buildwas (Bildewas), Sa., abbey, 428c

Bullington (Bollyngton), Li., priory, 164, 174
   can. (named), 164

Bunbury, Chs., coll. ch., 39e, 435e

Burbage on the Wye, Db., inh. of, *see* Hunt, Hugh

Burford, John, can. of Taunton, 357c

Burgchyer, *see* Bourgchier

Burgh le Marsh (Burgh), Li., ch., 174, 255a

Burlescombe (Burlecombe, Burlyscombe), De., ch., 274, 332d

Burlond, John, 361

Burman, John, r. of Radbourn, Wa., 417

Burnard, Thomas, cur. of Lostwithiel, Co., 331

Burneham, John, master of St Thomas's hospital, Southwark, 79

Burnell:
   Robert, r. of Dyrham, Gl., 483
   Thomas, m. of Buckland, 53b

Burnham (Burneham), Bk.:
   abbey, 232a
   dy., 232b

Burrington (Borington), De., ch., 333a

Burscough (Burscogh), La., priory, 396
   cans. (named), 396
   prior, see Scarisbroke, Hector

Burtle in Sprawlesmede, So., priory, 53c

Burton Lazars, Lei., hospital, 163, 231, 424

Burton on Trent, St.:
   abbey, 27, 39d, 384, 428d, 429b, 435a

abbot, *see* Fligh, William
  m. (named), 384
inh., *see* Normanton, William
Burton (Borton):
  John:
    apostate can. of Arbury, 377
    Mr, can. of Exeter cath., 276a
    Mr, prebendary of Crantock coll.
      ch., 288
    Mr, prior of Kalends in All
      Saints ch., Bristol, 482, 502
    Mr, r. of Whimple, De., 270,
      338
    Mr, v. of St David's chapel,
      Exeter, 267
    Mr, v. of St Nicholas, Bristol,
      482, 501
    Mr, 130
  Richard, Mr:
    r. of Warboys, Hu., 204
    r. of Wood Walton, Hu., 211
  Robert, Mr, r. of Rockhampton,
    Gl., 481
Bushbury (Buysshebury, Bysshbury),
  St., ch., 39d, 435d
Bushell, Thomas, ord., 428c
Bussher, Walter, cantarist of
  Thornbury, Gl., 481
Butleigh (Butley), So., ch., 364
Butler (Botiller):
  John, esq., 412
  Richard, 222a
Butterleigh (Boterleigh, Botislegh), De.,
  ch., 273, 332e
Byconell, John, kt., 305, 318
Byddill, Richard, chap. of Boxwell, Gl.,
  483
Bydfeld, Walter, r. of Cranham, Gl.,
  484
Byggys, John, ord., 357a
Bykcomb, William, v. of Payhembury,
  De., 273
Byllowe, Nicholas, v. of Exeter cath.,
  276c
Byllynghey, John, *dominus*, 226
Byngley, William, v. of Dronfield, Db.,
  425
Byrchold, Thomas, Mr, r. of
  Rodmarton, Gl., 494
Byrday, John, chap. of Morchard
  Bishop, De., 275
Byrdsey, John, chap. of St Nicholas,
  Gloucester, 480

Byrley, Roger, 43
Byrne, Simon, cantarist of Cambridge
  chantry, Slimbridge, Gl., 481
Byrom, James, ord., 428a
Bysshop, *see* Bisshop

Cabe, Thomas, 438
Cadbury (Cadbery, Cadburye), De.:
  ch., 275, 308, 332c
  dy., 265, 275, 332c
Caddall, John, *dominus*, 226
Cade, Thomas, r. of Buckworth, Hu.,
  208
Cadeleigh (Cadlegh), De., ch., 275,
  332c
Cadington, Thomas, 437
Cadney, Li., ch., 216e
Calceby, Li., ch., 159, 219a
Calcewaith (Calcewath), Li., dy., 138
Caldon, George, abbot of Rocester, 385
Caldwell (Caldewell), Bd., priory, 238a
Calmady, Stephen, *generosus*, 305
Calow, Thomas, cur. of Sheldon, De.,
  272
Calstock (Calstoke), Co., ch., 334a
Calton, William, chap. of Frampton on
  Severn, Gl., 481
Calverleigh (Cadwoodlegh), De., ch.,
  274
Calwich (Calwick), St., priory, 398,
  428d
  cans. (named), 398
  prior, *see* Elderbeke, Robert
Cam (Camme), Gl., ch., 481
Camberton, John, S.T.P., 82
Camberwell (Camerwell), Sy., ch.,
  106a
Camborn (Cambron), Co., ch., 334e
Cambridge, Ca., university:
  Clare Hall, 246, d, f
  King's College, 39e
  King's Hall, 240b
  Pembroke College, 206
Cambridge chantry, *see* Slimbridge
Campden, Gl.:
  ch., 477, 504, 508
  dy., 477, 504-5, 507
Candeler, Thomas, 175
Candleshoe (Candeleshou), Li., dy.,
  138
Canlayn, Robert, B.C.L., v. of St
  Oswald's altar in ch. of St
  Werburgh, Chester, 414

Cannington (Canyngton), So., priory, 60, 67

Canons Ashby (Asshby), Np., priory, 252b

Canonsleigh (Canonlegh), De.:
   abbey, 265, 269–70, 274, 281, 323b, 336a, 338
   abbess, *see* Stabba, Joan
   nuns (named), 281
   ch., 274

Cantell:
   Alice, 485
   Robert, 485

Canterbury, Kent:
   abp., *see* Morton, John; Savoy, Boniface of
   cath. priory of Christ Church, 135, 380, 481
   Convocation of, 60, 66

Cantevell, John, chap. of chantry of SS Mary and Michael, Melbourne, Db., 421

Cantlow, John, prior of Bath, 347

Canwell (Canwal, Canwall), St., priory, 428b, c

Canwik, John 222c

Canyngton, John, m. of Muchelney, 357d

Capell, John, v. of Axmouth, De., 271

Capnest, Robert, m. of St Werburgh's, Chester, 428d

Caproun, Thomas, Mr, cantarist of Lechlade, Gl., 486

Cardinham (Cardynan), Co., ch., 334b

Careby (Coreby), Li., ch., 172, 223a
   r. of, 222a

Carew (Carewe):
   Alexander, esq., 328
   Isabella, 328
   John, 328
      Mr, prebendary of Glasney coll. ch., 289

Carlell, John, v. of Fotherby, Li., 158

Carlisle dioc., l.d. from, 428d

Carlton, Great (Carleton Magna), Li., ch., 216e

Carmynow, Thomas, esq., 317

Carnok (Carnyk), John:
   clerk, 61
   r. of Talaton, De., 273

Carpenter:
   John, perpetual fellow of Westbury coll., 462
   Richard, prebendary of Laurensweston in Westbury coll., 462
   William, chap. of St Nicholas, Bristol, 482

Carshalton (Crashalton), Sy., ch., 106b

Carter:
   John, 222b, 236
   Thomas:
      chap. of St Nicholas, Bristol, 482
      ord., 220

Cartwryght, Thomas, r. of Folksworth, Hu., 207

Carvanell, John, v. of Crediton coll. ch., 282

Carwardyn, James, r. of Ayot St Lawrence, Hrt., 203

Carwynek, Benedict, annuellar of Exeter cath., 276d

Cary, So., dy., 76b, 359b

Caryhays (Caryhoes) *alias* St Stephen in Brannel, Co., ch., 334c

Caslegh, William, r. of Powderham, De., 268

Casse, John, r. of Cruwys Morchard, De., 315

Castellar (Castillar), Db., dy., 38c, e; 40b; 429c, 430c

Castellesi, Adrian, protonotary of the apostolic see, papal collector in England, 29

Castle Acre, Nf., priory, 175

Castle Cary (Cary), So., 361

Castle Combe (Castelcombe), Wlt., 557
   inh., *see* Lambert, Thomas

Castle Donington (Casteldonyngton), Lei., ch., 217b,d

Castel Morton (Castelmorton), Wo., ch., 479

Catell, John, r. of Missenden, Gl., 484

Caterham (Chaterham), Sy., ch., 106b

Catesby *alias* Shopes, Np., priory, 251a

Cateson, Richard, dean of Cirencester rural dy., 485

Catisbye, Walter, Mr, can. of Exeter cath., 276a

Cattister, William, 437

Caversfield (Caversfelde), Bk., ch., 235

Cawery, Edmund, 222c

Cawlecott, Thomas, chap. of chantry at Nettlecombe, So., 49

Cawthryn, John, chap. of Shipton Sellars, Gl., 487

Cockes (Cockys, Cokkes, Cokkys):
  (blank, probably Lawrence),
    prebendary of Hurstbourne
    Priors, Ha., 121
  Lawrence, Decr. D., can.-
    residentiary of Salisbury,
    Official *sede vacante* Salisbury
    dioc., 511–58
  Robert, ord., 428d
  William:
    prebendary of Glasney coll. ch.,
    289
    prior of Arbury, 377
Coffyn, Richard, 316
Cogan, Robert, m. of Newenham, 323b
Cokke, Robert, 222a
Cokkes, *see* Cockes
Colan, Co., ch., 334f
Colaton Raleigh (Colaton, Coleton
    Ralegh, Coliton), De., ch., 270,
    332h, 338
Colborne, Roger, 437
Colbronde, Richard, 361
Coldale, John, r. of Holton, Ox., 195
Cold Aston, *see* Ashton, Cold
Cold Norton, *see* Norton, Cold
Cold Salperton, *see* Salperton, Cold
Cole (Coole):
  John, 325
  Margaret, 325
  William, 325
Coleby (Colby), Li., ch., 216e
Coleridge (Colrigge), De., ch., 282,
    333a
Coleshill (Collsul, Colshil), Wa.:
  ch., 405
  inh. *see* Jakes, John
Colett, Robert, chap., 23
Colfoxe, John, can. of Haughmond,
    428d
Colinson, Edward, can. of Welbeck, v.
    of Coates by Stow, Li., 176
Collumpton (Columpton), De.:
  ch., 265, 273, 332e
  inh., *see* More, John
Collys, John:
  clerk of Westbury coll. ch., 462
  ord., 65b, 75c
Colman:
  Edmund, v. of Romsey, Ha., 110
  Robert, M.A., v. of Lower Swell,
    Gl., 490
  Roger, 222c
  Thomas, 323a

Colmer, Henry, m. of Glastonbury,
    53b, 65c
Coln Rogers (Culme Rogers), Gl., ch.,
    485
Coln St Aldwyn (Culne Aylwyn), Gl.,
    ch., 486
Coln St Denis (Culme Denyes), Gl.,
    ch., 485
Colom, Henry, *dominus*, 225
Colt, Thomas, notary public, 30
Colton, John, 43
Columbele, Hugh, ord., 428b
Colvylle, John, *generosus*, 146
Colwich (Colwyche), St., prebend of
    Lichfield cath., 38a, 430b
Colwyn, Robert, v. of Lower Swell,
    Gl., 487
Coly:
  Robert, v. of Wilcote, Ox., 197
  Roger, 437
Colyar, Richard, 361
Colyn, Robert, sacrist of Slapton coll.
    ch., 294
Colyton, De., ch., 332g
Comb, John, Mr, precentor of Exeter
    cath., 276a
Combdorowe, Thomas, r. of Combe-
    Raleigh, De., 271
Combe, Ha., ch. of St Swithun, 114
Combe, Wa., abbey, 252b
Combe Florey (Comb Flory), So.,
    chantry, 61
Combe-in-Teignhead (Combyntynhede,
    Comyntenehed), De., ch., 268,
    332a
Combe Martin (Combmartyn), De.,
    ch., 333e
Combepyne (Combpyne), De., ch.,
    271, 332g
Combe-Raleigh (Combralegh), De.,
    ch., 271–2, 332f
Combermere (Cumbermere,
    Cumbremere), Chs., abbey,
    428b–d
Compton (Cumpton), Ha., ch., 98c
Compton, Sy., ch., 106c
Compton Dundon (Comptondandon,
    Comptondunden), So., ch., 362,
    365
Compton, Little (Compton), Wa., ch.,
    487, 508
Compton:
  John, m. of Bath, 65d

Richard, chap. of Hanham, Gl., 483
Condon, Thomas, v. of Drayton in
    Hayles, Sa., 8
Congresbury (Congarisby), So., inh. of,
    see Knyght, William
Conisholme (Conyngesholm,
    Conyngshold), Li., ch. of St
    Peter, 152, 219a
Conner, Richard, ord., 323b
Constable (Constapill):
    Marmaduke, kt., 162
    Robert, ord., 323b
Constantine (Constantyne), Co., ch.,
    334d
Cook (Cooke):
    John, 325
        literate, 165
        Mr, r. of Ashbury, De., 310
        (*alias* Oke), prior of Pilton, 284,
        301
        r. of Morchard Bishop, De., 275
    Richard, chap. of Westbury coll.
        ch., 462
    Robert, can. of Worspring, 65b
    Thomas:
        D.C.L., abp.'s chancellor and
            auditor of causes, 85–7
        treasurer, Crediton coll. ch., 282
    Vincent, r. of Slapton coll. ch., 294
    William:
        chap. of St Nicholas, Gloucester,
            480
        prior of Totnes, 296
Cookbury (Cokebury), De., ch., 335h
Cookes, John:
    cur. of Silverton, De., 273
    r. of Butterlegh, De., 273
Cook Hill (Cokhill), Wo., priory, 508
Coole, *see* Cole
Cooper, Richard, r. of Dunkerton, So.,
    58
Coppingford, Hu., r. of, 246a
Corbett, William, r. of Backwell, So.,
    72
Corby (Coreby), Li., ch., 255a
Cordy, Walter, chap. of Arlingham,
    Gl., 480
Corner, William, Br, r. of Swarraton,
    Ha., 119
Cornish (Cornysh):
    Thomas:
        bp. of Tenos, 53, 65, 75, 323,
        357

warden of Ottery St Mary coll.
    ch., 280
William, v. of Horsley, Gl., 484
Cornwall:
    archd. of, or Official, 297, 311,
        317–8
    see also Silke, William
    archdeaconry, 297, 334, 336d
    deans of, 338
Cornwall (Cornewaile, Cornewale,
    Cornewall, Cornewayle):
    Robert:
        r. of Churchstanton, De., 272
        r. of Farway, De., 271
    Thomas:
        esq., 203
        kt., 178
Cornwood (Cornwode), De., ch., 335e
Cornworthy, De.:
    ch., 335c, 338
    priory, 75d, 295, 338
    nuns (named), 295
    prioress, *see* Dynham, Thomasina
Corringham (Coryngham), Li., dy.,
    139
Corscombe, Do., ch., 514
Coryngdon, John, Mr:
    can. of Exeter cath., 276a
    v. of Collumpton, De., 273
Coryton, De., ch., 335g
Cosshe, William, 105a
Cost, Walter, Mr, r. of St Mary
    Major, Exeter, 267
Coterell, Richard, cur. of Kentisbeare,
    De., 273
Cotesford, John, chap., 236
Cothay, William, Mr, r. of Widworthy,
    De., 271
Cotlegh, Robert, cur. of
    Doddiscombsleigh, De., 269
Cotleigh (Cotelegh, Cotlegh), De., ch.,
    271, 332g
Cotterstock (Coterstoke), Np., ch.,
    252a
Cottesbrook (Cottisbroke, Cottysbroke),
    Np., ch., 182, 219d
    r. of, 254
Cottismore (Cottysmore), John:
    esq., 116
    r. of Tusmore, Ox., 196
Cotton (Coton), Db.:
    inh., *see* Prentosle, William
    prebend, *see* Tamworth coll. ch.

Cottysmore, *see* Cottismore
Cotys, Thomas:
  Mr, r. of Oddington, Gl., 487
  r. of St Peter's, Rushton, Np., 181
Coulsdon (Collusdon), Sy., ch., 106b
Countas, Edith, 236
Countisbury (Conttesbury), De., ch.,
  333e
Couper, *see* Cowper
Courtenay (Courtnay):
  Edward, 324
  Margaret, 324
  Peter, 324
    bp. of Exeter, lately translated to
      Winchester, 278, 284, 338
    bp. of Winchester, 77, 105b
  William, kt., 267, 324
Cousyn, Richard, 222a
Cove:
  John, can. of Barlinch, 357d
  Robert, v. of Holy Trinity, Gl., 480
Coventre, William, r. of Manningford
  Abbots, Wlt., 526
Coventry (Coven'), Wa., 3, 16, 366,
  374, 404, 426, 433
  archd. of, or Official, 13–14, 32–3,
    369, 404–5, 417-2-, 424, 431
  see also Parkys, John (Official)
  archdeaconry, 38b, d; 39a, 40a,
    429a, 430a, 431, 434a, 435a
  cath. priory, 32, 40a, 366, 374, 427,
    429a, 508
  ms. (named), 374
  prior, *see* Share, Richard
  chap. of, *see* Gardiner, Henry
  chs. in or near:
    Holy Trinity, chantry of William
      de Allesley in, 32
    St Michael's, 405
  dy., 38b d; 40a; 429a, 430a
  inh., *see* Allewton, John; Bateman,
    John; Clerk, Robert; Forster,
    William; Prymerhose, John;
    Pultney, Margaret; Walker,
    Thomas; Wilkes, Clement;
    Wiston, Joan
  priory of St Anne, 39a, 428d, 434a
Coventry and Lichfield:
  bp., 395, 433
    see also Halse, John; Smith,
      William
  dioc., 1–43, 366–438
  Official *sede vacante*, 62

see, 261
Cowick (Carik, Cowik, Cowyk), De.:
  ch. of St Thomas the Martyr, 265,
    268, 332a
  priory, 292
  ms. (named), 292
  prior, *see* Dynham, Henry
Cowley, Gl., ch., 484
Cowley, Ox., ch., 248
Cowley:
  John, Mr, v. of Crondall, Ha., 97
  Thomas, r. of Corscombe, Do., 514
Cowlyng, Stephen, r. of Chudleigh,
  De., 268
Cowper (Couper):
  Henry, ord., 428a
  John:
    Decr. B., Official of archd. of
      Stafford, 406
    generosus, 214
    m. of Bath, 65b
    ord., 428d
    v. of Eldersfield, Wo., 479
  Thomas, chap. of chantry of
    B.V.M., Crich, Db., 34
Coxdon, John, ord., 357b
Cranham (Croneham), Gl., ch., 484
Cranleigh (Cranley), Sy., ch., 106c
Cransley (Cranesley), Lei., ch., 217d
Crantock (sancti Carentoci), Co., coll.
  ch., 288, 336d
  clergy (named), 288
  dean, *see* Edmund, John
Crayes, John, chap. of St Martin's,
  Exeter, 267
Creacombe (Crewcomb), De., ch., 333f
Crediton (Credyton, Cryditon), De.,
  coll. ch., 265, 275, 282, 336a
  clergy (named), 282
  precentor, *see* Bower, John
Creed (Crede), Co., ch., 334c
Crese, Thomas, 328
Cresham, John, esq., 181
Cretyng, William, dean of Westbury
  upon Trym coll. ch., 462
Crewe, John, ord., 428c
Crewkerne (Crokherne), So., dy., 76b,
  359c
Crich (Criche, Cruche), Db., ch.:
  chantry of B.V.M., 34
  chantry of SS Nicholas and
    Catherine, 12
Cristemas, John, 105a

Crofte, Edmund, 222b
Croke, Hugh, ord., 53d
Crokhay, John, cur. of Otterton, De., 270
Croley, David, chap. of Holy Trinity ch., Bristol. 482
Cromhall (Cromall), Gl., ch., 483
Crondall (Crondale), Ha., ch., 97
Crooke (Croke), De., ch. of St Mary, 327
Crosse, John, 361
   ord., 428c
   r. of St Michael, South St, Wilton, Wlt., 529
Croston (Crostone), La., ch., 39e
Crowan (Crewen), Co., ch., 334e
Crowder, John, ord., 428b
Crowhurst, Sy., ch., 106b
Crowther, Thomas, r. of Quatt, Sa., 7
Croxden (Crokisden), St., abbey, 428b, c, d
Croyland (Crowland), Li., 156
   abbey, 142, 147, 153, 156, 161, 207, 228
Crugge, John, Mr:
   r. of Shobrooke, De., 275
   r. of Tydecombe portion, Tiverton ch., De., 274
Cruwys Morchard (Crusmorchard, Cruys Morchard), De., ch., 315, 333f
Cruys:
   Alexander, r. of Cruwys Morchard, De., 315
   John, 322
   esq., 315
Cubert (Cuthbert), Co., ch., 334f
Cubley, Db., ch., 4
Cuddesdon, Ox., dy., 247b
Cuddington (Codyngton), Sy., ch., 106b
Cumbrebache, Roger, ord., 428d
Cumbregge, John, chap. of Clevelode, Wo., 479
Curry Mallet (Corymalett), So., inh. of, see Colyar, Richard
Curry Rivel (Corywell), So., ch., 364
Curson, John, 43
Curtes, Richard, chap. of Rodmarton, Gl., 484
Cury (Corantyn), Co., ch., 334d
Cury, William, m. of Athelney, 53b, 65c

Cusshe, John, chap. of Cirencester, Gl., 485
Cutboll, Thomas, v. of Ashill, So., 47
Cutler:
   John, clerk, 168
   Richard, chap. of Newington Bagpath, Gl., 481
Cutston, William, chap., 122

Dadyng, William, r. of West Kington, Wlt., 525
Daglingworth, Gl., ch., 485
Dainkys, Thomas, treasurer of Westbury coll., 462
Dalamere, see Delamer
Dalby, Little (Dalby Parva), Lei., ch., 217b
Dalby, Thomas, Mr, r. of Ashby Parva, Lei., 192
Dalderby, Li., r. of, 226
Dale, Db., abbey, 39b, 428b, d; 435b
Dale, Eugenius:
   ord., 65c
   v. of Hinton Monachorum, So., 64
Dalman, William, 222b
Dalton, Robert, r. of Woodchester, Gl., 484
Dameram, dominus John, 130
Damsell, John, chap. of Southwark, 79
Danyell, John, ord., 53c
Darley (Derlegh, Derley), Db.:
   abbey, 2, 18, 381, 428b, d; 429c
   abbot, see Ashby, John
   cans. (named), 381
   ch., 39b, 435b
Dartford (Derteford, Dertford), Kent:
   dy., 449a
   priory, 200, 529
Dartington (Dertyngton), De., ch., 335c
Datchett (Dachett), Bk., ch., 248
Daventry (Daventre), Np.:
   dy., 251b
   priory, 251a, 252b, 428c
David:
   John, ord., 357a
   Richard, clerk, 552, 554–7
Davidstow (Dewstow), Co., ch., 334h
Davies:
   Edward, chap. of Dursley, Gl., 481
   Richard:
      chap. of Woodchester, Gl., 484
      v. of Coaley, Gl., 481

Thomas, chap. of Olveston, Gl., 482
Davy:
John:
chap. of Sir William Courtenay,
267
chap. of Stapleton, Gl., 482
Mr, r. of Kimcote, Lei., 190
secondary of Exeter cath., 276e
Pascavius, r. of Blackborough, De.,
273
Richard, ord., 53d
Richard, ord. (another), 323c
Dawby, Thomas, v. of Studley, Wa.,
499
Dawe, Germanus, ord., 357c
Dawlish, (Dawlissh), De., ch., 303
Dawnsy, John, 57
Dayman, Elias, v. of Crediton coll. ch.,
282
Dean Prior (Deneprior), De., ch., 335c
Deane, Henry, prior of Llanthony, 461
Deddington (Dadyngtone,
Deddyngton), Ox.:
ch., 248
dy., 247b
Deer (Deere):
John, ord., 65b, 75c
William, ord., 53d
Deerhurst (Derhurst, Dierhurst), Gl.:
ch., 477, 504
priory, 459, 508
prior, see Prestbury, Robert
Delamer (Dalamere):
Matthew, clerk, 107
Thomas, 105b
Delapré, see Northampton
Delves, Richard, Mr, prebendary of
Lichfield cath., 395
Denbawe, Thomas, chap., 325
Denbury (Denebury), De., ch., 335b
Dene, John, 229b
Denford (Droneford), Np., ch., 42, 433
Denham, John, ord, 357a
see also Dynham
Denys:
John, r. of Gidleigh, De., 269
Thomas, 325
William, v. of St-Mary-Church,
De., 298
Derby (Derbei), Db.:
archd. of, or Official, 2, 4, 12, 15,
17–18, 24, 34, 371, 407, 411,
416, 421–3, 425, 431, 435

archdeaconry, 38c, e; 39b, 40b, 407,
429c, 430c, 431, 434c, 435b
ch. of St Mary, 18
dy., 38c, e; 40b, 429c, 430c
priory of King's Mead, 382, 428d
nuns (named), 382
prioress, see Chaundele, Margaret
Derby:
Edward, M.A., r. of Little
Rissington, Gl., 500
Thomas, v. of Elmton, Db., 24
William, r. of Hampnett, Gl., 485
Desborough (Desburgh), Np., ch., 184,
219d, 252b
Desedall, Thomas, Mr, cur. of
Bampton, De., 274
Deth, Robert, 222a
Devenold, Philip, Mr, can. of Exeter
cath., 276a
Deverlond, John, r. of Willand, De.,
274
Devonshire:
and Cornwall, sheriff of, 276a
parish chs. of, 324
Devoras:
Thomas, Mr, chap. of Cirencester,
Gl., 485
Walter, r. of Coln St Denis, Gl.,
485
Dey:
John, chap. of Iron Acton, Gl., 483
Thomas, r. of Gretford, Li., 155
Deyne, John, chap., 30
Deynys (Deyns), Alexander:
r. of Cottesbrooke, Np., 182
r. of mediety of Sedgebroke, Li.,
165
Dibbe, John, 134
Dicon (Dycon):
John, chap. of St Michael's altar in
Chesterfield ch., Db., 416
Richard, 437
Didbrook (Dudbroke), Gl., ch., 477,
504
Dier, see Dyer
Dieulacres (Dieulenacres), St., abbey,
428b, c, d
ms. (named), 428c
Diptford (Depeford), De., ch., 335c
Dittisham (Diddeham), De., 335c
Ditton, Long (Longdytton), Sy., ch.,
106b

Dixton, John, cur. of Huntsham, De., 274, 302
Dixwell, Henry, v. of Clifton, Wa., 418
Dobilday, Henry, 222b
Docheson, Richard, Mr, r. of Chilbolton, Ha., 118
Dodbrooke (Dodbroke), De., 335d
Doddington, Great (Dadington), Np., ch., 252a
Doddiscombsleigh (Legh), De., ch., 269, 332b
Dodford (Dudford), Wo., ch., 508
Doding:
    Elizabeth, 486
    William, warden of Winterborne Downe, Gl., 482
Dodson, John, r. of All Saints, Winchester, 107
Dokett, John, ord., 65a
Dolton (Donelton), De., ch., 333b
Don, John, v. of Awliscombe, De., 272
Dorchester, Ox., abbey, 247c
Dorking (Dorkyng), Sy., ch., 106c
Dormond, John, r. of All Hallows, Goldsmith St, Exeter, 267
Dorset:
    archd. of, or Official, 514, 516, 522, 524, 527, 531, 534–5, 540–1, 544
        see also Langton, Robert
    marquis of, see Grey, Thomas
Dortour, William, r. of All Saints, Wainfleet, Li., 168
Dotson, see Dottson
Dotton (Dadyngton), De., ch., 332h
Dottson (Dotson), Lawrence, M.A., ord., 65b, 75c
Doune, see Downe
Dowland (Doulond), De., ch., 333b
Dowles, Hugh, v.-choral of Wells cath., 75c
Downaby, Thomas, 229a
Down Ampney (Downeampney), Gl., ch., 486
Down, East (Estdowne), De., ch., 333e
Down, West (Westdowne), De., ch., 333e
Down-St Mary (Downe beate Marie), De., ch., 275, 332c
Downe (Doune):
    George, Mr, prebendary of Lichfield, 395

John:
    chap. of St Peter's, Bristol, 482
    r. of Easthampstead, Brk., 546
Downys, Robert, 222b
Doynton (Dyneton), Gl., ch., 483
Drake, Robert, v. of Driffield, Gl., 485
Draper:
    John, prior of Christchurch, Twynham, 133
    Richard, Mr, r. of Boxwell, Gl., 483
    Thomas:
        ord., 220
        v. of Tytherington, Gl., 483
Draycot Cerne (Draycote Cerne), Do., ch., 545
Drayton in Hayles, Sa., ch., 8
Drayton, John, par. chap. of St George's, Southwark, 79
Drewe:
    John, secondary of Exeter cath., 276e
    William, ord., 75c
Drewsteignton (Teyngton, Teyngtownedrewe), De., ch., 269, 332b
Driffeld (Driffeld), Gl.:
    ch., 485
    inh. of, see Clerke, John
Droitwich (Wiche), Wo., dy., 476, 503, 507
Dronfield (Dronefeld, Dronfeld), Db., ch., 39b, 425, 432, 434c
Droxford (Drokenesford), Ha., dy., 98b
Dudbrook (Dudbroke), Gl., ch., 508
Dudley, Wa.:
    inh. of, see Sayer, Roger
    priory, 6
Dudley, Richard, Mr, r. of Sutton-by-Brailes, Gl., 487
Dudlyn, Henry, v. of Spondon, Db., 424
Duffield, Db., ch., 39b, 435b
Duke, Edward, clerk, 552, 554–7
Duloe (Dulo), Co., ch., 334b
Dunchideock (Dunshidiok, Dunsydyok), De., ch., 268, 332a
Dunkerton, So., r. of, 65b
Dunkeswell (Dunkeswill, Dunkiswill), De.:
    abbey, 65c, 75c, 272, 323b
    ch., 272, 332f
    dy., 265, 272, 332f

Dunn, Richard, v. of Dronfield, Db., 425

Dunnyng, William, v.-choral, Exeter cath., 276c

Dunsby (Dunnesby), Li., r. of, 226

Dunsford, De.:
ch., 269, 332b
dy., 265, 269, 332b

Dunstable (Dunstaple), Bd.:
ch. of St Peter, r. of, 240a
dy., 238b
priory, 238a, 240b

Dunster, So.:
dy., 359c
inh. of, *see* Harris, Catherine
priory:
ms. (named), 347
prior, *see* Eyles, William

Dunterton, De., ch., 335g

Dunthorp, Thomas, 222b

Duntisbourne Abbots (Duntisburn Abbatis), Gl., ch., 485

Duntisbourne Rous (Duntisburn Militis), Gl., ch., 485

Durant (Duraunt), Thomas, 416, 423

Durban, John, ord., 65b

Durgin, Henry, ord., 75b

Durham, see of, 340

Durkyn, Thomas, 361

Dursley (Durseley), Gl.:
ch., 477, 481, 508
dy., 477, 481, 504–5, 507

Dursley, John, v. of Kempsford, Gl., 486

Dutton:
John, ord., 229b, 428d
Richard, ord., 428d

Dycon, *see* Dicon

Dyer (Dier, Dyere):
John:
B.A., fellow of New College, Oxford, 75c
chap. of St Nicholas, Bristol, 482
chap. of St Werburgh's, Bristol, 482
J.U.B., Official of archd. of Wells, 62

Dyker, Humphrey, ord, 65a, 75c

Dymer, Thomas, chap. of Yate, Gl., 483

Dymmerghion (Dynmerchian), Flints., prebendal ch., 428d

Dynham (Denham):
Charles, esq., 305
Henry, prior of Cowick, 292
Joan, 305
John:
kt., 305
lord, 305
Oliver, Mr:
archd. of Surrey, 95, 130
prebendary of Lichfield cath., 395
Thomasina, prioress of Cornworthy, 295

Dyrham (Dyrram), Gl., ch., 483

Dyryet, Thomas, cantarist of Stone, Berkeley, Gl., 493

Easthampstead (Esthamstede), Brk., ch., 546

Eastington (Estington), Gl., ch., 484

Eastleach (Estalache), Gl., ch., 486

Easton (Burghest), Lei., ch., 252b

Easton, Great (Burghest), Np., ch., 259c

Easton on the Hill (Estone iuxta Stanford), Np., ch., 252b

Easton Royal (Eston), Wlt., Trinitarian house, 538
minister, *see* Toppyng, John

Eastwyvelshire (Est'), Co., dy., 334

Eaton (Etone), Bd., dy., 238b

Ebrington, Gl., ch., 508

Eccleshall, St., prebend of Lichfield cath., 38a, 430b

Ecgleston, Thomas, prior of Upholland, 400

Echington, Robert, prior of St Sepulchre's, Warwick, 469

Eckington (Ekyngton, Ekynton), Db., ch., 39b, 41, 434c

Eckington (Ekington), Wo., ch., 508

Ede, Richard, chap. of Pendock, Wo., 479

Edersley, *see* Milborne

Edgeworth (Eggisworthy), Gl., ch., 484

Ediall (Edyall), Henry, Mr:
archd. of Rochester, Offical *sede vacante* in Coventry and Lichfield dioc.,1
prebendary of Lichfield cath., 395

Edlesborough (Edelesburg), Bk., ch., 246f

Edlington (Edlyngton), Li., ch., 173, 255a
v. of, 256

187

Edmond (Edmund), John:
  Mr, dean of Crantock coll. ch., 288
  Mr, prebendary of Glasney coll. ch.,
    289
  v. of Parranzabulo, Co., 313
Edward IV, king, 284
Edwards (Edwardes):
  Alan, chap. of Miserden, Gl., 484
  Stephen, Mr, succentor of Exeter
    cath., 276c
  Thomas, chap. of Marshfield, Gl.,
    483
Edworth, Bd., r. of, 243
Edyall, see Ediall
Effingham, Sy., ch., 106c
Egg Buckland (Egebokelond), De., ch.,
    335f
Eggesford (Egesford), De., ch., 333a
Egginton (Eginton), Db., ch., 17
Egham (Egam), Sy., ch., 106c
Eglesfeld, John, preceptor of Beverley,
    deputy of prior-provincial of
    Hospitallers in England, 52
Egloskerry (Egliskery), Co., ch., 334h
Eisey (Eysy), Wlt., ch., 539
Ekles, Thomas, ord., 428c
Elande, Richard, can. of Haverholme,
    v. of Anwick, Li., 160
Elcocke, Ralph, can. of Tong, 399
Elderbeke, Robert, prior of Calwich,
    398
Eldersfield (Ellisfeld), Wo., ch., 479
Elington (Elyngdon) alias Wroughton,
    Wlt., ch., 94n, 512
Eliott (Elyot, Elyott):
  Thomas, Mr, 338
  William:
    cur. of Powderham, De., 268
    Mr, archd. of Barnstable, 276b,
      278
    Mr, can. residentiary of Salisbury
      cath., 288
    master of Godshouse,
      Portsmouth, 88–91
    prebendary of Crantock coll. ch.,
      288
Elkstone (Elkeston), Gl., ch., 484
Ellerton (Eylberton), Gl., chapel, 482
Elmeley, William, prior of Leonard
    Stanley, 460
Elmore, Gl., chapel, 480
Elmton (Helmetone), Db., ch., 24

Elryn, John, secondary of Slapton coll.
    ch., 294
Elsham (Ellesham), Li., priory, 142,
    228
Elstow (Elmestow), Bd., abbey, 484
Ely (Elien'), bp. of, 209
Ely:
  John, Mr, r. of Alwalton, Hu., 215
  William, 437
Elyngham, Richard, chap. of St
    David's, Exeter, 267
Elyott, see Eliott
Elys:
  John:
    Mr, r. of All Saints, Huntingdon,
      202
    r. of Wimborne Minster, Do.,
      534
  William, chap., 226
Emelyn, Hugh, Mr, prebendary of
    Crantock coll. ch., 288
Endellion (Endelyvent, sancte
    Endeliente), Co., ch., 334g, 338
Enderby, Walter, esq., 58
England, king of, 296
  see also Edward IV; Henry VII
Enkbarough (Inkebarough), Robert:
  Mr, notary public, 457, 494
  Official of archd. of Worcester, 476
Epsom (Ebbisham), Sy., ch., 106b
Epworth, Li., chantry, 177, 219b
Ermethstede, Christopher, v. of
    Elmton, Db., 24
Ermington (Ermyngton), De., ch., 335e
Esher (Esshere), Sy., ch., 106b
Esmond (Esmonde):
  Agnes, 226
  Richard, Mr, 365
Esterfeld, John, Mr, r. of St Stephen's,
    Bristol, 482
Eton, Bk., coll. ch., 232a
Eton, Humphrey, v.-choral of Gnosall
    coll. ch., 403
Evan, John, ord., 323b
Evelegh, Michael, chap. of Clyst St
    Lawrence, De., 273
Ever, John, 361
Everard, Thomas, r. of St Michael's,
    Wareham, Do., 516
Everyngham, Robert, v. of
    Killingholme, Li., 143
Evesham, Wo., abbey, 472, 484, 508

Ewell, Sy.:
  ch., 106b
  dy., 106b
Ewerby (Iwardby), Li.:
  ch., 216d, 258a
Ewhurst (Iwerst), Sy., 106c
Exbourne (Ekisborn), De., ch., 335j
Exeter (Excester, Exon'), De., 285-6, 329
  archd. of, or Official, 265, 299-300, 302, 308, 319-20
    see also Hopton, David; Nix, Richard (archd.); Tyak, John (Official)
  archdeaconry, 265, 336a
    deans of, 338
  bp. of, 285, 338
    see also Fox, Richard
  cath. ch., 91, 265, 331
    annuellars (named), 276d
    cans. (named) 276a
    cemetery, 329
    dean and chapter, 267, 270, 272-3, 275, 298, 303, 307, 313, 319, 357c
    dignitaries (named) 276b
    Official of peculiar jurisdiction of, 298, 303, 313-4
    secondaries (named), 276c
    vs. (named), 276c
    vs.-choral, 270
  chapels in or near:
    St David's, 267
    St Mary in parish of St John Arches, 267, 332j
    St Mary-on-Exe-Bridge, 267
    St Sidwell's, 267
  chs. in or near:
    All Hallows, Goldsmith St, 267, 332j
    All Hallows-on-the-Wall, 267, 332j
    Holy Trinity, 267, 332j
    St Edmund-on-Exe-Bridge, 267, 332j
    St George's, 267, 332j, 325
    St John's, 267
    St John Arches, 267, 332j
    St Kerian's, 267, 332j
    St Lawrence's, 267
    St Leonard's, 267, 332j
    St Martin's, 267, 332j
    St Mary Major, 265, 267, 332j

    St Mary Steps, 267, 332j
    St Olave's, 267, 332j
    St Pancras, 267
    St Paul's, 267, 307, 332j
    St Petrock's, 267, 325, 329, 332j
    St Stephen's, 267, 332j
    St Thomas, see Cowick
  dy. of Christianity, 265, 267
  dioc., 264-338
    l.d. from, 53a, d; 65a-d; 75b-d; 357a-c
  friars, 324-5, 329
  guildhall, 293
  hospital of St John the Baptist, 265, 267, 278, 329
    cans. (named), 278
    prior, see Oliver, John
  inh., see Gefferey, John; Sayer, John
  priory of St Nicholas, 53d, 75c, 265, 270, 273, 275, 277, 300, 308, 323b, 329, 336a
    ms. (named), 277
    prior, see Herford, John
Exminster (Exmynstre), De., ch., 268, 332a
Exton, So., inh. of, see Crosse, John
Eycote, Gl., inh. of, see Meysy, John
Eye, Sf., priory, 165
Eyer, see Eyre
Eyford, Gl., ch., 508
Eyles, William, prior of Dunster, 347
Eynsham (Eynesham), Ox., abbey, 247c, 248
Eyre (Eyer):
  Roger, chap. of altar of St Michael in Chesterfield ch., Db., 423
  Thomas, v. of Hathersage, Db., 422
  Thurstan, v. of Hathersage, Db., 422
Eyton:
  Robert, ord., prebendary of Langarmewe and Dymmerghion, 428d
  William, 43
Eyworth, Bd., ch., 240c

Fairfax, Guy, kt., 179
Fairford (Faireford, Fayreford), Gl.:
  ch., 477, 486, 504
  dy., 477, 486, 504-5, 507
Falows, John, Mr, chap. of Hanley Castle, Wo., 479
Farewell (Ferwall), St., priory, 428b, d
Farley (Farlegh), Sy., ch., 106b

Farley:
   Henry, chap. of Grace Lane,
      Gloucester, 480
   Nicholas, v. of Hartpury, Gl., 480
Farmington (Thormerton), Gl., ch.,
   485
Farnham, Sy., ch., 95
Farringdon (Faryngdon), De., ch., 270,
   332h
Farthyng, Robert, ord., 75b
Farway (Fareway), De., ch., 271, 332g
Felmersham, Bd., ch., 240b
   v. of, 241, 243
Feniton (Fenyton, Fynaton), De., ch.,
   273, 332e
Fenne, Mr, prebendary of Ottery St
   Mary coll. ch., De., 280
Feock (Feok), Co., ch., 334c
Fer, William, 437
Ferrers:
   lord, see Grey, Thomas
   Martin, generosus, 88
Ferror, Gilbert, v. of Lower Guiting,
   Gl., 487
Ferseman, William, ord., 357a
Ferthmores, John, chap. of All Saints,
   Bristol, 482
Fetcham (Feccham), Sy., ch., 106c
Feygon, John, v. of St-Mary-Church,
   De., 298
Feylond, Robert, 72
Feyrcastell, David, chap. of All Saints,
   Bristol, 482
Feyrefeld, Richard, ord., 428c
Feyrehere, John, ord., 53d
Fichepole, John, chap. of St Mary's
   coll. ch., Warwick, 470
Fiddelere, Thomas, r. of Swarkestone,
   Db., 411
Filleigh (Fillegh), De., ch., 333d
Fillerey, William, v. of St Swithun's,
   Combe, Ha., 114
Filton Fishponds (Fylton), Gl., ch., 482
Fineshade (Fynneshede, Fynsherd),
   Np., priory, 251a, 252b
Fissher, Robert, 222c
Fitzjon, Robert, abbot of Lilleshall, 392
Fitzwaren, lord, see Bourgchier, John
Fitzwilliam:
   Humphrey, Mr, r. of Ingoldmells,
      Li., 170
   Thomas, kt., 224
Flamstead, Hrt., priory of St Giles in
   the Wood, 205

Flandria, Malinus de, O.E.S.A., of
   Bristol, 53c
Fleccher:
   Edmund, ord., 428a
   Elizabeth, 437
   Oliver, ord., 428c
   Roger, 214
Flede, Robert, ord., 53d
Fleet (Flete), Li., ch., 175, 255a
Fleete (Flytte), Bd., dy., 238b
Flete, John, v. of Ottery St Mary coll.
   ch., De., 280
Fligh, William, abbot of Burton on
   Trent, 384
Floude, Thomas, clerk of Westbury
   coll. ch., 462
Folksworth (Folkesworth, Folkysworth),
   Hu., ch., 207, 219h
Foorde, see Ford
Ford (Forde, Foorde, Fourde):
   Henry, ord., 428c
   John:
      cur. of Collumpton, De., 273
      v. of Dawlish, De., 303
   Richard, r. of Bridford, De., 269
   Robert, 105a
Forde (Ford), Do., abbey, 271, 273,
   357b
Fordingbridge (Fourde), Ha., dy., 98b
Fordington (Forthington), Li., see
   Ulceby (near Alford)
Forestar, Thomas, r. of St Michael
   Major, Stamford, Li., 156
Forlere, John, chap. of Southwark, 79
Forrabury (Forebury), Co., ch., 334g
Forster:
   Richard, r. of St Lawrence, Rode,
      63
   Robert, esq., 45
   Thomas, prior of Wombridge, 391
   William, 437
Forswild, John, can. of Canonsleigh,
   274
Forth:
   Ralph, Mr, r. of Eggington, Db., 17
   Thomas, bp. of Achonry, prior of
      Stone, 286
Forthey (Fortey), John, Mr:
   v. of Ampney Crucis, Gl., 486
   v. of Olveston, Gl., 482
   v. of Thornbury, Gl., 481

Foster, William, chap. of St Mary's chantry, All Saints, North Wraxall, Wlt., 520

Fotherby (Foterby), Li., ch., 158, 219a

Fotheringhay (Fodringay), Np., coll. ch., 251a

Founteyne, William, 321

Fourde, see Ford

Fowell, William, Mr, r. of Exminster, De., 268

Fowey (Fowy), Co., ch., 334c

Fowler, Joan, widow, 195

Fowy, Richard, v. of Glasney coll. ch., 289

Fox:
John, chap. of chantry of B.V.M., Crich, Db., 34
Richard:
bp. of Bath and Wells, 340
bp. of Exeter, 264

Foxcote, William, v. of Seagry, Wlt., 536

Framland, Lei., dy., 141

Frampton, Li., ch., 216d, 258a

Frampton Cotterell (Frampton Coterel), Gl., ch., 483

Frampton on Severn (Frampton super Sabrinam), Gl., ch., 481

Frankyssh, Luke, abp.'s apparitor in city and dioc. of London, 78

Fraunces, Thomas, Mr, can. of Exeter cath., 276a

Freman:
Henry, ord., 53d
John, prior of Maxstoke, 276

Fremington (Fremyngton), De., ch., 333d

French (Frensch, Frenshe, Frenssh):
German, r. of Combpyne, De., 271
Henry, 438
John, 361
Ralph, priest, 130
William, annuellar of Exeter cath., 276d

Frend, John, chap. of St Nicholas, Bristol, 482

Frene, Robert, ord., 428c

Frensch, see French

Frere:
Richard, 361
Thomas, 437

Fresby, William, 242

Fretherne (Frethorn), Gl., ch., 480

Frigon, John, 325

Friskney (Friskeney), Li., v. of, 256

Frithelstock (Fridelstok, Frithelstok), De.:
ch., 333c
priory, 283, 323b
cans. (named), 283
prior, see Osborn, John

Frocester (Frowcetter), Gl., ch., 480

Frodingham (Frothingham), Li., ch., 216c, e

Frodsham (Frodesham, Frawesham), Chs., dy., 40e, 429e

Frome, So., dy., 76b, 359b

Froste, Robert, Mr, r. of Bradninch, De., 273

Froucetter (Frowcettre), Edmund, S.T.P., 461
r. of St John's, Gloucester, 480

Frowlesworth (Frolesworth, Frollesworth), Lei., ch., 194, 255c

Frye, John:
ord., 323b
v. of Harpsford, De., 270

Fulford, John, Mr, r. of Bridestowe, De., 293

Fulstow (Fullestowe, Fulstowe), Li., ch., 216c, e

Furberer (Furborer), Thomas, cantarist of fraternity of Kalends, Bristol, 482

Fychet (Fychett):
John, v. of Exeter cath., 276c
Robert, ord., 428a
Thomas, chap. of St Nicholas, Bristol, 482

Fynde, John, ord., 75c

Gainsborough (Gaynesburgh), Li., ch., 139
third part of chantry in, 219b

Gale (Gaale), John, ord., 53c, 65c

Gararde, Joan, 487

Gardiner (Gardyner):
Henry, chap., 437
Thomas, 361

Garret, Ralph, 510

Garthorpe (Garnthorpe), Li., ch., 216e

Gartree (Gartre), Li., dy., see Horncastle

Gartree (Gartre), Lei., dy., 141

Gaskyn, John, O.P., of Bristol, 53b

Gatton, Sy., ch., 106b

Gaucyny, William, ord., 357a

Gawsell, Nicholas, esq., 437
Gay, Philip, ord., 323b
Gays, John, 30
Gayton le Marsh (Gayton), Li., r. of,
    225
Gednay, George, 151
Geffe, Geoffrey, ord., 323d
Gefferey, John, 437
Gens, Eliseus, par. chap. of St
    Nicholas, Bristol, 482
George, r. of Broadwell, Gl., 487
George, John, abbot of Athelney, 354
Georgeham (Ham sancti Georgii), De.,
    ch., 333e
Georgenympton (Nymet sancti
    Georgii), De., ch., 312
Gerard, Cecily, widow of Thomas, kt.,
    21
German, Henry, v. of Rockbeare, De.,
    270
Germansweek (Weke sancti Germani),
    De., ch., 335j
Gerveys, Henry, chap. of Ampney St
    Mary, Gl., 485
Geryng (Gerynge), John:
    chap. of Bampton, De., 274
    ord., 53d
Geynard, Edward, r. of Siston, Gl.,
    483
Gidleigh (Gydlegh), De., ch., 269, 332b
Giglis, John de, bp. of Worcester, 453
Gilbert, Mr, prior-elect of Bruton, 363
Gilbert, Richard, 222a
Gill, Thomas, 222b
Gittisham (Gyddisham, Gydesham),
    De., ch., 271, 332g
Glase, William, ord., 53d
Glasion, Alan, r. of Stoke Pero, So., 45
Glasney (Glaseney, Glasneya in
    Cornubia), Co., coll. ch., 53d,
    65b, 289, 336d, 357b
    clergy (named), 289
    provost, see Obye, John; Pascow,
        John
Glastonbury, So., abbey, 76a, 348
    abbot, see Bere, Richard
    ms. (named), 53b, d; 65b–d; 75b,
        348, 357b–d; 358
Glendon, Np., ch., 180, 219d
Gloucester (Gloucestrie), Gl., 496
    abbey, 115, 460, 480–1, 484–6, 504,
        508
    abbot, see Malverne, John

ms. (named), 460
archd. of, or Official, 474, 477, 481,
    489–91, 493–4, 497–8,
    500–02, 508
    see also Holforde, Thomas
        (Official)
archdeaconry, 504–5
chs. in or near:
    All Saints, 480
    Grace Lane (Gracelond), 480
    St Aldate's, 480
    St John's, 480
    St Mary before the Abbey Gate,
        480, 508
    St Mary in the South, 480
    St Michael's, 477, 480
    St Nicholas, 480
    St Owen's, 480
    dy., 477, 480, 504–5, 507
    priory of St Bartholomew, 480
Glossop (Glossope), Db., inh. of, see
    Berde, Thomas
Glover (Gloviere):
    Henry, 43
    John:
        chap. of Cirencester, Gl., 485
        chap. of Thorverton, De., 275
Glyn, Dr, 129
Gnosall (Gnavesall, Gnowsale), St.,
    coll. ch., 11, 40d, 403, 429b
    prebendaries (named), 403
    vs.-choral (named), 403
Gobbys, John, Mr, r. of Cherrington,
    Gl., 484
Godalming (Godalmyn), St., 106c
Godolgham, Thomas, ord., 53d
Godshill (Goddeshull), I.o.W., inh. of,
    see Chesthull, Robert; Smith,
        Elizabeth
Godstone (Wolkestede), Sy., ch., 106b
Godstow (Godstowe), Ox., abbey, 247a
Gold, Maurice, chap. of Cold Ashton,
    Gl., 483
Goneld, John, 222a
Goodeale, John, 43
Goodefelawe, John, Decr.D., 19
Goodeman, John, cur. of Alphington,
    De., 268
Goodleigh (Godelegh, Goodlegh), De.,
    ch., 306, 333e
Goodson, Thomas, chap. of Leonard
    Stanley, Gl., 484

Goodyer, William, v. of Ashley, Ha., 109
Gooldwyn, Nicholas, notary public, 457
Goran, Co., ch., 334c
Gore, William, 361
Goring (Goryng), Ox., priory, 247a
Gorwey, William, ord., 428d
Goscote, Lei., dy., 141
Gossage, Richard, Mr, r. of Nympsfield, Gl., 484
Gough, John, v. of Little Houghton, Np., 185
Gowle, John, ord., 75b, 323d
Grade (Grada), Co., ch., 334d
Graffoe (Grafhou), Li., dy., *see* Longoboby
Gransden, Great (Magna Grandesden), Hu., ch., 246d, f
Grantham (Graham), Li.:
  ch., 138
  dy., 138
Grantham (Grauntham):
  Joan, 222a
  Richard, 222c
  William, 229a
Grave, William, r. of Ulceby and Fordington, Li., 147
Graveley, Hrt., r. of, 246f
Grayingham (Geryngham), Li., ch., 216c
Greatford (Gretford), Li., ch., 155, 219a, 223a
  r., 222a
Grecson, Oliver, parish pr., St Mary's coll. ch., Warwick, 470
Greder, John, v. of Ottery St Mary coll. ch., De., 280
Greenfield (Grenefeld), Li., priory, 142, 228
Gregory, William, can. of Taunton, 357c
Grendon (Grendone), Np., ch., 252a
Grene:
  Henry, 222c
  Hugh, r. of Wistaston, Chs., 410
  John, 236
    chap. of Stratford coll. ch., 468
  Reginald, r. of Coln Rogers, Gl., 485
  Richard, notary public, 185
  Thomas, ord., 428c
  William, 222a
Grenefeld, John, 361

Grenehyll, William, chap. of Southwark, 79
Grenelefe, Robert, cur. of Yarcombe, De., 272
Grenewode (Grenewoode), John:
  r. of Notgrove, Gl., 487
  v. of Shipton Bellinger, Ha., 117
Gresley, Church (Greseley), Db., priory 379, 428c
  cans. (named) 379
  prior, *see* Mogge, Robert
Grete, Walter, cur. of Poltimore, De., 270
Greves, Peter, Mr., preb. of St Michael's coll. ch., Warwick, 495
Grevile (Grevyle):
  Thomas, Mr, r. of Bourton on the Water, Gl., 487
  William, 494
Grey:
  John, 222b
  Thomas, marquis of Dorset, lord Ferrers, Groby and Astley, 3, 13, 198
Griffith (Griffyth), John:
  chap. of St Philip's, Bristol, 482
  chap. of Whaddon, Gl., 480
  Mr, 482
  Mr, v. of St Augustine's, Bristol, 482
Grimsby (Grymesby), Li.:
  abbey (*alias* Wellow), 142, 228
  ch., 138
  dy., 138
Grobers, lord, *see* Grey, Thomas
Grobham, Richard, ord., 65b, 75c
Gryme, Richard, Mr, r. of St Olave's, Southwark, 79
Grymsby, Henry, esq., 172
Grymston, Henry, Mr, r. of Chagford, De., 269
Gryndell, John, r. of Braceborough, Li., 163
Guildford (Gildeforde, Guldeforde), Sy.:
  ch. of Holy Trinity, 106c
  ch. of St Mary, 106c
  ch. of St Nicholas, 106c
  dy., 106c
  priory (New Place), 117
Guiting, Lower (Gayton Inferior), Gl., ch., 487

Guiting, Temple (Gayting Temple),
	Gl., ch., 487
Gulval (Lanyskelegh), Co., ch., 334e
Gundys, Robert, ord., 428d
Gunne, Henry, m. of Totnes, 323c
Gunthorp, John, Mr:
	dean of Wells, abp.'s commissary,
		44, 57
	prebendary of Bitton, Gl., 492
Gussage All Saints (Gyssage), Do., ch.,
	531
Guthlaxton (Gudlaxton), Lei., dy., 141
Gwennap (Weneppe), Co., ch., 334d
Gwinear (Wynnyer), Co., ch., 289,
	334e
Gwithian, *see* Phillack
Gwynne, Hugh, ord., 75a
Gyam, Richard, Mr, r. of
	Minchinhampton, Gl., 484
Gybbys:
	John, ord., 75d
	Thomas, chap., 331
Gyffard:
	John, 325
	Leonard, 325
Gylbert, John, Mr, can. of St Mary's
	coll. ch., Warwick, 470
Gylle:
	John, r. of Rakenford, De., 322
	Thomas, chap. of Kilmington, De.,
		271
Gylmyn, John, abbot of Keynsham,
	349
Gylyngham, Thomas, ord., 65a
Gymmyll, Alexander, 222a

Haccombe (Haccomb), De., ch., 268,
	332a
Hache, Thomas, esq., 312
Hacket, John, v. of Down Ampney,
	Gl., 486
Hackthorn (Hakthorn), Li., ch., 216e
Haddon (Haddone), Np., dy., 251b
Haddowe, Richard, chap. of
	Cirencester, Gl., 485
Hagbourne, East (Hakebourne), Brk.,
	ch., 523
Hailes, Gl., abbey, 508
Hainyes, *see* Haynes
Hake, John, r. of Sampford Peverell,
	De., 274
Halberton, De., ch., 274, 332d

Haldman, Thomas, cantarist of
	Newport chantry, Berkeley, Gl.,
	481
Hale, Li., ch., 216c, e
Halefax, John, 222a
Halesowen, Wo.:
	abbey, 428d, 503, 508
	ch., 476, 503
Halkewurth, Christopher, 43
Hall (Halle):
	James, r. of Northenden, Chs., 5
	Nicholas, 222a
	Otvel, ord., 428c
	Peter, ord., 428a
	Richard:
		abbot of Hyde, 129
		cantarist, Suckley, Wo., 479
		chap., scribe of Convocation, 62
		ord., 428a
	William, 229a
		chap. of Cold Salperton, Gl., 487
Halliswill, John, Mr, r. of Uffculme,
	De., 274
Halse:
	Edmund, Mr:
		can. of Gnosall coll. ch., 403
		r. of Clyst Hidon, De., 273
	John, bp. of Coventry and Lichfield,
		1, 43
Halton, William, Br, r. of Ulceby and
	Fordington, Li., 147
Halwill (Haywill), De., ch., 304, 335h
Hambledon (Hamyldon), Ha., ch., 100
Hambledon (Hamolden), Sy., ch., 106c
Hamond, John, 105a
	r. of Withcote, Lei., 193
Hampnett (Hampnet), Gl., ch., 485
Hampstede, Richard, cantarist of
	Combe Florey, So., 61
Hampton, Meysey (Hampton), Gl.,
	ch., 486
Hanchurche, John, Mr, r. of Great
	Rissington, Gl., 487
Hancock (Hancoke):
	John, cur. of St Lawrence's, Exeter,
		267
	Robert, 361
Hande, Thomas, cur. of Gnosall coll.
	ch., 11
Handeley, William, 437
Handsworth (Handisworth), St., inh.
	of, *see* Walker, William

Hanforth:
Elizabeth, 329
Henry, 329
Juliana, 329
Hanham, Gl., chapel, 483
Hanley Castle (Hanley), Wo., ch., 479
Hanmer (Hannemere), Sa., ch., 39c, 435c
Hanneys, *see* Haynes
Hannington (Hannyngton), Ha., ch., 98c
Hanyngton, John, 105a
Hapton, La., inh. of, *see* Truflove, John
Harberton (Huberton, Hurberton), De., ch., 330, 335c
Harbury (Harburburye), Wa., inh. of, *see* Amyth, John
Harding (Hardyng):
Henry, 361
John:
r. of St Michael Major, Stamford, Li., 153, 156
r. of St Peter's, Conisholme, Li., 152
Matthew, r. of Chelvey, So., 72
Hardwick (Hardwyke), Gl., chapel, 480
Hardyng, *see* Harding
Harecourt, Robert, kt., 517
Harescombe with Pitchcombe (Harshcombe et Pethnichcombe), Gl., ch., 480
Haresfield (Harsfeld), Gl., ch., 480
Harford (Hardford, Herpforde), De., ch., 321, 335e
Harford, Thomas, chap. of St Werburgh's, Bristol, 482
Haringdon (Haryngton):
Richard, 290
Simon, 438
Harleston, Richard, 229a
Harnewill, Nicholas, r. of Cotleigh, De., 271
Harnhill, Gl., ch., 485
Harnston (Harneston), Li., ch., 216e
Harold, John, Mr, r. of Hezleton, Gl., 487
Harper:
Mr, v. of St Nicholas, Bristol, 501
Robert, 222b
Thomas:
chap. of Moreton in Marsh, Gl., 480
Mr, v. of Halberton, De., 274

Harpford (Harford, Herpford), De., ch., 270, 332h
Harpswell (Harpeswell), De., ch., 216c
Harptre, John, par. chap. of Thornbury, Gl., 481
Harpy, John, prior of Breamore, 134
Harris (Harres, Harreys, Harryes, Harrys):
Catherine, 361
David, v. of Haresford, Gl., 480
John, 105a
Richard, r. of Doynton, Gl., 483
Thomas, Mr:
abp.'s commissary, Bath and Wells dioc., 44–8, 55–60, 67, 71
can. of Exeter cath., 276a
r. of Stoke upon Tern, Sa., 3
William, 72
ord., 65c
Harrowden (Haroden, Harouden), Np., 183, 219d
Harry:
John, r. of Upton Hellions, De., 275
Philip, v. of Crantock coll. ch., 288
Ralph, annuellar of Glasney coll. ch., 289
Thomas, ord., 65a, 75b
Harryson, George, r. of Tusmore, Ox., 196
Hartland (Hartland, Hertlond, Hertlonde), De:
abbey, 75c, 285, 336b, 357b
abbot, *see* Lorymer, Richard
cans. (named), 285
ch., 333c
dy., 333c
Hartpury (Harpbury), Gl., ch., 480
Haryngton, *see* Haringdon
Haryson, John, r. of Kentisbeare, De., 273
Hasley, Edward, Mr, prebendary of Cotton in Tamworth coll. ch., 26
Hassall, Humphrey, ord., 428c
Hasulwode, William, v. of Little Houghton, Np., 185
Hathersage (Hathersag, Hathersege), Db., ch., 422, 432
Hatherop (Evrthrup), Gl., ch, 486
Hatton, William, m. of Dieulacres, 428c
Haughmond (Hagmond, Haumond), Sa., abbey, 39c, 389, 428b, 435c

abbot, *see* Pontisbury, Richard
cans. (named), 389, 428d
Haugner, Edmund, esq., 203
Haverholme, Li., abbey, can. of
    (named), 160
Hawardyn, Humphrey, D.C.L.:
    Official of consistory court of
        Lichfield, 30
    prebendary of Lichfield cath., 395
Hawkesbury (Hawkysbury), Gl.:
    ch., 483
    dy., 477, 483, 504–5, 507
    dean, *see* Paynter, John
Hawkesby, Robert, v. of Mayfield, St.,
    25
Hawky, Richard, cantarist of Combe
    Florey, So., 61
Hawkys:
    Edward, cantarist of Hanley Castle,
        Wo., 479
    William, chap. of St Werburgh's,
        Bristol, 482
Hawlet, Richard, chap. of Berkeley,
    Gl., 481
Hawley, John, Mr, r. of St Mary in
    the Market Place, Bristol, 482
Hawling (Halling), Gl., ch., 487
Hay, Thomas, v. of Exeter cath.,276c
Hayes, John, ord., 53b, 65d
Hayfeld, John, Mr, r. of St Lawrence,
    Wathe, I.o.W., 116
Haynes (Hainyes, Hanneys):
    John, ord., 428a
    Ralph, Decr.B.:
        commissary of abp. for visitation
            of Surrey archdeaconry, 80
        commissary of Official *sede
            vacante*, Lincoln dioc., 136,
            138–41, 229, 231
    Ralph, Mr, can. of Reigate, 92
Haywode, David, ord., 53b, 65c, 75d
Hazleton (Halsitton), Gl., ch., 487
Heanor (Henor, Henore), Db., ch.,
    39b, 435b
Heanton Punchardon (Heghhampton),
    De., ch., 333e
Heathcote (Haselosa), Wa., ch., 508
Hechyns, William, warden of
    Breadstone chantry, Berkeley,
    Gl., 481
Heckington (Hekyngton), Li., ch.,
    216c, e

Heide, Thomas, S.T.B., r. of St
    Mary's, Orton Waterville, Hu.,
    206
Heilde, Richard, r. of Waddingham St
    Mary, Li., 179
Helland (Hellond), Co., 334g
Helmswell (Helmeswell), Li., ch., 258a
Helpringham, Li., ch., 188, 216e
Helston, Co., ch., 334d
Helyare, Nicholas, cur. of Broadclyst,
    De., 270
Hempstead (Hempstede), Gl., chapel,
    480
Hempston, Little (Hempston Parva),
    De., ch., 335b
Henslay, Robert, v. of Burgh, Li., 174
Henyock (Hemyok), De., ch., 272, 332f
Henbury (Hembury), Gl., ch., 482
Hendlowe, Nicholas, v. of Waltham St
    Lawrence, Brk., 548
Henley, Ox., dy., 247b
Hennock (Heanok), De., ch., 335a
Henry:
    chap. of Bradninch, De., 273
    VII, king of England, 11, 26, 60,
        62, 112, 118, 124, 150, 191,
        276a, 495–6
Henshawe, John, 437
Henton, John, prior of Bruton, 350
Herberd, William, 222a
Hereford:
    cath., dean and chapter of, 480
    dioc., l.d. from, 323d
Herefordshire, inh. of, *see* Butler, John
Herford, John, prior of St Nicholas,
    Exeter, 277
Hernbroke, John, cur. of St Sidmole's
    chapel, Exeter, 267
Hert, Humphrey, ord., 428b
Herterlond (unid.), De., ch., 332d
Hervy (Hervey):
    John, Mr, prebendary of Lichfield
        cath., 395
    Richard, ord., 53b
    Thomas:
        chap. of St Nicholas, Gloucester,
            480
        cur. of Washfield, De., 274
        ord., 428d
Herytt, John, ord., 323a
Heth:
    Richard, 43

196

Thomas, cantarist of Quatt, Sa., 7

Hethcote (Hethcote, Hethercote), Ralph, Decr.B., 88
  prebendary of Lichfield cath., 395
  prebendary of Salisbury cath., 93, 121n
  r. of Sherborne St John, Ha., 94
  r. of Wroughton, Wlt., 94n

Hetherlegh (Hatherlegh), De.,ch., 335j

Hewe, John, ord., 428b

Hewell, John, ap, r. of Easthampstead, Brk., 546

Hewes (Hewys):
  John, 226
  Richard, r. of Winterbourne Downe, Gl., 482

Hewich (*unid.*) (Hewish *or* Huish Episcopi), So., inh., of, *see* Towker, John

Hey, John, chap. of Cherkenhill, Wo., 479

Heydon, William, v. of Frampton on Severn, Gl., 481

Heyfond, Ralph, v. of Studley, Wa., 499

Heywood, Thomas, ord., 428a

Hezleton (Halsitton), Gl., ch., 487

Hicheman, John, v. of Windrush, Gl., 487

Hichinson, Ralph, ord., 428b

Hickys, Ralph, chap. of St Ewen's, Bristol, 482

Higden, Robert, v. of Ulceby, Li., 222a

Higges (Higgys):
  John, chap. of Uley, Gl., 481
  Nicholas, chap. of Ozleworth, Gl., 481
  Robert, r. of Alderley, Gl., 483
  Thomas, chap. of Stratford coll. ch., 468

Higham, Kent:
  ch., 451
  priory of Lillechurch, 445, 449b
  nuns (named), 445
  prioress, *see* Bradfeld, Elizabeth

Higham Ferrers, Np., dy., 251b

Higham on the Hill, Lei., ch., 217a, c

Highhampton (Heghampton), De., ch., 335j

High Peak (Alto Pecco), Db., dy., 38c, e; 40b, 429c

Highweek (Hewike), De., ch., 335a

Hill, Gl., ch., 481

Hill (Hille), Li., dy., *see* Horncastle

Hill Farraunce (Hilferons), So., inh. of, *see* Turner, Ralph

Hill (Hille, Hyll, Hylle):
  Edward, v. of Powick, Gl., 478
  John, 321
    chap. of Berkeley, Gl., 481
  Thomas
    can. of Lincoln cath., 135
    ord., 220
  William:
    ch. of Coberley, Gl., 484
    r. of Mathon, Wo., 479

Hillingdon, Mx., tithes of, 506

Hillmorton (Hulmerton, Hylmorton), Wa., ch., 39a, 435a

Hillyng, William, Mr, sacrist of Ottery St Mary coll., ch., 280

Hilton, John, proctor, 49

Hinton (Henton), So., priory, m. (named) of, 357c

Hinton Blewett (Henton Blewett), So., ch., 56

Hinxley, Thomas, ord., 428a

Hirst, John, v. of Coates by Stow, Li., 176

Hitchen (Hichen), Hrt., dy., 244b

Hittisleigh (Hittereslegh, Hytteslegh), De., ch., 269, 332b

Hobbys, Thomas, M.A., r. of Wood Walton, Hu., 211

Hockere, John, v. of Ottery St Mary coll. ch., 280

Hockworthy (Hockeworthy, Hokworthy), De., ch., 274, 332d

Hode, William, Mr, r. of All Saints, Wainfleet, Li., 168

Hodnet (Hudnett), Sa., inh. of, *see* Coly, Roger; Woode, Richard

Hogeson, Richard, v. of Saleby, Li., 148

Hogsthorpe (Hoggesthorp), Li., ch., 216e

Holand:
  Ralph, ord., 428b
  Richard, ord., 428a

Holbeach (Holbeche), Li., ch., 227

Holbeine (Holbaine), Robert, 325

Holbeton, De., ch., 335e

Holcomb, William, Mr, precentor of Ottery St Mary coll. ch., 280

Holcombe Burnell (Holcombe,
    Holecomb), De., ch., 269, 332b
Holcombe Rogus (Holcomb, Holcomb
    Rogus), De., ch., 274, 332d
Holcot (Holcottes), Np., ch., 186, 255d
Holcote, Robert, Mr, r. of Goodleigh,
    De., 306
Holdom, see Oldham
Holes, Thomas, Mr, prebendary of
    Bitton, Gl., 492
Holford (Holforde):
  John, 199
  Thomas, Mr:
      Official of archd. of Gloucester,
          477, 487
      r. of Rodmarton, Gl., 484, 494
      v. of Tetbury, Gl., 484
Holiwell, Lawrence, ord., 428d
Hollacombe (Holcombe), De., ch.,
    335h
Holland (Holand), Li., dys. of north
    and south parts, 138
Holland Bridge (Holand, Holande),
    Li., priory, 428b–d
Holne (Hall), De., ch., 335c
Holsworthy (Hall', Hallisworthy), De.:
  ch., 335h
  dy., 335h
Holton (Halton), Ox., ch., 195, 219g
Holyburton, Patrick, Mr, can. of
    Exeter cath., 276a
Holyns, Thomas, ord., 428d
Homfrey, John, ord., 428d
Honeychurch (Honychurch), De., ch.,
    335j
Honington (Honyngton), Li., v. of, 225
Honington (Hunynton), Wa., ch., 508
Honiton (Honyton), De., 265
  ch., 271, 332g
  dy., 265, 271, 332g
Honywell, John, v. of Exeter cath.,
    276c
Hoo:
  John, cantarist of Quatt, Sa., 7
  William, r. of St John Arches,
      Exeter, 267
Hooker, Richard, 361
Hooper (Hoper):
  John, v. of Sidmouth, De., 270
  William, chap. of Frampton
      Cotterell, Gl., 483

Hoore:
  Richard, O. Carm., of Sutton, De.,
      323c
  Walter, ord., 53a, b; 65d
Hoper, see Hooper
Hopkins (Hopkyns):
  Henry, chap. of St John's,
      Gloucester, 480
  John, chap. of St John's, Gloucester,
      480
Hopkyn, William, prior of Launceston,
    286
Hopton, David, Mr, archd. of Exeter,
    324
Horley, Sy., ch., 106b
Horncastle (Hornecastre), Li., ch., 138,
    216e
Horncastle, Hill and Gartree, Li., dy.,
    138
Horne:
  John, chap. of Elmore, Gl., 480
  William, chap. of Ardyngton
      chantry, Aston, Wa., 33
Horneby:
  Henry, Mr, r. of Thrapston, Np.,
      187
  Robert, v. of St Lawrence, Morden,
      Sy., 96
Horridge (Holrigge), De., ch., 332a
Horsey, Robert, chap. of St Mary's
    coll. ch., Warwick, 470
Horsley, Db., inh. of, see Smith, Henry
Horsley (Horseley), Gl.:
  ch., 484
  inh., see Jones, Nicholas
Horsley, West (Westhorseley), Sy., ch.,
    106c
Horsley, Isabelle, 361
Horsman, William, r. of Babstock,
    Wlt., 533
Horton Kirby (Horton), Kent, ch., 450
Horwill, Thomas, cur. of Holy Trinity
    ch., Exeter, 267
Horwood (Horwoode), De., ch., 333d
Horwood Magna (Horwoode Magna),
    Bk., ch., 235
Hose (Howes, Howse), Lei., ch., 189,
    219c, 223b
  v. of, 222b
Hosier, Isabelle, 236
Hoskyn, Lawrence, v. of Wendron,
    Co., 299

Hoskyns, John, chap. of North Nibley, Gl., 481
Hospital of St John of Jerusalem in England, prior-provincial of, 119, 166, 180, 186, 192, 304, 489
see also Kendall, John
deputy of, see Eglesfeld, John
Houghton, Ha.:
ch., 98c
inh., see Jay, Robert
Houghton, Little (Houghton Parva), Np., ch., 185, 219d
Houghton:
Seth, ord., 428b
William, chap. of Tiverton, De., 274
Houson, John, 222a
Howe, William, prior of Marsh Barton, 293
Howell:
David, v. of prebendal ch. of Bathwick, So., 50
John, can. of St Augustine's, Bristol, 53b
Howton:
Roger, chap., 226
Thomas, 222a
Hoye, Thomas, r. of Feniton, De., 273
Hubbow, John, 361
Huberd, Robert, Mr, v. of Farnham, Sy., 95
Huchyns, Thomas, chap. of St John's, Bristol, 482
Huckmor, William, 330
Huddelston, John, kt., and Joan, 521
Huddesfeld, William, kt., 305
Hudson, John, ord., 428d
Hugh, cantarist of Stone, Gl., 481
Hugh, John, ord., 53d
Huish (Hiwish, Huissh), De., ch., 333b, 335e
Hulle, John, clerk of Westbury coll. ch., 462
Hulton, St., abbey, 39d, 434b
Humberstone (Humbreston), Lei., ch., 217d
Hungerton, Lei., ch., 217d
Hunt (Hunte, Huntt):
Hugh, 438
John:
ord., 65b, 75d
v. of Tilsworth, Bd., 205
Robert, r. of Siddington, Gl., 498

Thomas:
ord., 428a
v. of Ottery St Mary coll. ch., 280
William, chap. of Cirencester, Gl., 485
Huntbache, Thomas, cur. of coll.ch. of Gnosall, 11
Hunteley, Richard, chap. of Haresfield, Gl., 480
Huntingdon, Hu.:
archd. of, or Official, 200-12, 245
archdeaconry, 200-12, 219h, 244-6, 255d-e
ch. of All Saints, 202, 219h
dy., 244b
priory, 244a, 246f
Huntsham (Hunsesham, Hunsham), De., ch., 274, 302, 332d
Huntshaw (Hunshaue), De.,ch., 333d
Huntyngdon, Richard, ord., 428d
Hurdman, John, chap. of St Nicholas, Bristol, 482
Hurdyng, Walter, v. of Brampford Speke, De., 275
Hurley, Brk., priory, 546, 548
Hursley (Hurseley), Ha., ch., 98c
Hurlysfrensche, John, v. of Tickenham, So., 72
Hurstbourne Priors (Husborne Prioris), Ha., prebendal ch., 121
Hurste, Thomas, ord., 428c
Husee, John, Mr, r. of Corscombe, Do., 514
Hutt, Thomas, v. of Ottery St Mary coll. ch., 280
Hutton, Thomas, Decr.D., r. of Warboys, Hu., 204
Huxham, De., ch., 270, 332h
Huyssh, Robert, 361
Hyckes, Henry, v. of Tachbrook, Wa., 427
Hycoke, John, O.P., of Chester, 428c
Hyde (Hyda), near Winchester, Ha., abbey, 98a, 129, 526
abbot, see Hall, Richard; Strowde
ms. (named), 129
Hyde:
John, Mr, prebendary of Ottery St Mary coll. ch., 280
Richard, 105a
Hygar, John, v. of Glasney coll. ch., 289

Hygdon, Robert, v. of Ulceby, Li., 149
Hyll, *see* Hill
Hyngdon, Walter, Mr, prebendary of
    Crantock coll. ch., 288
Hynkys, Ralph, r. of Ladock, Co., 317
Hyrnyng, Robert, r. of Peatling Parva,
    Lei., 229b

Iddesleigh (Ideslegh), De., ch., 333b
Ideford, De., ch., 335a
Idsall (Edyshale), Sa., ch., 39c, 435c
Idsworth (Iddeswourthe), Hu., inh. of,
    see Banastre, Thomas
Ienkyn, *see* Jenkin
Ilchester (Yelve, Yllcestre), So., dy.,
    76b, 359b
Ilfracombe (Ilfradecombe), De., ch.,
    333e
Ilkeston (Illeston, Ilveston), Db., ch.,
    39b, 435b
Illogan (Illogans), Co., ch. 334e
Ilsington (Ilsyngton), De., ch., 335a
Inge (Ynge):
    Edmund, Mr, v. of Cadbury, De.,
        308
    Hugh, prebendary of Aust in
        Westbury coll. ch., 462
Inglyssh, John, r. of Bagenderby, Li.,
    151
Ingoldmells (Ingolmellys), Li., ch. of St
    Peter, 170, 255a
    r. of, 256
Inkebarough, *see* Enkbarough
Instow (Instowe), De., ch., 333d
Inwardleigh (Inwardelegh), De., ch.,
    335j
Ipplepen (Ipp'), De.:
    ch., 335b
    dy., 335b
Irby in the Marsh (Irby), Li., ch., 216e
Irchester (Irchestre), Lei., ch., 217a, c
Ireland, proctors of Llanthony priory
    in, 461
Iremonger, Richard, r. of Linkenholt,
    Ha., 115
Iron Acton (Ureacton), Gl., ch., 483
Irthlingborough (Irtlingbourgh), Np.,
    coll. ch., 251a
Isenhampstead Chenies (Isenhamstede,
    Isnamstede), Bk.:
    ch., 214, 219f
    lord of, *see* Philip, David and Anne
Isham, Robert, Mr, r. of Meysey
    Hampton, Gl., 486

Isle of Wight (Insula Vecta), dy., 98b
Islip (Islepe, Islyppe), Ox., ch., 157,
    219g
Itchington, Bishop's (Echington,
    Ichynton), Wa., ch., 39a, 434a
Ivinghoe (Ivynge, Ivynhoo), Bk., ch.,
    234b, 248
Ivychurch (Ederos'), Wlt., priory, 518,
    543
Iya, David, Mr, r. of Slimbridge, Gl.,
    481

Jacobstow (Jacobistow), Co., ch., 334h
Jacobstow (Stow sancti Jacobi), De.,
    ch., 335j
Jagons, William, r. of St Peter's,
    Wareham, Do., 544
Jakes:
    Henry, clerk of Westbury coll. ch.,
        462
    John, 437
Jakson:
    Henry, 222a
    John, 222a
Jamett, John, can. of Bruton, 357c
Jamys:
    Robert, chap. of Tiverton, De., 274
    Thomas, r. of Dunchideock, De.,
        268
    William, 555
Janyns:
    John, perpetual fellow of Westbury
        coll. ch., 462
    Thomas, r. of Norbury, St., 412
Janys, Roger, chap. of St Martin's
    chantry, Wells cath., 59
Jay, Robert, 105a
Jaybard, Margaret, 222a
Jeffrey, Alan, 229a
Jeffys, John, v. of Turkdean, Gl., 487
Jenkin (Ienkyn), Geoffrey ap, ord., 75d
Jenyvere, William, r. of Chale, I.o.W.,
    111
Jobe, John, pr. of Kennerleigh, De.,
    275
Johannys, *see* Jones
John:
    cur. of Uffculme, De., 274
    inh. of Wells, So., 361
John:
    Henry ap, Mr:
        Official of archd. of Lincoln, 138
        precentor of Lincoln cath., 135

John:
v. of Cadbury, De., 275, 308
v. of Wendron, Co., 299
Philip, chap. of Honiton, De., 271
Richard, cur. of St Olave's, Exeter, 267
Robert, v. of Thorncombe, De., 271
Thomas ap, ord., 357a
William, prior of Bodmin, 287
Johns, William, Mr, prebendary of Lichfield cath., 395
Johnson (Jonson):
Christopher, ord., 428a
John, chap. of Little Rissington, Gl., 487
Jones (Johannys, Johnys, Jonys):
David, r. of Little Rissington, Gl., 487, 500
see also Philip, David
Geoffrey:
chap. of Hempstead, Gl., 480
chap. of King's Stanley, Gl., 484
v. of Haresfield, Gl., 480
John:
r. of Duntisbourne Rous, Gl., 485
v. of Great Barrington, Gl., 487
Nicholas, 510
Richard, chap. of Tetbury, Gl., 484
Thomas, chap. of Rodborough, Gl., 484
William, Mr, r. of Holy Trinity ch., Bristol, 482
Jordan (Jurden):
John, ord., 65c
Thomas:
ord., 53c
r. of Knebworth, Hrt., 201
Josepp, Henry, ord., 65b
Juker, Thomas, ord., 53c
Jule, Richard, cur. of Colaton Raleigh, De., 270
Jurden, *see* Jordan

Kalends, fraternity of, *see* Bristol, ch. of All Saints
Karre, Gregory, literate, 157
Kay, John, chap. of St Mary's coll. ch., Warwick, 470
Keelby (Keleby), Li., ch., 138, 216e
Keepe (Kepe), William, ord., 53b, 65c, 75d
Kelligrewe, Benedict, Mr, prebendary of Glasney coll. ch., 289

Kelly, De., ch., 335g
Kelsey, North, Li., prebendal ch., 150, 219a
Kelshall (Kelsall), Hrt., ch. of St Faith, 209, 255d–e
Kempsey (Keamsey), Wo., ch., 508
Kempsford (Kemysforde), Gl., ch., 486
Kemsing (Keamsyng), Kent, ch., 450
Kemyll:
John, r. of Fretherne, Gl., 480
Nicholas, r. of St Aldate, Gloucester, 480
Kendall (Kendale), John:
prior-provincial of Hospitallers, *see* Hospital of St John of Jerusalem
v. of Exeter cath., 276c
Kenier, John, v. of Luppit, De., 272
Kenilworth (Kenelworth, Kenely), Wa.:
abbey, 375, 429a, 508
abbot, *see* Maxstoke, Ralph
cans. (named), 375
ch., 405
Kenn (Kenne), De.:
ch., 268, 332a
dy., 265, 268, 332a
Kennerleigh (Kenerlegh), De., ch., 275
Kent:
Nicholas, clerk, 331
William, v. of Box, Wlt., 547
Kentisbeare (Kentisbere), De., ch., 273, 332e
Kentisbury, De., ch., 333e
Kenton, De., ch., 268, 332c
Kenwall, Edward, chap. of St Lawrence's, Bristol, 482
Kenwyn (Kenewyn), Co., ch., 334c
Kere, Barnaby, chap. of Upton on Severn, 479
Kerier (Ker'), Co., dy., 334d
Ketyll, Gervase, r. of St Lawrence, Wathe, I.o.W., 116
Key, Thomas, ord., 323d
Keynsham (Keynesham, Keynessham, Keynysham), So.:
abbey, 76a, 349, 357b, 358
abbot, *see* Gylmyn, John
inh., see Keynysham, John
Keynysham (Kynsham), John, 361
Keyton, Robert, v. of Clevedon, So., 72
Kidderminster (Kyddermynster), Wo.:
ch., 476, 508

dy., 476, 503, 507

Kidderminster (Kedermyster), Richard, abbot of Winchcombe, 466

Kilkhampton (Kylkhampton), Co., ch., 334h

Killingholme (Kelingholme), Li., ch., 143, 219a

Kilmington (Kilmyngton, Kylmyngton), De., chapel, 271, 332g

Kimbolton (Kymbalton), Hu., ch., 246d

Kimcote (Kilmerdcote, Kilmyncote), Lei., ch., 190, 219c

Kineton (Kington), Wa., dy., 476, 503, 507

King (Kyng, Kynge):
　Humphrey, ord., 428a
　John, chap. of Great Sodbury, Gl., 483
　Lawrence, v. of Desborough, Np., 184
　Oliver, Mr, can. of Exeter cath., 276a
　Richard, r. of Pendock, Wo., 479
　Thomas, chap. of Painswick, Gl., 484

Kingsbridge (Kyngisbrige), De., ch., 335d

Kingsbury (Kynnesbury), Wa.:
　ch., 39a, 435c
　inh., see Bricebridge, Simon

Kingscote (Kyngscote), Gl., ch., 481

King's Stanley, see Stanley

Kingsteignton (Teyngton Regis), De., ch., 335a

Kingston (Kyngiston), So., inh. of, see Brice, Thomas; Morys, Walter; Slappe, Richard

Kingston (Kingeston), Sy., ch., 106b

Kington St Michael (Kington), Wlt., priory, 65c

Kington, West (Westkynton), Wlt., ch., 525

Kinver (Kynsare), St., ch., 39d, 435d

Kirk Langley, see Langley, Kirk

Kirkby St Denis (Kyrrkeby Dionisii), Li., ch., 167, 219a

Kirkman, Thomas, v. of Hose, Lei., 189

Kirnell, John, 236

Kneboon, John, v. of St Merryn, Co., 311

Knebworth, Hrt., ch., 201, 219h

Knightly, William, can. of Arbury, 428b

Knoddy, Robert, B.A., v. of East Hagbourne, Brk., 523

Knole, Kent, 11, 94, 455–6, 511

Knolles (Knollys):
　Alexander, literate, 169
　David, Mr, r. of Linkenholt, Ha., 115

Knottysford, John, chap. of St Philip's, Bristol, 482

Knowstone (Knoudeston), De., ch., 333f

Knyf, John, v. of Buckerell, De., 273

Knyght:
　Joan, abbess of Malling, 447
　Nicholas, r. of Combe-in-Teignhead, De., 268
　Peter, 437
　Richard, v. of Cam, Gl., 481
　Robert, 103
　　Mr, Official of archd. of Northampton, 259
　William, 361

Knyveton, Matthew, Mr, v. of Ashwell, Hrt., 210

Kocke, Robert, r. of Kirkby St Denis, Li., 167

Krive [unid.], Co., ch., 334c

Kyme, Li., priory, 159

Kympe, William, cur. of Chagford, De., 269

Kyng, see King

Kyngeston, Thomas, esq., 94

Kyngeswoode, William, prior of Pilton, 301

Kyngman, William, r. of Brockley, So., 72

Kynnardesley, William:
　r. of Ayot St Lawrence, Hrt., 203
　r. of Knebworth, Hrt., 201

Kynsham, see Keynysham

Kyntishall, Robert, r. of Trusham, De., 268

Kyrke, John, 30

Kyrkham, Thomas, esq., 306

Kyrdeman, Thomas, 222b

Kyrlagh, Roger, B.A., v. of North Morton, Brk., 532

Kyrse, Agnes, 361

Kyton, John, v. of Hanley Castle, Wo., 479

William, chap. of Cherrington, Gl., 484
Lecher, Thomas, v. of Waltham St Lawrence, Brk., 548
Lechlade (Lichlade, Lychelade), Gl.:
  ch., 486
  chantry in, 508
  inh., *see* Doding, Elizabeth; Stone, Thomas
  priory, 508
Ledbury, Maculinus, prior of Great Malvern, 478
Ledsham, Oliver, ord., 428d
Ledys, Christopher, can. of Lilleshall, 428a
Lee:
  Isota, prioress of Wroxall, 471
  John, esq., 513
  Richard, chap. of St Michael the Archangel, Norridge, Wlt., 513
Leek (Leke), St.:
  archdeaconry, *see* Alton
  inh., *see* Byrley, Roger; Heth, Richard; Lokwode, Thomas; Sondell, Nicholas
Leek (Leke):
  John, 222b
  Thomas, 437
Lefe, Robert, r. of Isenhampstead Chenies, Bk., 214
Legatt, Thomas, ord., 65a, 75c
Legbourne (Legborn, Legburn), Li.:
  ch., 216a
  priory, 142, 228
Legge, Robert, Decr. B., r. of Weddington, Wa., 13
Legh (Lee), Co., ch., 334c
Legh, Richard, r. of Stockleigh Pomeroy, De., 275
Leghmore, William, r. of Lasham, Ha., 126
Lehee, Hugh, Mr, prebendary of Lichfield cath., 395
Leicester (Leicestr'), Lei:
  abbey of St Mary de Pratis, 33, 142, 418
  archd. of, or Official, 141, 189–94, 218
    see also Shorman, John (Official)
  archdeaconry, 141, 217–8, 219c, 221, 223b, 226, 229b, 252b, 255c, 258b

ch. of St Martin, 141
coll. ch. of Newark, 39b, 191, 219c, 435b
dy., 141
hospital of St John, 217d
Leigh, Chs., ch., 39e, 435a
Leigh (Ligh), Sy., ch., 106c
Leigh (Lygh), Wo., ch., 479
Leightonstone (Leitamstone), Hu., dy., 244b
Leke, *see* Leke
Lelant (Lananta), Co., ch., 334e
Lemyng, John, chap. of Stogursey, So., 56
Lenton, John, v. of St Mary's, Derby, 18
Leonard Stanley, *see* Stanley, Leonard
Lesnes (Lesnys, Lesunnes), Kent, abbey, 442, 449b
  abbot, *see* Bright, William
  cans. (named), 442
Lesnewth, Co., ch., 334g
Letcombe Bassett (Letombassett), Brk., r. of, *see* Whitehorn, John
Levemore, Thomas, 361
Levet, John, chap. of Beverstone, Gl., 481
Lewannick (Lawanak), Co., ch., 334a
Lewellen, Robert, v. of Wapley, Gl., 483
Lewes:
  John:
    ord., 53d
    r. of Potsgrove, Bd., 213
  Thomas, r. of Christon, So., 51
  William, chap. of Bagendon, Gl., 485
Lewis (Lewys), John:
  m. of Witham, 357d
  ord., 428d
Lewtrenchard, De., ch., 335g
Lewys, *see* Lewis
Leydes, Robert, v. of Ashby, Li., 166
Leyland (Leylond, Leylonde), La.:
  ch., 39e, 435e
  dy., 429e
Leylond, Richard, S.T.P., chap. of Allesley chantry in Holy Trinity ch., Coventry, Wa., 32
Lichefeld, *see* Lichfield
Lichfield, St., 2, 4–8, 10, 12–15, 17–18, 20, 23–9, 30–7, 369–73,

London:
John, Mr, v. of Almondsbury, Gl.,
482
see also Stratton
Lawrence, r. of Washfield, De., 274
Richard, chap. of Tiverton, De.,
274
Long (Longe, Lonnge):
John:
r. of Southleigh, De., 271
v. of Chedworth, Gl., 485
Peter, cur. of Clyst Hidon, De., 273
Philip, r. of Clyst-St Mary, De., 270
Thomas, esq., 545
Longborough (Langbarough), Gl., 477
ch., 504
Longbridge (Longbregge), see Berkeley
Longdon, St., prebend of Lichfield
cath., 38a, 430b
Longdon, Wo., ch., 479, 508
Longe, see Long
Longford, Ralph, ord., 428a
Longforth, Henry, ord., 428d
Longman, Robert, chap. of Bampton,
De., 274
Longney, Gl., ch., 480
Longney, Walter, v. of Arlingham, Gl.,
480
Longoboby (Langhouboby) and
Graffoe, Li., dy., 138
Lonnge, see Long
Longtre, Margaret, 35
Lorymer:
John, par. chap. of Holy Trinity,
Bristol, 482
Richard, abbot of Hartland, 285
Loscombe, John, r. of Stoke Abbot,
Do., 522
Lostwithiel (Lostwythiol), Co.:
ch. of St Bartholomew, 331
inh., see Martin, William
Louth, Li., 158
ch., 138
Louthborough (Louthburgh), Lei., ch.,
141
Loutheske and Ludborough, Li., dy.,
138
Lovebond, John, ord., 53c
Lovedon (Loveden'), Li., dy., 138
Lowden, John, cantarist of St Nicholas,
Heckington, Li., 162

Lowe:
Henry, v. of Ottery St Mary coll.
ch., 280
Thomas, cur. of Membury, De.,
271
Lowre, John, 331
Loxhore (Lokishare), De., ch., 333e
Lubbenham (Lubenham), Lei., ch.,
223b
r., 222b
Lucas:
John, Mr, chap. of Stinchcombe,
Gl., 481
Richard:
notary public, 154
r. of Silk Willoughby, Li., 154
Ludborough (Louthburgh), Li., see
Loutheske
Luddington (Lodington), Wa., v. of, see
Bloke, John
Ludgvan (Ludvan), Co., ch., 334e
Luffincott (Lofyngcote), De., ch., 335h
Luke, John, prebendary of Glasney
coll. ch., 289
Luker, John, 361
Luky, John, v. of Glasney coll. ch., 289
Lulle, William, second treasurer of
Westbury coll. ch., 462
Lulsley chapel, see Suckley
Luppitt (Lovepit, Lovepitt), De., ch.,
272, 328, 332f
Lupton, Roger, Mr, prebendary of St
Michael's coll. ch., Warwick,
470, 495
Lustleigh (Lustlegh), De., ch., 335a
Lutt (Lutte), William, r. of Berrington,
Sa., 9
Lutterworth, Lei., ch., 141
Luxulyan (Luxawn), Co., ch., 331
Lychefelde, see Lichfield
Lydda, bp. of, see Church, Augustine
Lydeard, Bishop's (Lydyard Episcopi),
So., inh. of, see Nasshyng,
William
Lydford, De., ch., 335g
Lydtister, John, chap. of Sparsholt,
Brk., 549, 551
Lympstone (Lympston), De., ch., 270,
332h
Lynckhall, Thomas, chap. of Holy
Trinity, Bristol, 482

Lynke:
Hugh:
Mr, prebendary of Glasney coll.
ch., 289
r. of Goodleigh, De., 306
r. of Shirwell, De., 309
Philip, chap. of Collumpton, De.,
273
Lynse, William, can. of Arbury, Wa.,
428b
Lynton, De., ch., 333e
Lynton, John, can. of Church Gresley,
428a
Lyrd, Thomas, prior of Barlinch, 353
Lytill, Hugh, chap. of Upton St
Leonard, Gl., 480

Macclesfield (Macfild, Mayfild), Chs.,
dy., 40e, 429e
Macy, William, ord., 357b
Madely (Maddeley), St., ch., 39d, 434b
Maderer, Thomas, ord., 428d
Mades, Thomas, Mr, 365
Madiow, Thomas, Mr:
r. of St Michael Major, Stamford,
Li., 153
r. of St Peter's, Conisholme, Li.,
152
Madok:
Ralph, ord., 428c
Richard, ord., 428d
Madresfield (Mattysfeld), Wo., ch., 479
Madron (Madren), Co., ch., 334e
Maisemore, Gl., chapel, 480
Major (Maior, Maiour):
John:
ord., 357c
secondary of Exeter cath., 276e
Nicholas, Mr:
r. of Braceborough, Li., 163
r. of Greatford, Li., 155
r. of Toft, Li., 161
Maker, Co., ch., 328, 334a
Malbone, John, abbot of Norton, 397
Malborough (Malburgh), De., ch.,
335d
Malden (Maldon), Sy., ch., 106b
Maliverer, Halnatheus, esq., and Joan,
317
Malling (Mallyng), Kent:
abbey, 447, 449b
abbess, see Knyght, Joan
nuns (named), 447
dy., 449a

Malmesbury, Wlt., abbey, 301
Malpas, Chs., dy., 40e, 429e
Malpas:
Richard, ord., 53d
Thomas, chap. of Duntisbourne
Abbots, Gl., 485
Malton, John, O.Prem., r. of Chale,
I.o.W., 111
Malvern, Great (Magna Malverne),
Wo.:
ch., 479
priory, 477, 479–80, 503, 508
prior, see Ledbury, Maculinus
Malvern, Little (Malverne Minor),
Wo.:
ch., 476
priory, 479, 482, 487, 503
Malverne, John, abbot of Gloucester,
460
Mamhead (Mamhed, Mamhede), De.,
ch., 268, 332a
Man, John, cantarist of Thornbury,
Gl., 481
Manaccan, Co., ch., 334d
Manaton, De., ch., 335a
Manby, Peter, chap. of Henbury, Gl.,
482
Mancetter (Mancestr'), Wa., ch., 39a,
435a
Manchester (Mancestr'), La.:
coll. ch., 39e, 435e
dy., 429e
Maners, John, 105b
Mangotsfield (Mangarsfeld), Gl.,
chapel, 482
Manlake (Manlak), Li., dy., 139
Manningfold Abbots (Mannyngford
Abbatis), Wlt., ch., 526
Mannyng, William, chap. of
Cirencester, Gl., 485
Manson, Richard, ord., 428d
Marable, Henry, 222a
Marchall, see Marshall
Marchington, St., inh. of, see Smith,
Robert
Mareshall, see Marshall
Margam (Morgan), Glam., abbey, 53d
Marhamchurch, Co., ch., 334h
Mariansleigh (Marlegh), De., ch., 333f
Mariot (Mariott), Richard, 189, 222b
Market Harborough (Harborowe), Lei.,
ch., 141

Markham:
  John, esq., 182
  Robert, 222b
Markyate (Markeyate), Hrt., priory,
    39a, 238a, 262, 435a
  prioress-elect, *see* Akworth, Denise
Marlow, Little (Merlow), Bk.:
  ch., 234b
  priory, 234b
Marshall (Marchall, Mareshall):
  John:
      chap. of Bibury, Gl., 485
      chap. of St John's, Bristol, 482
  William, cantarist of St Nicholas,
      Heckington, Li., 162
Marsh Barton (Merssh), De., priory,
    293
  prior, *see* Howe, William
Marshfield (Mershfeld), Gl., ch., 483
Marston (Merston), So., dy., 76b, 359b
Marston Moretaine (Merston), Bd., r.
    of, 241, 243
Martin V, pope, 395
Martinhoe (Martynghoo), De., ch.,
    333e
Marton, Wa., dy., 38b, d; 40a, 405,
    429a, 430a
Martyn:
  Amicia, 331
  Edmund, J.U.D.:
      chap. of free chapel of
          Athelhampton, Do., 524
      r. of St Mary's, Steeple
          Langford, Wlt., 521
  Joan, 331
  John, 331
  Richard, ord., 53d
  Robert, r. of Ladock, Co., 317
  Thomas:
      Decr.D.:
          r. of Semley, Wlt., 537
          v. of North Morton, Brk., 532
          v. of Tilshead, Wlt., 518, 543
          v. of East Wellow, Ha., 108
      William, 324, 331
          esq., 524
Marwood (Merewood), De., ch., 333e
Maryns, Thomas, chap. of Stratford
    coll. ch., 468
Marys, Thomas, v. of Ashill, So., 47
Marystow (Stow Marie), De., ch., 335g
Marytavy (Tavy Marie), De., ch., 335f

Mason:
  John, 222c
      Mr, cantarist of Lechlade, Gl.,
          486
  Richard, ord., 428d
Massingham, Henry, clerk of Westbury
    coll. ch., 462
Massy, William, ord., 428d
Massymere, Nicholas, 105a
Mathon (Mathom), Wo., ch., 479
Matson (Matstone), Gl., ch., 480
Maunce, John, r. of Ozleworth, Gl.,
    481
Mawe, John, chap. of Epworth
    chantry, Li., 177
Mawgan (in Kerrier), Co., ch., 334d
Mawgan (in Pydar), Co., ch., 334f
Mawnan, Co., ch., 334d
Maxstoke (Machestok), Wa.:
  ch., 39a, 434a
  priory, 39a, 376, 429a, 434a
  cans. (named), 376
  prior, *see* Freman, John
Maxstoke, Ralph, abbot of Kenilworth,
    375
Mayfield (Mafeld), St., ch., 25
Mayne, Thomas, v. of Anwick. Li.,
    160
Mayow (Mayowe):
  Edward, v. of Landrake, Co., 314
  Richard, Mr, can. of Exeter cath.,
      176a
Meavy (Mewy), De., ch., 335f
Meburne, Thomas, chap. of Saul, Gl.,
    480
Mecy, *see* Mey
Medcalfe, William, v. of Shipton
    Bellinger, Ha., 117
Mede, George, chap. of St Mary's coll.
    ch., Warwick, 470
Medycok, John, r. of Cottesbrook, Np.,
    182
Meeth (Methe), De., ch., 333b
Melbourne (Melborn), Db., chantry of
    SS Mary and Michael, 421, 432
Melconek, Nicholas, prebendary of
    Endellion, Co., 338
Meldy, John, r. of Honiton, De., 271
Melhuysh, Richard, 325
Melton Mowbray (Melton Moubray),
    Lei., ch., 141
Membury (Memby), De., ch., 271,
    332g

Menheniot (Mahynyet), Co., ch., 334a
Mens, John, annuellar of Glasney coll.
    ch., 289
Menwynnyk, William, r. of South Hill,
    Co., 318
Meon, East (East Mean), Ha., ch., 100
Meraunde, Walter, 556
Mere, Li., ch., 216e
Meredith, William, r. of Filton
    Fishponds, Gl., 482
Merevale (Meryvall, Miravalle), Wa.,
    abbey, 39a, 419, 428b, 435a
Merifeld (Meryfeld, Meryfild):
    Alexander, ord., 357b
    Thomas:
        cantarist of the Kalends, Bristol,
        482
        r. of St Paul's, Exeter, 267, 307
Merrow (Merewe), Sy., ch., 106c
Merton, De., ch., 333b
Merton, Sy.:
    ch., 106b
    priory, 80, 83, 85–6, 106d
    cans. (named), 83
Merydewe, William, 437
Meryfild, see Merifeld
Mesaunt, John, Mr, r. of Thrapston,
    Np., 187
Meshaw (Meshaue), De., ch., 333f
Messingham, Li., ch., 139
Mevagissey (Mevagisby), Co., ch.,
    334c
Mey (Mecy):
    John, ord., 53b, 65d
    William, 361
Meysey Hampton, see Hampton,
    Meysey
Meysy, John, 510
Michaelstow, Co., ch., 334g
Michell:
    John, ord., 53d
    Matthew, r. of Ashcombe, De., 268
Michelson (Myghelson), John, m. of
    Witham, 65b
Mickleham (Mykylham), Sy., ch., 106b
Mickleton (Mekylton), Gl., ch., 508
Middelham, John, ord., 53d
Middleton (Middylton, Mydulton), La.,
    ch., 413, 432
Middleton, Robert, Mr, v. of Ashwell,
    Hrt., 210
Middlewich (Medii Wici), Chs., dy.,
    40e, 429e

Milborne [unid.] (Milborn), Do.,
    Endersley in, 554
Miller, William, notary public, 136,
    181, 205, 255–8
Millys (Mylles), William, Official's
    apparitor, Salisbury dioc., 555–7
Milner:
    John, v. of Hose, Lei., 189
    Thomas, 189
Milton (Myddleton, Mydleton), Do.,
    abbey, 53d, 357b
Milton Abbot (Milton Abbatis), De.,
    ch., 335g
Milton Damarel (Milton Damerell),
    De., ch., 335h
Milton, South (Milton), De., ch., 335d
Milverton stall, see Astley
Milward (Mylward), Robert, ord., 65b,
    75c
Mimms, North (Mymmes), Hrt., ch.,
    246f
Minchinhampton (Hampton), Gl., ch.,
    484
Minehead (Mynehede), So., inh. of, see
    Slyme, Nicholas; Smarte, Patrick
Minster (Mynstre), Co., ch., 334g
Miserden (Myserdene), Gl., ch., 484
Missenden (Myssenden), Bk., abbey,
    232a
Mitcham (Mycheham), Sy., ch., 106b
Modbury, De., ch., 335e
Moderby, William, 222b
Moge, Robert, chap. of East Ogwell,
    De., 268
Mogrige, Richard, chap. of Plymtree,
    De., 273
Molland (Malland), De., ch., 333f
Molton, De., dy., 333f
Molton, North, De., ch., 333f
Molton, South, De., ch., 333f
Mome, Robert, Mr, prebendary of
    Lichfield cath., 395
Monkleigh (Monklegh), De., ch., 333c
Monk Okehampton (Monkokhampton),
    De., ch., 335j
Monksilver, So., inh. of, see Chilcote,
    John
Monkton Farleigh, Wlt., priory, 357c,
    547
Monmouth (Monemouth), Mon.,
    priory, 498

Montacute (Montis Acute,
　　Montegewe), So., priory, 53b,
　　60, 65b, d; 75c, 274
　　m. (named), 357d
Moore, John, 61
　　Mr, prebendary of Lichfield cath.,
　　　395
　　v. of Shirley, Db., 2
　　see also More
Morchard Bishop (Morteherd Episcopi),
　　De., ch., 275
Morden (Mordon), Sy., ch. of St
　　Lawrence, 96, 106b, 125
More:
　　John, 324
　　　chap. of Almondsbury, Gl., 482
　　　Mr, r. of Stow on the Wold, Gl.,
　　　　487
　　　prebendary of Goodringhill in
　　　　Westbury coll. ch., 462
　　　r. of Offwell, De., 271
　　　v. of Great Malvern, Wo., 479
　　William, chap. of Holy Trinity ch.,
　　　Bristol. 482
Morebath (Morepath), De., ch., 274,
　　332d
Moreleigh (Morlegh), De., ch., 335d
Moren, Thomas, v. of East Wellow,
　　Ha., 108
Morepathe, William, m. of
　　Glastonbury, 357d
Mores, see Morys
Morestead (Morestede), Ha., ch., 98c
Moretonhampstead (Morton'), De.:
　　ch., 335a
　　dy., 335a
Moreton in Marsh (Moreton), Gl., ch.,
　　480
Moreton Morell (Morton Morell), Wa.,
　　ch., 508
Moreys, see Morys
Morgan:
　　John, v. of Lilleshall, Sa., 10
　　Thomas ap, r. of Siddington, Gl.,
　　　498
　　Walter ap, literate, 203
Morrock, John, Mr, r. of Cottesbrooke,
　　Np., 254
Morthoe (Morthoo), De., ch., 333e
Morton, North, Brk., ch., 532
Morton, John, abp. of Canterbury,
　　123, 251a
　　acts done in the name of, passim

bull addressed to, 261
charitable subsidy granted to, 62
clerk of, see Rise, John
collation by, 107, 120, 311
commissions issued by, 1, 22, 44,
　　77, 80–1, 85, 92, 136–7, 264,
　　339–40, 366–8, 439–40,
　　452–3, 456–7, 511
institutions by, 11, 89–91, 94–6, 427
letters of attestation from, 124
mandate issued by, 62, 78, 262–3
payment to, 338
visitation conducted in person by, 82
Morton (Moorton):
　　John, Mr, prebendary of Lichfield
　　　cath., 395
　　Thomas, Mr, r. of Beverstone, Gl.,
　　　481
Mortymer, Lawrence, Mr, v. of
　　Broadhembury, De., 273
Morval (Morvall), Co., ch., 334b
Morwenstow (Morestow), Co., ch.,
　　334h
Morwyn, John, literate, 199
Morys (Mores, Moreys):
　　Edmund, r. of St Michael's, Bristol,
　　　482
　　John, alias Pardener, canon of Tong
　　　coll. ch., 399
　　Maurice, chap. of St Michael's,
　　　Gloucester, 480
　　Philip, perpetual fellow of Westbury
　　　coll. ch., 462
　　Thomas, r. of Wraxall, So., 72
　　Walter, 361
　　　J.U.B., v. of prebendal ch. of
　　　　Yatton, So., 71–2, 365
Moston, Thomas, ord., 428c
Mottisfont (Mottesfont, Mottisfonte),
　　Ha.:
　　inh., see Boston, Richard
　　priory, 65d, 98a, 109
Motton, Alexander, chap. of Stratford
　　coll. ch., 468
Moulton (Mauton), Np., ch., 252b
Mountegue, William, r. of St Edmund-
　　on-Exe-Bridge, Exeter, 267
Mountgomery, Nicholas, kt., 4
Mount Grace (Monte Gre), Yk.,
　　priory, 39b, 435b
Mower, John, 229a
Mownt, Nicholas, ord., 53c

Muchelney (Mochelney), So.:
    abbey, 53c, d; 59; 65b, c; 76a, 351,
        358
        abbot, *see* Somerton, John de;
            Wyke, William
        ms. (named), 323d, 357d
    ch., 360
Muckeley, George, par. chap. of
    Redmarley d'Abitot, Gl., 479
Mullion (Melian), Co., ch., 334d
Munby, Li., ch., 227
Mursley (Murseley), Bk., dy., 232b
Musbury (Musberye, Musbyri), De.,
    ch., 271, 332g
Myghelson, *see* Michelson
Myles (Mylis, Mylys):
    David, Mr, r. of St Michael's,
        Wareham, Do., 516
    John, 510
        prebend of, *see* Endellion
Mylles, *see* Millys
Mylmett, John, r. of Halwill, De., 304
Mylton, John:
    chap. of St John's, Exeter, 267
    clerk of Westbury coll. ch., 462
Mylward, *see* Milward
Mylym, William, clerk of Westbury
    coll. ch., 462
Mynde, Thomas, abbot of Shrewsbury,
    390
Mynet, Henry, chap. of Quedgeley,
    Gl., 480
Mynshull, Charles, ord., 428c
Mytton, William, esq., 438

Nailsea (Naylesey), So., inh. of, *see*
    Wheler, John
Nakes (Nakys), Richard:
    r. of Gittisham, De., 271
    r. of St Stephen's, Exeter, 267
Nantwich (Vici Malpani, Wico
    Malbano), Chs., dy., 40e, 429e
Napton, Wa., ch., 434a
Naseby, Np., ch., 242a, b
Nasshyng, William, ord., 65a, 68, 75c
Naunby, John, 229a
Naunton (Newyngton), Gl., ch., 487
Navenby, Li., ch., 138
Neath (Neth), Glam., abbey, 53d, 75d
Neele (Nele):
    John, v.-choral of Wells cath., 53b,
        65d
    William, Mr, r. of North Cerney,
        Gl., 485

Neleson, Thomas, Mr, prebendary of
    Lichfield cath., 395
Nempnet Thrubwell (Nempnet), So.,
    inh of, *see* Crosse, John
Ness, Great (Ness Strange,
    Nissestrange), Sa., ch., 39c, 435c
Ness (Nesse) and Stamford, Li., dy.,
    138
Nether Wallop (Netherwallopp), Ha.,
    105a
Netley, Ha., abbey, 108
Nettlecombe (Netilcombe, Netlecombe),
    So.:
    chantry, 49
    inh., *see* Durkyn, Thomas
Nettleham (Nettilham), Li., bp.'s
    manor, 135
Nettlestead (Netilstede), Kent, r. of,
    450
Neucomb, John, r. of St Mary Steps,
    Exeter, 267
Nevell, Edward, chap. of Wotton under
    Edge, Gl., 481
Newark coll., *see* Leicester
Newbold, Thomas, ord., 428d
Newbold Pacey (Newbold), Wa., ch.,
    508
Newbury, Brk., hospital of St
    Bartholomew, 517
Newcastle under Lyme, St., inh. of, *see*
    Bolton, John
Newchurch (Nyghchurch in Insula
    Vecta), I.o.W., ch., 99
Newdigate (Nudegate), Sy., ch., 106c
Newenham (Newham, Nuham), De.,
    abbey, 53d, 65b, 272
    m. (named), 323b
New Forest, inh. of, *see* Pecok, Peter
Newington Bagpath (Nawnton), Gl.,
    ch., 481
Newland:
    John, 222a
        abbot of St Augustine's,
            Canterbury, 463
    Richard, r. of Isenhampstead
        Chenies, Bk., 214
Newlyn, Co., ch., 334f
Newnant, Roger, founder of Totnes
    priory, 296
Newnham (Newenham,), Bd., priory,
    238a, 240b
Newport (Novi Burgi), Sa., 412
    coll. ch., 28, 31

dy., 38f, g; 40c, 429d

Newport chantry, *see* Berkeley

Newport Pagnell (Newport), Bk., dy., 232b

Newsham *alias* Newhouse, Li., abbey, 143

Newstead by Stamford (de novo loco), Li., priory, 228, 428d

Newton (*unid.*), inh. of, *see* Dicon, Richard

Newton Ferrers, De., ch., 335e

Newton St Cyres (Newton, Newton sancti Cyriaci), De., ch., 275, 332c

Newton St Petrock (Pedrok), De., ch., 333b

Newton Tracey (Newton), De., ch., 333d

Newton:
  Elizabeth, lady, 51
  Hugh, chap. of Bermondsey, Sy., 79
  John, Mr, r. of St Lawrence's, Bristol. 482
  Ralph, 236
  Roger, ord, 428a

Nibley, North, Gl., ch., 481

Nicholl (Nicchol, Nycholl):
  John, 222a
    annuellar of Exeter cath., 276d
    Mr, r. of ch. of St Thomas the Martyr, Winchester, 120
  Richard, r. of Holcot, Np., 186
  Stephen, *presbiter de ponte*, Glasney coll. ch., 289
  William, Mr, sacrist, Glasney coll. ch., 289

Nicollys, Robert, parish pr., Stratford coll. ch., 468

Niker, William, 229a

Nix (Nikke, Nyck), Richard, Mr:
  archd. of Exeter, 276a
  prebendary of Cranctock coll. ch., 288
  prebendary of Westbury coll. ch., 462

Nocton Park (Nokton), Li., priory 228

Nonne, Robert, Mr, can. of Gnosall coll. ch., 403

Norbury, St.:
  ch., 412, 432
  inh. of, *see* Turnour, Richard

Norfolk, Elizabeth duchess of, 177

Normanton, Db., ch., 15

Normanton, William, 437

Norres:
  Christopher, Mr, r. of Aldford, Chs., 23
  Richard, esq., 23

Norridge (Norrige), Wlt., chapel of St Michael the Archangel, 513

Northam, De., ch., 333c

Northampton, Np.:
  abbey of Delapré (de pratis), 251a, 252b
  abbey of St James, 251a
  archd. of, or Official, 140, 180–8, 253
    see also Knyght, Robert (Official)
  archdeaconry, 219d, 230, 251–4, 255d, 259
  dy., 251b
  priory of St Andrew, 185

Northenden (Nortendene), Chs., ch., 5

Northeren (Northoryn):
  Richard, 325
  Walter, Mr, r. of St Leonard's, Exeter, 267

Northill (Northale), Bd., coll. ch., 238a

Northill, Co., ch., 334a

Northleach (Northlache), Gl., ch., 485

Northleigh (Northlegh, Northley), De., ch., 271, 332g

Northlew, De., ch., 335j

Northorpe (Northorp), Li., ch., 216c, e

Northoryn, *see* Northeren

Northwycke, John de, chap. of Henbury, Gl., 482

Norton, Chs., abbey, 397, 428c
  abbot, *see* Maltone, John
  cans. (named), 397

Norton, So., ch., 360, 365

Norton, Cold, Ox., priory, 247c, 248

Norton, King's (Norton), Lei., ch., 217c

Norton, Richard, Mr:
  r. of Algarkirk, Li., 198
  r. of Islip, Ox., 157

Norwich dioc., l.d. from, 65c

Norwich, Richard, r. of mediety of Sedgebroke, Li., 165

Norys, John, r. of Clayhidon, De., 272

Notbroke, John, r. of Little Sodbury, Gl., 483

Notgrove (Note Greve), Gl., ch., 487

Notley (Notteley), Bk., abbey, 232a, 234a, 487, 490

...

214

Pawlyn, Nicholas, cur. of Withycombe
    Raleigh, De., 270
Payhembury (Payhemby,
    Payhemburye), De., ch., 273,
    332e, 338
Payne:
    John, 510
        chap. of St John's, Gloucester,
        480
    Nicholas, ord., 428b
    Thomas, ord., 357b
Paynter (Peynter):
    John:
        chap. of Burlescombe, De., 274
        m. of Cleeve, 65d
        Mr, r. of Great Sodbury, Gl.,
            and rural dean of
            Hawkesbury, 483
    Robert, ord., 53d
Paythnoll, George, v. of Calceby, Li.,
    159
Paytrell, John:
    r. of Babstoke, Wlt., 533
    r. of St Andrew's, West
        Chelborough, Do., 535
Peatling Parva (Petlyng Parva), Lei., r.
    of, 229b
Pecok, Peter, 105a
Pedder:
    John, 242
    William, Mr, r. of Brimpsfield, Gl.,
        484
Peers (Peerse):
    John, can. of St Augustine's,
        Bristol, 53d
    Reginald, ord., 53c, 65d
    Robert, 56
    William, 236
Peke, John:
    chap. of St Mary in the South,
        Gloucester, 480
    m. of Tywardreath, 357d
Pelynt (Plenynt), Co., ch., 334b
Pemberton, Robert, Decr. B., 71-2
Pembroke, earl of, see Tudor, Jasper
Pendilton (Pendulton):
    Robert, chap. of St Michael's,
        Bristol, 482
    Thomas, v. of Eisey, Wlt., 539
Pendock (Pendocke), Wo., ch., 479
Penkivel, Co., see St Michael Penkivel
Penney, Robert, ord., 65a

Pennok, Peter le, D.C.L., prebendary
    of North Kelsey in Lincoln cath.,
    150
Penrose, William, ord., 65a, 75c
Penryn, see Glasney coll. ch.
Pensford, So., inh. of, see Petigrue,
    John
Penwith, Co., dy., 334e
Penwortham (Penthwortham,
    Penwurtham), La., priory, 39e,
    435e
Peper Harow (Pepurharow), Sy., ch.,
    106c
Peresall, Thomas, chap. of Wotton
    under Edge, Gl., 481
Perkyn:
    John, ord., 65a
    Michael, annuellar of Exeter cath.,
        276d
    Thomas, 222b
    William, v. of Ashby, Li., 166
Perott, William, v. of Ottery St Mary
    coll. ch., 280
Perranuthnoe (Uthno), Co., ch., 334e
Perranzabulo (sancti Pierani), Co., ch.,
    313
Pers:
    Edward, friar, 324
    Richard, chap. of Holy Trinity ch.,
        Gloucester, 480
    William:
        Mr, prebendary of Glasney coll.
        ch., 289
        r. of Bradford Peverell, Do., 540
Pershore, Wo.:
    abbey, 467, 483, 503, 508
        ms. (named), 467
    ch., 476
    dy., 476, 503, 507
Peter, Mr, r. of St George's,
    Southwark, Sy., 79
Peterborough (Petisburgh), Np.:
    abbey, 215, 230, 251b, 252b
    dy., 230, 251b
Peter's Marland (Merlond), De., ch.,
    333b
Petertavy (Tavy Petri), De., ch., 335f
Pethell, John, ord., 222a
Petherwin, North (Northpederwyn),
    Co., ch., 334h
Petrigrue, John, 361
Petrockstow (Pendrok), De., ch., 333b

Petyde, Richard, Mr, v. of Stonehouse, Gl., 484

Petyr, Thomas, r. of Quenington, Gl., 486

Pewe, John, ord., 75a, 323b

Pewsey (Peuesey), Wlt., ch., 129

Peynter, *see* Paynter

Peyrson, John, chap. of Oddington, Gl., 487

Philip the treasurer, 127

Philip (Phelip, Philippe, Phillip):
  David:
    alias Jonys, v. of Eisey, Wlt., 539
    esq., and Anne, lords of Isenhampstead Chenies, Bk., 214
  John:
    Mr, dean of Crediton coll. ch., 275, 282
    Mr, r. of St Olave's, Exeter, 267
    ord., 357a
    secondary of Slapton coll. ch., 294
  Richard, v. of Etwall, Db., 41
  William, cur. of St Margaret's, Southwark, Sy., 79

Philips, William, ord., 53a

Phillack and Gwithian (Felys et Conor), Co., ch., 334e

Philleigh (Eglosros), Co., ch., 334c

Phillip, *see* Philip

Pillaton (Pylaton), Co., ch., 334a

Pillerton (Pyllarton), Wa., ch., 508

Pilton (Pylton), De.:
  ch., 333d
  priory, 284, 301, 336b
    ms. (named), 284
    prior, *see* Cook, John; Kyngeswoode, William

Pinhoe (Pynhoo), De., ch., 270, 300, 332h

Pipewell, Np., abbey, 252b

Pitchcombe, Gl., *see* Harescombe

Pitminster (Pitmystre), So., inh. of, *see* Colbronde, David

Pitstone (Patesdoune, Potesden), Bk., ch., 234b, 248

Pitt portion, *see* Tiverton

Plemonstall (Plegmonstowe, Pleymystowe), Chs., ch., 39e, 434d

Plomer, William, Mr, r. of Naunton, Gl., 487

Plumgar (Plumgarth), Li., ch., 258a

Plymouth (Sutton), De., 328
  ch., 335e
  friars:
    O.Carm. (named), 323c
    O.P. (named), 65d

Plympton, De:
  ch., 336c
  dy., 335e
  priory, 53c, 65b, c; 75b, 275, 293
    cans. (named), 293
    prior, *see* Berklegh, David

Plymtree (Plymptre), De.:
  ch., 273, 332e
  dy., 265, 273, 332e

Plynmouth, John, annuellar of Exeter cath., 276d

Pole (Poole):
  Edmund, cantarist of Crich, Db., 12
  Elizabeth, widow of Ralph, 172
  John:
    cur. of Cheriton Fitzpaine, De., 275
    r. of Halwill, De., 304
  Ralph:
    esq., 12, 17, 34
    r. of Corby, Li., 172
  William, r. of St Peter's, Rushton, Np., 181

Polesworth (Pollesworth), Wa., abbey, 378
  abbess, *see* Ruskyn, Margaret
  nuns (named), 378

Poleyn, William, r. of Tortworth, Gl., 483

Polle, William, 222b

Polsloe (Polsloo), De., priory, 265, 270, 279, 336a
  nuns (named), 279
  prioress, *see* Trewranok, Isabelle

Poltimore (Poltemore, Poltymore), De., ch., 270, 332h

Pomeroy, Stephen, cantarist of Nettlecombe, So., 49

Pontisbury:
  Edward, ord., 428b
  Richard, abbot of Haughmond, 389

Pool, South (Poole), De., ch., 335d

Poole, *see* Pole

Pope, John:
  v. of Sopley, Ha., 123
  v. of Windsor, Brk., 519

Quatt, Sa.:
 chantry, 7
 inh., *see* Whiche, Thomas
Quedgeley (Quaddisley), Gl., chapel,
 480
Quenington (Quenynton), Gl.:
 ch., 486
 preceptor of, 486–7
Quethiock (Quedek), Co., ch., 334a

Rackenford (Rakinford), De., ch., 333f
Rackenford, West (Westraker Nefford),
 De., ch., 333e
Radbourn (Radbourne, Rodburne),
 Wa., ch., 417, 432
Radbourne, Db., inh. of, *see* Pole,
 Ralph
Radnare, John, v. of Wellow, So., 361
Radon, Richard, 105a
Radway, William, r. of Cheriton
 Bishop, De., 269
Raffeson, Thomas, v. of Seagre, Wlt.,
 536
Ragdale (Rakedale), Lei., ch., 217b
Rage:
 Oliver, ord., 428d
 Ralph, ord., 428d
Rakenford (Rakerneford), De., ch., 322
Ralph, Mr, r. of Clare portion in
 Tiverton ch., De., 274
Rame, Co., ch., 328, 334a
Ramsey, Hu., abbey, 204, 211, 244a
Rand (Randes), Lei., ch., 217a, c
Randoll, Thomas, ord., 428d
Randwick (Renwyke), Gl., chapel, 480
Ranowdon, John, r. of Kimcote, Lei.,
 190
Ranton (Rannton, Ronstone, Ronton),
 St.:
 inh., *see* Barwell, Richard
 priory, 388, 428b, d
 cans. (named), 428b
 prior, *see* Smith, Richard
Rasen, East (Estrasen), Li., ch., 138
Rasen Tupholme, Li., ch., 216e
Rasen, Thomas de, 229a
Ratclif, Ralph, ord., 428a
Ratheby, (blank), 229a
Ratley (Roteley), Wa., ch., 39a, 435a
Rattery (Rattre), De., ch., 335c
Ravenstone (Ravistone), Bk., priory,
 232a
Rawcliff, John, Mr, prebendary of
 Lichfield cath., 395

Rawlyn, John:
 cur. of Feniton, De., 273
 r. of Poltimore, De., 270
Rawson, William, Mr, r. of Orton
 Waterville, Hu., 206
Ray (Raye):
 Agnes, 222a
 John, v. of Sopley, Ha., 123
Raynold, *see* Reynold
Rayny, William, Mr, r. of Plymtree,
 De., 273
Reading (Redyng), Brk., gaol of liberty
 of, 553
Reculver, John, prior of St Mary
 Overy, Southwark, 79
Redbert, Thomas, ord., 357d
Redcliffe (Radcliff, Radcliffe, Ratclyff),
 So.:
 dy., 72, 76b, 359a
 inh., *see* Barton, John
Redelake, Henry, ord., 323a
Redmarley d'Abitot (Rydmerley), Gl.,
 ch., 479
Redruth (Redruyth), Co., ch., 334e
Redyng, Walter, r. of Pylle, So., 48
Reed, Robert, 222a
 chap. of Southwark, Sy., 79
Reigate (Reygate), Sy.:
 ch., 106b
 priory, 92, 106d
 can., *see* Haynes, Ralph
Rendcombe (Rencombe), Gl., ch., 485
Repton (Repyngdon, Rypingdon), Db.,
 9
 dy., 38c, e; 40b, 429c, 430c
 priory, 380, 429c
 cans. (named), 380
 prior, *see* Preiste, Henry
Restell, William, r. of Staunton, Wo.,
 479
Reston, North (Northrestone), Li., inh.
 of, *see* Ratheby
Rewe, De., ch., 273, 332e
Rewes, William, ord., 53a
Rewley (regali loco prope Oxon'), Ox.,
 abbey, 299, 337
Rewstone, John, r. of St Peter's,
 Wareham, Do., 544
Reynesford, William, 236
Reynford (Reyneford):
 Henry, Decr. B.:
  r. of Holy Trinity ch., Chester,
  20

v. of St Oswald's altar in St
Werburgh's, Chester, 414
Richard, r. of Windsor, Brk., 519
Reynold (Raynold):
John, v. of Budleigh, De., 270
Thomas, Mr:
can. of Lichfield cath., 22, 31,
35–7
vicar-general of abp. in Coventry
and Lichfield dioc., 31, 35–7
Rice (Ryce):
Richard ap. chap. of St John's,
Bristol, 482
Thomas, ap, 357a
Richard, can. (? of Canonsleigh),
274
Richard:
Michael, ord., 65a
Roger, ord., 323b
Richman, Robert, ord., 357c
Rigby, Robert, ord., 428d
Rigeway, Otvel, ord., 428c
Rigge, Thomas, 145
Rilston, William, esq., 179
Rime, Lawrence, v. of Holcombe
Burnell, De., 269
Ringmore (Ridmore), De., ch., 335d
Rise (Ryse), John:
abp.'s clerk, master of God's House,
Portsmouth, 89–91
can. of Exeter cath., 276a
ord., 53c, 75d
prebendary of Ottery St Mary coll.
ch., 280
Rissington, Great (Resington Magna),
Gl., ch., 487
Rissington, Little (Resingdon Parva,
Resington Parva), Gl.:
ch., 487, 500, 509
inh., see Gararde, Joan
Rissington Wick (Wyche Resingdon),
Gl., ch., 487
Roborough (Roburg), De., ch., 333b
Roby, Odo, presbiter de ponte, Glasney
coll. ch., 289
Robyns:
John, 361
Thomas, ord., 428a
Robynson:
John, literate, 198
Thomas:
r. of Draycot Cerne, Do., 545
v. of Killingholme, Li., 143

Rocester (Rowcetter), St., abbey, 385,
428c
abbot, see Caldon, George
cans. (named), 385, 428c
Roche, Co., ch., 334c
Roche, Simon, ord., 53b, 65d
Rochester (Roffen'), Kent, 439, 441–8
archd. of, or Official, 441, 448
bp., see Savage, Thomas
cath. priory, 439, 446, 449b, 450
ms. (named), 446
prior, see Bishop, William
dioc., sede vacante, 439–51
dy., 449a
Rockbeare (Rokebear, Rokebeare),
De., ch., 270, 332h
Rockhampton (Rochampton), Gl., ch.,
481
Rodborough, Gl., chapel, 484
Rodde, John, ord., 65d
Rode (Roode), So.:
ch. of St Lawrence, 63
inh., see Dawnsy, John
Rodeway, John, esq., 72–4
Rodmarton (Rodmerton, Rodmorton),
Gl.:
ch., 484, 494, 509
lord of, see Whitington, Thomas
Rogers (Roger):
John:
proctor, 58
v. of Bisley, Gl., 484
Thomas, r. of Upper Slaughter, Gl.,
487
William, r. of Dunkerton, So., 58,
65b, 69, 75d
Rolleston:
Henry, 411
Richard, r. of Kirk Langley, Db.,
415
Roger, 411
Rolowe:
Hugh, 7
Humphrey, 7
Romansleigh (Romondesley), De., ch.,
333f
Rome, 35–7, 276a
basilica of St Peter, 261
hospital of St Thomas the Martyr,
221
Romsey (Rumsey), Ha., 102
abbey, 98a, 110, 130
abbess, see Broke, Elizabeth

St John by Antony (sancti Iohannis), Co., ch., 334a

St Juliot (Julyt), Co., ch., 334h

St Just (in Penwith) (Juste), Co., ch., 334e

St Just (in Roseland) (St Juste), Co., ch., 334c

St Keverne (Kewryn), Co., ch., 334d

St Kew (Kewa), Co., ch., 334g

St Lawrence, Ha., ch., 129

St Mabyn (Mabyn), Co., ch., 334g

St Martin by Looe (Martyn), Co., ch., 334b

St Mary Church (Sentmarychurch), De., ch., 298

St Mellion (Melanne), Co., ch., 334a

St Merryn (Meryn), Co., ch., 311

St Mewan (Mewan), Co., ch., 334c

St Michael Penkivel (Penkevell), Co., ch., 334c

St Neot (Nyott), Co., ch., 334b

St Neots, Hu.:
  ch. of St Mary, 212, 255d
  dy., 244b
  priory, 244a

St Nicholas Melaneak, prebend of, see Endellion

St Pinnock (Pynnok), Co., ch., 334b

St Seiriol (Penmon), Ang., abbey, 428d

St Stephen in Brannel, see Caryhays

St Teath (Tetha), Co., ch., 334g

St Tudy (Tudi), Co., ch., 334g

St Veep (Wepe), Co., ch., 334b

St Wenn (Wenna), Co., ch., 334f

Saintlowe, Walter, Mr, r. of Tormarton, Gl., 483

Saleby, Li., ch., 148, 219a
  v. of, 229a

Salisbury (Nova Sar', Sarum), Wlt., 512–21, 523–30, 534, 536–9, 541–8, 553–7
  archd. of, or Official, 513, 515, 518, 521, 529–30, 533, 537, 543, 545, 547
  bp., 492
    see also Blythe, John; Langton, Thomas
  cath. ch., 549
    dean and chapter, 268, 542
    cans. residentiary, see Cockes, Lawrence; Eliott, William; Russell, William

prebends:
  Alton Borealis, 542
  Hurstbourne and Burbage (Hurstbourne Priors), 93
ch. of St Edmund, 549
ch. of St Thomas, 549
consistory court, 549, 552–4
dioc.:
  l.d. from, 53a, 65d, 75b, 323d, 357a, c
  sede vacante, 511–58
inh., see David, Richard; Duke, Edward; Lane, Richard; Underwoode, Bartholomew; Woodeward, Richard
market place, 549

Salle, John, r. of Edgeworth, Gl., 484

Salperton, Cold (Salvyrton), Gl., ch., 487

Saltash (Saltaissh), Co.:
  chapel of St Nicholas, 328
  ch., 337

Salte:
  James, 437
  John, 437

Salter:
  Richard, Decr.D.:
    Official of consistory court of Lichfield dioc., 30, 368
    prebendary of Lichfield cath., 395
  Roger, B.A., 29
    warden of Newport coll. ch., Sa., 28, 31

Saluse, Robert, Mr, par. chap. of St Olave's, Southwark, Sy., 79

Sampford Courtenay, De., ch., 335j

Sampford Peverell (Sampford), De., ch., 274, 332d

Sampson (Sandson), Robert, notary public, 28, 30

Sancreed (Sancrede), Co., ch., 334e

Sanderstead (Soundstede), Sy., ch., 106b

Sandes, William, chap., 421

Sandsone, Robert, see Sampson

Sandwell (Sandewell, Saundwell), St., priory, 40d, 429b

Sanyng, William, v. of Holcombe Rogus, De., 274

Saperton, James, r. of Cubley, Db., 4

Sapperton (Sapurton), Gl., ch., 484

Sare:
  Roger, r. of Whitstone, Co., 305

William, chap. of St Leonard's,
    Bristol, 482
Satterleigh (Saterlegh), De., ch., 333f
Saul (Salle), Gl., chapel, 480
Saunder (Sawnder):
    Matthew, par. chap. of Dursley,
        Gl., 481
    William, v. of Northleach, Gl., 485
Saunders, John, 554
    r. of Eastleach, Gl., 486
Saunderton, Bk., ch., 234a
Sause, Richard, r. of Uplyme, De., 271
Savage:
    George, Mr, r. of Upton on Severn
        and Redmarley d'Abitot, Gl.,
        479
    Thomas, bp. of Rochester,
        translated to London, 440
Savoy, Boniface of, abp. of Canterbury,
    135, 511
Say, Nicholas, ord., 75b
Sayer:
    Godfrey, 6
    John, 293
    Roger, 6
    Thurstan, v. of Sedgley, St., 6
Scaltocke, Richard, v. of Brookthorpe,
    Gl., 480
Scanyngton, John, Mr, chap. of
    Adlestrop, Gl., 487
Scarisbroke, Hector, prior of
    Burscough, 396
Scarsdale (Scarisdale, Scarvesdale),
    Db., dy., 38c, e; 40b; 429c, 430c
Scawby (Scalby), Li., ch., 216e
Schawe, see Shawe
Scilly, Isles of (insula de Sillegh),
    estates of Tavistock on, 292
Scolemaister, Richard, chap. of
    Crediton, De., 275
Scopwick (Skaupewik), Li., v. of, 226
Score, Alice, 325
Scott:
    Roger, ord., 428a
    ·William, 437
Scounide, William, v. of Southrop, Gl.,
    487
Scriche, Peter, fellow of Slapton coll.
    ch., 294
Scrope, Geoffrey, Mr, r. of St Faith,
    Kelsall, Hu., 209
Scurlock, Henry, Mr, chap. of
    Almondsbury, Gl., 482

Scyb, Edmund, clerk, 54
Seagry (Segre), Wlt., ch., 536
Seaton (Seton), De., ch., 271, 332g
Sedgebroke (Segbroke), Li., ch., 165,
    219a
Sedgley (Seghley), Db., ch., 6
Sele, John, 222b
Selle, John, annuellar of Exeter cath.,
    276d
Selman, William, chap. of Stoke-in-
    Teignhead, De., 268
Selworthy, So., inh. of, see Gore,
    William
Semley (Semely), Wlt., ch., 537
Send (Sende), Sy., ch., 106c
Sengere, Thomas, chap. of Bampton,
    De., 274
Serjaunt, John and Christine, 493
Serle, James, ord., 357a
Sevenacre, John, v. of South Cerney,
    Gl., 485
Seward, John:
    chap. of Budleigh, De., 270
    esq., 55
Sewardsley (Sweresley), Np., prioress
    of, 252b
Seyffe, William:
    chap. of St Nicholas, Gloucester,
        480
    ord., 428b
Shackerstone (Shakerston, Shakreston),
    Lei., ch., 217c, 258b
Shacsper, Elizabeth, prioress of
    Wroxall, 471
Shaffespere, Thomas, par. chap. of St
    Peter's, Bristol, 482
Shalford (Chalford), Sy., ch., 106c
Shank, William, r. of Shillingford, De.,
    268
Shardeley, William, chap. of Stratford
    coll. ch., 468
Share, Richard, prior of Coventry, 374
Sharp:
    John, Decr. B., Official sede vacante,
        Coventry and Lichfield dioc.,
        1–2
    Richard, v. of Sedgley, St., 6
Sharsford (unid.), inh. of, see Thirkill,
    Robert
Shawe (Schawe):
    John, chap. of Stow on the Wold,
        Gl., 487
    Ralph, ord., 428a

William, r. of Baxterley, Wa., 419
Shebbear (Shebbeare), De., ch., 333b
Sheen, Sy., priory, 8, 516, 544
Sheepstor (Shittister), De., ch., 335f
Shefford, Bd., dy., 238b
Sheldon (Shildon), De., ch., 272, 332f
Sheldon, William, chap. of St Aldate's,
    Gloucester, 480
Shepard (Sheparde, Sheppard):
  John, ord., 53d
  Ralph:
    ord., 428d
    r. of Kirk Langley, Db., 415
Sherard:
  Ralph, 222b
  William, chap. of St Mary's coll.
    ch., Warwick, 470
Sherborne, Do., 522
  abbey, 271, 514, 522, 527
Sherborne (Shurborne), Gl., ch., 486
Sherborne St John, Ha., ch., 94
Sherborne (Sherbourne, Shirborne,
    Shyrborne):
  Hugh and Anne, 36
  Robert, M.A.:
    archd. of Shrewsbury, 30
    master of St Cross hospital,
      Winchester, 112, 124
    Official sede vacante, Bath and
      Wells, dioc., 44, 49
    Official sede vacante, Coventry and
      Lichfield dioc., 12, 19, 30
    Official sede vacante, Exeter dioc.,
      264–5, 277–97, 338
    Official sede vacante, Winchester
      dioc., 77, 93, 107–11, 113–4,
      118–20, 122–3, 125–6, 127–34
    r. of Crondall, Ha., 97
    treasurer of Hereford cath., 44,
      77
Shere (Shire), Sy., ch., 106c
Sherowe, John, r. of Stockleigh
    English, De., 275
Sheviock (Shebik, Shevioche), Co., ch.,
    328, 334a
Shillingford (Shelyngford, Shilyngford),
    De., ch., 268, 332a
Shipton Bellinger (Shipton), Ha., ch.,
    117
Shipton Moyne (Shepton Moyne), Gl.,
    ch., 484
Shipton Sellars (Shipton Solas), Gl.,
    ch., 487

Shirborne, see Sherborne
Shirley (Shyrley), Db., ch., 2
Shirwell (Shirwill), De.:
  ch., 309, 333e
  dy., 333e
Shobilworth, Roger, ord.,. 428b
Shobrooke (Shodbroke, Shogbroke),
    De., ch., 275, 328, 332c
Shoore, Hugh, r. of Wimborne
    Minster, Do., 534
Shoper (Shoppare), John:
  r. of Hinton Blewett, So., 55
  v. of Kilmersdon, So., 52
Shopes (Shopis), see Catesby
Shoppare, see Shoper
Shordych, John, cur. of Gittisham,
    De., 271
Shorman, John, Mr, Official of archd.
    of Leicester, 141
Shorne, Kent, ch., 450
Shortgrave, Bd., manor, 240b
Shoter, William, 222c, 229a
Shotteswell (Shoteswell, Shotwell), Wa.,
    ch., 39a, 435a
Shrewsbury (Salop', Shroisbury,
    Shroysburye), Sa., 409
  abbey, 9, 28, 39c, 390, 429d, 435c
  abbot, see Mynde, Thomas
  ms. (named), 390
  archd. of, or Official, 3, 8–10, 28,
    372, 408, 430d, 431
  archdeaconry, 38f, g; 39c, 40c, 408,
    429d, 430d, 431, 435c
  coll. ch. of St Chad, 40c
  dy., 38f, g; 40c, 429d
  hospital of St Giles, 428c, d
  inh., see Merydene, William;
    Wentnor, Richard
Shrewsbury, Ralph de, bp. of Bath and
    Wells, 60
Shropshire, inh. of, see Woode, Roger
Shuldham, Edward, D.C.L.:
  commissary of Official, Lincoln
    dioc., 136
  prebendary of Newark coll. ch.,
    Leicester, 191
Shurley, Robert, esq., 421
Shustoke, Wa., ch., 39a, 434a
Shyrborne, see Sherborne
Shyrive, Henry, chap. of Stratford coll.
    ch., 468
Siddington Mary (by Cirencester), Gl.,
    ch., 485, 498, 509

Siddington Peter (Sedington Petre),
    Gl., ch., 485
Sidmouth (Sydmouth), De., ch., 270,
    332h
Sileby, Lei., ch., 217d
Silk (Silke, Sylk), William, Mr:
    archd. of Cornwall, 276a, 289
    prebendary of Crantock coll. ch.,
        288
    prebendary of Glasney coll. ch., 289
Silk Willoughby (Northwillugby alias
        Silwillughby, Silk Willuby), Li.,
        ch., 144, 154, 219e
Silverton (Sylverton), De., ch., 273,
    332e
Simon, John, r. of Stoke-in-Teignhead,
    De., 268
Siston (Syseton), Gl., ch., 483
Sithney (Sithny), Co., ch., 334d
Sixhill, William, proctor, 174
Sixhills, Li.:
    ch. of All Saints, 171, 255a
    priory, 148
Skay (Skey):
    John, chap. of Westleigh, Gl., 483
    Richard, Mr, v. of Painswick, Gl.,
        484
Skebiria, Richard, ord., 65c
Skey, see Skay
Skinnand (Skynnand), Li., ch., 223a,
    255a
Skipwit (Skypwitt):
    Agnes, widow of William, kt., 170
    William, 256
Sklater, see Slater
Skybury, Richard, v. of Exeter cath.,
    276c
Skynner:
    Richard, chap. of Combe-in-
        Teignhead, De., 268
    William, 105a
        Mr, v. of Fairford, Gl., 486
Skypwitt, see Skipwit
Slade, William, chap. of Ottery St
    Mary coll. ch., 270
Slappe, Richard, 361
Slapton, De., coll. ch., 294, 335d,
    336c, 337
    clergy (named), 294
    r., see Cooke, Vincent
Slater (Sklater), Richard, v. of Romsey,
    Ha., 104, 110

Slatter, John, alias Wynyngton, v. of
    Charlbury, Ox., 199
Slaughter, Upper (Sloucestrie Superior),
    Gl., ch., 487
Sleaford (Sleford), Li., ch., 138
Sleford, Henry, r. of Kirkby St Denis,
    Li., 167
Slimbridge (Slymbregg), Gl., ch., 481
Slimbridge, Robert, Mr, prebendary of
    Lichfield cath., ch., 395
Slyme, Nicholas, 361
Smalwoode (Smalwode):
    John, v. of Crondall, 97
    Thomas, perpetual chap. of hospital
        of St Thomas the Martyr,
        Birmingham, 14
Smarte, Patrick, 361
Smith (Smyth):
    Clement, Mr, can. of St Mary's
        coll. ch., Warwick, 470
    Elizabeth, 105a
    Henry, 437
    John, 222b
        ord., 323a, 428d
        chap. of Temple Guiting, Gl.,
            487
        par. chap. of North Nibley, Gl.,
            481
        r. of Northleigh, De., 271
    Nicholas, ord., 428c
    Richard:
        chap. of Shipton Moyne, Gl.,
            484
        prior of Ranton, 388
    Robert, 250, 437
        chap. of St Werburgh's, Bristol,
            482
        ord., 428a
        S.T.P., abp.'s commissary in
            Oxford, 263
    Roger, ord., 428c
    Thomas, M.A., prebendary of
        Bathwick, So., 50
    Thurstan, proctor, 143
    Walter, ord., 53a
    William:
        bp. of Coventry and Lichfield,
            translated to Lincoln, 261–2,
            367, 369
        can. of Tong coll. ch., 399
        chap. of Tyknall, Gl., 485
        generosus, 193
        Mr, prebendary of Lichfield, 395

Mr, r. of prebendal ch. of Holy
Trinity, Wherwell, 113
ord., 53d
v. of coll. ch. of Ottery St Mary,
280
Snape, John, ord., 428d
Snellyng, William, 325
Snelshall (Snelsale), Bk., priory, 232a
Snodsbury, Upper (Snodsbury), Wo.,
ch., 508
Sodbury, Gl., dy., dean of, 492
Sodbury, Great (Sobbury), Gl., ch.,
477, 483
Sodbury, Little (Sobbury Parva), Gl.,
ch., 483
Sombourne (Sombourn), Ha., dy., 98b
Somer (Somor):
John, chap. of Stratford coll. ch.,
468
Thomas, apparitor-general,
Canterbury province, 78–9
Somerby, Old (Somerbye), Li., ch.,
146, 219a
r., 222a
Somerby, Li., v. of, 225
Somerby, John, 227
Somerford, John, par. chap., Stone,
Gl., 481
Somerton, So., ch., 360
Somerton, John de, abbot of
Muchelney, 59
Somor, see Somer
Sondell, Nicholas, 43
Sopley (Sopeley), Ha., ch., 123
Sotherey, William, r. of Withcote, Lei.,
193
Souch, see Zouche
Sourton, De., ch., 335g
Southam, Wa., ch., 405
Southampton, Ha., 102
dy., 98b
inh., see Clouth, John; Massymewe,
Nicholas; Trussel, Thomas
priory of St Denys, 98a, 132
cans. (named), 132
Southford, William, ord., 428d
Southill (Southyll), Co., ch., 318, 334a
Southleigh (Southlegh), De., ch., 271,
332g
Southoe (Southo), Hu., ch., 246f
Southrop (Sothrop, Southrup), Gl., ch.,
486, 489, 509

Southwark (Southwerk, Suthwerke),
Sy.:
borough, 78
chs.:
St George, 78–9, 106a
St Margaret, 78–9, 106a
St Mary Magdalene, 78–9, 106a
St Olave, 78–9, 106a
dy., 106a
Southwick (Sothewicke, Suthwyke),
Ha., priory, 98a, 122, 131
cans. (named), 131
prior, see Stanbroke, Philip
Sowderne, Thomas, r. of Baxterley,
Wa., 419
Sowton (Cliste Famison), De., ch.,
332h
Spalding (Spaldyng), Li.:
ch., 138, 216d
priory, 142, 228
Sparkenhoe (Sperkenhou), Lei., dy.,
141
Sparsholt (Sparsold), Brk., chap. of, see
Lydtister, John
Spelhurst, Kent, ch., 450
Spiller, John, chap., 328
Spilsby (Spillisby), Li., ch., 216e
Spital-in-the-Street (Spitel of the
Strete), Li., chapel, 139
Spoltte, William, ord., 323b
Spondon, Db., ch., 424, 432
Spreyton (Sprayton), Db., ch., 269,
320, 332b
Spridlington (Sprydlyngton), Li., ch.,
216d
Sprot (Sprote):
John, warden of Cobham coll. ch.,
443
Robert, 437
Squyer, John, r. of Clopton in
Gordano, So., 72
Stabba, Joan, abbess of Canonsleigh,
281
Stafford, St.:
archd. of, or Official, 6–7, 25–7,
370, 406, 412, 431
see also Cowper, John (Official)
archdeaconry, 38h, j; 39d, 40d, 406,
429b, 430b, 431, 434a, 435d
inh., see Bale, Malus; Eyton,
William; Tirlaund, Thomas

priory of St Thomas the Martyr
(Baswich), 39d, 394, 424,
435d
cans. (named), 394
prior, see Chedull, William
Stafford and Newcastle under Lyme
(Novo Castro), St., dy., 38h, j;
40d, 429b, 430b
Stafford, Richard, r. of Glendon, Np.,
180
Stainton Burneth (Steynton Burneth),
Li., ch., 216e
Stainton (*unid.*), Li., r. of, 226
Stakesley, see Stokisley
Stalls (Stallis), So., dy., 76b, 359a
Stalworth, Simon, Mr:
subdean of Lincoln cath., 150
r. of Algarkirk, Li., 198
r. of Islip, Ox., 157
Stalys, Oliver, notary public, 206
Stamford (Stamfordie, Staunford), Li.,
138
ch. of St George, 226
ch. of St Michael Major, 153, 156,
219a
dy., see Ness
priory, 228
Stanbridge (Stanbrigge), Do., ch., 534
Stanbroke, Philip, prior of Southwick,
131
Standerwike (Standerwyke), John,
notary public, 63, 72
Standish, Gl., ch., 480
Stanford on Avon (Stainford super
Haven), Np.:
ch., 252a
inh., see Cabe, Thomas
Stanground (Stangre, Stangrounde),
Hu., ch., 246a, e
Stanley, King's (Stanley Regis), Gl.,
ch., 484
Stanley, Leonard (Stanley Leonarde),
Gl.:
ch., 484
priory, 460
prior, see Elmeley, William
Stanley, John, esq., 23
Stanlowe, John, esq., 144
and Margaret, his wife, 154, 167
Stanton (Staunton), Gl., ch., 491, 509
Stanton (Staundon), Sa., 39c, 435c
Stapleford (Stapilford), Li., v. of, 225

Staplegrove (Stapulgrove), So., inh. of,
see Burlond, John
Stapleton (Stapulton), Gl., ch., 482
Stary, George, par. chap. of Lechlade,
Gl., 486
Staughton, Great (Stokton), Hu., ch.,
246f
Staunton, Wo., ch., 479
Stavordale (Staverdale), So., priory,
53c, 65b
Steeple Langford (Stepillangford), Wlt.,
ch. of St Mary, 521
Stenigot (Stanygoode), Li., r. of, 225
Stephen, cur. of Clayhanger, De., 274
Stephins (Stephyns):
John, r. of Hatherop, Gl., 486
William, Mr, 118
Steward, John, chap. of Barnwood,
Gl., 480
Stickford (Stikford), Li., ch., 216e
Stillingford, Robert, bp. of Bath and
Wells, 44, 56
Stinchcombe (Stynchcombe), Gl., ch.,
481
Stirche, Robert, chorister of Slapton
coll. ch., 294
Stithians (Stediane), Co., ch., 337
Stixwould (Stikeswolde, Stikkiswold),
Li., priory, 142, 228
Stockleigh English (Stokeleghenglys,
Stokeleghinglish), De., ch., 275,
332c
Stockleigh Pomeroy (Stokeleghpomeray,
Stokelegh Pomery), De., ch., 275
Stogumber (Stokegumer), So., v. of,
326
Stogursey (Stokecursy, Stowegurcy),
So.:
chap. of, see Lemyng, John
cur. of, 56
inh., see Frere, Richard; Peers,
Robert
Wyke in, 56
Stoke Abbot (Stoke Abbatis), Do., ch.,
522
Stoke by Clare, Sf., coll. ch., 484, 508
Stoke Climsand (Stoke), Co., ch., 334a
Stoke d'Abernun (Stoke Daberun), Sy.,
ch., 106b
Stoke Damarel (Stokedamerell), De.,
ch., 335f
Stoke, East (Est Stoke), Do., ch., 541

Strood (Strode), Kent, hospital of
B.V.M. of the New Work, 444,
449b
master, *see* Barber, William
Stroud (Strode), Gl., chapel, 484
Strowde, abbot, of Hyde, 129
Stroxton (Strawston), Li., ch., 256
Stryngare, Thomas, ord., 428b
Studley (Stodelegh), De., ch., 333f
Studley (Stodeley), Ox., priory, 247a,
248
Studley (Stodeley), Wa.:
ch., 499, 509
priory, 473, 487, 499
cans. (named), 473
prior, *see* Woode, Thomas att
Sturdyvale, John, Mr, chap. of
Southwark, Sy., 79
Style:
Ralph, *dominus*, 274
Thomas, v. of Harrowden, Np., 183
Stythians (Stedyans), Co., ch., 334d
Suckley, Wo., ch., 479
Lulsley chapel in, 479
Sulby, Np., abbey, 39a, 183, 252b,
435a
Sulhampstead Bannister (Selhamstede
Banaster), Brk.:
ch., 552
cur., 553
inh., *see* Russell, Stephen
Summaster (Summaister), William, Mr:
r. of Rewe, De., 273
r. of Silverton, De., 273
subdean of Exeter cath., 276a
Sumnour, Roger, ord., 428d
Sundon (Sundonne), Bd., v. of, 241,
243
Suppeley, John, 554
Surrey:
archd. of, or Official, 95–6, 115
see also Dynham, Oliver (archd.)
archdeaconry, 80, 101, 106
Sutcombe (Suttecombe), De., ch., 335h
Sutton, De., *see* Plymouth
Sutton, Sy., ch., 106b
Sutton-by-Brailes (Sutton), Gl., ch.,
487
Sutton Coldfield, Wa., inh. of, *see*
Wyott, Cornelius
Sutton Veny (Venney Sutton), Wlt.,
ch., 515

Sutton:
John, chap. of Crediton, De., 275
Richard, ord., 428b
Swan, Richard, Mr, v. of Upottery,
De., 272
Swarkeston (Swerkeston), Db.:
ch., 411, 432
inh., *see* Rolleston, Henry
Swarraton (Swarveton), Ha., ch., 119
Swaton, Li., ch., 216c
Swell, Lower (Swell Inferior, Swellys),
Gl., ch., 487, 490, 509
Swell, Upper (Swell Superior), Gl., ch.,
487
Swepson, John, can. of Church Gresley
priory, 428c
Swynerton:
Richard, chap. of Bourton on the
Water, Gl., 487
Thomas, v. of Drayton in Hayles,
Sa., 8
Swynestone (*unid.*, ? Syncombe, Ox.),
ch., 235
Sydall, Roger, v. of Dawlish, De., 303
Sydecoke, Henry, v. of Abbots
Bromley, St., 27
Sydenham Damarel (Siddenham), De.,
ch., 335g
Sylk, *see* Silk
Syll, (blank), v. of St Swithun's,
Combe, Ha., 114
Syllys, Matthew, chap. of Siston, Gl.,
483
Sylson, Thomas, chap. of Southwark,
Sy., 79
Sylwyn, John, r. of Hawling, Gl., 487
Symeon, Geoffrey, chancellor of
Lincoln cath., 168
Symmes, Thomas, r. of East Stoke,
Do., 541
Symon, John, Mr, prebendary of
Crantock coll. ch., 288
Synton, William, r. of Oldbury-upon-
Severn, Gl., 483
Syon, Mx., abbey, 270–2, 485
Syston (Siston), Li., ch., 216e

Tachbrook (Tachebroke), Wa.,
prebendal ch., 427
Tadersall, Robert, ord., 428a
Tailour, *see* Taylor
Talaton (Taleton), De., ch., 273, 332e

Talbot (Talbott):
Christopher, Mr, archd. of Chester, 19
Joan, lady, 190
Talland (Tallan), Co., ch., 334b
Talys, Robert, M.A., r. of Alwalton, Hu., 215
Tamerton, De., dy., 335f
Tamerton Foliot (Tamerton), De., ch., 335f
Tamworth (Tameworth, Tomworth), St.:
coll. ch., 40d, 429b
prebend of Coton in, 26
dy., 38h, j; 40d, 429b, 430b
Tancrett, John, annuellar of Exeter cath., 276d
Tandridge (Tanrigge), Sy.:
ch., 106b
priory, 106d
Tanner, Peter, v. of Crantock coll. ch., 288
Tapiscote, Thomas, chap. of St Stephen's, Bristol, 482
Tardebigge (Terbick, Terbycke), Wo., ch., 476, 503
Tattershall (Tateshal, Tatteshall), Li., coll. ch., 142, 228
Taunton, So.:
archd. of, or Official, 45, 49, 61, 345–6
archdeaconry, 359c
dy., 76b, 359c
inh., see Ash, John; Hooker, Richard
priory, 53b–d; 65b, 66–7, 76a, 323b, d; 326, 357c, 358
cans. (named), 357c
prior, see Prowce, John
Taverner, Robert, r. of Wistaston, Chs., 410
Tavistock (Tavestok, Tavistok), De.:
abbey, 65b, 268–9, 292, 320, 323b, 336c
abbot, see Banham, Richard
ms. (named), 292
ch., 335g
dy., 335g
Tawstock (Tawstok), De., ch., 333d
Tawton, North (Tawton), De., ch., 327, 333a
Tawton, South (Southtawnton), De., ch., 269, 332b, 337

Tay, Elias, ord., 528a
Taylor (Tailour, Taylor, Tayllor, Taylour):
Humphrey, chap. of St Mary's coll. ch., Warwick, 470
John:
chap. of Great Sodbury, Gl., 483
Mr, chancellor of Exeter cath., 276a
r. of Bagenderby, Li., 151
Thomas:
chap. of Tormarton, Gl., 483
v. of Lilleshall, Sa., 10
William:
ord., 43d
v.-choral of Gnosall coll. ch., 403
Teack (Teak), John:
r. of Harford, De., 321
r. of Littleham, De., 319
Tedburn St Mary (Tedborne, Tetteborn), De., ch., 269, 332b
Tegan, John, cur. of Wedworthy, De., 271
Tele, Nicholas, chap. of Grace Lane, Gloucester, 480
Temple Guiting, see Guiting
Temse, William, chap. of Market Lavington, Wlt., 555
Tenos (Tinen'), bp. of, see Cornish, Thomas
Terbock, receiver of Romsey abbey, 130
Tetbury, Gl., ch., 477, 484
Tetcott (Tettecote), De., ch., 335h
Tetford, Li., ch., 169, 255a
Tetryngton, William, 437
Tew, Great (Tewe), Ox., inh. of, see Smith, Robert
Tewkesbury, Gl.:
abbey, 459, 481–3, 486–7, 497, 504, 508
abbot, see Cheltynham, Richard
ms. (named), 459
inh., see Payne, John
Theddlethorp (Thedilthorp), Li.:
ch. of All Saints, 216c, e
ch. of St Helen, 216c
Thelbridge (Thelbrigge), De., ch., 333f
Thingden, Lei., ch., 217d
Thirk, David, minister of Ottery St Mary coll. ch., 270
Thirkill, Robert, 438

Thomas:
David, ord., 53a
ap Philip ap, ord., 75b
John:
Mr, v. of All Saints, Bristol, 482
ord., 65c
William:
Mr, r. of St John's, Bristol, 482
ord., 65c
Thomasson (Thomeson):
John, v.-choral of Gnosall coll. ch.,
403
Robert, v. of Edlington, Li., 173
Thomkyn, Otto, cur. of Kenn, De.,
268
Thomlyns, John, r. of Hinton Blewett,
So., 52, 55
Thomson, Christopher, cur. of
Sampford Peverell, De., 274
Thomyowe (Tomyowe), Thomas, Mr,
286
can. of Exeter cath., 276a
Thoresway (Thoreswey), Li., r. of, 226
Thormerton, *see* Farmington
Thornburgh (Thornebourgh), William,
D.C.L.:
r. of St Faith's, Kelshall, Hu., 209
r. of St Mary's, Steeple Langford,
Wlt., 521
Thornbury, De., ch., 335h
Thornbury (Thornebury), Gl., ch.,
481, 508
Thorncombe (Thorncomb,
Thornecombe), De., ch., 271,
332g
Thornebourgh, *see* Thornburgh
Thorne Falcon (Thorne Fawkyn), So.,
ch., 360
Thorney, Ca., abbey, 202, 246a, e
Thorney, John, m. of Muchelney, 323d
Thornhaugh (Thornehoo), Np., ch.,
252b
Thornton, Li.:
abbey, 142, 149, 228
ch., 138
Thorp, Robert, v. of Edlington, Li.,
173
Thorpe (*unid.*), v. of, 226
Thorverton, De., ch., 275, 332c
Thrapston, Np., ch., 187, 259c
Throwleigh (Throwlegh), De., ch., 269,
332b
Thurbarn, Richard, 72

Thurgarton, Nt., priory, 24
Thurleman, Richard, chap. of
Cirencester, Gl., 485
Thurlestone (Thurleston), De., ch.,
335d
Tilshead (Tydilside, Tyleshede), Wlt.,
ch., 518, 543
Tilsworth (Tylesworth), Bd., ch., 219e
Tintagel (Tyndagill), Co., ch., 334g
Tirlaund, Thomas, 43
Titchfield (Tychefeld), Ha., abbey, can.
of (named), 111
Titsey (Tichesey), Sy., ch., 106b
Tiverton, De.:
ch., 265, 274, 332d
portions and prior's quarter in,
274, 332d
dy., 265, 274, 332d
Todde, John, can. of Rocester, 428c
Toft (Tofte), Li., ch., 161, 219a, 223a
Tofte, John, chap. of Minchinhampton,
Gl., 484
Tolle, William, can. of Drewsteignton,
De., 269
Tomkynson, Henry, 43
Tomlynson:
John, r. of Winstone, Gl., 484
Robert, 222c
Tong (Tonge), Sa., coll. ch., 39c, 399,
428d, 435c
cans. (named), 399
warden, *see* Brown, Thomas
Tonge, Thomas, ord., 428c
Tonyowe, *see* Thomyowe
Top (Toppe):
Andrew, minister of Slapton coll.
ch., 294
John, chorister of Slapton coll. ch.,
294
Toples, William, chap. of chantry of SS
Mary and Michael, Melbourne,
Db., 421
Toppe, *see* Top
Toppyng, John, Mr, minister of Easton
Royal, Wlt., O. Trin., 538
Torbryan (Torrebrian), De., ch., 335b
Torksey (Torkesey), Li.:
ch. of St Peter, 139, 216e
priory, 142
Tormarton (Thormerton, Thormorton),
Gl., ch. 483
Torre (Torre Abbatis), De:
abbey, 323b

ch., 335b

Torre, William, chap. of Exeter, 267

Torrington (Toryton), De., dy., 333b

Torrington, Black (Blaktoriton), De.,
 ch., 335h

Torrington, Great, De., ch., 333b

Torrington, Little (Toryton Parva),
 De., ch., 333b

Torrington, West (Westrington), Li.,
 ch., 164, 219a

Tortworth (Torteworth), Gl., ch., 483

Totnes (Totton', Totnesse), De.:
  archd. of, or Official, 277, 304, 310,
   321
  see also Chaderton, Edmund
   (archd.)
  archdeaconry, 335, 336c
  deans of, 338
  borough, 330
  ch., 330, 335c
  dy., 335c
  priory, 53d, 270, 296, 323b, c; 336c
  ms. (named), 296, 323c
  prior, *see* Cooke, William

Tottington (Tetryngton), La., inh. of,
 see Stonys, Roger

Towcester, Np., Sponne's chantry at,
 255d

Towker, John, 361
 chap. of Berkeley, Gl., 481

Townkys, John, chap. of St Nicholas,
 Bristol, 482

Townstal (Townestall), De., ch., 335c

Trad, John, 250

Trafford (Trafort):
 Henry, esq., 5
 John, ord., 428d

Travelowe, Matilda, 236

Trebnyth, Thomas, ord., 323a

Treborough (Treborugh), So., r. of,
 361

Treftry, John, kt., 63

Tregarthen, Thomas, 305

Tregonwell, John, ord., 65b, 75d

Tregony (Tregonye), Co., ch., 334c

Tregose, Peter, prebend of, *see*
 Endellion

Treman, John, r. of Bicton, De., 270

Trencher, John, chap. of St John's,
 Exeter, 267

Trenethall, John, r. of Ashbury, De.,
 310

Trentham, St., priory, 387, 428c, d

cans. (named), 387
 prior, *see* Williams, Thomas

Trentishoe (Trenshoo), De., ch., 333e

Tresuthen, Robert, Mr, prebendary of
 Glasney coll. ch., 289

Trevalga, Co., ch., 334g

Trevenande, William, ord., 428d

Treviglas (Treweglis), Co., ch., 334h

Trevilian, John, esq., 49

Trevranok, Isabelle, prioress of Polsloe,
 279

Treway, Lawrence, v. of Newton St
 Cyres, De., 275

Trewola, John, v. of Kenton, De., 268

Treworga, John, ord., 65b, 75d

Triesham, Richard, Mr, r. of
 Tendcombe, Gl., 485

Trigg Major (Maioris Trigge), Co.,
 dy., 334h

Trigg Minor (Minoris Trigge), Co.,
 dy., 334g

Trigis, John, secondary of Exeter cath.,
 276e

Troutbeke:
 Joan, *alias* Butler, 30
 William, kt., 30

Trowbridge, Thomas, B.A., ord., 53b,
 65d

Truflove, John, 437

Truro (Truru), Co., ch., 334c

Trusham (Trisma, Trysham), De., ch.,
 268, 332a

Trussel, Thomas, 105a

Trysull (Trisill), St., dy., *see* Lapley

Tudor (Tudur):
 Jasper, duke of Bedford and earl of
  Pembroke, 197
 Lewis ap Ievan ap, ord., 428d

Tuke, Elizabeth, 254

Tunstall, Richard, can. of Ranton,
 428b

Tunthewe, William, cur. of Stockleigh
 Pomeroy, De., 275

Tupholme, William, r. of Waddingham
 St Mary, Li., 179

Turelehall, Thomas, v.-choral of
 Gnosall coll. ch., 403

Turkdean (Thurkdene), Gl., ch., 487

Turle, John, chap. of St Mary's coll.
 ch., Warwick, 470

Turner (Turnar, Turnour, Turnur):
 Edmund, ord., 428d

prebendary of Gnosall coll. ch., 11
prebendary of North Kelsey in
Lincoln cath., 150
Uttoxeter (Otoxhatre, Uttoxhater), St.,
ch., 39d, 435d

Vaghan, *see* Vaughan
Vale Royal (Valle Regali), Chs.,
abbey, 428c, d
Vale, Richard, chap. of St Stephen's,
Bristol, 482
Varyatt, John, ord., 65a, 75c
Vaughan (Vaghan), John, Mr:
cantarist of the Kalends in All Saints
ch., Bristol, 502
r. of Avening, Gl., 484
Venaunce, Robert:
chap. of St Stephen's, Bristol, 482
ord., 357a
Venymecum, John, Mr, r. of St
Ewen's, Bristol, 482
Verdon, John, chap. of altar of St
Michael, Chesterfield, Db., 416
Vernay, Alexander:
ord., 65b, 75d
subdeacon of Bridgewater, So., 70
Veryan (Elerky), Co., ch., 334c
Veysye, John, D.C.L., commissary of
Official, Lincoln dioc., 136,
232–46, 260
Vicarie (Vicary, Vyvkrye), John:
cur. of Rewe, De., 273
r. of Huntsham, De., 274, 302
Vienne (dép. Isère, France), hospital of
St Anthony, 221, 231
Vikaries, John, Mr, v. of Great
Badminton, Gl., 483
Virginstow (Virgynstow), De., ch.,
335g
Volvell, Richard, can. of Bruton priory,
357c
Vowell, William, Decr.B.:
r. of Holy Trinity ch., Wareham,
Do., 522
r. of Stoke Abbot, Do., 522
Vowles, Thomas, 72

Wacy, John, v. of Axminster, So., 271
Waddesdon (Woddestone), Bk., dy.,
232b
Waddingham St Mary (Staynton
Wadyngham, Wadyngham), Li.,
ch., 179, 255b
Wade, John, 357b

ord., 65b, 75d
Wadynton, John, chap. of Naunton,
Gl., 487
Wainfleet (Wayneflete), Li.:
ch. of All Saints, 168, 255a
r., 256
ch. of St Mary, 216c, e
Wakeham, Richard, 324
Walborne, Hugh, r. of Cromhall, Gl.,
483
Walding, William, 438
Wales:
borders of, 293
Prince of, 276a
Wales, Henry, 242
Walkdene, William, v. of Mayfield, St.,
25
Walkfelde, Richard, r. of All Saints,
Winchester, 107
Walker:
Maurice, Mr, chap. of St Mary-in-
the-Market Place, Bristol, 482
Richard:
chap. of Cobham coll. ch., 443
prior of St Frideswide's, Oxford,
263
v. of Tachbrook, Wa., 427
Robert:
chap. of St Nicholas, Bristol, 482
chap. of St Owen's, Gloucester,
480
r. of Westcote, Gl., 487
Thomas, 438
chap. of Cirencester, Gl., 485
chap. of St Mary before the
Abbey Gate, Gloucester, 480
William, 437
Walkhampton, De., ch., 335f
Wall (Walle):
Richard, M.A., v. of Farnham, Sy.,
95
Thomas, chap. of Bibury, Gl., 485
William, Mr, prior of Longbridge
hospital, Berkeley, Gl., 481
Walles, John, Mr, can. residentiary of
Lincoln cath., Official *sede vacante*
Lincoln dioc., 135–8, 216–31,
255–8, 262
Walley, Robert, r. of Madresfield, Wo.,
479
Walowfield, John, cur. of Hardwick
chapel, Gl., 480
Walrage (*unid.*), ch., 292

Walrond, William, chap. of Silverton, De., 273
Walsall (Walshale, Walshall), St., inh. of, *see* Fer, William; Fletcher, Elizabeth; Sprote, Robert
Walsall, Robert, *generosus*, 194
Walsh (Walshe, Walsshe):
  David, chap. of Mangotsfield, Gl., 482
  Edmund, Mr, r. of Stoke Pero, So., 45
  Elias, v. of Aylesbeare, De., 270
Walshcroft (Walescrofte), Li., dy., 138
Walter, chap. of Little Compton, Gl., 487
Walter, Richard, ord., 357a
Waltershire, John, 242
Waltham Holy Cross, Ess., abbey, 519
Waltham, North, Ha., ch., 98c
Waltham St Lawrence, Brk., ch., 548
Waltham, Robert, 222a
Walton, Bk., ch., 234a
Walton-on-the-Hill (Walton), Sy., ch., 106b
Walton-on-Thames (Walton), Sy., ch., 106c
Walton, Wood (Walton), Hu., ch., 211, 225d
Walton:
  John, 222a
  Richard, r. of Weddington, Wa., 13
  Thomas, v. of Saleby, Li., 148
Walweyn, William, v. of Charlbury, Ox., 199
Wamyslay, Thomas, chap. of one third of chantry, Gainsborough, Li., 178
Wandsworth (Wannysforth), Sy., ch., 106a
Wapley (Wapeley), Gl., ch., 483
Wappenbury (Wapynbury), Wa., ch., 39a, 435a
Warboys (Wardeboys), Hu., ch., 204, 219h
Warbstow (Warbistow), Co., ch., 334h
Ward (Warde):
  John, 229b
  Peter, ord., 428d
  Richard, r. of Folksworth, Hu., 207
  Robert, r. of St Mary Magdalene, Bermondsey, Sy., 79
  William, r. of Corby, Li., 172

Warderoper:
  Robert, 361
  Thomas, annuellar of Exeter cath., 276d
Wardon (Verdone), Bd.:
  abbey, 240d
  ch., 240d
Wareham (Warham), Do.:
  ch. of Holy Trinity, 527
  ch. of St Michael, 516
  ch. of St Peter, 544
Wareham, William, D.C.L., Official *sede vacante*, Coventry and Lichfield dioc., 1
Waren:
  John, Mr, prebendary of Milverton in Astley coll. ch., 16
  Richard, chap., 112
  Thomas, v. of Milverton stall in Astley coll. ch., 16
Waresley (Weresley), Hu.:
  chantry, 246e
  v., 246e
Warleggan (Walregan), Co., ch., 334b
Warkleigh (Warkelegh), De., ch., 333f
Warlingham (Warlyngham), Sy., ch., 106b
Warmouth, Richard, Mr, r. of St George's, Stamford, Li., 226
Warner:
  John and Joan, 105a
  Robert, chap. of St Stephen's, Bristol, 482
Warrington (Werington), La., dy., 429e
Warwick, Wa.:
  ch. of St Nicholas, 508
  ch. of St Peter, 508
  coll. ch. of St Mary, 39a, 434a, 470, 503, 508
    cans. (named), 470
    dean, *see* Brakinburgh, Richard
    prebend of St Michael, 495, 509
  dy. of Christianity, 476, 503, 507
  hospital of St John, 508
  hospital of St Michael, 496, 509
  inh., *see* Maners, John
  priory of St Sepulchre, 469, 503
    cans. (named), 469
    prior, *see* Echington, Robert
Warwik, Robert, *dominus*, 229a
Waryn:
  John, r. of Clyst St Lawrence, 273

Richard, v. of Landrake, Co., 314
Washfield (Waisshfeld, Wasshefeld),
De., ch., 274, 332d
Washford Pyne (Waisfeld), De., ch.,
333f
Wathe (Southwath), I.o.W., ch. of St
Lawrence, 116
Watson:
Richard, r. of Musbury, De., 271
Walter, Mr, r. of Cadelegh, De.,
275
Wawton, Thomas, 242
Way, Richard, v. of Exeter cath., 276c
Wayneflete, William, bp. of
Winchester, 127
Waynsford, John, subdean of Wells,
prebendary of Ashill, So., 47
Waty, John:
r. of St Kerian's, Exeter, 267
r. of St Lawrence's, Rode, So., 63
Weare Giffard (Were), De., ch., 333c
Webbe:
George, r. of Siddington Peter, Gl.,
485
John, chap. of St Mary's coll. ch.,
Warwick, 470
William, chap. of Holy Trinity ch.,
Gloucester, 480
Webber, Thomas, v. of Exeter cath.,
276c
Webster, John, chap. of Lechlade, Gl.,
486
Weddington, Wa., ch., 13
Wedmore, Nicholas, m. of
Glastonbury, 75b
Week St Mary (Weke sancte Marie),
Co., ch., 334h
Weke, Simon, cur. of Exminster, De.,
268
Welbeck, Nt., abbey, 176
can. (named), 176
Welby, Li., r. of, 225
Welby, Thomas, esq., 227
Well (Wellie), Li.:
inh., see Trad, John
r., 226
Welland (Wellond), Wo., ch., 479
Welles (Wellys):
John, viscount, 152
Richard, chap. of Slimbridge, Gl.,
481
Thomas, O.F.M., bp. of Achonry,
21

Wellow, Li., see Grimsby
Wellow (Wellowe), So., v. of, see
Radnare, John
Wellow, East (Welow), Ha., ch., 108
Wells (Wellen'), So., 45-53, 55-6,
58-67, 71, 73, 341-6
archd. of, or Official, 48, 51-2, 58,
62-4, 343-4
see also Dyer, John (Official)
archdeaconry, 359b
cath., 269, 356, 358, 365, 483
dean, 47, 59
prebend, see Whitchurch
precentor, see Overay, Thomas
subdean, see Bokett, William
vs.-choral (named), 65b, 75c, d
chapel of St Mary by the cath.
cloister, 56
ch. of St Andrew, 362
ch. of St Cuthbert, 362
dioc., see Bath and Wells
hospital of St John the Baptist, 53c,
d; 65b, c; 75, 323b, 357
inh., see Bartholomew, John; John;
Kyrse, Agnes
market-place, 56
Wellys, see Welles
Wellywe, John, subdean of Westbury
coll. ch., 462
Welson, Christopher, chap. of
Hatherop, Gl., 486
Welton (Weldone), Np., dy., 251b
Welton le Marsh (Welton), Li.,
perpetual chantry of B.V.M.,
145, 219a
Wembworthy (Wemmeworthi), De.,
ch., 333a
Wendover, Bk., dy., 232b
Wendron (sancte Wendrone), Co., ch.,
299, 334d
Wenlok, William, prior of Worcester,
452-5, 460
Wentnor, Richard, 438
Weryn, Thomas, r. of All Hallows-on-
the-Wall, Exeter, 267
West:
John, ord., 75c
Richard, chap. of Ardyngton
chantry in Aston ch., Wa., 33
Robert, Mr, 171
William, perpetual fellow of
Westbury coll. ch., 462

Westbury upon Trym (Westbury), Gl.,
coll. ch., 462, 482, 504, 508
cans. (named), 462
dean, see Cretyng, William
Westbury, Maurice, r. of Stanton, Gl.,
491
Westcombe, John, chap. of Ottery St
Mary coll. ch., 270
Westcote, Gl., ch., 487g
Westerleigh (Westurley), Gl., ch., 483
Westlake, John, v. of Pinhoe, De., 270,
300
Westleigh (Westlegh), De., ch., 333d
Westlonde, William, r. of Fleet, Li.,
175
Westminster (Westm;), Mx., 60, 67
abbey, 96, 125, 157, 210, 246b, e;
479, 508
coll. ch. of St Stephen, 234a, b
Weston Birt (Weston Byrte), Gl., ch.,
483
Weston in Gordano (Weston), So., ch.,
72
Weston, South (Weston), Ox., ch., 248
Weston under Lizard (Lusyard), Sa.,
inh. of, see Mytton, William
Weston-upon-Trent (Weston), St., ch.,
39d, 435d
Weston (unid.), inh. of, see Bagshawe,
William; Salte, James and John
Westwode:
John, 229a
William, v. of Fotherby, Li., 158
Westwyvelshire (West'), Co., dy., 334b
Wever:
Lewis, 361
Thomas:
r. of Coberley, Gl., 484
r. of Shipton Sellars, Gl., 487
Wey, John, ord., 65b, 75c
Whaddon (Waddon), Gl., chapel, 480
Whalley, La., abbey, 428b, c, d
Whalley, William, prior of Tutbury,
383
Wheatenhurst (Whetynhurst), Gl., ch.,
484
Wheler (Whiler):
John, 72
v. of Aston Blank, Gl., 487
Richard:
chap. of Meysey Hampton, Gl.,
486

chap. of St Lawrence's, Bristol,
482
Roger, v. of Yarcombe, De., 272
Thomas, clerk, 554–7
William, 222c
Wherwell (Wharwell), Ha.:
abbey, 98a, 113
abbess, see Overey, Juliana
prebendal ch. of Bathwick
pertaining to, 50
prebendal ch. of Holy Trinity
Wherwell pertaining to, 113
inh., see Wodecock, John
Whitecomb, Robert, cur. of
Lympstone, De., 270
Whiche, Thomas, 7
Whiler, see Wheler
Whimple (Whympell), De., ch., 270,
332h, 338
Whitchurch, De., ch., 335f
Whitchurch, So., prebendal ch. of
Wells cath., 60, 67
White (Whyte):
John, 222a
chap. of third part of chantry,
Gainsborough, Li., 178
par. chap. of St Mary
Magdalene, Southwark, Sy.,
79
r. of Duntisbourne Abbots, Gl.,
485
Richard, 256
Simon, v. of Thorverton, De., 275
William, see Whitechurche
Whiteaker, Richard, ord., 428d
Whiteby, Richard, can. of Bullington,
v. of West Torrington, Li., 164
Whitechurch, Do., dy., 554
Whitechurche, William:
alias White, chap. of North Cerney,
Gl., 485
prior of Alcester, 472
Whitehorn, John, r. of Letcombe
Bassett, Brk., 549–50
Whitestone (Whitstone), De., ch., 269,
332b
Whitewood, Thomas, secondary of
Exeter cath., 276e
Whitfare, Ralph, clerk of Westbury
coll. ch., 462
Whithede, John, chap. of Avening, Gl.,
484

inh., *see* Batell, William; Cristemas, John; Hamond, John; Hanyngton, William; Radon, Richard; Skynner, William
Winchcombe (Wynchcombe, Wynchecombe), Gl., 495, 497
  abbey, 466, 486–7, 491, 504, 508
  abbot, *see* Kidderminster, Richard
  ms. (named), 466
  ch., 477, 488
  dy., 477, 488, 504–5, 507
Windlesham (Windesleham), Sy., ch., 106c
Windrush (Wynregge), Gl., ch., 487
Windsor (Wyndesore), Brk., 519
  coll. ch. of St George in the castle, 39d, 114, 248, 269, 337, 435d
Winkleigh (Wynkelegh), De., ch., 333b
Winnall (Wynhale), Ha., ch., 98c
Winstone (Wynston), Gl., ch., 484
Winterbourne Doune (Wynterborne), Gl., 482
Winwick (Wynwyke), La., inh. of, *see* Troutbeke, Joan
Wirksworth (Worsworth), Db., inh. of, *see* Storere, Thomas
Wirral (Wyrall), Chs.:
  dy., 40e, 429e
  inh., *see* Cholmeley, John
Wirth, Richard, chap. of St Mary's chapel, Exeter, 267
Wise, Robert, r. of Alphington, De., 268
Wistaston (Wistauston, Wystaston), Chs., ch., 410, 432
Wiston, Joan, 43
Wistow (Wistowe), Lei., ch., 217d
Witham (Wytham), So., priory, m. of (named), 65b, 357d
Withcote (Withcok, Wythcoke), Lei., ch., 193, 255c
Witheridge (Witherigge), De., ch., 333f
Withiel, Co., ch., 334f
Withycombe (Withcombe), So., inh. of, *see* Luker, John
Withycombe Raleigh (Wethycombe, Wythecombe), De.:
  chapel, 270
  ch., 325
Witley, Sy., ch., 106c
Witney, Ox., dy., 247b
Witney, Henry, par. chap. of St Stephen's, Bristol, 482

Wodecock, John, 105a
Wodington, Thomas, Mr, r. of St Peter's, Bristol, 482
Wodthorp, Thomas, r. of Tetford, Li., 169
Woking (Wockyng), Sy., ch., 106c
Wolborough (Wolburgh), De., ch., 335b
Woldy, Henry, v. of Longdon, Wo., 479
Wolf (Wolfe):
  Richard, r. of Acton Beauchamp, Wo., 479
  Robert, r. of Chilbolton, Ha., 118
Wolfhamcote (Willfancote, Wolfamcote), Wa., ch., 39a, 434a
Wolford, Great (Wulford), Wa., ch., 476, 503
Wolkestede, Sy., *see* Godstone
Wollaston, Henry, r. of Desborough, Np., 184
Wolley, Richard, v. of St Mary's ch., St Neots, Hu., 212
Wolstanton, St., inh. of, *see* Henshawe, John
Wolverton (Wolecheston, Wolverheton), Wa., ch., 39a, 434a
Wolworth, Thomas, r. of Charfield, Gl., 483
Wombridge (Wombrigge), Sa., priory 391
  cans. (named), 391
  prior, *see* Forster, Thomas
Wonersh (Wogners), Sy., ch., 106c
Wonston, Ha., ch., 98c
Wooburn (Woburne), Bk., ch., 237
Wood (Woode):
  Alice, prioress of Brewood White Ladies, 393
  Dorothy, 327
  Emotte, 327
  Ivott, 327
  John, 321
    cur. of Canonsleigh, De., 274
    master of free chapel of Claverham, So., 71–3
    ord., 428c
  Mary, 327
  Richard, 327, 437
    chap. of Rockhampton, Gl., 481
    r. of St Werburgh's, Bristol, 482

Robert:
    perpetual fellow of Westbury coll.
        ch., 462
    proctor, 9
Roger, 43
Thomas:
    att, prior of Studley, 472
    chap. of St Mary before the
        Abbey Gate, Gloucester, 480
Thomasina, 327
William, *generosus*, 71–4
Woodbury (Woodebury, Woodebyri),
    De., ch., 270, 332h
Woodchester (Woodchestr'), Gl., ch.,
    484
Wooderof, *see* Woodruffe
Woodeward, *see* Woodward
Woodford (Woodeford), Np., ch., 252a
Woodhall (Woodehyll), Li., ch., 216e
Woodhouse, Thomas, chap. of Stow on
    the Wold, Gl., 487
Woodleigh (Wodelegh), De.:
    ch., 335d, 338
    dy., 335d
Woodmansterne (Wodmershom), Sy.,
    ch., 106b
Woodruffe (Wooderof):
    Robert, Mr, prebendary of Crantock
        coll. ch., 288
    William, cantarist of Crich, Db., 12
Woodsfield (Woodefeld), Wo., ch., 508
Woodstock (Woodestok), Ox., dy.,
    247b
Woodward (Woodeward):
    Richard, clerk, 552, 554–7
    Robert, Mr:
        r. of Elkstone, Gl., 484
        r. of Wickwar, Gl., 483
    Thomas, r. of All Saints ch.,
        Gloucester, 480
Woolfardisworthy (Wolfradisworthi) (in
    Hartland dy.,), De., ch., 333c
Woolfardisworthy (Wolfradesworthi) (in
    Molton dy.), De., ch., 333f
Wootton (Wotton), Li., ch., 216c
Wootton (Wotton), So., inh. of, *see*
    Lathwell, John
Wootton Wawen (Wotton), Wa.:
    ch., 476, 503
    priory, 503
Worcester (Wigorn'), Wo., 452, 454–5,
    457–77, 490–4, 498–9

archd. of, or Official, 474, 476,
    495–6, 499
    see also Enkbarough, Robert
        (Official)
archdeaconry, 476, 503
bp., 485
    see also Giglis, John de
cath. priory, 452, 458, 479, 483, 508
    chapter house, 452, 454
    ms. (named), 458
    prior, *see* Wenlok, William
ch. of St Helen, 476
ch. of St Peter, 508
consistory court, 457
dioc:
    l.d. from, 323a, b
    sede vacante, 452–510
dy., 476, 503, 507
hospital of St Wulfstan, 489, 494,
    503
inh., *see* Langford, Agnes
Worcetur, John, m. of Bath, 65d
Worfield (Worfild), Sa., inh. of, *see*
    Cattister, William
Worlington, East (Estwolrington), De.,
    ch., 333f
Worlington, West (West Wolryngton),
    De., ch., 333f
Wormeswell, Thomas, Mr, v. of
    Littleham, De., 319
Worplesdon (Warphiston), Sy., ch.,
    106c
Worseley, Thomas, Mr, prebendary of
    Lichfield cath., 395
Worspring (Worspryng), So., priory,
    53b, 60, 65b, 67, 75c, 355, 358
    cans. (named), 53d, 65b
Worthing, Roger, ord., 323d
Worthington (Worthynton):
    Edmund, master of St
        Bartholomew's hospital,
        Newbury, 517
    Roger, ord., 428a
Wotton under Edge (Wotton), Gl., ch.,
    481
Wotton, Edmund, chap. of St Mary's
    coll. ch., Warwick, 470
Wragby, Li., ch., 138
Wraggoe (Wraghou), Li., dy., 138
Wrangeford, William, clerk of
    Westbury coll. ch., 462
Wrangle, Li., v. of, 225
Wrawby (Wrauby), Li., ch., 216c, e

239

Yeott, John, annuellar of Exeter cath., 276d
Yeovil (Yevill), So., ch., 364
Yere, John, chap. of Kenton, De., 268
Ynge, *see* Inge
Yoman, William, 222b, 254
Yong (Yonge):
  Benedict, ord., 53d
  John:
    chap. of Tetbury, Gl., 484
    r. of West Ogwell, De., 268
    v. of Coln St Aldwyn, Gl., 486
  Robert, r. of Holy Trinity ch., Exeter, 267

Thomas, esq., 520
York minster, dean and chapter of, 271
Yotton, John, S.T.P., dean of Lichfield cath., 395
Youlgreave (Yolgrave), Db., inh. of, *see* Ely, William
Ylmynster, John, cur. of Dunkeswell, De., 272

Zeal-Monachorum (Sele Monachorum), De., ch., 333a
Zennor (Senar), Co., ch., 334e
Zouche, lord de la, 296

INDEX OF SUBJECTS

founder's intentions, neglect of, 130, 263
house of studies, religious not sent to, 127
household:
    of abbess, nuns maintained in, 130
    of prior, not maintained, 129
layman feeds animals at convent's expense, 134
letters of institution not produced, 282
library:
    construction of new, not yet begun, 129
    lack of free access to, 127
negligence:
    of deputy, 129–30
    of superior, 130, 263
obedientiaries, office of:
    plurality in, 127, 129
    retained in superior's hands, 127
office, divine, neglect of, 130, 263, 289
organ, defective, 276
pensions a burden on house, 134
pittances, withdrawal of, 127
priests, number in nunnery diminished, 130
prison, monks in, 296, 467
profession, seniority according to neglected, 130, 292
proprietas, 130
punishment of delinquents neglected, 127, 130, 263
religious, shortage in numbers of, 127, 129, 281, 286–7, 296
revenues, illicit detention of, 278, 281, 284, 290, 293
seal, abuse of, 130, 296
secondaries:
    vagrant, 276
    wages of in arrears, 280
secular business in chapterhouse, 276
sick, neglect of, 127, 129–30
statutes:
    infringed, 280
    no copy for secondaries, 280
    no copy in house, 283–4
    not read publicly, 282, 289
    tampered with, 289
steward, undue influence of, 130

superior:
    disobedient to visitor, 285
    misappropriates revenues of convent, 130
    tyrannical or rude, 127–8
taverns, frequenting of, 130
theft by monk, 296
tonsure, indecent, 277
town, illicit trips to, 130, 263, 282, 380
valuables, alienation of, 127, 130, 286
vessels and ornaments in poor condition, 127, 130
vicars:
    not properly paid, 289
    shortage of, 282, 289
vintner, office of in abeyance, 129
violence:
    of monk, 277
    shown to brethren, 128
visitors, illicit, 130
Composition concerning *sede vacante* administration, 135, 453, 511
Compurgation, 56, 552–7
    fees for, 225
Consistory court:
    commissions to preside in, 81, 368, 456–7
    proceedings in, 30, 549, 552–7
Convocation of Canterbury, 60, 62, 66
    scribe of, *see* Hall, Richard
Corrections:
    fees for, 226, 259b
    reserved to abp., 262
Corrody, request for exoneration from, 130
Cum ex eo, papal constitution, 31

Deans, rural:
    fees paid by, to abp., 338
    fees paid to, for services in visitation, 338
Dispensations:
    for marriage within prohibited degrees, 35–6
    for ordination notwithstanding illegitimacy, 37
    for ordination over age of twenty-two, 29
    for religious to hold parochial cure, 111